D1522149

Forty-six Lives

EARLY ENGLISH TEXT SOCIETY

Original Series No. 214

1943 (for 1940), reprinted 1970

O the moste hygh. moste
puysaunte, moste excellent and
moste chrysten kynge, my moste
redoubtede souereygne lorde hen
ry theighte by the grace of gode
of Englonde, ffraunce z Irelonde
kynge, Defender of the ffeythe. z
in erthe vndre gode. supreme ~
heede of the churche of enissonde
and Irelonde. Your moste humble
Subiecte Henry parcure knyght.
Lorde Morley desyreth thys newe
yere with infynyte of yeres to ~
your Imperiall maieste healthe
honoure and vyctory

IN the tyme the hoole worlde was
obediente to the Romaynes Moste victoriouse z glorouse
souereygne Lorde. Not onely by Armes they were Re //
noumede aboue all other naciones. But also in eloquence
and goode lernynge. as it apprethe by thyes Oratours
and poetes in the greate Augustine days. That is to saye.
Varro / Tullius, Cicero Virgill Ouace and Ouyde with
diuers others. / And all thoughe that those that ensuyde ~
frome one Empoure to another were excellently lernede
as bothe the plynys, Marciall / Quyntilian z Claudian.
and suche other. / Yet why it was so. that they coulde neuer attayne to the
afore rehersyde / Nather in profe nor yet in verse is to me a treate won //
der. ff for asmuche as they sawe the workes of the other. Whiche as my
reasone geuythe me shulde haue rather causede theym to haue bene in

f. 1a of the Chatsworth MS. containing Lord Morley's
Translation from De Claris Mulieribus

Forty-six Lives

TRANSLATED FROM

BOCCACCIO'S *DE CLARIS MULIÈRIBUS*

BY

HENRY PARKER, LORD MORLEY

EDITED BY

HERBERT G. WRIGHT

35996

Published for

THE EARLY ENGLISH TEXT SOCIETY

by

OXFORD UNIVERSITY PRESS

LONDON   NEW YORK   TORONTO

FIRST PUBLISHED 1943 (for 1940)
REPRINTED 1970

Reprinted Lithographically in Great Britain by
Fletcher & Son Ltd, Norwich

To

J. W. H. ATKINS

TUTOR, COLLEAGUE AND FRIEND

PREFACE

IN the preparation of this edition the following procedure has been adopted. The spelling of the manuscript is retained, the contractions being expanded and indicated by italics, while the capitalization and punctuation are modernized. However, to indicate the end of a page in the manuscript a vertical bar is inserted. The names of persons and places in the text and also in Morley's prefaces contained in the Appendix, which sometimes assume strange forms, have been treated conservatively. Quotations from manuscripts and from Morley's letters in the Introduction are given without any reference to contractions.

This last statement applies likewise to the Latin text of the original; here, too, apart from a few essential changes, the spelling has been left unaltered, but capitalization and punctuation have been made to conform to modern practice. All other changes are carefully recorded. In the footnotes the most important variants are also given, and it is hoped that these may be of use to Latin scholars. Of course, the readings adopted by me are not necessarily the best, as my task was to establish which text Morley had before him and to follow that closely, apart from the emendation of corrupt passages. However, full information is provided about the readings in other editions, and from these the most appropriate can be selected.

It now remains for me to thank those who have aided me in my work. In the first place, this edition was made possible by the Leverhulme Trustees, who in 1936 awarded me a Research Fellowship, and by the Council of my own College, which enabled me to have a sabbatical year. The owner of the manuscript of Morley's translation of *De claris mulieribus*, His Grace the late Duke of Devonshire, most generously permitted me to publish it. I am also deeply indebted to His Grace the present Duke of Devonshire, who allowed me to reproduce a page by way of illustration. To Mr. Francis Thompson, Librarian and Keeper of Collections at Chatsworth, I am under a similar obligation for the readiness with which he gave me access to the manuscript and for later confirmatory information.

Professor H. J. Thomson has displayed an exemplary patience in helping me to straighten out the often garbled text of *De claris mulieribus*, and I am most grateful for his advice. My introduction has been read by Professor Edna Purdie, by whose comments I have profited greatly. To Dr. Mabel Day I should like to express my thanks for the willingness with which she revised my footnotes and collated Morley's prefaces with the manuscripts, and also for useful remarks during the reading of the proofs.

My labours have been greatly facilitated by Mr. A. I. Ellis, Superintendent of the Reading Room at the British Museum, who with unfailing kindness has answered my inquiries. Mr. Victor Scholderer, too, sent me information when, owing to war conditions, one of the incunabula which I was investigating had been removed from London. Similarly, I am much indebted to Dr. H. Idris Bell and the members of the Department of Manuscripts at the British Museum, to Dr. H. H. E. Craster, Bodley's Librarian, and to the late Sir C. T. Hagberg Wright, of the London Library, as well as to their staffs.

From other scholars I have received valuable suggestions on a number of points. In addition to Henri Hauvette, whose account of *De claris mulieribus* in his *Boccace* I have found of great service, I would mention Sir W. A. Craigie, Dr. Robin Flower, Dr. L. F. Powell, and Mr. J. Isaacs. To the Rev. Canon D. B. Barclay, rector of Great Hallingbury, I am much obliged for rubbings of the epitaph of Lord Morley and for particulars relating to Hallingbury Place.

Finally, I would thank Dr. John Johnson for the skill and care with which this book has been printed and the Readers of the Oxford University Press for their expert observations.

H. G. W.

BANGOR NORTH WALES

June 17, 1940

CONTENTS

Contents

INTRODUCTION

I

THE LIFE OF LORD MORLEY

BEFORE Morley's translation of *De claris mulieribus* is considered, some preliminary account of his career is desirable, in order that his work may be envisaged, not as an isolated episode, but as one of numerous activities. In this way it will be possible to see its relation to his other versions and also to estimate his importance as a translator, while a survey of his life and writings will throw light on his personality.

Henry Parker, afterwards Lord Morley, was born in 1476,[1] and the family to which he belonged was distinguished and influential. The last holder of the title before him was Henry Lovel, who married Elizabeth de la Pole, daughter of the Duke of Suffolk by the Princess Elizabeth Plantagenet, sister to Edward IV and Richard III. When Henry Lovel was killed at Dixmude, he left no issue, and so his sister Alice became the heir to the baronies of Morley, Marshall, Hengham, and Rhie. She married Sir William Parker, who is said to have been in great favour with Edward IV and Richard, Duke of Gloucester, to have won the honour of knighthood for his prowess in the expedition against Scotland in 1483, and to have been made a Privy Counsellor and Standard-bearer to the King when Richard seized the throne. It is asserted likewise that he fell into disgrace on the accession of Henry VII and lay imprisoned in the Tower until 1510, when he died a violent death.[2] After this event his wife married Sir

---

[1] *Vide post*, p. xlvi, n. 3.

[2] These statements regarding Sir William Parker appear to rest upon the authority of A. Collins, *Peerage of England*, ed. Sir E. Brydges, London, 1812, vol. vii, p. 349. In part, at least, their accuracy is doubtful. Thus Lord Morley has recorded that when he was 15 years of age his father was present at the Christmas festivities in the house of the Lady Margaret. As Morley was 80 when he died in 1556, it is evident that in 1491 his father was not only free, but also a guest of Henry VII's mother. That Sir William Parker met with an untimely end, however, though not necessarily in the manner indicated by Collins, is proved by the epitaph on a tablet erected

Edward Howard, second son of the Duke of Norfolk and Knight
of the Garter, whom she survived. Her will, dated April 9th,
1518, is of interest, because it gives a glimpse of the environment
familiar to her son, Henry Parker, and mirrors a world of high
rank, wealth, and piety. She speaks of valuable jewels and plate,
and bequeaths to him 'my bed of cloth of gold and tawny veluet
withe all thynges to that belongyng' and 'all the ornamentes of
my chapell with a chalice belongyng therto'. Her numerous
servants are all remembered, and she commits Sir Thomas, her
blind priest, 'in to the handes and kepyng of my sonne, that
duryng the said prestes lyf he may be kepte in my sonnes housse
to praye for the soulis of my lorde my husband and me'. Among
her legacies was one of £3 'to the makyng of a pyx for the sacrament for the parissh church of Halyngbery Morley', and she also
provided that a priest should sing for her a whole year after her
interment 'in the parissh chirch of Sainte Andrewe of Hyngham
in Norffolk'.[1] Through his own marriage Henry Parker became
allied with another great family, for his wife Alice was the daughter
of Sir John St. John, who in his turn was related to the Dukes
of Somerset from whom Henry VII was descended.[2]

As was fitting for one of such high position, Henry Parker
while still a boy entered the household of Margaret Beaufort, the
mother of Henry VII. In this respect he was singularly fortunate,
as, by general consent, she was among the most remarkable
women of the age. She made a deep impression upon those in
daily contact with her by her zeal for learning. St. John's College
and Christ's College, Cambridge, were founded by her; both

to his memory by his son Henry, and still preserved in the church of Great
Hallingbury in Essex. The dead man is made to exclaim:
> Vi tamen heu perii. Quantum inimicitie
> Conquerar, an taceam mecumque ut luserit olim
> Fortuna instabili dum stetit illa rota?

[1] Prerogative Court of Canterbury Wills, Ayloffe, 15.
[2] The future Lord Morley was not unmindful of his distinguished
affiliations. The epitaph which he caused to be placed in the church of
Great Hallingbury in honour of Alice St. John refers to her as *regio sanguine
prognata*, and the marble tomb in which at his instance were buried the
bones of his grandmother, his father and mother, and his wife was evidently
intended to perpetuate the memory of his noble connexions. Presumably
the remains of his mother were transferred from Hingham when the tomb
was erected.

Caxton and Wynkyn de Worde were encouraged by her patronage,[1] and 'right studious she was in Bokes, which she had in grete number, both in Englysh and in Frenshe, and for her exercise, and for the profyte of others, she did translate divers maters of Devocyon out of the Frensh into Englysh'.[2]

Not less striking were her courtesy and graciousness, her piety and charity, while her solicitude for the welfare of her household won their entire devotion, so that her death was mourned by all. The account of her given by John Fisher, Bishop of Rochester, in the sermon that he delivered on the occasion of her funeral was confirmed and amplified by Henry Parker. Writing to Queen Mary in his old age, he said:

'Albeyt that I thinke ther is vnethe syxe men and women alyue at this present day, that then were about her godly person at that houre, yet my chaunce was ther to be, as one that vnworthy she so tendrid, that wher and to what place her Highnes went, I was ever one by her speciall comaundement about her person, either in that rovme to be her caruer or her cuppe bearer. And I do ensure your Highnes that Doctour Fysher, then Bishopp of Rochester, being her ghostly father, shewyd me not long before his death, that he had writen her liffe, which I suppose is in your Graces hande; then if yt so be, oh, good Jhesu! how ioyous wolde yt make me to se and to reade it, writen by so good a man, and so devine a clerk as that bishop was. But briefly I shall declare, as my rude witt is, her godly maners, as folowith. Thus did she vse her life. Her Grace was every mornyng in the chapple betwixt sixe and sevyn of the clock and dayly sayde matyns off the day with one off her chaplyns, and that sayde, from sevyn tyll yt was eleven off the clocke, as sone as one preist had sayd masse in her syght, another beganne. One tyme in a day she was confessyd, then, going to her dynner, how honorably she was seruyd—I think fewe kinges better. Her condityon alwaies at the begynnyng of her dynner was to be ioyous, and to heare those tales that were honest to make her mery. The myddes off her dynner either her amner[3] or I redde some vertuous tale vnto her of the life of Chryst or such like. The latter ende off her dinner agayne she was disposed to talk with the Bishop or with her chauncelour, which satt at her bordis ende, of some godly matter, and her Grace wolde often

---

[1] Cf. T. F. Tout in the *Dictionary of National Biography*, 1908–9, vol. ii, p. 49.
[2] *The Funeral Sermon of Margaret, Countess of Richmond and Derby*, London, 1708, p. 7.   [3] almoner.

say at her table, when she heard that the great Turke preuayled so against the Crysten men, she wolde wyshe that she were a launder to them that shoulde go against them.'

Next Morley describes her hospitality and generosity at Christmas and New Year.

'In Cristmas tyme she kept so honorable a house that vpon one Newe Yeares Day, I, being her sewer off the age of fyftene yeares, had fyve and twentye knightes folowing me, of whom myne owne father was one, and syttyng at her table the Erle off Derby, her husband, the Vicount Wellys, the olde Lord Hastinges, the Byshoppe of Lincolne, and by her person, vnder her clothe of estate, the Lady Cecyle, King Edwardes doughter, your awnte. In her hall, from nyne of the clock tyll it was sevyn off the clock at night, as fast as one table was vp, another was sett. No pore man was denayed at that sayde feast of Cristmas, if he were of any honestye, but that he might come to the buttrye or to the cellar, to drinke att his pleasure. Her liberalytie was such that ther came no man of honour or worship to her, as ther came many of the greatest of the realme, but that they were well rewardyd. I sawe my selff the Duke of Buckingham came to her vnto Collyweston, to whom she gaue a iewell to the value of one hundred pounde. Yf it were an erle, his reward was no lesse then fortye poundes; yf yt were a baron and his wife, his rewarde and hers was twenty poundes. To the ladies and gentylwomen that came to do ther duetye to her, she vsyd such hvmanitye that neuer pryncse coulde do more.'

However, her kindliness to her household was not confined to any special season. At all times she was solicitous of their welfare.

'Although that she had in her cheker roule contynually two and twenty score of ladies, gentylmen, yeomen and offycers, yet it ys a wonder to tell, ther was neither man nor woman, if thei were off any reputatyon, but she coulde call them by ther names. In that kynde of remembraunce I thinke she might haue ben comparyd vnto Methridatus, Kinge of Pontho. Ther were none off her sayd seruauntes but iff he were syck or in perell of his life, iff her phisicions did not forbydde her, she wolde in person visite hym, hauing no mo with her but one cheife gentylwoman and one gentylman vsher before her. And as he was in degre, so she wolde rewarde hym, geving hym good instructyons not to trust to the worlde, but only to put his mynde to God; iff he died, she wolde her selff see hym buryed '[1]

[1] MS. Add. 12060 in the British Museum, ff. 20*b*–22.

This passage is interesting, not only because of Morley's tribute to the Lady Margaret, but also because of the information that it contains about his youthful environment. Otherwise his early life is obscure. Anthony à Wood, it is true, claims that he was educated in most kinds of literature in the University of Oxford and that his youth was occupied with all kinds of superficial learning,[1] but his statements are so vague and his biography in other respects so inaccurate,[2] that he cannot be relied upon.

Nor can we treat seriously the assertion that owing to the disgrace into which his father fell on the accession of Henry VII, the family remained under a cloud in the reign of Henry VIII, with the result that Henry Parker was not summoned to take his seat in the House of Lords until 1530.[3] Actually, he appeared there as Lord Morley in 1523,[4] and it is difficult to believe that if he had to bear the royal disfavour, he would have been tolerated in the retinue of the Lady Margaret. Moreover, his son was a gentleman usher and page of the chamber ordinary to Henry VIII in 1516,[5] and ten years later he was still waiting on the King's person and as a sign of royal goodwill was granted the manor of Hasilbach, near Derby.[6]

Morley himself must have won and retained the confidence of his sovereign, for he figured prominently on ceremonial occasions. Thus he was one of the nobles who were required to attend the King at his meeting with Charles V in 1520 and was also present at the Field of the Cloth of Gold.[7] Again, in 1540 he took part in the procession of gentlemen which preceded Henry VIII when he went to welcome Anne of Cleves,[8] and six years later he was among those appointed to entertain the Lord Admiral of France

[1] *Athenae Oxonienses*, ed. P. Bliss, London, 1813–20, vol. i, col. 115.
[2] For example, he speaks of Henry Parker's property as lying in Northamptonshire, whereas the estates were in Essex.
[3] A. Collins, op. cit., London, 1812, vol. vii, p. 386.
[4] W. Dugdale, *A Perfect Copy of All Summons of the Nobility to the Great Councils and Parliaments*, London, 1685, p. 493. After that he was summoned regularly, not only in the reign of Henry VIII, but also in those of Edward VI and Mary. Cf. pp. 495, 498–500, 502, and 504–17.
[5] *Letters and Papers, Foreign and Domestic, of the Reign of Henry VIII*, vol. ii, pt. i, pp. 872–3.
[6] Ibid., vol. iv, pt. i, pp. 748, 867, and 870.
[7] Ibid., vol. iii, pt. i, pp. 326 and 240.
[8] Ibid., vol. xiv, pt. ii, p. 201, and vol. xv, p. 5.

at Greenwich.[1] At the christening of Prince Edward in 1537, when the Lady Elizabeth bore the chrisom, Morley was instructed to help to carry the princess 'for her tender age',[2] and a few weeks after this joyous event he was one of those who held aloft the canopy over the body of Jane Seymour, when she was buried in state at Windsor.[3]

Previously he had been entrusted with a mission to Ferdinand, Archduke of Austria, the brother of Charles V, who, having resolved on the suppression of heresy in Germany, had received the support of the Pope against Francis I, in consequence of which Wolsey had declared himself in favour of the Emperor. Accordingly, late in the summer of 1523, it was decided that Morley should go to Germany along with Edward Lee, Archdeacon of Colchester and Almoner to the King, Sir William Hussey, and Sir Thomas Wriothesley, and convey to the Archduke the Order of the Garter.[4]

The time at which Morley and his companions visited Germany was critical. Luther's ideas had spread rapidly among the German people and had even begun to sway the nobility. Many of the cities supported him openly, and in places his followers preached freely. That very year the Diet had rejected the demand of Hadrian VI that the Edict of Worms should be enforced against Luther and had refused to inferfere with the evangelical preachers at Nürnberg. The upheaval had also affected the Netherlands, and only a few weeks before Morley set out, two Augustinian monks belonging to the monastery at Antwerp had been burnt at the stake for their adherence to Lutheran doctrines.

The excitement caused by these events was increased by the writings of Luther. Pamphlet after pamphlet came from his busy pen, and among them was one which, as will be seen shortly, deserves special mention. In this tract, published in March 1523, Luther joined with Melanchthon to pour ridicule on the Papacy and the monks, by the interpretation of certain monstrosities which were looked upon as portents. One, with the head of an

---

[1] *Letters and Papers, Henry VIII*, vol. xxi, pt. i, p. 695.
[2] Ibid., vol. xii, pt. ii, p. 319.
[3] Ibid., vol. xii, pt. ii, p. 374.
[4] Ibid., vol. iii, pt. ii, pp. 1350 and 1359.

ass and the stomach of a woman, was said to have been fished out
of the Tiber in 1496; the other, a semi-human creature, with
a calf's head and something resembling a monk's cowl, was
reputed to have been born at Freiberg in Saxony. The Freiberg
monster had been regarded as foretelling the advent of Luther,
but Luther himself saw in it a representation of the monastic
orders, while Melanchthon explained the Tiber monster as an
embodiment of the Pope. This pamphlet, with two curious wood-
cuts portraying the monsters, enjoyed widespread popularity.[1]

To a man of scholarly bent this year was also important,
because it witnessed a violent quarrel between Ulrich von Hutten
and Erasmus. After the failure of his plans for a holy war
against priests and prelates in Germany, Hutten had wandered
to Basle, where he tried to visit Erasmus. The latter, however,
had refused to see him, and so, to revenge himself, Hutten had
attacked him and after endeavouring to blackmail Erasmus into
buying the manuscript, had published his *Expostulation*. Angered
by the charge of duplicity and cowardice brought against him,
Erasmus had replied in his *Spongia adversus aspergines Hutteni*.
By the time of its appearance in the summer of 1523 Hutten was
seriously ill, and his death at the end of August deprived Erasmus
of much of the satisfaction that he would otherwise have felt.[2]

The impressions of an English visitor to Germany at this
juncture are obviously of particular interest, and fortunately four
of Morley's letters relating to the mission have been preserved.[3]
Even though they are somewhat damaged by fire, they enable
the reader to form a clear idea of his journey and also to catch

---

[1] *Deutung der zwo greulichen Figuren, Bapstesels zu Rom und Mönchkalbs
zu Freiberg in Meissen funden.* Cf. Luther, *Werke*, Weimar, 1883– ,
vol. xi, p. 359. An English translation, *Of Two Woonderful Popish Monsters*,
was published in 1579 (item 17797 in A. W. Pollard and G. R. Redgrave,
A Short-Title Catalogue, London, 1926). For an account of the German
pamphlet, see J. Mackinnon, *Luther and the Reformation*, London, 1925–30,
vol. iii, pp. 153–4.

[2] Preserved Smith, *Erasmus*, New York and London, 1923, pp. 332–5.

[3] One to Henry VIII and three to Wolsey; one is presumably from
Mechlin, two are from Cologne, and one from Nürnberg. They are inaccurately described by J. Holmes (MS. Add. 20768, f. 3a) as 'Four Letters
to Cardinal Wolsey from Nuremberg in 1522'. Holmes's errors are repeated
by J. E. T. Loveday in the Roxburghe Club reprint of Morley's translation
of Petrarch's *Tryumphes*, London, 1887, p. xix.

a glimpse of his personality. The first is addressed to Wolsey, and the opening lines prove how anxious Morley was to propitiate him. He offers his 'humble servis' and significantly greets him as 'your Grace' and a 'prince of the Cherche', instead of styling him 'your Lordshipe' and a 'pillar of the Cherche', as he had done before revising the letter. He describes how they entered Flanders and, passing through Dunkirk and Bruges, reached Antwerp on September 20th. The next day they were given a civic welcome. When the spokesman of the city authorities had ended his speech in French, Morley replied.

'After my s[mal] lernyng', he says, 'I gave to theym aunswer that wher we wer not sufficie[nt] to geve theym due thankes, we doutyd not but our souerain lorde an[d] his honorable councell shuld, so that, if percase they hade to do with [our] Prince, he shuld in lyke maner with all humanitie in thar affayars b[e] favorable and gracious. This said, they presentyd vnto vs xxiiij [bottles] of wyne. So we requirynge theym to come and dyne with vs, th[ey wold] not, but departyd, levynge only ther spekar with vs, whiche don, [we] passyd our dyner with all honest communycacion.'

With these pleasant memories fresh in their minds, the party set out for Mechlin. As their arrival coincided with that of the Lady Margaret of Savoy, they were presented to her by Henry VIII's representative, Dr. Knight. In narrating to Wolsey how they fared at court, Morley contrives to interweave a little judicious flattery.

'I gave vnto her', he writes, 'the [Kinges] gracious lettre, which by her red, and she with good wordes thankyd the Kinges Highnes that he dyd not forget her dere [nevew, advancing] hyme to so honorable a norder,[1] I then presentyd to her your lettre, whiche also she gladly acceptyd and by that to vs promysyd, what in her was, other by lettre or otherwise, in the forderynge of [our i]orney at your Graces requeste she gladly wold do. Thus, and it please your Grace, we do take your presens in Inglonde to all well disposyd a sure defence and proteccion, and your lettres beyond the see to all your seruauntes a sure hyghe waye.'[2]

The second letter, written from Cologne, reported to Henry VIII that the mission had reached that city in safety and communicated

[1] That is, 'an order', the Order of the Garter.
[2] MS. Vitell. B. XX, f. 285a and b.

to the King the news of the death of Hadrian VI and such other
information as Morley had collected since his arrival.

'Rumour has it', he says, 'that the Popes Holynes shulde be
dede, whiche [I learnyd] be one of the greateste of auctoryte of the
citi of C[oleyn. He] shewyd vs thate yt was lyke to torne to greate
besyne[s in] Crystyndom, forasmoche as the said person affermyd
tha[t the] Venesyens were nowe of new confederat with the Turke
[and redy] to obey hym in all thinge, for fer leste that the said Turke
haue envadyde fourthewith bothe Sypres and Candy, whiche
[myght] in no wise haue resystyd his puyssauns. To this also, please
your Grace, yt ys said that the Cardynall Volt[erra, whiche] was ever
frendly to the Frenche kinge shulde be ded.'

Then Morley proceeds to speak of the death of Hutten and of
the controversy between him and Erasmus.

'Hutin', he says, 'that was a great frend to Luthere ys departyd.
[How] be yt, we haue suer knowlege that or he dyed, he wrot
[agaynst] Erasmus, and Erasmus ther vnto aunswerd, whiche
Mai[ster Almoner] and I bothe haue sene. But Hutins werke could
no[te be] gottyn; yf it might haue ben hade, I wold haue se[nt it]
vnto your Hyghnes.'

Of Luther, whose doings, as Morley well understood, Henry VIII
followed with keen attention, a full account is given, which
betrays the writer's anxiety about the spreading of heretical
doctrine in the Netherlands.

'Wher I wrote vnto yo[ur Hyghnes] that by your gracious lettres
sent ad principes German[iae] truste of retorne was of the Germayns
from Luthe[re], now I am compellyd agayn to forsake that, ass[uryng
your] Grace that as we can her, all the countre ys lyke [to go] from
the right way, for dayly nerar and nerar [to] Flaunders warde this
flame of herysy incresy[th and without] Godes helpe and th'assys-
tence of your Grace and [other] lyke prynces ys lyke to subverte all
auns[yent religion].'

Morley alludes also to the popularity of Luther, whose 'bokes
goythe abrode in euery place' and to the mockery poured upon
the Pope and the dignitaries of the Church. He likewise mentions
abominable anti-ecclesiastical pictures. One of these he sent to
the King, anticipating that it would amuse him, 'for Doctour
Morener, your frear and our gyde, ys one of th[e] sorte your
Grace may well see in the picture'. This would appear to have

been a caricature of a monk or friar, and in view of the extensive circulation of the *Deutung der zwo greulichen Figuren* by Luther and Melanchthon, one may surmise that what Morley referred to was the grotesque woodcut of the 'Mönchkalb' in that pamphlet. He had found it difficult to obtain at Cologne, no doubt because this city with its faculty of theology was a centre of orthodoxy, but 'in Franforde and Hyghe Almayn as well theys as other [. . .] worse then this may be hade great plenty'.[1]

It is significant that Morley should think that the King, good Catholic though he was, would not fail to relish a Lutheran caricature of a monk; but naturally he was not so lacking in tact as to speak of such matters in the letter which he addressed to Wolsey from Cologne on October 4th. Rather, after giving a condensed version of what he had told Henry VIII of the journey, he set himself once more to flatter the pride of 'my good, gracious Lorde, my Lord Cardinall' by implying that an introduction from him was an 'Open, Sesame' on the Continent. Hence he says:

'. . . the towne with divers prese[ntes shewyd] vnto vs vonders kynde and lovynge behav[your. In] esspeciall Sire Harman Ringe, by your gracio[us requeste,] handyllyd vs in the beste maner. He had vs to hi[s house and] ther made vs a goldin banket, tolde that what th[er] lakyde that he hade, at the contemplacion of y[e same,] we shulde haue it, takinge your favorable lettres in grat[e favour,] so that we myghte well perseyve by hym that h[e ys to] your good Grace a faythefull seruaunt.'[2]

It was to Wolsey also that Morley's fourth letter was written on November 19th to announce that he and his companions had arrived at Nürnberg and that according to information which he had received, the Archduke Ferdinand was expected there within six days in order to hold a Diet, at which most of the great princes of Germany were to attend, with the object of taking measures to cleanse the country of robbers. Furthermore, Morley had learnt

'that to[warde] the begynnynge of the yere shuld be sent a gr[eat] lorde of the countre with a pusaunte army to w[ar] apon the great Turke, whiche ys not a lytyll [hopyng] that without great resystence he shulde put th[e whole] of Hungery vnder hys subieccion.'

[1] MS. Vitell. B. XX, f. 286*a* and *b*.   [2] Ibid., f. 287*a*.

With regard to the strength of the Lutheran movement and its effect on the monasteries his news was, if anything, almost gloomier than before.

'As towchinge to [Luthere, we] vnderstaunde that lytyll mencion of hym [and his] fautours shall be spokyn of, for asmoc[he as by] the longe sufferaunce of the pryn[ces that heresy is] so rotyde that without perell to theym self it is not to be commonyde of, whiche ys great pytie, forasmoche as that the good relygious people be hade in derysion in all the countre, so that theys that be the fathers afferme that, after the dethe of theym that now be in the religious howsys, they shall stande desolate for eny that entende to enter to theym eny more.'[1]

There is no account by Morley of the ceremony when the Order of the Garter was handed over, but it is known to have taken place on December 8th,[2] and he seems to have reached England again early in February 1524.[3]

The journey to Germany must have been one of the most cherished experiences in Morley's life. It certainly remained a vivid memory even in his old age. Thus when he tells Queen Mary 'There is in Germany, in the Lowe or Base-Almayne, a cytye callyd Mastrick, the which stondyth vpon a ryver callyd the Mase; ther ys over the sayde ryver a fayre brydge, the which I my self have twise passed it', one can readily perceive that the

---

[1] Ibid., ff. 289a–290b.

[2] The receipt of the order was acknowledged in a letter drawn up in Latin (MS. Vitell. B. XX, f. 298a and b) and again in a letter written in French, a copy of which is extant in the Bodleian Library (MS. Ashmole 1110, ff. 53b–54a).

[3] Originally it had been contemplated that Morley should proceed from Germany to the court of the Duke of Ferrara and bestow the Order of the Garter on him (*Letters and Papers, Henry VIII*, vol. iii, pt. ii, pp. 1359 and 1373). Even on November 19th the intention had apparently not been abandoned, for on that date Morley reported to Wolsey that intelligence had been received by Archdeacon Lee from Italy that the Duke 'with great desyer abydythe the Kinges imbassatours' (MS. Vitell. B. XX, f. 289b). In the end, however, the plan seems to have fallen through, for in a letter to Cromwell in 1539 (*vide post*, p. xxx) Morley makes it clear that he had no acquaintance with the Italians. Moreover, he must have been back in England within two months of the ceremony at Nürnberg, since Lord Berners intimated to Wolsey on February 3rd, 1524, that Morley and his party were waiting for favourable weather to embark at Calais (*Letters and Papers, Henry VIII*, vol. iv, pt. i, p. 36) and they could hardly have travelled so far south as Ferrara and returned with such speed.

miracle of which he is about to speak gains in interest for him, because he has seen the place with his own eyes.[1] It is with manifest pleasure too that he recalls how 'in reverting home, being lodged in a denes house in the cytye of Mastrick in Base Almaine, he sayd vnto me, when I departyd from hym, these wordes: "God sende the, lorde embassadour, safe and sounde to thy golden contrey and most plentyfull region in the worlde"'.[2] But perhaps the most striking of all Morley's recollections was the unrest which culminated within one year of his return in the peasants' rising in Germany, at the excesses of which he shuddered, as he wrote to Mary.

'I beynge embassadour from your most victorious father vnto the noble King of Romaynes, Fardinando, bearing to hym the Garter, Luthers secte then newly begunne, scant was I retournyd vnto this your realme but that the contrey was in such a rebellion, that is to say, the vilaynes against the lordes, that, or they coulde be appeasyd, yt cost of both partes aboue the lyves of an hundred thousand men. And such crueltye was executyd by the vilaynes to certayne of the nobylytye, that I haue horrour to tell it. How many religious persons was slayne, how many churches burnt, how many virgines defyled, and harmes innumerable done and executyd, yt is impossible for me to tell.'[3]

Although England was spared these bloody struggles, she witnessed much strife and many gruesome deeds, and during the troubled years of Henry VIII's reign Morley played his part on momentous occasions. Thus in 1530 he joined the Lords in the appeal to Clement VII to consent to the King's desire, because of the evils that would arise from delay in granting the divorce.[4] From 1529 to 1547 he repeatedly sat in Parliament and attended the Council to which he was summoned.[5] He was present also at the numerous trials of noblemen who for one reason or another had incurred the wrath of Henry VIII. The list is headed by the

---

[1] MS. Add. 12060, f. 15a.
[2] Ibid., f. 10a.　　　　　　　　　　　　　　　　　　[3] Ibid., f. 9a and b.
[4] *Letters and Papers, Henry VIII*, vol. iv, pt. iii, p. 2929.
[5] Ibid., vol. iv, pt. iii, p. 2695; vol. vii, pp. 24 and 164; vol. xi, p. 48; vol. xv, p. 220; vol. xvi, p. 632; vol. xx, p. 512; vol. xxi, pt. ii, p. 388. See also W. Dugdale, *A Perfect Copy of All Summons of the Nobility to the Great Councils and Parliaments of this Realm*, London, 1685, pp. 495, 498–500, 502, and 504–8.

Duke of Buckingham in 1521 and continues with Lord Dacre,
Lords Darcy and Hussey, and the northern men after the
Pilgrimage of Grace, Lord Montague, and the Marquis of Exeter,
down to Lord Dacre of the south in 1541.[1]

However, the trial in which Morley himself was most deeply
concerned was probably that of Anne Boleyn and George,
Viscount Rocheford, her brother, in 1536,[2] to whom Morley's
daughter Joan was married. One can only surmise what his
feelings were as he sat in judgement upon them. That his mind
was not free from pain seems likely, when we reflect that only
four years earlier he had presented to Anne Boleyn, while still
Marchioness of Pembroke, one of his translations[3] with the
following preface, in which he refers to their kinship:

'Our frendly dealynges, with so diuers and sondry benifites,
besydes the perpetuall bond of blood, haue so often bownd me,
Madame, inwardly to loue you, dayly to prayse you, and continually
to sarue you, that in euery of theym I must perforce become your
debtour for want of pooire, but nothyng of my good wyll. And were
it not that by experience your gentilnes ys dayly proued, your meeke
fachon often tymes put in vre,[4] I myght wel dispaire in my self,
studyeng to acquitt your desertes towardis me, or enboldyng my
self with so poore a thyng to presente you. But knowyng these
perfectly to raigne in you with moo, I haue been so bold to send vnto
you, not iewels or gold, wherof you haue plenty, not perle or ryche
stones, wherof you haue ynough, but a rude translation of a welwyller,
a good mater meanly handelyd, moost humbly desyryng you with
fauour to way the wekenes of my dull wyt, and paciently to pardon
wher any faute ys, allwayes consideryng that by your commande-
ment I haue aduenturyd to do this, without the whiche it had not
been in me to haue perfourmyd yt. But that hath had pooire to
make me passe my wit, which lyke as in this I haue been redy to
fulfyll, so in all other thynges at all tymes I shall be redy to obey,
prayeng hym oon whoome this booke treatyth to graunt you many
good yeres to his plesure and shortely to encres in hartes easse with
honnor.'

If, as there is good reason to believe, these concluding words
are an anticipation of Anne Boleyn's elevation to the rank of

[1] *Letters and Papers, Henry VIII*, vol. iii, pt. i, p. 493; vol. vii, p. 370;
vol. xii, pt. i, pp. 550 and 556; vol. xiii, pt. ii, p. 417, and vol. xvi, p. 449.
[2] Ibid., vol. x, p. 361.
[3] MS. Harl. 6561. *Vide post*, pp. liii–liv.   [4] use, practice.

queen, the task that fell to Morley in 1536 affords a melancholy contrast.

Such scenes were a grim warning of the dangers that lay in wait for those in high places. Of set purpose, therefore, he renounced the excitement of a courtier's life and generally lived on his estates, carrying out the public duties that fell to one of his rank, and for the rest devoting himself to quiet communion with his books. He had two country residences, Mark Hall[1] and Hallingbury Place, both in Essex. The former was situated near the church in the parish of Latton, which extended to the borders of Epping on one side and to the river Stort on the other.[2] His chief seat, Hallingbury Place, stood, until its demolition in 1924, within easy reach of the church of Hallingbury Morley, now Great Hallingbury, at no great distance from Hatfield Forest and Bishop's Stortford. Thus it was not far from Hertfordshire, and indeed at the present day the road from Great Hallingbury to Bishop's Stortford runs partly in the one county, partly in the other. Consequently, it was but natural that Morley should occupy a prominent position both in Essex and in Hertfordshire. From 1530 to 1547 he figures among the Commissioners of the Peace,[3] and from 1540 to 1543–4 he was one of those responsible for supervising the drainage of these counties.[4] In 1544–5 he was appointed to the commission authorized to arrange and collect in Essex the benevolence for the French war,[5] and in 1546 he

[1] He wrote a letter to Cromwell from Mark Hall, the date of which is probably 1534 (*vide post*, p. xxv, n. 1), and other letters down to October 8th, 1549 have been preserved (cf. *Calendar of State Papers, Domestic Series, of the Reigns of Edward VI, Mary and Elizabeth, 1547–80*, p. 25), which show that he resided there at intervals. On August 3rd, 1538, licence was given to Thomas Shawe to alienate the manor of Mark Hall to Lord Morley and his heirs (cf. *Letters and Papers, Henry VIII*, vol. xiii, pt. ii, p. 98).

[2] P. Muilman, *A New and Complete History of Essex*, Chelmsford, 1770–2, vol. iv, p. 78.

[3] *Letters and Papers, Henry VIII*, vol. iv, pt. iii, p. 3076; vol. v, pp. 54, 399, 702, and 703; vol. xi, p. 85; vol. xii, pt. ii, p. 408; vol. xiii, pt. i, pp. 486 and 565; vol. xiv, pt. i, p. 485; vol. xv, pp. 106 and 111; vol. xvi, p. 280; vol. xvii, p. 642, and vol. xx, pt. i, p. 322. Also *Calendar of the Patent Rolls, Edward VI*, vol. i, pp. 83–4.

[4] *Letters and Papers, Henry VIII*, vol. xvi, p. 172, and vol. xx, pt. i, pp. 314 and 317.

[5] Ibid., vol. xx, pt. i, p. 325.

filled a similar office in the assessment of a 'loving contribution' from Hertfordshire.[1] Again, in 1550 he appears as one of the commissioners empowered to collect in Essex and Hertfordshire the relief granted by Parliament.[2] The following year Morley's name occurs in the commission for Hertfordshire which was to inquire into the rise of prices as the result of 'the insacyable greadynes of dyvers covetous persons' and report to the Privy Council,[3] and he is mentioned as one of the justices chosen to deliver the jail at Colchester.[4]

Morley was also to the fore in organizing the activities of his district. When the northern rebellion broke out in 1536, he was required to furnish a hundred men to withstand the insurgents.[5] Three years later he was made one of the commissioners in Hertfordshire for dealing with the musters,[6] and in 1546 he was again authorized to raise levies.[7] Not only did he have to provide footmen himself, sometimes four hundred, sometimes six hundred strong, but he was obliged to see to the equipment of the levies and conduct them from Essex and Hertfordshire to Dover.[8] In view of Morley's position and experience in this kind of work, a recommendation of a soldier by him doubtless carried weight,[9] and in a national emergency it was but natural that the authorities should seek to obtain his support in rallying to their cause the counties where his influence was so great. Thus in 1549, when Edward VI was thought to be in danger at the hands of the Duke of Somerset, the Council appealed to Morley. In spite of his seventy years and more, he sent a prompt reply in these terms:

'Plese it your good Lordchyppis to be aduertysyd that I have resayvyd your most honorabill letters declaryng and expressyng vnto me the dangerovs estate of the Kynges most riall parson, hys

---

[1] Ibid., vol. xxi, pt. i, p. 484.

[2] *Calendar of the Patent Rolls, Edward VI*, vol. v, pp. 352 and 354.

[3] Ibid., vol. iv, p. 141.

[4] Ibid., vol. iv, p. 153.

[5] *Letters and Papers, Henry VIII*, vol. xi, pp. 234 and 236.

[6] Ibid., vol. xiv, pt. i, p. 275.

[7] Ibid., vol. xxi, pt. i, p. 40.

[8] Ibid., vol. xviii, pt. i, pp. 391 and 467; vol. xix, pt. i, pp. 150 and 166; vol. xix, pt. ii, p. 255; vol. xx, pt. i, p. 440, and vol. xxi, pt. i, p. 313.

[9] State Papers, Henry VIII, 3/6, f. 55*a*. See also *Letters and Papers, Henry VIII*, vol. vii, p. 30.

dominions and remes, by the Lord Protectour. To that I mak your
good Lordchyppes thys true and faythefull subiectes anser, that
likevyse as above all thynges, next vnto God I am most bounden to
defend the Kyng, evyn so am I most bounden to defend hys reme,
my . . .¹ and dere contre. Wherfore so to do I schall acordyng to
your comandment put my selfe in redynes with that pore pover I
have, vythin one hovrs varnyng, so ether to lyve or to dy. And thus
Crist Jhesu preserve you, most honorabill lordes, all.'²

Morley's usefulness was recognized in June 1536, when he was
granted the offices of 'chief steward of the manor or lordship,
master of the hunt of deer of the whole forest, and keeper of the
park of Hatfield Regis'.³ One cannot help noticing, though the
connexion may only be fortuitous, that this mark of the King's
goodwill came to him almost immediately after the trial and
execution of Anne Boleyn.

Whether this is a mere coincidence or not, it is likely that
Cromwell had a hand in the appointment, for Morley was on
excellent terms with him. After the fall of Wolsey the shrewd
nobleman was quick to see that Cromwell was to be a power in
the land, and in later years he asked for his help in various matters.
The first time that we find Morley approaching Cromwell is on
behalf of an unfortunate canon who had belonged to a priory
suppressed by Wolsey. It seems that he had been granted the
farm of Bromefelde which had been in the possession of the priory
of Christ's Church, but that one John Smith having challenged
his claim to it, Morley and others had been ordered by the King
to investigate the dispute and had given their decision in favour
of the canon. On these grounds Morley appealed to Cromwell
to lend his support.

'Yn your so doyng,' he says, 'ye shallnott only bynde thys pore
man dayly to pray for you, but me also to be redy at all tymes to
do you ony plesure I cann, whych⁴ at my comyng to the Parlyament

---

¹ The word is illegible. Most of the letter is difficult to decipher. As
a rule Morley employed a secretary, but on this occasion the necessity for
speed as well as secrecy led him to write hastily in his own hand.
² State Papers, Edward VI, 10/9, f. 45*a*. Cf. also *Calendar of State
Papers, Domestic Series, Edward VI, Mary, Elizabeth, 1547–80*, p. 25.
³ *Letters and Papers, Henry VIII*, vol. x, pp. 358 and 526.
⁴ MS. wchych.

wyll shewe you more clerely off thys pore chanons wronges, whom
yet ones agayne I pray you to favour yn the mene tyme.[1]

When Morley next addresses Cromwell, the latter is no longer
'my synguler goode frende and olde aqwayntanse Master Crome-
well' but 'Master Secretary', and this time Morley himself is
involved in a controversy, with a body of ecclesiastics as his
opponents. He maintains his rights stubbornly, for in spite of
his early pious environment he was not the man to bow to an
assembly of monks, and the temper of the age was not conducive
to meek forbearance on the part of laymen. Consequently, though
he might see that justice was done to a helpless canon who had
fallen on evil days, he resisted what he considered to be monkish
encroachments. He therefore begs Cromwell for support in 'the
besynes betwyxt me and the Pryor of Cry[st]e Chyrche in Nor-
wyge'.[2] Evidently Cromwell had previously advised him on the
best course of action, and he had referred the question to the
Council, knowing full well that he could rely on the influence
of Cromwell. For all that, however, the monks of Norwich had
persisted with their litigation.

'They contrary', Morley writes, 'by froward and malycyus wyll
haue gotten oute serten wrytys agaynste my pore tenantes, wyche
indyfferently holdys aswele of them as of me, to areste them and
feche them vp at thys nexte terme, to the pore mens grete charge
and to my grete rebuke, wyche for the goodnes schuyde to them by
my pore blode lokyd to haue bene other wyse handled on them then
after so cruell a facyon; but, to aduertyse you of the trewthe, I know
they wolde neuer wythe oute grete beryng so haue done. And yt
more greuythe me, the trobyll of the pore men for my cawse then

---

[1] State Papers, Henry VIII, 1/65, f. 48a. Cf. also *Letters and Papers,
Henry VIII*, vol. v, p. 10. The letter is dated January 1st, but no year is
given. However, as it only styles Cromwell 'Master', it must have been
written before Cromwell had been made Secretary. Consequently, it must
be earlier than the spring of 1534. Another clue is provided by Morley's
reference to his intention of coming to London for the meeting of Parliament. On looking into the records, we observe that in 1531 and 1534
Parliament assembled in January. If we take account of all the facts,
it seems likely that the year in question was 1534.

[2] Although what is now Norwich Cathedral is dedicated to the Holy
Trinity, it was often known as Christ Church in the sixteenth century.
The prior referred to by Morley was presumably William Castleton, who
held office from 1531 until the Dissolution and became the first Dean of
the Cathedral in 1538.

the lose of all my ryghtfull tytyll. I therfore, hauyng no seurer porte
to fle to in thys grete tempest then to yow, refare yt holey to God,
to my Prynse and to yow, to do wythe me as yt shall plese you in
the sauyng of my pore honeste.'[1]

This letter, which was skilfully calculated to flatter Cromwell's
sense of importance and to create in him the feeling that his
authority had been flouted by Morley's antagonists, probably
had the desired effect, and there may well be a connexion between
this incident and the present of a greyhound which Morley made
to Cromwell as a grateful acknowledgement of favours received.

'For that I know well,' he says, 'after your grete laboures, wyche
ye hovrly take for the welthe of meny, you vyll now and then go
thys summer of sportyng and solassyng, I do sende you wythe thys
my letter a greyhownd, wyche, I trust, shall not myslyke you, for,
and ys goodnes be to ys gentyllnes as I suppose yt ys, he ys mete
fore suche a gentyllman to dysporte wythe all as ye be—I wolde he
were the best. I offer hym wythe my hole harte and my harty love
wythe all to do you or eny that longes vnto you for your sake all and
suche pore plesuer as that I can, to the extremyte of my small
power—God my iuge, who kepe you!'[2]

The Dissolution of the monasteries, when it began in earnest in
1536, plunged Morley into difficulties once more. Like so many
other noblemen, he was on the look out for his share of the spoils,
but, powerful though he was, he could not immediately satisfy
his desires, as may be seen from his correspondence in the
year 1537. A letter to Sir Thomas Wriothesley, his former companion on the mission to the Archduke Ferdinand, written on
February 28th, makes it clear that Morley had succeeded in
obtaining the lands belonging to the priory of Aldeby, but that
the monks were still in occupation of the priory itself. The
problem, as he explains to his friend, was to dislodge them,

'for I not being in possessyon of the howse, albeit I haue the landes
in my handes, no man will gladly medell with them, wherby I haue
grett losse, in so moche that this last yere I lost by hit twenty markes,
and now, if afore Oure Lady Day I haue not oute this lycens, I schall
lose as moche'.

---

[1] State Papers, Henry VIII, 1/239, f. 231*a*. See also *Letters and Papers, Henry VIII, Addenda,* vol. i, pt. i, p. 359.

[2] State Papers, Henry VIII, 1/93, f. 207*a*. See also *Letters and Papers, Henry VIII,* vol. viii, p. 375.

These circumstances caused him anxiety, as may be gathered from his plea for Wriothesley's intervention.

'Most effectually', he tells him, 'I pray youe to labor in hit and schortly to get it oute. And surly I schall geue youe for youre payns as good a gelding as ever ye rode on, with all and suche plesure elles that I may schew youe whilles I lyve.'[1]

Presumably it was this difficulty about which Morley had approached Cromwell on January 18th, at the same time thanking him for his good offices to his brother and son.

'Albeit that nothing is in me, nother p[o]wer[2] nor otherwyse to recompense youe,' he declares gratefully, 'I shall pray youe to thinke that not only for this youre goodnes, but for meny other benyvolences done to me and myne, that if youre Lordship schall call me to go with youe, with the lysens of my Prynse, vnto the fardyst part of Chrystendome, I and all myne shalbe at youre commaundement.'

Thus encouraged, he alludes to 'the matter betwyxt the marveolus monke of Norwyche and me' and hopes 'that syns your Lordship so meny tymes hathe taken payne to se and order betwyxt hym and me, that at the sute of this my sun youe will se hit brought to a fynall effecte'.[3]

In response to Morley's appeals Cromwell agreed to come to his aid, as is proved by a communication dated March 25th, in which he thanks Cromwell for his letter to the Prior of Norwich, 'wherby I ame now clerly at a poynt wythe him, whiche I thinke [I] schuld never haue bene at but wythe youre speciall helpe in that behalf'.[4]

Not even Cromwell, however, could always secure immediate compliance with his wishes, and if Morley had counted on the rapid satisfaction of his claims, he was to be disappointed. The Chapter of Norwich offered resistance, as is evident from a communication addressed to Cromwell on April 15th. In this, while politely declaring themselves his 'dayly poure oratours and beade-

---

[1] State Papers, Henry VIII, 7/1, f. 6*a*. See also *Letters and Papers, Henry VIII*, vol. xii, pt. i, p. 242.

[2] MS. Pewer.

[3] State Papers, Henry VIII, 1/114, f. 171*a*. See also *Letters and Papers, Henry VIII*, vol. xii, pt. i, p. 61.

[4] State Papers, Henry VIII, 1/117, f. 126*a*. See also *Letters and Papers, Henry VIII*, vol. xii, pt. i, p. 321.

men', they made objections to the desire expressed in his 'honourabyll and gentyll lettres' of April 1st that Morley should be granted the late priory of Aldeby in feefarm.[1] Nor was Morley long in discovering that his hopes were frustrated, for on April 21st he complained bitterly to Cromwell of 'the harde heddyd cannons of Norwyche' who, egged on by his enemies in those parts, had raised obstacles which caused him intense annoyance. He therefore implores Cromwell to support him:

'Praying your Lordshipp further to goo thorowe with me and not to forsake me in this my sute, for, onelesse that your pleasur be to the contrarye, I had rather forsake all my poore lordshipps then to be subiecte vnto so vngentle a sorte of prestes as they be, for as concerning aunswer, I knowe assuredly thei haue preventyd me, before this my lettre came vnto your handes. But as your seruaunt Philipp Morice can aduertise you, thei haue not ordered me after no good sorte, for amonges other harde wordes, thei demaunde, yf I were attaynted of treason, what my bondes shoulde availe them for the payment of their rent. And I trust the Kinges Maiestye taketh me as his true subiecte, and in thes wordes, saving your honour, I defye them!'[2]

Yet for all the skill displayed by the Chapter of Norwich in postponing the fulfilment of Cromwell's desires, it appears likely that in the long run they had to acquiesce and that Morley had his way; in 1547 the manor of 'Albeye' is mentioned as being his property.[3]

But these were not the only monastic lands on which Morley had turned an eager eye. From his correspondence we learn that in accordance with the pious leanings which he had acquired in the household of the Lady Margaret he had founded a priory at Beeston in Norfolk[4] and that now, in an age when worldly greed was stronger than religious devotion, he determined to retrieve what he could from the ecclesiastical wreckage. At least, in this

[1] State Papers, Henry VIII, 1/150, f. 143a. See also *Letters and Papers, Henry VIII*, vol. xiv, pt. i, p. 374.

[2] State Papers, Henry VIII, 1/150, f. 172a. See also *Letters and Papers, Henry VIII*, vol. xiv, pt. i, p. 387.

[3] *Letters and Papers, Henry VIII*, vol. xxi, pt. ii, p. 418.

[4] According to W. Dugdale, *Monasticon Anglicanum*, London, 1817–30, vol. vi, pt. i, p. 568, it was founded by Lady Margery de Cressy 'in the latter end of King John's reign or the beginning of King Henry the Third'.

instance he might reasonably plead, if his claim was just, that amid the general upheaval he was merely regaining what had once been his. The first step that he took was to broach the plan to Cromwell. Afterwards, on March 25th, 1537, when he believed the dissolution of the priory to be imminent, he touched on the subject again. The caution with which he sounded Cromwell and the deference that he displayed are a silent witness to the ascendancy of Henry's minister at this juncture.

'As I dyd fyrst desyer youre favor in hit,' says Morley, 'so I most hartely pray youe that I may know youre plesure, whyther I may sew to the Kynges Highnes with his gracyous favor for hit or nay. I schewid youe, if it plese youe to call to youre rememb[r]auns[1] that other I woldc by youe obtayne hit or never speke in hit, and youre Lordschip vpon that movyd the Kynges Maiestie in hit, and he most gracyously consentyd to youre swet[2] for me. The tyme then now cum, my specyall good Lorde, other now or never to put my sewte forwarde, alwayes I put my will into youre handes as my sure port to fly vnto in all tempestes, for no dought of hit, there will be inoughe that will be agaynst me, but God and youe with me, I fere no enemys.'[3]

There was some delay before measures were taken against Beeston, but on March 29th, 1538, Sir Richard Ryche informed Cromwell that he intended to suppress the foundation.[4] In the following year this was done,[5] but Morley can have derived no advantage from it, since the priory was granted, not to him, but to a certain John Travers, in consideration of his services.[6]

On this occasion Morley's association with Cromwell had not yielded the fruits for which he had hoped, but he was not so foolish as to neglect further intercourse with one so powerful. Hence, in recognition of Cromwell's services to him and in anticipation of substantial aid in the future, Morley in 1539[7] presented to the Lord Privy Seal Machiavelli's *Istorie Fiorentine* and *Il Principe*, probably in the Florence edition of 1532. Morley

---

[1] MS. remembauns.   [2] suit.
[3] State Papers, Henry VIII, 1/117, f. 126a. See also *Letters and Papers, Henry VIII*, vol. xii, pt. i, p. 321.
[4] *Letters and Papers, Henry VIII*, vol. xiii, pt. i, p. 232.
[5] Ibid., vol. xiv, pt. i, p. 596.
[6] Ibid., vol. xv, p. 553, and *Addenda*, vol. i, pt. ii, p. 530.
[7] Henry Ellis, *Original Letters*, London, 1846, vol. iii, p. 63, assigns this letter to the year 1537, but the editors of *Letters and Papers, Henry VIII*, date it 1539.

thought that they would appeal to Cromwell, because he had been in Italy and also because these books were valuable guides to one in his position. The *Istorie Fiorentine*, which he had carefully marked and annotated for Cromwell's benefit, seemed to him especially valuable on account of the precedents which it contained for the measures to be taken by Henry VIII in his quarrel with the Pope, but he recommended *Il Principe* too as a manual for the handling of political problems. Actually, Cromwell was already familiar with Machiavelli's ideas,[1] but this does not detract from the interest of the letter that accompanied Morley's gift.

Incidentally, he touches on the plotting and treachery recorded by Machiavelli, and it is evident that though men were not squeamish in the England of Morley's generation, he recoiled in horror from the deeds of the Florentines. Hence his exclamation to Cromwell:

'Youre Lordschip, I haue oftentymes hard youe say, hath bene conuersant among them, sene theyere factyons and maners, and so was I never. But yf they vse suche fraudes, myscheves, treasuns and conspyrasys as he wryttyth that they do, I do not skant account them worthy to be nomberyd amongest Chrysten men.'

However, Morley was most concerned with the information given by Machiavelli about the history of the Papacy in its struggle with the secular power.

'The auctor . . . as yt apperythe in the boke,' he says, 'wrote yt to Clement the seventhe, late Bysschop of Rome. Youre Lordschip will marvell moche, when ye do reade yt, how he durst be so bolde to present suche a warke vnto hym, for he so declaryth theyer petygrew[2] that yf one schulde reade a hundrethe bokes, he myght lake to know of theyere vsurpacion, whiche he schall fynde aparant in his fyrst boke. . . . And forbecause that, as I say, sythens the great Charles[3] the Bysschop of Rome hathe wythe all the prynces medlyd, and bene now in lege with them and somtyme otherwyse at war and stryf, now cursyng, now blessyng, which they lyttell pas vpon, he so accountyth the myschef that they haue vsyd to maynteyne theyer vsurpyd power and dingnyty that I do know very well youre Lordship will affyrme to haue redd no suche thing. At the last . . . he

---

[1] Henry Ellis, *Original Letters*, p. 67.
[2] That is, 'pedigree'.
[3] Charlemagne.

declaryth of the warre which the Florantyns hadd agaynst the Bisschop of Rome and Farnando, that tyme Kyng of Naples,—I think yt passys lyttell fyfty yeres sythens that war was—and how vniustly he vsyd them. And forbycause the Kyng oure soueraigne lordes cause and theyers be sumwhat lyke, for asmoche as agaynst all reason he dothe what in hym ys agaynst the Kyng, aswell by cursyng as by sowyng off devysyon with all nacyons agaynst the Kynges Magestie and the realm, I do exort youre Lordschip to note well what the Florantyns dyd agaynst the Romysche Bysschop and how lyttle they reputyd his cursynges; what shamfull abusyons they leyde to his charge; how to maynteyne theyre righteus cause they callyd a counsell of all the Bysschopes of Tuskan and causyd the prystes, wyll they, nyll they, to do as they com[a]undyd them and appeele vtterly frome his evyll dysposyd court vnto the generall counsell. And this one example ys for oure Prynce so great a declaracion of his rightfull defens that I woold to God that not only all Inglysche men, but all other nacyons, hadd redd the same, therby to see whyther a cytie may resyst in theyre right the wronges done to them by a bysschop—better then one of the most nobelyst kynges of Crystendome! And, my most especyall good Lord, I most hartely pray youe to schew the very wordes vnto the Kyng, for I do thinke his Magestie schall take great pleasure to see them. In conclution, bycause my letter schuld not be to tedyous to youe, in suche places as the auctor touches any thing consernyng the Bysschop of Rome, I haue notyd yt with a hand or with wordes in the mariant, to the intent yt schuld be in a redynes to youe at all tymes in the redyng.'[1]

Another famous writer who links together the names of Morley and Cromwell is Plutarch. The *Lives* were well known to Morley in Latin versions, and he translated five into English, one of which, the Life of Agesilaus, he dedicated to 'the right honorable Baron the Lorde Cromwell, Lord privy-seal'.[2] This compliment was doubtless intended as another mark of Morley's gratitude to Cromwell for complying with his requests.

In 1540, however, Cromwell's career was abruptly ended. Obviously the loss of one on whom he had been able to rely with such confidence must have disconcerted Morley, but it did not prevent him from deriving still more personal advantages from the crisis through which England was passing. In 1543 he pur-

---

[1] State Papers, Henry VIII, 1/143, f. 74a and b. See also *Letters and Papers, Henry VIII*, vol. xiv, pt. i, p. 110.
[2] *Vide post*, pp. liv–lvi.

chased various lands from the King,[1] and the following year he
received a substantial grant of property in Essex and Hertfordshire, which had at one time belonged to the monasteries of
Bermondsey and Bury St. Edmunds, the priories of St. Osyth
in Essex and Merton in Surrey, and to the Marchioness of Exeter
and Thomas Cromwell, Earl of Essex.[2] Some of these estates
Morley afterwards sold,[3] quite possibly at an enhanced price.
In any case, he must have profited substantially by the King's
measures against the Church and the nobles that incurred his
displeasure.[4] Such rewards were no more than could be expected
by one who had faithfully supported Henry VIII throughout his
contention with the Pope. That support had been given in
Parliament and by means of the printing-press. The contempt
with which Morley referred to 'the Bysschop of Rome' in his
letter to Cromwell in 1539 is mingled with defiance in the book
which he published the same year, *The Exposition and Declaration
of the Psalme, Deus ultionum Dominus*. The dedication, which
refers to Henry as 'in erthe supreme heed immediatly vnder
Christe of the church of Englonde', is significant of the challenge
to the Papal power, and the challenge is repeated in the preface,
where the King is hailed as the great deliverer:

'For where as vnto this presente tyme of your moste happy reigne,

[1] See the accounts of the Court of Augmentation in *Letters and Papers,
Henry VIII*, vol. xviii, pt. ii, item 231, p. 121.

[2] This comprised the manors of Tednambury, More Hall, and Monkesbury
or Hallingbury, the farm of Wickham Hall in Stortford, Farnham and
Albury, lands in Tolleshunt Knights, and appurtenances in various places,
including Great and Little Hallingbury, in addition to woods in Sawbridgeworth, Thorley, Stortford, Farnham, Albury, Tolleshunt Knights, and
Salcott (cf. *Letters and Papers, Henry VIII*, vol. xix, pt. i, p. 174).

[3] He was authorized to sell to Clement Newce, a London mercer, the
manor of More Hall in May 1544 (ibid., vol. xix, pt. i, p. 385), and two
months later to sell to the same purchaser the manor of Tednambury
(ibid., vol. xix, pt. i, p. 639). In November of that year he was permitted
to sell to Thomas Darcy of Tolleshunt Darcy certain lands in Tolleshunt
Knights (ibid., vol. xix, pt. ii, p. 419).

[4] Under Edward VI Morley continued to obtain possession of former
monastic property. Thus on June 11th, 1552, he was granted the manor
of Shingle Hall, near Sawbridgeworth, as well as a messuage in Epping,
both of which had belonged to Waltham monastery. Further, he received
the portion of tithes in Great Hallingbury which had appertained to the
monastery of St. John at Colchester (*Calendar of the Patent Rolls, Edward VI*,
vol. iv, p. 337).

this youre Empire mooste triumphant hath ben wrongfully kept as tributarie vnto the Babylonicall seate of the Romyshe byshop, your moste sage and polytike wisedome hath benne suche, that as it maye be well thoughte, by diuine inspiration, ye haue taken a very kynges harte, whiche seketh, as it ought, to rule and nat to be ruled, and hath set the englysshe nation at fredoome and lybertie. What worthy thankes for so noble a dede, and so beneficial an acte, can your mooste bounden subiectes render vnto your high maiestie? We may moche better say to you, than euer might the Romans vnto the most noble Emperour Augustus, that ye are not onely the noblest kynge that euer reigned ouer the english natiõ, but also *Pater patriae*, that is, the father of our countrey, one by whose vertue, lernyng, and noble courage, England is newe borne, newly brought from thraldome to freedome. For where as there is nothing more swete than libertie, nothynge more bytter than bondage, in so moche that death hath ofte ben chosen to aduoyde seruitude, what owe we vnto you most gracious soueraigne lorde, which ar by you, as by a most natural father, the bondes broken, set out of danger, from the captiuite Babylonical, so that we may say plainly as the Jewes dydde to Judith: You are our beautie, you are oure honour, you are our glorie.'

After more extravagant praise of this kind Morley ends by wishing prosperity to the King and 'to youre ennemye the Babylonicall byshoppe of Rome, reproufe, shame, and vtter ruine'.

Nor was the Bible the only kind of literature that Morley turned to account in his polemics against the Papacy. Even fiction was pressed into the service of Henry VIII, and so Masuccio's tale of the treachery of Honorius to the Emperor Frederick is alluded to in the above-mentioned *Exposition* and elsewhere translated in its entirety.[1]

On other occasions Morley sought to combine an appeal to the King's love of learning with a flattering tribute to his personal qualities. Thus his translations from Plutarch of the Lives of Theseus, Paulus Aemilius, Scipio, and Hannibal all have this double aim.[2] Similarly, his translation of the *Commentario del [le] cose de Turchi* by Paolo Giovio is prefaced by an exhortation to

---

[1] MS. Royal 18. A. LXII.

[2] MSS. Royal 17. D. II, Laud Misc. 684, and Royal 17. D. XI. His translation of the Life of Agesilaus was also meant to praise Henry VIII. *Vide post*, p. lv.

Henry VIII to act as a leader against these fierce invaders from the East. Morley speaks of the wealth, power, and military strength of the Turk and compares him to 'that dragon that with hys tayle, as Saincte John wryteth in the Apocalippes, pulleth vnto hym the three partes of the heuyn', which he interprets as a symbol of the way in which three-quarters of the world had been overrun. There was a grave danger that the Turk would establish a universal dominion, but Morley declared that he placed his hope in Henry VIII:

'With Goddes helpe he shall fayle of his peruers and frowarde wyll, for emongest other moste Christene kynges, God hathe electe your moste royall persone, not onely to be victoriouse of your ennemyes, but also made youe Defendour of the Feithe and the verey true setter forthe of hys moste holy and dyuyne wourde. To youe than, moste gratiouse souereigne lorde, I thoughte itt expedyent to translate thys booke oute of the Italion in to oure maternall tonge, that when it shulde please your exellent Mageste for your recreation and pastyme to see itt, that your hyghe wysdome myght counsell with other Christen kynges for a remedye agaynste so perlouse an ennemye to oure feythe. And I darre say, so holy, so noble and so graciouse a hart haue youe, that yf all the rest wolde folow your holsome ways, all ciuill warres shulde sesse, ande onely they with youe, moste Christen Kynge, as the chef of theim all, shulde brynge thys Turke to confusion.'[1]

Sometimes, however, the works that Morley translated had no political value, and he relied solely on their ethical and literary qualities to gain the approval of the King. This is true of his version of Boccaccio's *De claris mulieribus*[2] and of Petrarch's *Trionfi*,[3] of which more will be said later.

Presumably it was because Morley knew that the work of famous authors would give little pleasure to the Duke of Somerset that he returned to the sphere of religion and offered to the Lord Protector a commentary on the Book of Ecclesiastes. The preface is less violent in tone than the *Exposition* which he had written some eight years earlier and for the most part confines

---

[1] MS. Arundel 8, f. 1*a* and *b*.

[2] Formerly MS. Phillipps 10314 and now in the possession of the Duke of Devonshire at Chatsworth.

[3] After the death of Henry VIII it was printed, with a dedication to Lord Maltravers. *Vide post*, pp. xlviii–l.

itself to respectful praise of Somerset's encouragement of evangelistic preaching and the instruction of the people in the Bible. He describes Somerset as being divinely appointed to his office, 'aswell for the wittie defence of vs alle frome our foreyne enymies as for th'advauncement of Goddes veritie, alle vayne supersticion and Romysshe errour troden vnder foote'. And he claims that his opinion is shared by others who see in Somerset the chosen instrument for spreading light among Englishmen, in preparation for the time when Edward VI himself can govern.

'It is also beleved of many faithfull hartes,' he says, 'the furderaunce of the Gospell also witnessing the same, that God hathe ordeyned your Grace to make so godlie a redie waie in the hertes of alle the Kinges Maiesties loving subiectes that when God shall appoynte his Highnes to ruele and governe in his owne parsone they shall not oonlye receyve hys Grace as their headd and kinge, as other nations are accustomed to do, for feare of his aucthoritie and sworde, but also throughly enstructed in the Gospell, therin learnyng their moost bounden dueties, they shall with alle herte and mynde acknowledge his Maiestie to be the veraie same their spirituall heade, by whome God hathe appoynted his spirituall temple to be reedified and buylded vp agayne, that longe hathe lyen waste, overwhelmed with the Romysshe vsurped aucthoritie and moost pestiferous and erronyous lawes of the same. For the perfect and fulle perfeccion and performaunce wherof I shall, as I am mooste bounden, dailly praie vnto the ever-lyving one God, whiche hathe begonne this moost godlie enterprise and purpose, to prosper it and bringe it to suche effect that the thinge so godlie begonne may the same persever and contynue, and that throughe the strength of his almightie hande, no storme of false appostles and teachers, the onelie disturbers and destroiers of alle godlines, maye hereafter be able to putt owte and exstincte the syncere and pure light that now begynneth moost purely to shyne.'[1]

Yet, however emphatically Morley may dwell on the advantages accruing to a people schooled in the Bible, however severely he may condemn monasticism, and however fiercely he may hurl abuse at the Pope, he never questions the fundamentals of the Catholic faith. It is true that he inveighs in general terms against Romish error and superstition, but there is nothing to show that he ever abandoned the tenets of the creed in which he

[1] MS. Royal 17. D. XIII, ff. 1b–2a.

had grown up. To emphasize them on all occasions was doubtless inexpedient, but that he remained a Catholic at heart is suggested by his relations with the future Queen Mary, even though his skill in suiting his words to his reader may now and then seem to lend a different colour to his writings. The first sign that the Lady Mary was acquainted with him appears when she was twenty years of age. At that time, and even long after, her situation was humiliating and, indeed, dangerous. The marriage of Henry VIII to Catherine of Aragon having been declared illegal, it followed that Mary could not be regarded as his lawful daughter, and hence she was deprived of the rank of princess. To bestow the title on her was perilous, as was demonstrated by the arrest of Lady Anne Hussey in 1536. She was imprisoned in the Tower and had to answer the charge of having visited Mary at Hunsdon and referred to her as 'the Princess', instead of calling her 'the Lady Mary'. In the course of her examination she stated that Lord Morley and his wife and daughter were at Hunsdon at that time. This fact is notable, for it required some strength of mind to court the King's wrath by any step which might be taken to indicate sympathy for one under the cloud of the royal displeasure.[1] That Morley was regarded for a while with some suspicion is highly probable, to judge by the hints which the Prior of Norwich let fall in 1537 concerning the possibility of his being accused of treason.[2] Moreover, this incident would explain the great zeal that Morley displayed during the next few years in supporting the King's anti-papal measures. He had seen too many heads roll from the block not to feel anxious about his own.

The preface to one of Morley's translations alludes to his meeting with Mary at Hunsdon, and it seems likely that this took place on the occasion just mentioned.

'I do remembre, moste noble Lady Mary,' he says in the preface to his rendering of Giovanni de Turrecremata's exposition of the 36th Psalm, 'that I apon a certeyn tyme waytynge on your Grace at Honesden, and youe, after your accustomede maners, talkynge with me of thynges touchynge to vertue, that ye dyd greatly commende thys same psalme.'

---

[1] *Letters and Papers, Henry VIII*, vols. vii, p. 405, and xi, p. 97.
[2] *Vide ante* p. xxviii.

If they spoke of it, evidently it was because the theme of the psalm had some bearing on Mary's position at that juncture. Knowing that Mary would recall this episode, Morley afterwards turned the Italian writer's commentary into English and accompanied it with the following remarks on the instability of fortune:

'O, how many is ther of those that, hauynge the goodes of this worlde, weene thay shall neuer departe frome theym, yea, and weene that they be wyser then other and more to be extemyde then other, vntyll suche tyme as that sodeynly, eyther by fortune, whyche cannot stande stable, or seknes, or suche lyke aduersyte, they be dispoylede frome all theyr pleasures and lefte in the ryght shappe of men! As Senek wryteth, that noone be more honourede then those that haue on theym purple robes and golden garmentes on theyr backes, and yet, when suche goo to theyr beddes to slepe, as nature requyrethe, then cum they vnto the comune shappe of all men. I say to youe, fayre Lady Mary, that not onely ar fayre in verey deede of outewarde beautye, but muche fayrer of inwarde vertue, that as for my parte, seynge the continuall mutation of the worlde, I dreade when I do here the name of felycyte, as a thynge vncertayne, vnstable, and thynke myself in felicyte, because I neuer desyrede to haue it.'[1]

It was the knowledge of Mary's interest in the Psalms that induced Morley to present to her a translation of the introduction of St. Athanasius to his treatise on the Psalms, which in the Latin rendering of Angelus Politianus had enjoyed considerable popularity since the end of the fifteenth century. He was confident that his version would appeal to her, not only because of the excellent style of Politianus, but also because 'yt is manefestly knowen to all those that knowe your vertuous lyfe that daly ye exarcyse your selfe in the Salmes, in saynge with your chaplen the service of the daye'. This emphasis on Mary's piety is repeated at the close of Morley's preface, when he affirms his devotion to her 'as well for the heyghe, excellent bloude that ye are comme of as also for that vertu in yow, whiche ys suche that ones yt shalbe manyfest to all the worlde'.[2]

While Morley esteemed this work of St. Athanasius so much, he also appreciated other writings on the Psalms. In particular, he thought well of the commentary which is now attributed to

---

[1] MS. Royal 18. A. XV, f. 2*a* and *b*.
[2] Ibid. 17. C. XII, ff. 2*a*-3*a*

Richard Rolle of Hampole. Morley had come across it in an old manuscript, and as he calls it a castaway, it is possible that it was one of the many manuscripts scattered in prodigal fashion by the dissolution of the monasteries. At any rate, it found in him a zealous rescuer, who afterwards gave it to the royal lady by whom it would be treasured with sincere piety.

'Moste vertuouse lady,' he says, 'thoughe percase sum that knowythe not what a preciouse thyng ys hyde in thys so rude a letter,' might regard him as overbold in presenting it to her, 'yet that hyghe and exellent wytt of yours wyll in the redynge of thys exposition of thys Psalter deme all other wyse. Orace saythe: "Phisisiens promyse, smythes trete of their forgys." Euery man wyll say and thynke his fantasy. But your Grace, that vsythe that holy craft of Goddes worde, specially in that that is Catholyke, wyll well wourke with thys holy exposition of thys rude Psalter and fynde thynges in itt more preciouse then perle or stoone.'[1]

This quotation from Horace was made in the assurance that his reader was versed in the classics, and occasionally he turned to the works of the ancients to find matter for the translations that he intended to offer to her. Thus he combined the ninety-first epistle of Seneca, which dealt with the destruction of Lyons by fire, with a part of the one hundred and twentieth, which advocated steadfastness in adversity. Evidently he was of opinion that such a philosophy would be in harmony with the austerity of Mary and that the ideal thus inculcated—'to suffre all evill fortune that maie fall' with equanimity—might be applied to her circumstances. Of course, Morley prudently disclaims any intention to associate the ideas of Seneca with her position. He had good reason to be cautious. But it is extremely probable that his translation was meant to lend her fortitude in her troubles. He commends these epistles to her:

'Thei ar no lesse worthey to be loked vpon then a fayer dyamonde or saphyre, whiche in value farr surmountethe an huge rocke of stone. Not that the matier of them any thing apperteynethe vnto you, being so gratious, so mightye and so victorious a kinges childe as ye be, and by his fauour and loue in most highe felicitye, but for other, whiche harde fortune bloweth here and there in to so soundry daungiers that when they wene to haue escaped from Sylla, that most perilous monstre, they furthe with fall in to Caribdis, a farr

[1] MS. Royal 2. D. XXVIII, f. 1*b*.

worse confusion. They then that be so wrapped in suche dysease, lett them loke tha[t] can knowe the Latyne tong, of this golden epistle of this vertuous Sen[e]cke; thos that can but rede the mother tong, to loke on this my poore translacion, which I nowe with a loving minde present vnto your Grace, as I am wont yerely to do.'[1]

Obviously Morley's translations were presented at New Year as something more individual and distinctive than the customary jewels or objects made of precious metals. There is another reference to this practice in the preface to his rendering of the 'Somnium Scipionis' from Cicero's *De Republica*, when he speaks of himself as being 'accustomed allways afore this present tyme, either to send youe sum notable wourke concernynge sum Christen doctours wrytynge in the Laten tonge,[2] or ells sum of their workes by me translated in to our tounge'.

By the time this gift was sent to Mary, her position was somewhat improved. Henry VIII was dead, and she could be called princess without danger, a privilege of which Morley makes use again and again in his dedication and preface. But her difficulties were not ended. On the contrary, pressure was harshly exercised to force her to change her religion, and it is conceivable that Morley is glancing at these trials when he vows that he will pray to Christ 'after this transitory and troubleouse sea to brynge you to the courte celestiall for youre merytes'. In any case, he was so keenly aware of Mary's preoccupation with books of a devotional order that he deemed it advisable to explain that if he has on this occasion resorted to a pagan author, it is because Cicero seems to corroborate the teaching of the Church about the after-life. He sends it to her therefore

'surely, to this entent—yf parcase that when your goode Grace had at your pleasure redde it, as I thynke that in the Laten ye haue allredy seene yt, that the booke myght be seene of sum of those that by their lyfe shew theymselfes rather to be of Epicurs secte then of Tullius secte, whiche proueth many ways, and with wonderfull wourdes, the soule of man to be immortall, and after this lyfe, lyuynge vertuously, that ther is a place in heauen sure and certeyn, where ther is beatitude eternall. And I do professe, noble lady, that I, that am a Christen man, am muche worthy of blame that, seynge

---

[1] Ibid. 17. A. XXX, ff. 1*a*–2*b*.
[2] Most likely he alludes to ibid. 2. D. XXVIII.

a paynyme that knew not Chryste nor his blessed religion to folow vertue so as Tully dyd, and I, taught by Chrystes wordes, so often fall frome vertue into vyce. But all thoughe I confesse me so to do, and haue doone, yett I thank that eternall God, I neuer had in my hert, nor wyll haue, any false faith to thynke otherwyse but that to theym that beleue well and in tyme amende their faltes—but that suche shall haue joy eternall, and contrary, that beleue otherwyse, payne in hell euerlastynge, as, to my poore vnderstandyng, this moste eloquent paynyme playnly declareth.'[1]

Similarly, he translates for her some works relating to the Holy Virgin. Thus he turned into English the 'Ave Maria' of St. Thomas Aquinas and the account of the stature and form and life of our Blessed Lady and of our Saviour Christ by St. Anselm. His task was performed to the honour of the mother of God, 'whiche is so highe a worde that, as Anselme sayes, "only to thinke of the Virgin that she ys the mother of God excedis all height that, nexte God, maye be thought or spoken"'. In addition, the preface eulogizes Princess Mary for her 'beautyfull and most stedfast mynde' and her unceasing cultivation of virtue and rejection of false worldly pleasure, even from her tender infancy. But its chief interest lies in a passage which shows that Morley's acquaintance with her dated back to her childhood and that at the early age of twelve she possessed such a command of Latin as recalls the proficiency of Henry VIII. For his part, Morley was so much impressed by her skill that he kept a copy of one of her translations and held it up as a model to his wife and children, who, it is to be hoped, were stirred to emulate so precocious a scholar!

'I do well remember', he writes, 'that skante ye were cum to xij yeres of age, but that ye were so rype in the Laten tonge, that rathe dothe happen to the women sex, that youer Grace not only coulde perfectly rede, wright and constrewe Laten, but farthermore translate eny harde thinge of the Latin in to ouer Inglysshe tonge. And amonge all other youer most vertuus ocupacions I haue sene one prayer translatyd of youer doynge of Sayncte Thomas Alquyne that, I do ensuer youer Grace, is so well done, so neare to the Laten that when I loke vppon yt, as I haue one of the exemplar of yt, I haue not only meruell at the doinge of yt, but farther, for the well doynge, set yt as well in my boke or bokes as also in my pore wyfes, youer

[1] MS. Royal 18. A. LX, f. 1*b*.

humble beadwoman, and my chyldern, to the entent to gyue them ocasion to remember to praye for youer Grace, to thinke that yt is a honor to all women to se that youer Grace, beinge the moste noblest kinges daughter of the worlde, be to all other a myrrour, to follou so right a waye and soche a vertuus pathe as ye do.'[1]

The devotional tone at the end of the preface is notable; it is still more clearly audible in the introduction to Morley's version of Erasmus's 'Laude or prayse to be saide vnto the Virgyn Mary'. In fact, the translator here reveals more fully than in any work that has so far been considered how fervent was his attachment to the worship of the Virgin. His opposition to the encroachments of the Papal power in the secular sphere and his advocacy of the diffusion of the Bible among the people did not imply that he was willing to accept far-reaching changes in doctrine. He was, indeed, horrified at the growth of sectarianism and the spread of erroneous teachings, as may be seen from this passage:

'Albeit that sythen Chryste was borne of the Virgyne, vnnethe was ther noo renoumyde clerke but that he sumthynge saide in the laude of the mayde, yett we haue clerkes in our tyme that dar affyrme that to honour hyr is a dymynysshynge of the honour of Godd, and so, fallynge frome oone hereticall opynyone to another, at last deny the honoure due to God hymsellf in the moste holy and dyuyne sacrament of the aulter. And ne were the blessyd stay of our moste victoryouse and moste Chrysten Kynge, your deare father, I thynk noone other but that ther be dyuers that wolde be verey Epecurs, that doubted whether God was, "Ye" or "Nay"; and if ther were God, that he was in heuen, idle and in quyete, nother carynge nor regardynge vs mortall, but lettynge vs runne at large, and sufferyng vs withoute ordre to do what we wyll, withoute either to punyshe theym that spende their tyme abhomynably in vyce and synne, or to rewarde theym that vertuously passe theyr daies in vertuouse lyuynge.'

And in bewildered indignation Morley exclaims: 'O, noble and vertuouse kynges doughter! How is it that men in oure tyme ar so blynded? I can thynke noone other but that the ende of the worlde hastythe apasse.'[2]

When 'the secunde Mary of this worlde' had succeeded to the throne, Morley again attempted to devise some means of winning

---

[1] Ibid. 17. C. XVI, f. 2a and b.   [2] Ibid. 17. A. XLVI, ff. 1b and 2a.

her favour. From various sources he compiled a narrative about miracles which showed the power and efficacy of the Holy Sacrament. But nearly two-thirds of his work is taken up with matter which is but indirectly related to the main theme, though it had an obvious interest for the Queen. Thus he interweaves the account of the death of Richard III given by a gentleman called Bygott whom he had known in the household of the Lady Margaret. He would tell, says Morley, how on the day of Bosworth

'Kyng Richard callyd in the mornyng for to have had masse sayd before hym, but when his chappelyns had one thing ready, evermore they wanted another; when they had wyne, they lacked breade, and ever one thing was myssing. In the meane season King Henry commyng on a pace, King Rychard was constrayned to go to the battayle, wher God shewed his puissaunce, that the noble King, your grauntfather, having but a fewe, vanquished hym that had thre men for one, and King Richard, layd vpon a horse nakid, was caryed through the felde with shame infynyte.'

Morley pleaded that the introduction of this episode was justified, because there was something miraculous in the prevention of Richard from hearing Mass 'for his horrible offence comytted against his brothers children'.[1] But he would have had more difficulty in proving the strict relevance of his description of the pious and charitable life of the Lady Margaret. However, he knew that in writing at length of her he could count on the indulgence of Queen Mary.

'She kept her chapple', he says, 'egall with the King, her sonne; she buylt two colledges in Cambridge, that is, Cristes Colledge and S. Jones Colledge, and was off suche a benygne nature that neuer man went from her hevy nor sadde . . . neither prosperitye made her proude, nor aduersytye overthrewe her constant mynde, for albeyt that in King Richardes daies she was often in ieoperdy off her lyfe, yet she bare paciently all trouble in such wyse that it ys wonder to thinke it. And in that she was like to Seneca or Socrates. But what shuld I more say? Yff I had Demosthenes eloquence or Tullius or Lactantius fayre style, I could not suffyciently laude nor commende her high vertues and her honour. But, as I tolde before, . . . this redolent floure, this precious Margaryte is past from this worlde, not as other floures be, that to-day be fayre and to-morowe withered

[1] MS. Add. 12060, ff. 19b–20a.

and drye, but this our fayre floure, as long as the sea hath fyshes and the skye twinkling starres, vntyll the sounde of the last trompet shall call all creatures to iudgment, her fame, her honour, her liberalitye, her prudence, her chastytye and her excellent vertues shall be commendyd for euer.'[1]

The tribute rings true, and the sense of loss which assailed Morley, though he was now an old man, with but a few years to live, appears equally sincere. The very recollection of her death fills him with emotion, for at the time when it occurred, he was still in her service.

'Vpon S. John Baptystes Daye', he tells Queen Mary, 'she sawe the coronatyon of the worthy prynce, your father, in a place apointyd on the right syde off Westminster Hall, and that day, I being her cup-bearer and a gentilman callyd Hynyngham being her carver, it is thought she toke her infyrmytye with eating of a cignet, and so, being syck vntyll S. Peters Day in the mornyng, calling her ghostly father, being shryven and receyving the blyssed sacrament off the aulter, the Bishop sayd masse before her, and as he lifte vp the precyous Hoost, this worthy lady expyred. And so, as she had honoured the blissyd sacrament, even so the laste thing that ever she sawe, as I do thinke, was God in his essence, and ys now ioyfull in that celestiall court of heauen, wher she shall be in eternall felycytie for euer.'[2]

Morley speaks not only of his association with the Lady Margaret, but also of his acquaintance with Queen Mary herself. In this connexion he acknowledges her kindness, saying: 'I haue receyuyd of you, my most gracious lady and maistres, a rewarde more precyous then golde or stone, that is, libertye to ende myne olde dayes in quyet.'[3] These words are significant, for they suggest that underlying Morley's reminiscences was perhaps something more than the desire to record his impressions of a great lady. His main purpose may well have been to propitiate one whose religious zeal impelled her to extreme measures. Possibly he was ill at ease, when he thought of what violent language he had used against the Pope, even though it had been in support of Mary's father. This would explain the ardour with which he now set himself to champion the cause that she had at heart.

[1] Ibid., ff. 22a–23a. [2] Ibid., f. 23a and b.
[3] Ibid., f. 20b.

The preface to Morley's narrative embraces far more than one would expect to find in an introduction to a collection of miracles connected with the Holy Eucharist, for in it he tries to demonstrate the perils attendant on any departure from orthodoxy. The conclusion that he drew from world history was that heresy spelt disaster. Thus the Peasants' Rebellion had been inflicted upon Germany as a punishment for the false doctrines of Luther, whose writings he condemns vigorously:

'Luther, the aucthor of all mischeife, and, as I do thinke, the very Antechrist for our synnes sent from God to persecute Cristendome, in his writinges is so vyle and abhomynable in certayne places that, although, excellent Quene, I professe I haue redde Alkarom, Machomettes lawe, lately translatyd into the Italyen tonge, yet is ther nothing so spurke and detestable wordes wryten in that lawe as is writen by hym.'[1]

Another conspicuous example that Morley cites is the wretched fate which overtook Bohemia, after Jerome and Huss had spread the teachings of Wyclif, so that 'the hole contrey came vtterly to ruyne, and specyallye by a gentilman, whose name is called Johannes Ciskay, who so burnt churches, pulled downe religious houses, defyled virgins, and made suche racket in that realme that it coulde never prosper as it dyd, vnto this present day'.[2] And in England the failure of Edward III to suppress these same doctrines rigorously brought him misfortunes in war to which he had earlier been a stranger.

The England of Morley's own time provided him with yet another illustration of his thesis. He discusses at length the state of religion and paints a dark picture of sectarianism and heresy rampant. So gloomy is this picture, indeed, that the reader must find it irreconcilable with much of what Morley had written during the reigns of Henry VIII and Edward VI. In particular, one is struck by the change in his attitude towards the Papacy. Addressing the Queen, he says:

'For wher that off late dayes this your most noble realme was brought to that barbarous estate that ther was in the headis off the people as many dyvers argumentes as ther hath ben heretyckes synce Christes churche began, by reason wherof the vulgar was so amased that many thought ther was no religion at all but to do as

[1] MS. Add. 12060, f. 9*b*.   [2] Ibid., f. 9*a*.

Epicure or vile Sardanapavlus dyd, that folowed so his vityous liffe that vnto this day he is despised off all, lernyd and vnlernid, euen in lyke maner this your realme was brought to that sedytion that first they denyed the head of the Church, the Popes Holynes, next wolde have no saintes honored, but threwe vile matter at the crucifyx, and, adding mischeife to myscheife, denyed the sevyn sacramentes of the Church—some of them willing to have but thre, some none at all—and by ther desertes fyll into so reprobable a will that they not only expulsed the name off the precyous Mary, mother to Christ, out off ther common prayers, but thervnto wolde not the "Aue Maria" to be sayde. This was greatly to be lamentyd, but this that folowith moche more, for the most devine Holy Sacrament of the aulter, the very Sancta Sanctorum, which all Cristen realmes hath belevyd to be really the very body off Christ, these heretyckes without sence or wytt, more abhomynable then Machomet, the false prophete, hath so despised yt and handlyd yt, and in such an herytycall sorte, that, as the excellent Maro sayeth, to tell yt, "Animus meminisse horret,[1] luctuque refugit." '[2]

Truly, it behoved Morley to walk charily, for he was on difficult ground, since Henry VIII, in spite of his general maintenance of Catholic tradition, had his share of responsibility for subsequent departures from it. Yet it would have been untactful on Morley's part to criticize the King, all the more so because of his own participation in abusive anti-papal propaganda. Hence he makes little mention of Henry VIII, and when he does, ignores his contribution to the work of the Reformation, as may be seen from the contrast that he draws between the condition of England in the days of Henry VII and his son and its state on the accession of Mary:

'Now to this your realme, most excellent Princesse,' he remarks, 'I dare not say what I thinke, but thus moche with your pacyence I may say. Wher is become all the plentye that was in your wyse grauntfathers daies, King Henry the Seventh, and my godly maistres, the Lady Margaret, your great-grandame, and in your worthy fathers dayes, King Henry the Eight? Wher is the plentye off corne, the haboundaunce of cattall, the frutefulnes of all thing, as well of the water as of the londe? Wher is become the quyetnes of subiectes and obedience to ther headis? Wher is the golde and silver

---

[1] MS. Orret.
[2] MS. Add. 12060, ff. 2a–3a. Cf. *Aeneid*, book ii, l. 12.

that in such haboundaunce was in this realme? . . . All this, gracious lady, is past and gone, our golde is turnyd vnto copper, our sylver to brasse, and ne were the hope that we have in God and you, swete, delycate red rose, the very maynteyner off faythe, I thinke that we shulde be in worse case then other Grece or Boheme.'[1]

Granted the truth of Morley's premiss, it followed logically enough that a remedy for economic distress was to be found in abandoning the pursuit of erroneous doctrine, and so his survey culminates in a flattering presentation of Mary as the supreme hope of the age. Did not the religious tradition of the English throne go back to that ancient Briton Lucius, who was baptised before there was any Christian king in France, and did it not thus bestow on Mary an undeniable precedence? Again, had not her grandfather Ferdinand won back Granada from the heathen Moors and established himself as the Christian ruler of all Spain? And finally, had she not inherited the title of 'defendoresse off the faythe'? Hence Morley foretold the dawn of a new era of true faith and prosperity:

'The golden worlde shall in processe come againe, and this your realme prosper in peace and in haboundaunce, and if ther be any of your obedient subiectes that by false teaching of the heretyckes haue had, or have, any vngodly opinyon in ther stomack, with Goddes mercy and your most Cristen example they shall revert home to ther mother, Holy Church, againe, which, I pray to God and to his blessyd mother, may in your most happy raigne come to passe, and that I may se it, or I die.'[2]

Morley's wish was unfulfilled. He passed away in November 1556,[3]

---

[1] MS. Add. 12060, ff. 9*b*–10*a*.   [2] Ibid., f. 10*b*.

[3] T. Warton, *History of English Poetry*, London, 1774–81, vol. iii, p. 85, wrongly states that Morley died in the latter end of the reign of Henry VIII. The error was repeated even as late as W. C. Hazlitt's edition of this work, London, 1871, vol. iv, p. 79. The correct month and year are to be found in an epitaph which still hangs upon the wall of the church at Great Hallingbury. This was originally placed upon the marble tomb that Morley had erected there to receive his body along with those of his family. It was evidently composed by his grandson and heir and runs thus:

'Epitaphium Henrici Parkar, equitis aurati, Morlei domini. Henricus, auratus eques, Morlei dominus, vere nobilitatis specimen, qui semper in deum optimum maximum, parentes ac sanguine coniunctos praestanti pietate fuit, marmoreum hoc monumentum commune sepulchrum suis esse uoluit, aui namque auie et parentis vtriusque clarissimaeque femine vxoris suae ossa, vt sub hac mole conderentur, effecit. Quo heroe

and was laid to rest a few days later with the ceremony befitting
a Tudor nobleman.[1]

II

ACCOUNT OF HIS PUBLISHED WORK

According to John Bale, Morley's literary activities were far
more extensive than would be supposed from the specimens of
his work that have come down to us. Bale speaks of him with
esteem as 'uir literiś clarus ac generis nobilitate conspicuus',
and adds

'in Anglico sermone edidit

Comoedias et tragoedias .	.	Lib. plures.
Vitas sectariorum .	.	Lib. i.

Rhythmos quoque plures.'[2]

viuente vere affirmare licet multo illustriorem fuisse Essexiam, erat
enim in cetu nobilium gemma veluti preciosissima, bonarum literarum
splendore omnique virtutum genere refulgens. Cuius suauissimis manibus
optabis, hospes, quietem placidissimam. Vixit annos 80, obijt anno
domini 1556, mense Nouembris; bene merenti posuit nepos et heres
Henricus Parkar, eques auratus, Morlei dominus.'
It is not clear whether the marble tomb was still in existence in the
eighteenth century. Muilman, writing in 1770–2 (*A New and Complete
History of Essex*, vol. iv, p. 143), merely says: 'Against the north wall of
the chancel is a large tomb stone, and over it six plates of brass, containing
six Latin inscriptions in old English letters for the family of Morley.' At
present all trace of the tomb has disappeared, except for a figure, which in
1938 was situated, along with the six brasses, so high up in the tower as to be
accessible only with difficulty. The figure and the brasses were doubtless
transferred to this position when the church was restored some sixty
years ago.

[1] There is no record of the funeral in the parish registers, for although
these go back to 1538, the page which presumably contained the entry in
question is missing. However, Arthur Machyn, the furnisher of funeral
trappings, whose diary, much scorched by the fire in the Cottonian collection, is preserved in the British Museum, records that 'The iij day of
Desember was bered in [Essex] Lord Morley, with iij harolds, Master
Garter and odur [harolds, a] standard and a banor of ys armes, and iiij
bane[rs. . . .] and iiij baners of emages and elmett and cott [-armour,]
targett and sword and viij dossen of skochyon[s], . . . dosen of torchys and
ij whytt branchys [and many] mornars, and after the masse a grett dener'
(MS. Vitell. F. V, f. 63a). The reference to Lord Morley's helmet is interesting, because two helmets are still to be seen in Great Hallingbury Church,
one of which is probably his. In all likelihood, as was the custom, it formerly
hung over his tomb.
[2] *Scriptorum illustrium maioris Brytannie* . . . *Catalogus*, Basle, 1547–9,
pt. ii, p. 103.

Though signs are not lacking in Morley's writings of an interest both in the drama and in sectaries,[1] the compositions mentioned by Bale under these heads have apparently been lost. It was also denied by Joseph Ritson that any of Morley's verses were extant,[2] but four years later Thomas Park[3] discovered an epitaph on Sir Thomas West, Knight of the Garter, in G. Legh's *Accedens of Armory*,[4] and Sir Egerton Brydges introduced it into his edition of Collins's *Peerage of England*.[5] This epitaph was reprinted in the Roxburghe Club edition of Lord Morley's translation of Petrarch's *Tryumphes*.[6]

In 1813 P. Bliss found in MS. Ashmole 48, now in the Bodleian Library, a poem beginning 'All men the do wysshe vnto them selffe all goode', which he printed in his edition of Wood's *Athenae Oxonienses*.[7] Shortly afterwards another poem, entitled 'Henry Lord Morley to his Posteritye' and derived from the same manuscript, was included by Brydges and Haslewood in *The British Bibliographer*.[8] The versions of these poems thus made accessible to the public were reprinted in the edition of Morley's rendering of Petrarch's *Tryumphes* issued by the Roxburghe Club.[9]

This translation was originally published by John Cawood 'at London in Powles churchyarde at the sygne of the holy Ghost'. It was undated, but it is possible to estimate approximately when it appeared. Miss E. P. Hammond has pointed out[10] that *The Tryumphes* was dedicated to Lord Maltravers, the son and heir apparent of Morley's friend, the Earl of Arundel, and on the

---

[1] *Vide post*, pp. lxxiii.

[2] *Bibliographia Poetica*, London, 1802, p. 291.

[3] In his edition of Horace Walpole's *Catalogue of the Royal and Noble Authors*, London, 1806, vol. i, p. 321.

[4] Park quoted from the 1597 edition. The copy in the British Museum, which is ascribed to the year 1562, contains the poem on f. 89a. P. Bliss mentions this epitaph in his edition of Wood's *Athenae Oxonienses*, London, 1813–20, vol. i, col. 116. But he refers to an edition of 1568, f. 51b.

[5] London, 1812, vol. v, p. 15.   [6] London, 1887, p. xxvii.

[7] London, 1813–20, vol. i, col. 117.

[8] London, 1810–14, vol. iv, p. 107.

[9] *Ut supra*, pp. xiv–xvi. The two poems were also printed by T. Wright, *Songs and Ballads . . . chiefly of the Reign of Philip and Mary*, London, Roxburghe Club, 1860, pp. 22–3; E. Arber, *The Surrey and Wyatt Anthology*, London, 1900, pp. 128–9, and E. Flügel, *Neuenglisches Lesebuch*, Halle, 1895, vol. i, pp. 37–8.

[10] *English Verse between Chaucer and Surrey*, Durham, N.C., 1927, p. 383.

evidence of a poem lamenting his death in Tottel's *Miscellany*,[1] Maltravers must have passed away unexpectedly in 1556. The fact that Cawood's publications extend only from 1546 to 1557[2] and that in the colophon of Morley's version he is described as 'Prynter to the Quenes hyghnes' indicates the period 1553–6 as the date of its appearance.[3]

However, it is evident that the translator must have ended his task some time before the book was published. In fact, it must have reached the finished state before 1547, the year of Henry VIII's death, because Morley told Lord Maltravers that the King had seen and praised it. He says:

> [I] dyd as your Lordshyppe doth se, translate the sayde booke to that moost worthy kynge our late soueraygne Lorde of perpetuall memorye kynge Henrye theyghte, who as he was a Prynce aboue all other mooste excellente, so toke he the worke verye thankefullye, merueylynge muche howe I coulde do it, and thynkynge verelye I hadde not doone it, wythoute helpe of some other, better knowynge the Italyen tounge then I: but when he knewe the verye treweth, that I hadde traunslated the worke my selfe, he was more pleased therewith then he was before, and so what his highnes dyd with it, is to me vnknowen.'

The last sentence perhaps indicates that Morley had presented a copy to Henry VIII, though so far no such manuscript has been traced, but it does not necessarily imply, as has been thought,[4] that Morley must have undertaken a new translation before his book could appear in Mary's reign. If the gift was ever made, it

---

[1] Arber's edition, London, 1897, pp. 118–19, contains the poem 'Vpon the death of lord Mautrauers, out of doctor Haddons latine', and on p. 119 we read:
>   And thus, O thus (good lord) this ymp, of heuen most worthy wight
>   His happy life with blisfull death concluded hath aright:
>   When, in fourt yere quene Maries raign proceeded: and what day,
>   Was last of Iulie moneth, the same his last took him awaye.
>   From yeres twise ten if you in count wil but one yere abate:
>   The very age then shall you finde of lord Mautrauers fate.

[2] Cf. H. R. Plomer's bibliography of works from his press in *Hand-lists of Books printed by English Printers, 1501–1556*, London, 1913.

[3] J. Holmes in MS. Add. 20768, f. 23a, wrongly claims that the book must have been published before 1543.

[4] J. P. Collier, *The Poetical Decameron*, London, 1820, vol. i, p. 80.

was doubtless, in accordance with Morley's practice, a handsome manuscript written out by a skilful calligrapher, and Morley would still retain the draft version.

The book is now very rare, only five copies being known.[1] One is in the Bodleian Library,[2] and two are in the British Museum.[3] The second of these copies was sold at auction by Sotheby in July 1832 and bought by Thorpe for Grenville.[4] Subsequently it found its way back to the British Museum with the rest of the Grenville Library. As a note inserted in Grenville's copy proves, he was unaware that there was one in the Bodleian, but he had heard of another which Richard Heber had purchased for thirty guineas. J. P. Collier was acquainted with these four,[5] as was W. C. Hazlitt.[6] Heber's copy was sold to Thorpe for £20 in 1836 and ultimately passed into the Britwell Court Library. It was bought by Dr. A. S. W. Rosenbach for £560 in 1923,[7] and is at present in the Henry E. Huntington Library at San Marino, California. A fifth copy has recently come to light in the library of Sion College.[8]

A reprint of the whole work was issued by the Roxburghe Club in 1887. It was based on a transcript made by J. P. Collier, this being afterwards collated with the two copies in the British Museum. A part of the translation, *The Tryumphe of Loue*, had already been somewhat inaccurately reproduced by G. F. Nott in his edition of the works of Wyatt and Surrey.[9] Miss E. P. Hammond embodied the first chapter of the same canto in her anthology, as well as part of the dedication.[10] Flügel inserted twenty lines from the opening of the canto in his *Neuenglisches*

[1] At one time it was believed that only three were in existence. Cf. *Bibliotheca Grenvilliana*, ed. J. T. Payne and H. Foss, 1842–72, vol. i, p. 540, and J. Holmes, MS. Add. 20768, f. 23*a*.   [2] Catalogued as 4° P. 57. Jur.

[3] The press-marks are C. 13. a. 7 (2) and G. 10713.

[4] See J. P. Collier's note in *A Catalogue of Heber's Collection of Early English Poetry*, p. 232.

[5] Ibid., p. 232. Somewhat earlier he had heard only of two. Cf. his *Poetical Decameron*, vol. i, p. 78.

[6] *Handbook to the Popular, Poetical, and Dramatic Literature of Great Britain*, London, 1867, p. 455.

[7] *The Britwell Handlist*, London, 1933, vol. ii, p. 758.

[8] The press-mark is K. 12. 5/P. 44 E.

[9] London, 1815–16, vol. i, Appendix, pp. lxxxix–xcvi.

[10] Op. cit., pp. 386–7 and 387–90.

Account of His Published Work li

Lesebuch,[1] and Paget Toynbee quoted from the fourth chapter in which the poet sees 'Dant with beatryce'.[2]

Appended to Morley's rendering of *The Tryumphes* was a translation, entitled 'Vyrgyll in his Epigrames of Cupide and Dronkenesse', to which attention was drawn by W. C. Hazlitt.[3] It was included in the above-mentioned reprint issued by the Roxburghe Club.[4] Another verse translation is to be found at the end of Giovanni de Turrecremata's exposition of the thirty-sixth Psalm.[5] It is from *De utilitate psalmorum* by Mapheus Vegius, a writer of the fifteenth century.[6]

In addition to these compositions in verse, there appeared in Morley's lifetime a work in prose. This was *The Exposition and Declaration of the Psalme, Deus ultionum Dominus, made by Syr Henry Parker knight, Lord Morley, dedicated to the Kynges Highnes*. The printer was Thomas Berthelet, and although the title-page bears the date 1534 the book was really published in 1539, as the colophon indicates. Three copies are known—in the British Museum,[7] the Bodleian Library,[8] and the archiepiscopal library at Lambeth.[9]

Of greater interest at the present day, however, are Morley's prefaces to his numerous translations. These have been unduly neglected, though the importance of three has been recognized. Thus Flügel printed a part of the preface to the above-mentioned

---

[1] Halle, 1895, vol. i, p. 111.
[2] *Dante in English Literature*, London, 1909, pp. 35–6.
[3] Op. cit., p. 455. [4] pp. 100–2. [5] MS. Royal 18 A. XV, f. 9b.
[6] Hazlitt, op. cit., p. 402, erroneously speaks of 'some Sonnets translated by Lord Morley from Maphei Vegio' and also in his edition of T. Warton's *History of English Poetry*, London, 1871, vol. iv, p. 80. The mistake is repeated by J. E. T. Loveday in the Roxburghe Club's edition of Morley's translation of *The Tryumphes*, p. xxii, and by Sir Sidney Lee, *Dictionary of National Biography*, London, 1908–9, vol. xv, p. 239. It was left for E. Flügel to draw attention to the error in *Anglia*, vol. xiii, p. 73, note 1. He printed the sonnet at the same time (p. 75) and again in his *Neuenglisches Lesebuch*, Halle, 1895, vol. i, p. 110. The sonnet was also quoted by Miss Hammond, op. cit., p. 391.
[7] The press-mark is 292. a. 33 (2). [8] Press-mark, Mason CC. 37.
[9] Not mentioned in *A Short-Title Catalogue*, ed. A. W. Pollard and G. Redgrave, London, 1926, p. 439. It is, however, recorded by S. M. Maitland, *An Index of such English Books, printed before the year MDC., as are now in the Archiepiscopal Library at Lambeth*, London, 1845, p. 84, and also in his *List of some of the Early Printed Books in the Archiepiscopal Library at Lambeth*, London, 1843, p. 205. The press-mark of the Lambeth copy, which contains the initials of Archbishop Bancroft, is xxxi. 9. 3 (3).

exposition of the thirty-sixth Psalm by Giovanni de Turrecremata,[1] and F. Brie reproduced the whole of the foreword to
Morley's version of a tale by Masuccio,[2] along with the story itself.
In addition, the preface to Morley's rendering of forty-six lives
from Boccaccio's *De claris mulieribus* appeared along with other
extracts in Waldron's *Literary Museum*,[3] and a part of the
preface was printed by P. Toynbee[4] and J. Raith,[5] though not,
it would seem, from the manuscript.

III

MANUSCRIPTS CONTAINING HIS WRITINGS

More varied and substantial than Morley's published writings
are those which are unpublished and still extant in manuscript.
It was his custom, as the prefaces to these manuscripts prove, to
give them as presents at New Year, instead of the usual gifts
of precious stones or vessels of gold and silver.[6] In all, sixteen
have been preserved, in addition to one containing work other
than his own, but with a preface composed by him. This one
manuscript, together with six others, was presented to the Lady
Mary, and yet another was sent to her while she was Queen. Six
were gifts to Henry VIII, one to Cromwell, one to the Duke of
Somerset, and one probably to Anne Boleyn. Undoubtedly,
Morley received something in return. There are records of gifts
to him by Henry VIII[7] and of rewards bestowed on his servant,
obviously when he handed over the present from his master to
the King.[8] Similar entries occur in the accounts of the Lady Mary,
and on two occasions it is stated specifically that Morley's
messenger had brought her a book. It is a matter of interest to

---

[1] *Anglia*, vol. xiii, pp. 73–4.

[2] *Archiv für das Studium der neueren Sprachen und Literaturen*, vol.
cxxiv, pp. 49–57. *Vide post*, pp. lxi–lxii.

[3] *Vide post*, p. lxiii, n. 6.

[4] *Dante in English Literature*, London, 1909, vol. i, pp. 33–5.

[5] *Boccaccio in der englischen Literatur. von Chaucer bis Painters Palace
of Pleasure*, Leipzig, 1936, pp. 74–6.

[6] *Vide ante*, p. xxxix.

[7] In January 1532 and 1533. Cf. *Calendar of State Papers, Henry VIII*,
vol. v, p. 327, and vol. vi, p. 14.

[8] In January 1529, 1538, and 1540, 20s., and in 1541, 13s. 4d. (ibid.
vol. v, p. 307; vol. xiii, pt. ii, p. 538; vol. xvi, pp. 179 and 699).

note that the number of these entries is six, and this tallies with the number of manuscripts containing his translations which Morley sent to Mary before her accession to the throne.[1]

In the following pages some particulars are given concerning these seventeen manuscripts, including a special chapter on the one that contains a translation of part of Boccaccio's *De claris mulieribus*.

I. MS. Harleian 6561 in the British Museum is that which Morley presented to Anne Boleyn. As the title-page indicates, it contains 'The Pistellis and Gospelles for the .lij. Sondayes in the yere | begynnyng at the furst Sonday of Aduent' in French, and after each of them, in English, 'a brief exhortation accordyng to the vnderstondyng of the same'. It is on vellum and there are 202 leaves. The *Catalogue of the Harleian Manuscripts in the British Museum*[2] says with regard to it: 'The arms contained in several illuminations are those of a female, who bears the Royal Arms of England, in the second quarter. Many of the initial letters have these Arms, others have a Monogram in Gold, and others A.P. in different forms. These three devices are repeated throughout the book.' However, the author of the catalogue did not attempt to identify 'A.P.' This was done by J. Holmes, who believed that the manuscript was a gift to Anne Boleyn while she was still Marchioness of Pembroke.[3] He was struck by the allusion in the preface to 'the bond of blood' that united the donor and the recipient, and he examined the genealogy of Anne Boleyn to see who might make this claim of kinship. Only three persons seemed to him likely. The first was John Bourchier, Lord Berners, who married Anne Boleyn's maternal grandfather's half-sister, a relationship which could hardly justify the term 'close'; the second was Henry Howard, Earl of Surrey, her first cousin—but in 1532 he was only sixteen years old and therefore

---

[1] In January 1537 Morley's servant received 10*s*.; in December, 3*s*. 4*d*.; in January 1538, 1540, 1543, and 1544, 5*s*. The entries which refer to a book are in 1543 and 1544. Cf. MS. Royal 17 B. XXVIII, ff. 4*b*, 31*b*, 33*b*, 55*b*, 64*b*, and 93*a*. The reason for the two gifts in 1537 was perhaps that in January of that year Mary acted as godmother to the child of Lord Morley's son, Sir Henry Parker. Cf. ibid., f. 7*a*.

[2] 1808–12, vol. iii, p. 375.

[3] MS. Add. 20768, f. 4*a*.

might be eliminated; the third, Lord Morley, was the father-in-law of Anne Boleyn's brother, and Holmes concluded that it was he who gave the present.[1]

Unfortunately, the manuscript is damaged, and the dedication which precedes the preface is almost illegible. With the aid of the ultra-violet ray, however, it is possible to read: 'To the ryght honorable ladye, the Ladye Marchionesse of Pembrooke, her moost lovyng and fryndely brother sendeth gretyng'. On the last page the figures 'xxxij', probably of the date 'M D xxxij', are visible. As Anne Boleyn was created Marchioness of Pembroke on September 1st, 1532, and was recognized publicly as Queen on April 12th, 1533,[2] it is manifest that Holmes was correct in thinking her to have been the recipient of the manuscript. But so far no evidence which would prove Lord Morley to have been the donor has emerged. There is, indeed, one point that makes us hesitate to accept Holmes's conjecture in its entirety, namely, that in all other manuscripts presented by Morley his name is expressly mentioned. Moreover, the word 'brother' is ambiguous and might be taken in the narrower sense. On the other hand, it has to be borne in mind that Morley was particularly attracted to religious subjects such as that of the manuscript in question, that he was in the habit of presenting such devotional works, and that he was related to Anne Boleyn by the marriage of his daughter to her brother. Moreover, the way in which the donor apologizes for his inadequacy as a translator and ends by wishing long life to his friend displays a remarkable similarity to Morley's practice in the prefaces accompanying the versions presented by him to others. Thus there seems to be very good reason for assuming that MS. Harleian 6561 was a gift from him.

II. The translation of Plutarch's life of Agesilaus has already been mentioned in the account of Morley's relations with Cromwell.[3]

---

[1] Loc. cit. A genealogy is inserted by Holmes, based mainly on pedigrees in MS. Harl. 1529, ff. 59b and 60a, and MS. Harl. 6136, ff. 45b and 46a.

[2] Cf. P. Friedmann, *Anne Boleyn*, London, 1884, vol. i, pp. 162 and 199. Incidentally it may be noted that Sir Sidney Lee, in the *Dictionary of National Biography*, London, 1908–9, vol. xv, p. 238, refers to Anne Boleyn as Marchioness of Wiltshire. This was, of course, the title of her mother.

[3] *Vide ante*, p. xxxi.

The version is recorded by Horace Walpole in his *Catalogue of the Royal and Noble Authors of England.*[1] He says:

'In an old catalogue of a sale of books I found this article: "Lyff of the good Kyng Agesilaus, wretten by the famous Clerke Plutarche in the Greke Tounge, and traunslated out of the Greke into Latyn by Antony Tudartyn, and drawen out off Latyn into Englishe by me Henry Lord Morley, and dedycated unto the right honorable Baron the Lorde Cromwell, Lord privy-seal; with a comparison adjoyned of the life and actions of our late famous King Henrie the Eighth, MS. wrote in his Lordship's own hand-writing, as appears by letter to the Lord Zouch, President of the Queene's counsaill in the marches of Wales, wrote by William Henrick, one of the clerkes of that court in 1602. Price ten shillings and six-pence".'

In his edition of Walpole's book Thomas Park was able to add, on the authority of Dr. Lort, that the catalogue alluded to in the above passage was issued by Osborn in 1756, the translation being No. 18137.[2] Subsequently this manuscript reappears in the collection of Sir Thomas Phillipps, where it was No. 9375.[3] The Latin rendering, which was Morley's immediate source, was that of Antonius Tudartinus, which was available in the edition of Plutarch published at Venice in 1491, ff. xxvi*b*–xxx*a*. It is evident that Morley wrote his dedication some time between July 9th, 1536, when Cromwell was made a baron, and July 28th, 1540, when he was executed. The reference in the catalogue to 'our late famous King Henrie the Eighth' raises a difficulty, as Henry did not die till 1547. If the words are Morley's, they must have been added after the dedication was made. But it is possible that this part of the description of the manuscript was appended by some other person at a later date. The statement that the manuscript is in Morley's own hand must be treated with caution. Even in order to write a letter Morley usually employed a secretary, and only in exceptional circumstances did he pen one himself.[4] The manuscripts that he presented were invariably the work of a skilful calligrapher. Unfortunately, I have been unable

---

[1] Strawberry Hill, 1758, vol. i, pp. 80–1.

[2] London, 1806, vol. i, p. 315, note 4.

[3] The reference given by Sir Sidney Lee in his biography of Morley is incorrect. Cf. *Dictionary of National Biography*, London, 1908–9, vol. xv, p. 239.   [4] *Vide ante*, p. xxiv, n. 1.

lvi *Introduction*

to inspect the manuscript containing the Life of Agesilaus. Mr. T. FitzRoy Fenwick, the owner of that portion of the Phillipps collection which remains unsold, informs me that it is not in his possession, and I have not succeeded in tracing it, either in Great Britain or America.

III. The one manuscript given by Lord Morley to the Duke of Somerset is Royal 17 D. XIII in the British Museum. As is proved by the dedication, it was intended for the Duke during the period of his Protectorship, that is, between 1547 and 1549.[1] It is on paper and contains 103 leaves, the matter being a commentary, written by Morley, on the Book of Ecclesiastes.

IV. Among the gifts from Morley to the Lady Mary was a fifteenth-century manuscript, Royal 2 D. XXVIII, now in the British Museum. The preface makes it clear that Henry VIII was still alive and that Prince Edward had been born; this places it in the period 1537–47. It is on vellum and has 148 leaves. Only the dedication to the Lady Mary and the preface (ff. 1b–2a) are by Morley; the rest consists of a commentary on the Psalms in Latin, followed on f. 138b by comments on some of the Old Testament Canticles. This exposition is attributed to Richard Rolle of Hampole.[2] The contents of this manuscript have often been inaccurately described. David Casley speaks of the commentary as being upon 'seven of the first Psalms',[3] and his error was repeated by Tanner[4] and, in a slightly different form ('the first seven Psalms'), by J. Holmes.[5] Warton made the confusion still worse by referring to 'seven of the first penitential psalms', and on the strength of his own blunder criticized the donor's lack of taste in sending to a royal lady such a gift as a commentary on this theme![6] In spite of the singularity of this mistake, which not only betrays the writer's unfamiliarity with the manuscript, but also ignores the fact that there are no more than seven

[1] T. Tanner, *Bibliotheca Britannico-Hibernica*, London, 1748, p. 573, wrongly says that it was dedicated to Henry VIII.
[2] Cf. *Catalogue of Western Manuscripts in the Old Royal and King's Collections*, London, 1921, vol. i, p. 59, and H. E. Allen, *Writings ascribed to Richard Rolle, Hermit of Hampole*, New York, London, and Oxford, 1927, p. 166.
[3] *A Catalogue of the Manuscripts of the King's Library*, London, 1734, p. 278.   [4] Op. cit., p. 573.   [5] MS. Add. 20768, f. 17a.
[6] *History of English Poetry*, London, 1774–81, vol. iii, p. 86.

penitential psalms, it was given new life by Thomas Park,[1] and lingered on in Bliss's edition of Wood's *Athenae Oxonienses*,[2] and in Sir Sidney Lee's account of Morley.[3] In some respects Horace Walpole was nearer to the truth than all these scholars when he said that in the King's Library there was a book entitled 'Expositio in Psalterium', in which was written 'Henricus Parker, eques, baro Morley, hunc codicem dono dedit Dominae Mariae, regis Henrici VIII. filiae'.[4] Yet even these data are faulty, for the 'book' is a manuscript, and the dedication, which is not in Latin, is incorrectly reproduced.

In addition, it may be noted that Casley was responsible for another incorrect statement, in that he recorded the press-mark of the manuscript as 18 B. XXI.[5] His error was faithfully repeated by a whole succession of bibliographers.[6] Park examined MS. Royal 18 B. XXI and discovered that it did not tally with the description that he had found in Warton,[7] and Madden also commented on the error,[8] but neither of them managed to trace the manuscript actually presented by Morley.

V. MS. Royal 17 C. XII in the British Museum was also a gift to the Lady Mary. The preface alludes to Henry VIII as still alive and to Prince Edward. Hence the presentation must have taken place between 1537 and 1547. It is on paper and has 23 leaves. The translation is from the Latin rendering by Angelus Politianus of the preface of St. Athanasius to the Psalms.

VI. MS. Royal 18 A. XV in the British Museum was likewise presented to the Lady Mary. It contains a translation of the exposition of Psalm xxxvi by Giovanni de Turrecremata. The

---

[1] Horace Walpole, *A Catalogue of the Royal and Noble Authors*, ed. T. Park, London, 1806, vol. i, p. 317.

[2] London, 1813–20, vol. i, col. 116.

[3] *Dictionary of National Biography*, London, 1908–9, vol. xv, p. 238.

[4] *A Catalogue of the Royal and Noble Authors*, Strawberry Hill, 1758, vol. i, p. 80.   [5] Op. cit., p. 278.

[6] T. Tanner, op. cit., p. 573; T. Warton, op. cit., vol. iii, p. 86; Bliss in his edition of Wood's *Athenae Oxonienses*, vol. i, col. 116; J. Holmes, MS. Add. 20768, f. 17*a*; J. E. T. Loveday, in the preface to the Roxburghe Club edition of Morley's translation of Petrarch's *Tryumphes*, London, 1887, p. xix, and Sir Sidney Lee, loc. cit., vol. xv, p. 238.

[7] Op. cit., vol. i, p. 317, note 8.

[8] T. Warton, *History of English Poetry*, ed. W. C. Hazlitt, London, 1871, vol. iv, p. 79, note 4.

references in the preface to Henry VIII as the reigning king and to Prince Edward indicate that it was given to Mary between 1537 and 1547. It is on paper and has 9 leaves. On f. 9*b* there is the Latin text of a poem by Mapheus Vegius, after which there follows an English version 'In an Italion Ryme called Soneto'.[1]

VII. MS. Royal 17 A. XLVI in the British Museum is less easy to date. The preface to this translation of Erasmus's *Paean Virgini matri dicendus* refers to Henry VIII as still being on the throne and therefore must be earlier than 1547. There is no clue to a more definite date, but as Morley's literary activities seem to begin about 1532, the manuscript was probably written between 1532 and 1547. It is on vellum and contains 22 leaves. The calligraphy is especially beautiful. Contrary to Flügel's assertion, however, there is no ground for saying that it is in Morley's own hand.[2]

VIII. MS. Royal 17 C. XVI in the British Museum, which, like the manuscript just described, was a gift to Mary, is also a handsome piece of work. The larger part of the manuscript, which is of vellum and has 12 leaves, is devoted to a translation of *The Angelical Salutacion* by St. Thomas Aquinas; after this there follows *The stature and forme and lyfe of ouer blessed Lady and of ouer Sauior Criste Iesu* by St. Anselm. Here again the only clue to the date is the fact that Henry VIII was still reigning. On the grounds given in connexion with MS. Royal 17 A. XLVI it may be assigned to the years 1532–47.

IX. The same remark applies to MS. Royal 17 A. XXX in the British Museum, though the only guidance on this occasion is to be found in the dedication to the 'Ladye Mary' and the reference to 'so mightye and so victorious a kinges childe'. The manuscript, which is of paper and has 19 leaves, contains a statement[3] that the translation thus offered to Mary consists of the ninety-second epistle of Seneca and part of the eighteenth.[4]

[1] *Vide ante*, p. li, n. 6.
[2] *Anglia*, vol. xiii, p. 73. *Vide ante*, pp. xxiv, n. 1, and lv.   [3] f. 3*a*.
[4] D. Casley, op. cit., p. 260, speaks as if the whole of the eighteenth epistle as well as the ninety-second had been turned into English by Morley. The error is left uncorrected by Tanner, op. cit., p. 573; Walpole, op. cit., 1758, vol. i, p. 78; Park in his edition of Walpole, op. cit., 1806, vol. i, p. 314; Bliss in his edition of Wood, op. cit., vol. i, col. 116; Holmes, MS. Add. 20768, f. 19*a*; Loveday, op. cit., p. xx, and Lee, *Dictionary of National Biography*, 1908–9, vol. xv, p. 239.

However, this numeration does not tally with that of modern editions. A close investigation shows that Morley translates a considerable portion of the ninety-first epistle, which deals with the destruction of Lyons by fire,[1] and then links to it a passage on virtue from Epistle CXX.[2] He also seeks to give a semblance of coherence to these two passages by adding at the close the following words: 'Thies thinges, my Lucillius, yf they be wysely called to rememberaunce shall cause not onely Liberalis, our dere frende, but also all men to suffre all evill fortune that maie fall.'

X. MS. Royal 18 A. LX in the British Museum is somewhat later than the manuscripts presented to Mary which have so far been described. The dedication 'To the ryght highe and exellent Prynces, the Lady Mary, suster to oure moste redoubted and victoriouse souereign Lorde, Kyng Edwarde the Syxt' points to the period 1547–53. The fact that the word 'Kyng' has been inserted as an afterthought can be accounted for, if we assume that Edward had but recently come to the throne and that the scribe had not yet acquired the habit of referring to him as 'King'. If this hypothesis were correct, the date of the manuscript, which is of vellum and has 7 leaves, would be about 1548. Morley here translates the 'Somnium Scipionis' from Book VI of Cicero's *De Republica*.[3]

XI. MS. Add. 12060 in the British Museum is the only one at present known to have been given by Morley to Mary after she had become Queen. It is to be observed that, although she is given the resounding titles of 'Qvene off Inglonde, Fraunce, Naples, Jerusalem and Irelond', she is only called 'Pryncesse off Spayne', which indicates that her husband Philip had not yet ascended the Spanish throne. The manuscript must therefore be assigned to the years 1553–5.

[1] Down to the passage: 'Itaque formetur animus ad intellectum patientiamque sortis suae et sciat nihil inausum esse fortunae, adversus imperia illam idem habere iuris quod adversus imperantes, adversus urbes idem posse quod adversus homines.'

[2] It begins with the words: 'Hinc intellecta est illa beata vita secundo defluens cursu, arbitrii sui tota' and continues as far as the question 'Quid hac re fieri impudentius, quid stultius potest?'

[3] J. Holmes, MS. Add. 20768, f. 18*a*, wrongly speaks of 'Macrobius, Scipio's Dream'.

A leaf before the text contains the inscription of a former owner: 'Ex dono Elisaei Ashpoole Rectoris de Bardfield magnâ Comitatu Essexie An° Dñi 1694', and a second, 'A.C. To Margaretta Phillippina [W]ale 1773'. Later, it was in the possession of Samuel Butler, Bishop of Lichfield, and was bought by the British Museum from Thomas Butler in 1841.

It is on vellum and contains 23 leaves. The dedication and preface are of unusual length, running from f. 1*a* to 11*a*; then follow a number of miracles connected with the Holy Sacrament (ff. 11*b*–19*a*); next comes an account of Richard III and Margaret, wife of Henry VII (ff. 19*a*–23*b*), and finally another miracle on f. 23*b*, which, however, is incomplete. This is the second place in which the manuscript is defective, for in addition f. 2*a* is so badly blurred as to be partially illegible. At the foot of f. 23*b* an entry has been made by some one who viewed sceptically the miracles related by Morley. It runs thus:

> Tantum religio potuit suadere nugarum
> Whatt can't religion doe! Men fools are made,
> When knaves are priests, and they the fools perswade.

XII. Of the group of manuscripts presented by Morley to Henry VIII, four are in the British Museum. Mention may first be made of MS. Arundel 8, which was known to Tanner[1] as Gresham 8. It is of paper and has 35 leaves. Formerly it belonged to Henry Howard, Duke of Norfolk, and was given by him to the Royal Society, as is shown by a stamp on f. 1*a*.[2] No doubt it came to the British Museum in 1831 along with the other Arundel manuscripts. The dedication to Henry VIII refers to him as 'supreme heede vnder Gode of the Churche of Englonde', and so the manuscript, which is a translation of the *Commentario del[le] cose de Turchi* by Paolo Giovio, Bishop of Nocera, must be later than 1534, when the Act of Supremacy was passed. If Morley used the edition of 1538 for his rendering, it may be supposed that his work was done between 1539 and 1547.

XIII. MS. Royal 17 D. XI, which is of paper and contains 40 leaves, is probably the earliest of the manuscripts given by Morley to Henry VIII, for the dedication does not allude to his

---

[1] Op. cit., p. 573.
[2] See also *Bibliotheca Norfolciana*, London, 1681, p. 126.

supremacy over the Church of England, and this fact points to its having been written before 1534. Morley here translates Plutarch's Lives of Scipio and Hannibal from the Latin version of Donatus Acciaiolus. This he most likely found in the edition of Plutarch printed at Venice in 1491, ff. lxviii*a*–lxxix*b*.[1]

XIV. MS. Royal 17 D. II, on the other hand, which is of vellum and has 38 leaves, must be later than 1534, since the dedication styles Henry VIII 'in earthe supreme head of the Churche of Inglonde'. Once more Morley translates from Plutarch, this time the Life of Theseus through the Latin rendering of Lapus Florentinus.[2]

In his preface he speaks of America, referring to 'these barberus pepyll of the late fownde contres, that be more lyke in maner to beastes then men but that they have the shap of men, withe owte eny knowlege of thinges paste or thinges to cum at all'.

XV. MS. Royal 18 A. LXII, written on vellum and containing 13 leaves, must be later than 1534, because the dedication speaks of Henry VIII's supremacy. Another clue is provided by the mention of Prince Edward, which implies that the manuscript was copied out after his birth in 1537. There is still more evidence in the passage where Morley conveys his good wishes to 'your noble wyfe, Quene Katheryn'. If Catherine Howard is meant, we should have to accept the date 1540–2; if Catherine Parr, 1543–7. There has been a disposition to conclude that it was most probably Catherine Parr to whom Morley alluded,[3] but if one attaches importance to the records of the New Year's gifts in the State Papers,[4] one may be inclined to think that the present was made in 1541, and that the reference was therefore to Catherine Howard. However, the evidence is insufficient to warrant any confident assertion. At any rate, the translation is of considerable importance, because it appears to be the first instance of an English

---

[1] The title-page, oddly enough, merely gives the title of the first life: 'Thesei vita per Lapum Florentinum versa' with the sub-title 'Thesei vita per Lapum Florentinum ex Plutarco Graeco in Latinum versa'.

[2] In the Venice edition of 1491 it occurs on ff. 1*a*–5*a*.

[3] Sir Sidney Lee, *Dictionary of National Biography*, London, 1908–9, vol. xv, p. 239, and F. Brie, *Archiv für das Studium der neueren Sprachen und Literaturen*, vol. cxxiv, p. 48.

[4] *Vide ante*, p. lii, n. 8.

version of an Italian tale derived from the source without a Latin or
French intermediary.[1] It is No. 49 in the *Novellino* of Masuccio.[2]
XVI. The Bodleian Library possesses one manuscript containing a translation by Morley. It is of vellum and has 38 leaves.
Inside the cover is the inscription 'Liber Roberti Hare, 1559',
and at the foot of f. 1*a* 'Liber Guilielmi Laud Archiepi Cantuar:
et Cancellarij Vniuersitatis Oxoñ. 1633'. At one time it was
catalogued as Laud H. 17,[3] but at any rate since 1885 it has been
known as Laud Misc. 684;[4] in spite of this, however, the former
press-mark has been cited by various scholars.[5] Tanner suggested
that the manuscript was in Morley's own hand,[6] and he was
followed by Bliss.[7] However, this opinion is certainly erroneous,
as may be seen by comparing the hand of the scribe with that of
a letter written by Morley himself.[8]

   The dedication to HenryVIII refers to him as supreme head of the
Church of England and also mentions Prince Edward, from which
we conclude that the manuscript belongs to the period 1537–47.
The translation that Morley here presents to the King is the Life of
Paulus Aemilius. It is based, not on the original Greek of Plutarch,
but on a Latin version, presumably that of Leonardus Aretinus.[9]

   [1] See the valuable article of F. Brie, loc. cit., pp. 46–57.
   [2] Park, in his edition of Walpole's *Catalogue of the Royal and Noble
Authors*, p. 315, wrongly criticized Tanner for stating that it was from the
Latin of Massuetius Salernitanus. Actually, Tanner wrote: 'Transtulit in
sermonem Anglicum . . . Historiam papae maletractantis Fridericum
imperatorem, per Massuetium Salernitanum' (op. cit., p. 573). It was
Walpole who was responsible for the idea that the story was translated from
the Latin, simply because he misinterpreted Tanner. In this connexion
attention may be drawn to the distortion of another accurate statement.
J. Holmes in MS. Add. 20768, f. 13*a*, had given a reference to 'Masuccio
Salernitano, *Novelle*, pt. v, n. 49'. But J. E. T. Loveday in the Roxburghe
Club edition of Morley's version of *The Tryumphes*, p. xxi, spoke of 'Masuccio Salernitano, *Novelle*', as if the manuscript contained all Masuccio's tales,
and the error was repeated by Sir Sidney Lee, loc. cit., vol. xv, p. 239.
   [3] Cf. T. Tanner, op. cit., p. 573; T. Warton, *History of English Poetry*,
London, 1774–81, vol. iii, p. 86; and P. Bliss, loc. cit., vol. i, col. 116.
   [4] Cf. H. O. Coxe, *Catalogi codicum manuscriptorum Bibliothecae Bodleianae
pars secunda*, Oxford, 1858–85, p. 494.
   [5] W. C. Hazlitt in his edition of Warton's *History of English Poetry*,
London, 1871, vol. iv, p. 79, note 6; Loveday, loc. cit., p. xix; Lee, loc.
cit., vol. xv, p. 239.   [6] Op. cit., p. 573.
   [7] Loc. cit., vol. i, col. 116.   [8] *Vide ante*, p. xxiv, n. 1.
   [9] In the Venice edition of 1401 it appears on ff. cia–cva.

XVII. The last of these manuscripts, now at Chatsworth, is described in the next chapter.

IV

THE CHATSWORTH MANUSCRIPT OF MORLEY'S TRANSLATION FROM *DE CLARIS MULIERIBUS*

A. HISTORY OF THE MANUSCRIPT

The statement has been made that this manuscript at one time belonged to Narcissus Luttrell,[1] but the first mention of it that I have been able to trace occurs in the latter part of the eighteenth century. Thomas Tanner[2] does not seem to have known it, nor does Horace Walpole,[3] nor Thomas Warton.[4] However, it appears in the catalogue of the Library of Edward Wynne of Chelsea in 1786.[5] Evidently the sale of this collection drew attention to it, for in 1792 extracts were published in *The Literary Museum*.[6] This brought the manuscript to the notice of T. Park, who in 1806[7] printed the dedication and prefatory epistle from the specimens given by Waldron with the statement that it was then in the possession of James Bindley. When Bindley's library was put up for auction on December 7th, 1818, the manuscript was sold for £3. 3s.,[8] the purchaser apparently being Sir Peter Thompson.[9] It is next heard of in the collection of Richard Heber, and

---

[1] *Bibliotheca Heberiana*, London, 1836, pt. 11, p. 32.

[2] *Bibliotheca Britannico-Hibernica*, London, 1748, p. 573.

[3] *A Catalogue of the Royal and Noble Authors*, Strawberry Hill, 1758, vol. i, pp. 77–82.

[4] *History of English Poetry*, London, 1774–81, vol. iii, pp. 85–6.   [5] P. 45.

[6] These consisted of (i) Morley's dedication and prefatory epistle to Henry VIII; (ii) his translation of Boccaccio's preface; (iii) Chapter I on Eve, and (iv) Chapter II on Semiramis. The latter ends abruptly 'And thus the wyfe of the sumtyme Nynus, faynynge hyr bothe his wyfe and his chylde, with a mervelouse diligence maynteyned the kyngly dignyte and the knyghtly'. Graesse in his *Trésor de livres rares et précieux*, Dresden, 1859–69, vol. i, p, 447, and A. Bacchi della Lega and F. Zambrini in their *Serie delle edizioni delle opere di Giovanni Boccacci*, Bologna, 1875, p. 26, erroneously assume that Waldron published the whole of Morley's translation.

[7] Horace Walpole, *A Catalogue of the Royal and Noble Authors*, ed. T. Park, vol. i, pp. 317–21.

[8] *A Catalogue of the Curious and Extensive Library of the late James Bindley*, London, 1818, No. 1283.   [9] MS. Add. 20768, f. 7a.

when his books were dispersed in 1836 it fetched £24.[1] The same year Thomas Thorpe offered it for £35.[2] Thence it seems to have passed into the library of Sir Thomas Phillipps, where it was MS. 10416. On June 9th, 1898, it came up for auction as lot 641 in the sale of that particular section of the Phillipps collection and was bought by Messrs. Bain on commission for the Duke of Devonshire for £98. It is now at Chatsworth.[3]

Morley's version has sometimes been confused with another translation of part of Boccaccio's *De claris mulieribus*. This was by an anonymous writer of about 1440, and was in verse.[4] The manuscript containing it was formerly in the library of Richard Heber, was sold in 1836 for £3. 18s.,[5] and is now MS. Add. 10304 in the British Museum. When Phillipps MS. 10416 was sold, the information given in the catalogue was so inadequate that Morley's rendering was assumed to be a variant of the older metrical translation.[6]

B. Description of the Manuscript

The Chatsworth manuscript is the work of a scribe who was frequently engaged by Morley to copy out his translations, when he wished to make a present of them. Six other manuscripts exist in this hand, Arundel 8 and Royal 18 A. LXII dedicated to Henry VIII, and Royal 17 A. XLVI, 18 A. XV, 18 A. LX,[7] and 2 D. XXVIII, dedicated to the Lady Mary. Of all these the Duke of Devonshire's manuscript is the most beautiful. It is of vellum and consists of 47 leaves, numerous initials being ornamented with human faces and grotesque figures, birds,

---

[1] *Bibliotheca Heberiana*, London, 1836, pt. 11, pp. 31–2. Lot 340.

[2] *Catalogue of upwards of Fourteen Hundred Manuscripts*, London, 1836, p. 29, item 109.

[3] W. C. Hazlitt mentions it in his *Handbook to the Popular, Poetical and Dramatic Literature of Great Britain*, London, 1867, p. 43, and in his edition of Warton's *History of English Poetry*, London, 1871, vol. iv, p. 80, but does not state who was then the owner. Neither does Sir Sidney Lee locate it in his day.

[4] See the edition of Gustav Schleich, *Die mittelenglische Umdichtung von Boccaccios 'De claris mulieribus'*, Leipzig, 1924, p. 106.

[5] *Bibliotheca Heberiana*, pt. 11, p. 8. Lot 81.

[6] Cf. Max Foerster in *Archiv für das Studium der neueren Sprachen und Literaturen*, vol. cx, p. 103.   [7] *Vide post*, p. lxvi, n. 2.

animals, and flowers of great delicacy and charm. Of especial
interest is the initial on f. 1a, where the capital of the word 'To'
is in the form of a rose, with the letters $\frac{\text{'H R}}{\text{VIII}}$, on the stalk, the
artist's idea being evidently to use the first initial for a compli-
ment to the Tudor sovereign. It is also notable that on f. 12b
the initial letter of the name 'Marpesia' embraces the inscription
'aue maria pro'. The translation of Boccaccio's preface breaks
off abruptly on f. 3b: 'I wyllnot also forgete to tell youe that
emonge all thies women, whiche were but panymes, our fyrste
mother Eue sett asyde, I'. This is followed on f. 4a by these
words: 'Of Eue, oure fyrste mother. The fyrst chapitre. Hauynge
intencion to wryte the exellent glory that the noble women in
tyme passyd haue obteyned, it semethe to me that it is not
incongruente to begynne at the commune mother of vs all.'[1]
Obviously something is lacking, and a glance at the original
makes it clear that a leaf is missing. When this went astray we
do not know, but it is possible to show that the manuscript must
have been imperfect in 1792, because Waldron, in his desire to
secure coherence, connected the end of f. 3b with the opening
of the Life of Eve, leaving out the title. Thus in his text[2] the
passage ran: 'I wyll not also forgete to tell youe, that emonge all
thies women whiche were but panymes (our fyrste mother Eue
sett asyde) I havynge intencion to wryte the exellent glory that
the noble women in tyme passyd have obteyned, it semethe to
me that it is not incongruente to begynne at the commune mother
of us all.'[3]

Quite apart from this defect in the manuscript, Morley's
translation is incomplete. The original contained one hundred
and four lives, beginning with Eve and ending with Joanna,
Queen of Naples,[4] but the manuscript breaks off after the forty-

[1] *Vide post*, pp. 7–8.

[2] *The Literary Museum*, p. v.

[3] In a few places the manuscript has been marked by a pencil. A
comparison of these passages with the extracts printed in *The Literary
Museum* leaves no doubt that this scribbling is the work of the vandalistic
Waldron.

[4] The editor of the Berne edition of 1539 inserted before the Life of
Joanna that of Brynhild, which he derived from Boccaccio's *De casibus
virorum illustrium*, thus bringing the total up to 105.

sixth, that of Lucrece. Whether Morley ever translated more is uncertain, but perhaps the somewhat vague words 'as farr as it gothe' in his preface indicate that he interrupted his labours at this stage.

C. Its Spelling and Punctuation

It is one of the peculiarities of the scribe who copied the Chats-worth manuscript that he frequently hesitated over the spelling of words beginning with 'exc'. Thus we sometimes find 'ex-cedyng' and sometimes 'exedyng'. However, the word 'excellent' almost invariably appears as 'exellent'.[1] This feature occurs in the other manuscripts that may be ascribed to him.[2] Another characteristic, though less distinctive, is the occasional spelling of the word 'peace' as 'peax'.[3] The only letter that is doubled to indicate a capital is 'f'. Now and then the scribe departs from his practice and writes 'F'.[4] The letters 'w' and 'v' are generally employed in accordance with the usage of the period, but sporadically such forms are found as 'wery' for 'very',[5] 'dewylles' for 'deuylles',[6] and 'eschewyde' for 'escheuyde', meaning 'accomplished'.[7] It may be observed also that the scribe often combines the adverb of negation with the preceding verb, as in 'shallnot',[8] 'shuldnot',[9] 'wyllnot',[10] 'woldenot',[11] 'couldenot',[12] 'hadnot',[13] and 'knownot'.[14]

---

[1] The form 'excellente' on f. 1b is unusual.

[2] MS. Royal 17 A. XLVI, ff. 4a, 7b, and 12b, *exellent*; ff. 11b and 21b, *exellente*; f. 15b, *exellently*; but ff. 9a and 14a, *excellent*, and f. 14a, *excellente*; MS. Royal 18 A. XV, f. 2b, *exellently*, and f. 3a, *exellent*; MS. Royal 18 A. LX, f. 1a, *exellent*, and f. 1b, *exellente*, whereas in the later part of the manuscript, which is in the hand of another scribe, the spelling is *excellent*; MS. Royal 18 A. LXII, f. 3a, *exellently*, f. 4b, *exellent*; MS. Royal 2 D. XXVIII, ff. 1b and 2a, *exellent*; MS. Arundel 8, ff. 3b, 8a, 13a, 14b, 15a, and 34a, *exellent*, and ff. 13b and 31b, *exellently*.

[3] Cf. the Chatsworth MS., ff. 13a, 13b, and 23b, and MS. Royal 18 A. LXII, f. 12b. On the other hand, in MS. Arundel 8 on ff. 8a, 8b, 9a, 9b, 12b, 13a, 15b, 17a, 18a, 21b, and 23b the scribe writes *peas* and on ff. 2a, 4a, 16b, and 17b *pease*.

[4] ff. 24b and 41a.

[5] f. 6a.

[6] f. 7a. Cf. *dewyll*, ff. 6b and 42b; *dewell*, f. 42b; *dewyles*, f. 29a, and *dewylyshe*, f. 28b.

[7] f. 5a.   [8] f. 14b.   [9] f. 1b.   [10] f. 3b.

[11] f. 2a.   [12] f. 5a.   [13] f. 15a.   [14] f. 44b.

The punctuation is based on an adequate system, which, however, is not always applied. It is of a rhetorical kind and seeks to mark the places where one would pause in reading aloud. To indicate these pauses the point and the virgule are available. They may be used singly or jointly. In combination they serve especially to emphasize a more important pause, as at the end of a sentence. For example: 'Not onely by armes they were renoumede aboue all other naciones. but also in eloquens and goode lernynge. as it apperethe by thyes oratours and poetes in the greate Augustus days. that is to saye. Varro / Tullius / Cicero / Virgill / Orace and Ouyde with diuers others./'[1] When the point and the virgule are combined, the former comes first in the great majority of cases. But the reverse order is found now and then.[2]

The two signs are also used singly or together after the word 'say', when a clause reporting a statement follows, or before 'that', introducing a dependent clause. Similarly, they may take the place of an exclamation mark or a mark of interrogation. It sometimes happens too that a parenthesis is completed by a point instead of one of the brackets.[3] Before and after a numeral a point is employed, and, as a rule, before and after the exclamations 'A' and 'O'. If the exclamation follows the end of a sentence, the first point may be preceded by a point and a virgule, e.g. 'She desyrede to bye noo more grounde of the inhabitantes. then she coulde compasse with an oxe hyde. which to hyr gladly grauntyde. / .O. wonderfull womans wytte. / she cutt the hyde in small lasys.'[4] On the other hand, the point before the virgule may be omitted, as in '.I. am a woman of fleshe / bloode and boone. and not of the harde yron / .O. wanton and scornefull excuse'.[5] Or, alternatively, the combined point and virgule are retained, but the point before the exclamation is dropped, e.g. 'And my neyghbours wilnot suffre me to be in quyete vntyll .I. mary. / A. goode lady. as who shulde say ye were so ignoraunte'.[6] And yet again the four signs may be simplified to a point before and after the exclamation, e.g., 'and emongst other sparede not hyr oune

---

[1] See p. 1, ll. 10–14.
[2] ff. 29a and 35a.
[3] See f. 17b and ff. 45b–46a.
[4] f. 40a. See p. 137, ll. 13–14.
[5] f. 41b. See p. 141, ll. 11–12.
[6] f. 42a. See p. 143, ll. 12–14.

sonne a yonge prynce of singler beautie and personage. O. shamefull and abhomynable fylthe /'.[1] The scribe adopts a similar practice with regard to the pronoun 'I', as may be seen from these instances:

(*a*) 'this valliaunt virago preasynge emonge the moste valliauntes of the Grekes to the entente to shewe to hyr loue what a noble hert she had / not withoute greate slaughter of theym was slayne. / .I. deny not but sum say that or she came to Troy Hector was deade /'[2]

(*b*) 'She was doughter to Solis. which he had by Perse hys wyfe that was doughter to Oceanus the suster to Oethes Kynge of Colchos / .I. thynke she is sayde to be the doughter of Solis. because that she floryshede in excessyue beautie.'[3]

(*c*) 'And forbecause that one shuldnot thynke. I. do feyne. / I. shall sett the wordes in the Italiane tunge.'[4]

It was no doubt the habit of writing a point before and after 'I' that led the scribe to insert it before and after the name 'Io',[5] and on one occasion before the adjective 'Iuorye'.[6]

Finally, attention may be drawn to the device of employing the point or the virgule, or both, to prevent confusion, when a word is repeated or when two similar words occur in succession. Generally it is the virgule that is found:

(*a*) 'toke to hyr / hyr armour'.[7]

(*b*) 'toke frome hyr / hyre lyfe'.[8]

(*c*) 'And when he wente hys waye after he had / had by hyr too children by the lawe that was made emonge the women / wylde she / nylde she / she was compellyde to sende theym oute of hyr londe.'[9]

(*d*) 'and had / had / afore that. by hym many chyldren.'[10]

(*e*) 'The day comen all bewepte with teares Lucres called to hyr / hyr father.'[11]

(*f*) 'she burnte not oonely Crewsa. but also the children that Jasone had . had. by hyr./'[12]

(*g*) 'hauynge with hyr. / hyr yonge brother callede Absoetes.'[13]

(*h*) 'And that. / that worste is the lyf of man shortyde therby by famyne /'[14]

(*i*) 'or he were / waare Jupiter was taken in loue with hyr /'[15]

[1] f. 6*a*. See p. 15, ll. 7–9.   [2] f. 31*a*. See p. 104, l. 17 to p. 105, l. 3.
[3] f. 35*a*. See p. 119, ll. 12–16.   [4] f. 1*b*. See p. 2, ll. 8–10.
[5] ff. 10*b* and 11*a*.   [6] f. 34*a*.   [7] f. 5*b*. See p. 14, ll. 8–9.
[8] f. 6*a*. See p. 17, l. 2.   [9] f. 17*b*. See p. 57, ll. 13–16.
[10] f. 33*a*. See p. 111, l. 2.   [11] f. 46*b*. See p. 158, l. 20 to p. 159, l. 1.
[12] f. 18*b*. See p. 61, ll. 11–12.   [13] f. 18*b*. See p. 60, ll. 14–15.
[14] f. 8*b*. See p. 24, ll. 14–15.   [15] f. 11*b*. See p. 36, ll. 12–13.

D. THE DATE OF THE MANUSCRIPT

The evidence for dating the manuscript is slender. In the dedication Henry VIII is referred to as 'suppreme heede of the Churche of Englonde and Irelonde'; this indicates that the translation is later than 1534. But there is no other definite clue, for the prayer at the end of the dedication that Christ may 'teche that right Christen hande of yours to batell agaynste youre auncyente ennemyes', though it probably alludes to Henry's feud with Rome, is too vague to be of any service. One can only conclude, therefore, that the manuscript belongs to the period 1534–47.

E. THE TEXT USED BY MORLEY

Theoretically, Morley might have based his version on a French intermediary, and at the time when he performed his task, the rendering of Laurent de Premierfait was accessible to him. It had been published by Anthoine Vérard in 1493 and reprinted with but slight modification by Pierre Hermier in 1538. However, this translation may at once be excluded from consideration, for it treats the original freely, often condensing the text, and elsewhere adding comment of a moralizing or anti-pagan tendency, to which there is no counterpart in Morley's version.

The Latin text was available in four editions, the first printed by Johann Zainer at Ulm in 1473,[1] the second, thought to have been printed by G. Husner at Strasburg about 1474–5,[2] the third printed at Louvain by Egidius van der Heerstraten in 1487,[3] and the last, published by Mathias Apiarius at Berne in 1539. If these editions are compared, we observe that though they all contain the substance of what Morley calls 'The preface of th'exellent clerc, John Bocasse, of his booke, intitlede in the Latyne tunge "De preclaris mulieribus."'' only one describes it in such a way

---

[1] Cf. *Gesamtkatalog der Wiegendrucke*, Leipzig, 1925–, vol. iv, No. 4483. The British Museum has two copies, of which the press-marks are IB. 9110 and G. 1449.

[2] Ibid., No. 4484. The British Museum has two copies; their press-marks are IB. 1023 A and 86. k. 12 (2).

[3] Ibid., No. 4485. The British Museum copy has the press-mark IB. 49350.

as to recall the wording of his title. That is the Louvain edition, which says 'Incipit Prologus Johannis Bocacij / in librum de claris mulieribus', and at the end of this passage it is again spoken of as the 'Prologus'. However, there is a discrepancy between Morley's 'De preclaris mulieribus' and the title here given to the work by van der Heerstraten. How can it be accounted for? The editions of 1473 and 1539 describe the book as 'De claris mulieribus' and therefore cannot explain Morley's nomenclature. But the Strasburg and Louvain editions, while calling it 'De claris mulieribus' in the section that Morley terms the preface, refer to it in the colophon as 'de preclaris mulieribus'. That there is any connexion between Morley's translation and Husner's edition is improbable, because the latter says nothing that would tally with the word 'preface'. Further, the different lives in his edition merely contain headings such as 'De Opi Saturni coniuge', but the work is not divided into chapters, one for each woman whose history is related, as are the texts of both van der Heerstraten and Morley. It would seem, therefore, that Morley had the Louvain edition before him and that, seeing the word 'Prologus', he rendered it by 'preface', but that, for the sake of consistency or some other reason he inserted here the title that he had read at the close of van der Heerstraten's text.

A scrutiny of the texts bears out this conclusion. The edition of 1539 was clearly founded on the same tradition as was followed by Zainer, but introduced such corrections and emendation as had become necessary in view of the growth of classical scholarship during the interval of sixty-six years. On the other hand, the text of the Louvain edition frequently has distinctive features, which bring it into more intimate relationship with that of Strasburg. In the spelling of names, in the choice of textual readings, and even in the incorporation of errors, they agree closely.[1] But as Husner's edition has already been eliminated on other grounds, the text of van der Heerstraten is manifestly what Morley must have employed. His translation corroborates this opinion, for, if allowance be made for the distortion caused by a scribe unfamiliar with the names of places and persons in ancient

---

[1] The textual variants have been given in some detail to prove the relationship of the different editions.

times, the forms in Morley's translation appear to correspond to those in the edition of Louvain.[1] In addition, where the text of his source was corrupt, one can note how he sought to overcome the difficulty by omitting the passage or rendering it freely.

V

MORLEY'S READING AND LITERARY INTERESTS

Nothing is more characteristic of Morley than his intellectual curiosity. He was always eager to read anything new, and it is typical of him that when on a diplomatic mission he made it his business to lay hands on the *Spongia* of Erasmus because of its attack on Hutten, and to discover what he could of Luther's publications. Similarly, when an Italian translation of the *Koran* appeared,[2] in spite of his seventy years and more, Morley studied it with zest.[3] As a result of this enthusiastic pursuit of knowledge, he acquired a store of learning which is continually displayed in his writings.

It is evident that he was fond of works of a devotional character. The Bible, in particular, must have been constantly in his hand, for at every turn he shows great intimacy, not only with the Old and New Testaments, but also with the Apocrypha. Its characters and events come to him unsought as illustrations of right and wrong conduct, and as manifestations of the workings of God in relation to man. Above all, he found food for his mind in the Psalms, which, as he told the Lady Mary, were his daily reading,[4] and on one occasion when he waited upon her, it was one of the Psalms that formed the subject of their conversation.[5] Commentators on the Psalms were also often at his side, for Morley maintained that in spite of the changes brought about by the Reformation, these writers had not been superseded. On the contrary, such expositions 'writton vppon Scripture and groundid vppon Godes worde hathe remaynid vnto thes days and shall contynwe vnto the laste days agaynst the mynde and power of

---

[1] Examples of forms peculiar to the Louvain edition, to which Morley's translation corresponds, will be found as follows: p. 5, n. 23; p. 5, n. 24; p. 5, n. 30; p. 14, n. 22; p. 37, n. 30; p. 68, n. 18 Sibillas; p. 108, n. 20; p. 154, n. 21.

[2] *L'Alcorano di Macometta*, 1547.   [3] MS. Add. 12060, f. 9*b*.

[4] MS. Royal 17 C. XII, f. 2*b*.   [5] Ibid. 18 A. XV, f. 2*a*.

all detracters, herytikes, sectes a[nd]¹ sacramentaryes'.² Holding such views, Morley thought it most fitting to present to the Lady Mary Richard Rolle's commentary on the Psalms and a translation of the preface of St. Athanasius to his exposition of the Psalms. The latter work, which had been turned into Latin by Angelus Politianus, had frequently been printed after its first publication in 1498 and ranked high in Morley's esteem. Indeed, although he had read many commentaries on the Psalms, he thought this 'the flower of them all'. However, his admiration did not prevent him from having also a special predilection for the exposition of the thirty-sixth Psalm by Johannes de Turrecremata. Here was a theme which appealed strongly to one who felt so acutely the mutability of things that the very mention of happiness filled him with dread.³ And to a determinist like Morley there was something more than usually congenial in a writer who 'blameth those that ymagyne, because that oftentymes the goode in this worlde lyue in laboure and payne, and the euyll in greate prosperite and ryches, they suppose all to cum by chaunce and not by the gouernaunce and prescyens of God'.⁴

Fathers of the Church such as St. Gregory were also at Morley's elbow, and from that moving document the *Confessions* of St. Augustine he had culled as an example of the bitterness of human affection the words: 'I was miserablye scorgid in the myddes of my loue.'⁵ The works of 'that great clarke' St. Thomas Aquinas, as well as the religious writings of Erasmus, doubtless lined the walls of Morley's library in his Essex home. His knowledge of ecclesiastical literature was indeed such as to stand him in good stead when he was dealing with the controversies of his day. Thus when he touches on the monastic system, he is able to refer not only to Silvanus and the fourteenth-century exegetist Nicholas of Lyra, but also to the great fathers such as St. Jerome and St. Anselm. In addition, he was well versed in the history of the Church from the time of Constantine's donation to Silvester I down to his own contemporaries Alexander VI, Julius II, Leo X, Clement VII, and Paul III.

¹ MS. a.   ² MS. Royal 17 D. XIII, f. 103a and
³ Ibid. 18 A. XV, f. 2a and b. *Vide ante*, p. xxxvii.
⁴ Ibid., f. 3a.   ⁵ Ibid. 17 D. XIII, f. 15b.

He was perhaps even better informed about secular history and could trace the successive rise and fall of Assyrians, Medes, Persians, Greeks, and Romans. The names of Codrus, Lycurgus, Cyrus, Themistocles, Epaminondas, and Alexander are cited as examples of virtues or vices to be imitated or eschewed. Above all, Morley was steeped in the history of Rome. He had read Livy and was familiar with the deeds of Catiline, Pompey, Julius Caesar, and Augustus. The later emperors too, Nero, Commodus, Heliogabalus, Justinian, and Theodosius, are led forth like so many puppets on the stage as by one who had them at his command.

On the other hand, Morley's references to Diogenes, Crates, Aristotle, and Epicurus do not prove conclusively that he was a student of ancient philosophy, and in the same way it would be hazardous to conclude from his allusion to Terence that he had read or seen his plays, though Bale's account of Morley undoubtedly appears to imply that he took an interest in drama.[1] Similarly, when he speaks of Varro, Ovid, the two Plinies, Martial, and Quintilian, he does not reveal how far they had come within his purview. However, it is possible that he had read some Claudian,[2] that he knew the *Miles Gloriosus* of Plautus, and that he had conned his Virgil[3] and the *Commentaries* of Julius Caesar. The fables of Aesop were manifestly a source of delight to him, and the stories of the dog and his shadow, the crow in borrowed feathers, the cock and the precious stone, and the dog in the manger, every now and then serve to reinforce his arguments.[4]

---

[1] *Vide ante*, p. xlvii.

[2] In addressing Queen Mary, he quotes the words of Theodosius to Honorius:

'componitur orbis
regis ad exemplum'

from Claudian's *Panegyricus de quarto consulatu Honorii Augusti*, ll. 299–300 (cf. MS. Add. 12060, f. 1*b*).

[3] He cites *Aeneid*, book ii, l. 12 (cf. MS. Add. 12060, f. 3*a*).

[4] There are grounds for thinking that Morley did not read Aesop in Caxton's translation of 1484. In the first place, the fable which he knows as that of the crow in borrowed feathers is related by Caxton 'of the Jaye and of the pecok' (book ii, no. 15). Again, in MS. Royal 18 A. LXII (f. 2*a* and *b*) Morley writes: 'What is he to be reputede but, as Isope saith in hys fables, a verey fox that promyseth frenshyppe and loue to smale, lytle beastes, to noone other entent but for to deuoure them?' This

He was able likewise to quote from the epistles of Horace[1] and had wrestled with Cicero's *De Republica*. In the latter work he had been struck by the dream of Scipio in the sixth book with its promise of everlasting bliss to the virtuous, and he humbly confesses his own sinfulness and failure to live up to his ideals. To one thus concerned with the necessity of right living, Plutarch's lives of the great figures of the ancient world naturally made a strong appeal. One can understand likewise that Seneca, who of all the ancient philosophers approaches nearest to the Christian outlook and believes so firmly in the justice of providence, should have been regarded by Morley with uncommon interest. He knew the *Epistles* and the *Moral Essays*, and in an age of upheaval he learnt from the Roman Stoic the art of combining the performance of public duties with the solace of quietistic contemplation.[2]

Of English no less than of ancient history, Morley had some knowledge. He could quote as the source of his information old chroniclers such as Higden and William of Malmesbury, as well as his own contemporary Polydore Vergil; but, on the other hand, English authors play a smaller part than the classics in his world. He certainly knew Caxton's *Life of Jason* and perhaps others of his translations. But apart from this he displays little familiarity with writers in his native tongue and is unappreciative in his judgement. Thus, as might be expected of one so much enamoured of literature with a moral, religious, or ethical content, he found nothing to praise in the tales of Robin Hood and in fact condemned them as utterly worthless. But if he has so little to say about English literature, it would be inadvisable to infer that he was unacquainted with it, just as it would be rash to contend that he was a complete stranger to French authors, because he mentions only one work in that language—a translation of Petrarch's *Trionfi*.[3] It may well be that in his desire to impress the great persons for whom his translations were made, he resolved to go farther afield in quest of devotional or instructive material.

appears to allude to the fable 'of the Foxe of the Cock and of the dogges', which Caxton ascribes, not to Aesop, but to Poggio.

[1] MS. Royal 2 D. XXVIII, f. 1*b*: 'Orace saythe "Phisisiens promyse, smythes trete of their forgys".' Cf. *Epist.* 2. 1, ll. 115–16.

[2] *Vide post*, p. xciii–xcix.   [3] *Vide post*, p. ci.

Be this as it may, his choice of Italian writers was unquestionably influenced by the same eagerness to discover useful themes as has already been noted. Only on one occasion does he translate a tale, and even then he selects it from Masuccio Salernitano on account of its anti-papal bias. Equally characteristic is the attraction that he finds in Machiavelli's *Istorie Fiorentine* and *Il Principe*, and in Paolo Giovio's *Commentario del[le] cose de Turchi*, because of their bearing on contemporary politics, and in the work of Andrea Alciati, because of his grave reflections on life. The same attitude is displayed in Morley's relation to the older Italian authors. Of these it might seem obvious that Dante would be the one to whom he would first turn, but it is not at all certain that he had seen the *Divine Comedy*. He speaks of Dante only once—in the dedication of his version of Boccaccio's *De claris mulieribus*, where the earliest account in English is given of the three masters, Dante, Petrarch, and Boccaccio. With a slight inaccuracy in regard to dates Morley tells Henry VIII:

' In the tyme of the flowre and honour of prynces, Kynge Edwarde, the thyrde of that name . . . there sprange in Italy three excellente clerkes. The fyrst was Dante, for hys greate learnynge in hys mother tunge surnamyde dyuyne Dante. Surely, not withoute cause. For it is manyfest that it was true, whiche was grauen on hys tumbe, that hys maternall eloquens touchede so nyghe the prycke that it semyde a myracle of nature. And forbecause that one shuldnot thynke I do feyne, I shall sett the wordes in the Italiane tunge, whiche is thys:

> Dante Alighieri son, Minerua oscura
> D'intelligenza e d'arte, nel cui ingegno
> L'eleganza materna aggiunse al segno
> Che si tien gran miracol di natura.'[1]

Attention has been drawn to the fact that Morley does not name any of Dante's writings, and hence his knowledge of them has been doubted.[2] Against this it might be argued that as the above verses occur without the name of their author Boccaccio at the end of the edition of the *Divine Comedy* printed by Wendelin of Speyer in 1477, Morley might have found them there and

---

[1] *Vide post*, p. 2, n. 1.
[2] P. Toynbee, *Dante in English Literature from Chaucer to Cary*, London, 1909, vol. i, p. 33.

erroneously conceived them to be an epitaph. But this is mere hypothesis, and the extent of his familiarity with Dante must remain an open question.

In connexion with Petrarch no such problems arise, for Morley gives ample proof that he had more than a nodding acquaintance with his work. This intimacy is shown in the first place by the passage in the above-mentioned dedication where he passes on from Dante to Petrarch and incidentally bears witness to the popularity in Italy of the latter's poetry in the vernacular.

'The next vnto thys Dante', says Morley, 'was Frauncis Petrak, that not onely in the Latyne tunge, but also in swete ryme, is so extemyde that vnto thys present tyme vnnethe is ther any noble prynce in Italy, nor gentle man, withoute hauynge in hys handes hys sonnetes and hys "Tryhumphes" or hys other rymes. And he wrote also in the Latyne tunge certeyn eglogges in versys and another booke namede "Affrica" and "Of the Remedyes of bothe Fortunes", with dyuers epistles and other wourkes . . .'[1]

But the vogue of Petrarch's poetry was, of course, by no means limited to Italy. Not only did his sonnets set the fashion for all Europe, but the *Trionfi* were greatly admired. The skill of the artists was lavished on them in illuminated manuscripts, and they were taken as subjects by the designers of magnificent tapestries.[2] For his part, Morley was glad to leave the sonnets to Wyatt and Surrey; his concern was with the weightier matter of the *Trionfi*. The dedication of the translation that he made contains what must now seem the most extravagant eulogy.

'I dare affirme, yea, and the Italians do the same, that the deuine workes set aparte, there was neuer in any vulgar speche or language,

---

[1] See p. 2.
[2] Cf. Prince d'Essling and Eugène Müntz, *Pétrarque*, Paris, 1902, pp. 122–267 and 269–76, where the extraordinary popularity of the *Trionfi* is illustrated from paintings, frescoes, manuscripts, engravings, sculpture, stained glass, pottery, and tapestry. See also W. G. Thomson, *A History of Tapestry from the Earliest Times until the Present Day*, London, 1930, pp. 183–5, 240, 242, 245, 246, 248, 249, 253, 259, 260, 316, 317, 318, 324, 326, 327, 329, 330, 367–8, and 379. Some fine specimens of tapestry with themes drawn from the *Trionfi*, which Professor A. W. Reed has brought to my notice, are preserved in the Victoria and Albert Museum and at Hampton Court. The set at Hampton Court belonged to Cardinal Wolsey. Cf. W. G. Thomson, *ut supra*, pp. 184–5 and 240, and A. F. Kendrick, *Catalogue of Tapestries*, London, 1924, pp. 30–4.

so notable a worke, so clerckely done as this his worke. And albeit that he setteth forth these syxe wonderfull made triumphes all to the laude of hys Ladye Laura, by whome he made so many a swete sonnet, that neuer yet no poete nor gentleman could amend, nor make the lyke, yet who that doth vnderstande them, shall se in them comprehended al morall vertue, all Phylosophye, all storyall matters, and briefely manye deuyne sentences theologicall secretes declared.'[1]

Yet Morley was not too hopeful that his countrymen would share his enthusiasm.

'There be a nomber of that sorte', he assures Lord Maltravers, 'that percase when they shall eyther heare redde, or them selfe reade this excellent tryumphes, of this famous clercke Petrarcha, shall lytle set by them, and peraduenture caste it from them, desyrynge rather to haue a tale prynted of Robyn Hoode, or some other donge-hyll matter then this . . . alas who is he that will so reade them, that he wyl marke them, or what prynter wyll not saye, that he may winne more gayne in pryntynge of a merye ieste, then suche lyke excellente workes? Suerlye[2] (my good Lorde) very fewe or none.'[3]

After listening with some surprise to Morley's hyperbolical praise of the *Trionfi*, the modern reader will be curious to learn the translator's opinion of Boccaccio. It is to be found in the passage which follows the lines referring to Dante and Petrarch in the dedication to Henry VIII, of which mention was made a little earlier.

'The last of thies three, moste gratiouse souereign lorde,' he says, 'was John Bocas of Certaldo, whiche in lyke wyse as the tother twayne, Dante and Petracha, wer moste exellent in the vulgare ryme, so thys Bocas was aboue all others in prose, as it apperythe by his hundrith tayles and many other notable workes. Nor he was noo lesse elegaunte in the prose of his oune tunge then he was in the Latyne tunge, wherin, as Petrak dyd wryte clerkly certeyn volumes in the Latyne tunge, so dyd thys clerke. And fyrst "Of the Fall of Prynces", "Of the Geonelogye of the Goddes", and emonge other thys booke namede "De preclaris mulieribus".'[4]

It was the book 'of the ryght renomyde ladies' that Morley chose to turn into English. In view of his personal tastes, this is readily understood. Just as he had passed over the sonnets of Petrarch in favour of an allegorical poem overlaid with learning

[1] See p. 189. [2] Text workes, suerlye. [3] See pp. 188, 189. [4] See pp. 2–3.

and tending to the promotion of virtue, so he left aside the *Decameron* for the more scholarly *De claris mulieribus*. This preference was characteristic of Morley's age, at any rate in England, for not only in the fifteenth, but also in the early sixteenth century Boccaccio was better known as a grave moralist than as a narrator of joyous, but by no means always decorous, tales. He was the 'glorieux historien . . . réciteur des fortunes du monde et des tristes malheureuses matières . . . le docteur de patience en adversité',[1] and was recommended along with Seneca and other weighty writers to students of politics.[2] And just as Spenser read *De claris mulieribus* with profit,[3] so Morley translated for the edification of the ladies at the court of Henry VIII. His explanation of his purpose runs thus:

'And for asmuche as that I thoughte howe that your Hyghnes, of youre accustomede mekenes and pryncely herte, woldenot disdayn it, so dyd I imagyne that if by chaunce it shulde cum to the handes of the ryght renomyde and moste honorable ladyes of your Highnes moste tryhumphaunte courte, that it shulde be well acceptyde to theym to se and reede the meruelouse vertue of theyr oune sexe, to the laude perpetuall of theym. And albeit, as Bocas wrytethe in hys proheme, he menglyssheth sum not verey chaste emongste the goode, yet hys honeste excuse declarethe that he dyd it to a goode entent, that all ladyes and gentlewomen, seynge the glorye of the goode, may be steryde to folowe theym, and seynge the vyce of sum, to flee theym.'[4]

In reality, there was nothing in this work from which even so devout a mind as that of Morley had cause to shrink.[5] Juno and Isis are linked to a condemnation of idolatry, and Venus, Semiramis, Circe, Clytemnestra, and Helen are stigmatized for wantonness. On the other hand, Hypermnestra, Argia, Penelope, Lucrece, and the wives of the Meniae are held up as supreme

---

[1] *Œuvres de Georges Chastelain*, ed. Kervyn de Lettenhove, Brussels, 1865, vol. vii, pp. 97–8.
[2] Cf. MS. Rawlinson A. 338, ff. 94a–96b, in the Bodleian Library, to which attention is drawn by Miss Rosemond Tuve, 'Spenser's Reading: The De Claris Mulieribus', *Studies in Philology*, April, 1936, p. 147, note 1.
[3] Miss Rosemond Tuve, *ut supra*, pp. 147–65.
[4] See p. 3.
[5] For a thorough analysis of Boccaccio's attitude to women in *De claris mulieribus* see Laura Torretta 'Il "Liber de Claris Mulieribus" di Giovanni Boccaccio', *Giornale storico della letteratura italiana*, vol. xxxix, pp. 260–73.

examples of conjugal fidelity. Lavinia's conduct in remaining a widow after the death of Aeneas is also commended, while Dido, unlike her counterpart in Virgil, prefers to plunge a dagger into her heart rather than to take a second husband, and forms the subject of a lengthy encomium of chastity. Yet in the same breath as he eulogizes these notable personifications of feminine virtue, Boccaccio reveals that he had not too high an opinion of the majority of women. He still thinks lightly of them as in his youthful work, but his point of view is modified, for whereas in the *Decameron* he had smiled tolerantly upon voluptuousness and condoned the breaking of the marriage tie, here he sets his face sternly against fleshly lust and lauds the institution of matrimony. But though he issues repeated warnings against concupiscence and rigorously censures what seemed to him the excessive freedom of women in society,[1] he has no faith in the nunneries of his day. Indeed, at the close of the Life of Rhea he indulges in a vigorous denunciation of the system, which, but for the note of moral indignation, appears for a moment to transport the reader back to the atmosphere of the *Decameron*. Perhaps also it was this dissatisfaction of the severe critic with his feminine contemporaries which led him to toy with the ideal of the martial, virile type of woman, such as Marpesia and Lampedo, Penthesilea and Camilla, or the woman of intellect, such as Nicaula, Sappho, and Amalthea Sibylla.

With much of what Boccaccio had said Morley must have sympathized cordially, for he held the monastic system to be vicious in its repression of powerful instincts, while at the same time he was a zealous advocate of the sober and upright life. He too could appreciate the woman with intellectual interests, as he showed in his various dedications to the Lady Mary. But he did not believe that it was for the good of women to enjoy too much liberty, lest they should forget their station and function in life. This view can be seen in the following passage, which makes his attitude perfectly clear:

'Woman ys the creature of God, and with reuerence she ys to be

[1] Cf. ch. ix, *De Europa*: 'Vagari licentia nimia virginibus et aures faciles cuiuscunque verbis prebere minime laudandum reor, cum contigisse sepe legerim his agentibus honestati nonnunquam notas turpes imprimi, quas etiam perpetue demum castitatis decus abstergere non potuit.'

taken as his creature; and to this she ys ordeyned and made, that she shulde be abought the man, bringe vpe children and instructe them godly and honestly, and to be subiecte vnto the man. Vnto men commaundment ys gevin that they shuld gouerne and haue rule ouer there wiffes and famylye, but yf the woman (her office set a parte) will take vppon her to rule ouer her husbond, then she doth not the office whervnto she was created and made, but that thinge commyth of her own will and malice, for in dede God did not create this kynde vnto rule and to haue gouernance, and therfor they neuer raygne prosperouslye.'[1]

Consequently, he rejected, as mere fables without practical application to life, the stories of the Amazons and the women of Ethiopia that he had read in Boccaccio.[2]

In addition to the Italian writer's commentary on the virtues and vices of women there were scattered about the pages of *De claris mulieribus* moralizations affecting humanity as a whole of which Morley doubtless approved. A notable example is the denunciation of the power of gold that is found in the Life of Procris and, even more fully, in the Life of Medusa:

'Infelix auri possessio est, quod, si lateat, possessori nullius est commodi: si fulgeat, mille concupiscentium nascuntur insidie: etsi stent violentorum manus, non cessant possidentis anxie cure; fugatur enim quies animi, subtrahitur somnus, timor ingreditur, fides minuitur, augetur suspicio et omnis breuiter vite vsus impeditur misero. Si vero casu quocunque pereat, anxietatibus excarnificatur pauper factus, auarus laudat, liberalis ridet, inuidus consolatur, inops et omne vulgus dolentis canit in fabulam.'

And such a maxim as 'studijs igitur et diuina gratia illustres efficimur'[3] would be dear to the heart of a pious scholar like Morley.

VI

MORLEY AS A WRITER

The first prose work by Morley which has been preserved is his *Exposition and Declaration of the Psalme, Deus ultionum Dominus*, and it is significant that he, who was so familiar with theological writings, should have chosen this means to convey his thoughts.

---

[1] MS. Royal 17 D. XIII, f. 69b.   [2] Ibid., f. 69b.
[3] Cf. ch. xxiv, *De Amalchea seu de Deiphebe Sibilla.*

The book was, however, something more than was implied by
Thomas Warton when he remarked: 'A theological commentary
by a lord, was too curious and important a production to be
neglected by our first printers.'[1] It certainly was not just 'a
pious lucubration',[2] but a contribution to the polemical literature
of the period. Such a commentary, which actually has little
relation to the ninety-fourth Psalm, but merely serves as a frame-
work for Morley's anti-papal views, suited him well, since it
saved him the labour of building up a closely knit argument.
His *Exposition* therefore, far from being an elucidation or interpretation of a part of the Old Testament, is a series of denuncia-
tions of ecclesiastical policy.

The pamphlet arose from Morley's desire to propitiate
Henry VIII by lending him support in his struggle with the Pope,
and it discusses their relations with all the distorting violence of
a partisan. In Morley's eyes the King could do no wrong, and
consequently he shows little sympathy with those faithful
Catholics who remained true to their convictions. Thus he
presents those Englishmen who obey the Pope as disloyal rebels.

'Those that be adherentes to his cursed courte, they murmure,
they grudge, and do that in them is, to resyste the holy zele, whiche
our kinge hath, to set forth the holy worde of god. But our prynce,
that hath goddis worde feruently and moste constantly fyxed in his
hart, wyll with his assistens, perseuer agaynst all them[3] that wolde
ought do to the contrary.'

The ruthlessness of Henry VIII towards those who opposed or
angered him is thus glossed over. In fact, Morley portrays the
King as of a singularly mild disposition. 'It is not to be douted',
he asserts, 'but his highnesse moste tender and gentil harte,
felte great dolour, whan he sawe suche to haue intended hym
moste hygh displeasure, whom he toke to be his trustiest seruauntes.' No names are given here, so that the modern reader
cannot tell whom the author had in mind. It is likely, however,
that, writing in 1539, he was alluding to the Marquis of Exeter,
Lord Montacute, and Sir Edward Neville.[4] Whoever they were,

[1] *History of English Poetry*, London, 1774–81, vol. iii, p. 86.
[2] Sir Sidney Lee in the *Dictionary of National Biography*, London,
1908–9, vol. xv, p. 239.   [3] Text comma after them.
[4] It is noteworthy that along with the British Museum copy of Morley's

Morley approved of their fate, for he boasted that in England there were 'none slayn, in especiall by proces and iudgemente, but suche as are vnworthy to lyue'.

In political agitation fomented by Rome Morley saw a grave danger, for he claimed that wherever a tendency to reform displayed itself, sedition was encouraged. Moreover, prince was egged on against prince, so that their dissensions might strengthen the Papal power. The desire for secular dominion, he contended, had been inimical to Christianity from the time when 'Syluester chalenged by gyfte, that that Constantyne neuer gaue hym', and his successors, abandoning the ideals of the apostles—humility, poverty, and obedience—had fallen victims to pride, pomp, and arrogance. The Pope 'is made of an humble sheparde, an ymage for pryncis to kisse his shoes', and the Christian faith lost ground in Asia, Africa, and even in Europe 'whan pristes presumptuously toke vpon theym[1] to rule goddis worde after their fantasyes, and not theyr lustes[2] accordyng to his lawes'. Moreover, to strengthen her position Rome had not scrupled to 'sette one priuate man to poyson an other, one cytezen to murder an other', and had wrongly condemned to death those who were martyrs for the truth. To such a pitch does Morley's indignation rise that, with an imaginativeness unusual in him, he exclaims: 'Gret mylles myght be driuen with bloude, if that that hath ben shedde, coulde runne together.' Finally, he brings his accusations to a head when he declares that this state of affairs could only be maintained by the propagation of erroneous doctrine, the setting up of idolatry, the inculcation of superstition, and the distortion of the Bible.

The remedy that Morley proposed was twofold. First, that the unlettered people should be given free access to the Scriptures, and second, that the princes of Europe should unite and oppose the 'dyuellyshe dreames' entertained in Rome of subjecting them to ecclesiastical domination. One man had been ordained to lead the way, for as divine aid had saved 'the noble Henry the fyfte

pamphlet is bound up '*An Invective Ayenste the Great and Detestable Vice, Treason, wherein the Secrete Practises, and Traiterous Workinges of theym, that suffrid of late are disclosed*', which was published in 1539. The author, Richard Morysine, denounces the above-mentioned men as traitors.

[1] Text comma after theym.   [2] Text comma after lustes.

frome the frenche men, the wyse Henry the seuenth[1] from the tyrant kynge Rycharde', so Morley affirmed that his sovereign was chosen to perform the great mission of re-establishing the secular power and restoring true Christianity. At the very thought he indulges in this panegyric:

'Blessed arte thou, whome god hath taught[2] to espie out the peryllous doctryne of the byshop of Rome, wherby the people of Englande ar brought from darkenes to lyght, from errour to the hygh way of righte knowlege, from daunger of dethe eternall, to life that neuer endeth, to be shorte, euen from hel to heuen. By the,[3] O sage kynge, the worde of god, that in tyme paste was cloked and hyd to the elders of the realme, is now manyfest to chylderne, that ceasse not to prayse with their mouthes god[4] and his holy worde. For the mayntenance wherof, most royall kynge, thy prayse shall styll continue vpon erthe, and than depart, whan all menne haue taken theyr leaue of it.'

And he calls upon other rulers to arise and follow in the path thus opened for them:

'Awake christen kynges awake, Englande blowethe the trompe, and sheweth you all[5] how ye may auoyde bondage, and howe accordinge to your title and name, ye may as kynges rule and Reygne. God chose not you his kynges[6] for to be reuled, but to rule. Ye maye haue offycers vnder you, as many as you wyll: beynge kynges, you oughte to haue none aboue you.'

As a contribution to the polemical literature of the age, Morley's tract is not without merit. Obviously, it is one-sided and full of prejudice, but it is written with a vigour and at times a passion which at least give the impression of sincerity. He speaks with a greater directness and lucidity than appears in much of his work, and he uses various devices—invective,[7] metaphor,[8] literary allusion,[9] and even punning,[10] to reinforce his argument.

---

[1] Text comma after seuenth.　　　　[2] Text comma after taught.
[3] Text lacks comma.　　　[4] Text comma after mouthes and god.
[5] Text comma after all.　　　　　[6] Text comma after kynges.
[7] 'bloud suckers'; 'this runnagate, this strayeng byshop'; 'this sect of Sathan'.
[8] 'monstruous hydra', 'Babylonicall monster', 'dronke with the wyne of her hooryshe fornication', and 'this dronken strompette, soused in the bloude of sayntes and martyrs'.
[9] 'I truste euery byrde woll take his fether, and that the prowde crowe of Esope, beinge ones naked, shal make the worlde to laughe, whiche a longe season hath made it to wayle.'
[10] 'as he and his pyrates, I wolde haue sayde prelates, can deuyse.'

Yet even in the heat of controversy, Morley could not refrain from turning aside to dwell for a moment on the inspiration that enabled St. John to make known the sublime mysteries of the Christian faith. 'He, whyche before was a fyssher man, vtterly vnlerned,' says Morley, 'nowe excellynge the reste of the Euangelistes, vttered manye hygh mysteries, and suche as the other thre left vntouched, writing that wonderfulle piece of worke, *In principio erat verbum.*' The passage is important, precisely because it is irrelevant. Here at any rate Morley is free from all suspicion of a desire to ingratiate himself with the King. He had nothing to gain by its insertion, nor to lose by its omission, and the reflection gives a glimpse of a truly religious mind, tinged with mysticism.

Morley's commentary on *Ecclesiastes* was not prompted by any such contemporary events as led to the publication of the pamphlet just examined. Hence, after he had paid his introductory compliments to the Duke of Somerset, he was free to use the scriptural text as a channel for the expression of his views on life as a whole. It is significant that, whereas he had previously quoted from the Vulgate, he now draws upon the English version of the Great Bible. And as the Reformation which had effected this change had passed beyond the initial stage, the violence of Morley's attacks on Rome had not unnaturally abated. He can still assert that 'the monkes and papistes wolde haue ruled the worlde, and loo! they did delude the worlde and drowned the same in most depe errours and ygnorance',[1] or rail at 'the Romysshe vsurped aucthoritie and moost pestiferous and erronyous lawes of the same',[2] indulge in a jeer at 'the mother churche, as they call yt',[3] or claim that 'at thes days the Pope ys ledde vnto iudgment and allmost condempnyd as an herytik, with all his adherentes, by the aucthorite of Godes worde'.[4] But all this is mild in comparison with the invective to which he had descended in the earlier phase. Even such a subject as the accumulation of wealth by the Church elicits only this remark:

'Our bishopes had gatherid together great riches, with so greate evill (for that none other were partakers of the same) that yt made

---

[1] MS. Royal 17 D. XIII, f. 56*b*.   [2] Ibid., f. 2*a*.
[3] Ibid., f. 41*b*.   [4] Ibid., f. 103*b*.

an vprore amonge the rude and common people. And nowe they goo abought to gather agayne, devowringe the people, and will not cease vntill such tyme as some shall com to take awaye the same with the distruccion of the gatherers therof.'[1]

Indeed, at this stage Morley seems to have been almost more concerned about the extreme innovators in religion. He sighed over the fact that just when the Bible had begun to circulate freely and sound teaching had been established, 'forthwith here-tykes and false preachers shuld avarte the hartes of men from the same'.[2] Nevertheless, he was convinced that 'no storme of false appostles and teachers (the onelie disturbers and destroiers of alle godlines) maye hereafter be able to putt owte and exstincte the syncere and pure light that now begynneth moost purely to shyne'.[3] This conviction disposed him to take a philosophical view of erroneous innovations, which, as it appeared to him, resulted from the innate restlessness of the human mind, so that 'we nowe a days, not contentid with the Gospell gevin vnto vs in the vulgar tonge, seake for newe disputacions of sacramentes; and when they be oulde, newe shall springe out without numbre'.[4]

For his part, like Martin Luther, he held a middle course between 'the Papistes reprouynge' and the sects disputing; and even though he regarded with aversion the introduction of new and vain doctrines, his remedy was not to repress them by force, but to set forth the truth and 'to suffre thoos that we cannot conuert vnto faith by our admonycions, to remayne vnto the ponishment and correccion of God'.[5] He took up a similar attitude, when events in Germany became less favourable to the spreading of the Bible. In a passage which probably alludes to the break-up of the Schmalkaldic League and the compromise arrived at by the Diet of Augsburg, he says:

'At thes days we willid the prefarment of the Germaynes, as towchinge the knowlege of the Gospell, and trustid that they all wolde haue embraced the same. But yt came to passe clene contrarye, for thoos that we toke to haue bene our ayeders and helpers for the furtherans of the said Gospell were our moste enymes, and trode vs vndre fote.'[6]

[1] MS. Royal 17 D. XIII, f. 47a. [2] Ibid., f. 101b.
[3] Ibid., f. 2a. [4] Ibid., f. 24a.
[5] Ibid., f. 75b. [6] Ibid., f. 34a.

This leads him to ask 'What shall we doo? Shall we not haue them in disdayne? Shall we not forsake all?' His answer is: 'Noo. Let other dispice, envye, hate, and parsecute vs, and let vs, to our powers, labore in preachinge and teachinge and expoundinge our Master Christes Gospell . . . and commyt the reste vnto hym'.[1]

But, even if Morley's methods are less bitterly controversial, he still leaves the reader in no doubt regarding his condemnation of the monastic life. His reason for this is not that abuses had crept in, but that the conceptions underlying that life were misleading. Why should any one take the vows of poverty and obedience, since these were the precepts of the Gospel and pertained to all Christians? And as for the vow of chastity, it was untenable, and therefore, by the test of St. Jerome and Nicholas of Lyra, to be condemned. Further, Morley held that for man to appoint fixed times for abstinence was to usurp the function of God who will ordain when fasting is necessary. Nor did he believe that the practice of asceticism, by the wearing of vile apparel, the observance of vigils and the maceration of the body, was the best way of despising the world. On the contrary, he recommended that men should use joyfully everything that was given them. He says:

'Yf the Lorde shall geve the meate, eate yt; yf he shall geve the fast, forbeare yt; yf he shall call the to honor, take yt; yf he shall sende the losse, suffre yt; yf he shall caste the in preson, take yt pacientlye; yf he will the to be a kinge, folowe his callinge; yf he shall caste the down, passe not of yt, . . . for thoos that wilbe taken in very deade for the trewe contemptors of this worlde must take all thinges paciently and vse all thinges with thankesgevinge when they be present, and abstayne from the same willinglye, when the Lord shall withdrawe them.'[2]

Here zeal is tempered by common sense and piety by humanism. But the humanistic ideal emerges still more clearly when Morley considers the fate of the young who were bereft even of innocent pleasures and doomed to be 'shet vp as birdes in a cage'.[3] By contrast, he praises the wisdom of Solomon who understood so much better the working of the child's mind.

[1] MS. Royal 17 D. XIII, f. 34*a*.   [2] Ibid., ff. 16*b*–17*a*.
[3] Ibid., f. 98*a*.

'Salomon . . .' he remarks, 'forbiddith not pleasures and thinges pertaynynge vnto a mery lyff, as the folish monkishe masters haue don, for that were none other thinge but as to make of men dome blokes, or to plant a gret tree in a litle pott. As Anselmus, the most manerly monk, affirmed, so they enclosed there youth, as yt were in a cave, and forbid them the sight and speche of men, to the ende thei shuld leorne nothinge and be without all experience, when in very dede there ys nothinge more pestilent for youthe then to lyve solitarilye. The mynde ought to be well instituted with good opinions and good leorninge, lest they shulde be corrupted with the continuance of evilles, but the body must be exersised in the thinges belonginge to this lyff. The world must be seene and harde . . . wherfor youth owght chefflye to avoyd hevines and the deserte lyff, for vnto youth myrth and gladnes ys as necessarye as meate and drink.'[1]

At the same time, those responsible for the guidance of the young should not think too much of the body, but devote themselves to the training of the mind.

'The body ys recreatid with a mery mynde, and so educacion, or bringyng vp of youth, ys not to be begonne at the body, but at the mynde, for when the myndes are well instituted, the bodyes be easlye gouerned.'

In any case,

'youth must haue liberte to be merye and to do all thinges with a glad hart, this onlye exceptid, that yt be not coruptid with the voluptuousnes of the fleshe, for thes bankettes, dronkennes and hauntynge of whores be not gladnes of harte . . . but rather occasion of hevines and sorowe.'[2]

On other grounds, too, Morley advocates that youth shall be allowed to move freely in the world. The cloistered existence seemed to him, as it did to Milton, a form of cowardice, in that the recluse fled from evil, instead of conquering it. Only one who has seen and faced the worst in life can hope for tranquillity in later years, and so Morley's advice is: 'Yf thou wilte attayne vnto this mark, or passe to haue thy hart pacifyed in the myddes of thes evylles, be conuersant in them from thy youth, for so shallt thou well avoyd all calamites and perelles.'[3]

In yet another respect Morley was typical of his age, namely,

[1] Ibid., ff. 97*b*–98*a*.   [2] Ibid., f. 98*a*.
[3] Ibid., f. 97*a*.

in his exaltation of the royal power, which followed naturally from the attempt to diminish that of the Pope. Luther himself had lent his influence in this quarter, and in his antipapal pamphlet Morley had acclaimed Henry VIII as the herald of a new era, in which the monarchs of Europe would recover their rightful position. He now turns to another aspect of a King's powers—his relation to his subjects. On this point he has no hesitation. Those placed in authority must always be held in reverence, partly because they are so troubled and afflicted for those over whom they rule, but chiefly 'for asmoch as yt ys not mans, but Godes ordinaunce'.[1] Of course, Morley recognizes that not all monarchs are good rulers and that often those who promise well in their youth prove themselves unfitted to govern others, as is shown by Nero, Commodus, and Heliogabalus. In fact, he goes so far as to declare that 'a good prince ys a phenix seldome sene'.[2] In spite of all this, obedience is essential: 'Yt often chaunsith that tyrantes do raynge and ocupye the higher powers to afflicte there subiectes, and yet this notwithstonding the commandment of the kynge must be observid, and no cause gevin by the subiectes of sedicion.'[3] It is evident that in such a case Morley sees no remedy but to await a change at the hands of the same inscrutable divine power as established the tyrant on his throne.

Yet those in attendance on kings were no more faultless than their masters. The courtiers of his day are especially criticized by Morley. He speaks bitterly of the way in which 'thoos pestilent devowrars and covetous men which be in the houses of princes regard nothinge but to haue plesant lyves and are nothinge profitable vnto there princes but to emtye there cooferrs and to put them to importunate charges, covetinge allways money, whether yt be to the hinderance of there princes or kyngdom or not'.[4] These self-seeking courtiers were all the more distasteful to Morley, because the covetousness with which the spirit of the age had infected them caused them to neglect the obligations that he felt it incumbent upon a nobleman to perform. He censures them for doing nothing 'but gape after promocions and

[1] MS. Royal 17 D. XIII, f. 93b.　　[2] Ibid., f. 38a.
[3] Ibid., ff. 74b–75a.　　[4] Ibid., f. 93a.

infynite treasure, wherbye yt commyth to passe that nothing
ys distributid vnto the pore, nothinge seene for the advansynge
of leornynge and soche other which be workes of godlines'.[1]
Even in their own interest Morley doubts the wisdom of the
course that they pursued, for whereas they might live com-
modiously at home, they chose to spend their days in discontent
and misery.

The lust for wealth that animated the courtier spurred on
others also. 'Howe many', exclaims Morley, 'haue ben in thees
our days slayne in there owne houses for there riches and money!'[2]
Nor was greed of gold the only failing that he discovered among
his contemporaries. There was much else to deplore—among
those in authority oppressions and false accusations, with innumerable other kinds of ungodliness, and among the people
envy, disdain, hatred, deceit, and guile. In spite of much
preaching of the Gospel, few became good and faithful, and
whereas 'in tymes past all thinges were gevin vnto the vngodly
prestes . . . nowe a days meate and clothe ys not gevin vnto the
godlye ; leornyd men are nothinge set by, but are troden vnderfote
euerywhere'. In his bewilderment, Morley could find no other
reason for so grievous a state of affairs than that it was in order
that men 'shuld leorne to knowe the worlde howe furious and
howe vnthankfull a best yt ys'.[3]

As a rule, however, Morley takes refuge in the belief that all is
divinely ordained and therefore must sooner or later prove conducive to the welfare of mankind. This attitude was closely
connected with a question which had been hotly debated in his
day, namely, whether man was a free agent or not. In 1524
Erasmus had contended in his *De libero arbitrio* that the human
will was free, to which Luther replied the following year in his
De servo arbitrio, which upheld determinism. For his part, Morley
sided with Luther.

'Yt may be spoken', he says, 'agaynst frewill, that yt ys not in
our power to prescribe nether tyme nor measure for the parformans
of the same, and that our stodies and councelles be vtterlye deceyvid
therin, for that they shall come to passe onlye when God shall

---

[1] Ibid., f. 92b.
[2] Ibid., f. 46b. [3] Ibid., ff. 76b–77a.

ordayne and assigne the tyme. Vnto this apartaynith the saynge in the Gospell, "His hower ys not yet com". Agayne, the woman, when she bringith forthe childe, sustaynyth dolor and payne, for that her hower ys com, and thus hathe Godes mighti power determynid all thinges, which man cannot alter or let. But, a man may saye, "howe ys man ordayned the lorde ouer all thinges, as yt ys said in the second chapter of Genisis, yf he cannot ordre all the same at his own will and vse them at his pleasure?" I answer, "We be so made lordes of thinges, that we maye haue the present vse of the same and not gouerne them with our cares and stodies. Neyther can ony man with his councelles or stodies do anythinge for to com, for howe shulde men determyn of thinges wherin they be ignorant"? '[1]

Morley goes on to argue that men cannot control their births, and it is in vain for midwives to fix a time and season. There can thus be no certainty, because it is beyond their power to have foreknowledge. Similarly, no one can say when he will die, for the hour will strike only when God wills it. One feels how Morley, living in an age of capricious despots, takes comfort from this thought and faces these unknown dangers with fortitude. He says:

'We shall not dye, all though we be in greate ieobardye and in extreme disperacion, but at the hower apoyntid. Wherfor shulde we then fere deathe? For we shall lyve no lenger then God hat[h] set the tyme, nor dye before the same. . . . . "But", thou saist vnto me, "manye haue perished thorough there own folye, or elles they might haue lyvid longer, and some other hathe willinglye murderid them selffes—colde not they haue kept there lyffes?" I answer "No, trewly, for God gaue the very same hower and kynde of deathe, the which thinge ys provid by experiens. Some men haue taken grevus and deadlye wondyes and haue ben sone made hole and haue lyvid; other, litell or nothinge hurt at all, dye forthe with. The astroligers ascribe the sam vnto the sterres and planettes; other ascribe yt to fortune. But the holy scriptures doth attribute yt vnto God, with whom the momentes of our lyffes and deathes be set, who also hathe no respectes vnto the greatnes of the wondes, therby confutinge all humayne wisdom and stodye. Wherfor vnto Christians this ys no small consolacion and comfort, for that they knowe there deathes to be nether in the handes and power of tyrantes, nor in ony other creature, but all onlye in the handes of the Lord, when he shall call them".'[2]

---

[1] MS. Royal 17 D. XIII, f. 27*a* and *b*.   [2] Ibid., f. 28*a* and *b*.

From the careers of great men Morley draws illustrations of the way in which God has determined their fate. The Scripture provides abundant material, not to speak of 'Mathias, Kynge of Hungarye', who 'in our days . . . out of preson ys made a moste mighty prince', and the Emperor Valerian, who, 'when he was taken, was made the fote stole vnto the Kynge of Peerce, and that vnto deathe'. How could such a reverse of fortune take place, Morley wonders? His explanation is simple—'for because his hower was come, so set and determyned by God'. That being so, it follows that man should not agitate himself unnecessarily. 'To what purpose then ys all this care and travell? Euery day ys able to sustayne yt selff by the own travelles.'[1] And again he says: 'So ys yt with God determined that this mane shalbe a man of ocupacion, a nother a curate, a nother a precher, a nother a ruler. Nowe seinge that both names and offices are before knowin and determinid of God, wherfor dothe man wander so folishly about thinges vncertayne?'[2] How unwise it is also for man to concern himself too deeply about future generations. We make our constitutions and ordinances, but they may not be held in esteem by posterity. Moreover, when the control of our destinies is outside our own hands, why should we take so much thought in erecting great and splendid buildings?

'Nero buyldid a somtuose and kynglye howse, but yet neuer had vse therof. The same ofte tymes chaunsith with vs; one takith stodye and labor in buyldinges, a nother hathe the pleasure there of . . . In like case Frederik, a prince of worthy memorye, buyldid manye thinges, but other men haue the possession therof. He lokid vnto thinges to comme, not content with thinges present; when he had buyldid one place, he sowght a nother. The prince that nowe ys occupyithe nothinge of the afforsaid buyldinges, but buyldyth other, streng[t]hnyth his townes and hathe a nother stodye; he that shalbe his successor shall delight in a cleane contrarye stodye. Therfor I say yt ys great myserye for a man to troble and vexe hymselff about the acomplishment of anye soche thinge that ether deathe, syknes or other impediment can deceyue him of the vse therof, and also when he that succedithe the shall ether haue no pleasure in thy former actes, or elles shall vtterlye destroye the same.'[3]

[1] Ibid., f. 37*a* and *b*.
[2] Ibid., f. 55*b*.   [3] Ibid., ff. 18*b*–19*a*.

To plan joy may well bring disappointment, if it does not happen to accord with the divine purpose.

'Manye tymes musicall instreumentes be prepared, to provoke myrthe and gladnes of harte, delicate dishes be prepared, and enterludes plaid to exitate and provoke gladnes of mynde. This not withstondinge, yt chaunsith some tyme all together other wyse, for eyther there be some that be gevin vnto sadnes or some vncherfull countenaunces, or elles some other thinge that trobleth all the reste, cheflye when men purpose and intende there ioie and pleasures of longe tyme before hande.'[1]

Nor are princes in any better plight than ordinary mortals, for

'when they intend to be merye and vse pastymes, there commyth some vrgent maters in hande which disturbith all the purposid ioys and make them hevy and sad.'[2]

Underlying all this anxiety about the future Morley discerns man's insatiable desire—whether he be an Alexander the Great, a Julius Caesar, or a contemporary. True happiness lies in limiting our wishes. 'We owght to be appeysed and contentyd with thinges preasent, and to extinguise and quenche the thirst of thinges to comme.'[3] However, Morley recognizes that this is a counsel of perfection and that the practice of mankind is different. 'To be breff, no man folowith yt, for we be evyn drownid with stodyes and cares abought the parformyng of our workes and labors. And this ys likwise vanite.'[4]

At times the world as seen through Morley's eyes is a sorry spectacle. Love, as St. Augustine had lamented long ago in his *Confessions*, turns to bitterness; wives prove unchaste and children become thieves, 'not meate to lyve apon the yerthe',[5] the actions of the father cause dissension in the family, and relatives spread calumny among neighbours and citizens; the punishment of the ungodly is delayed, evil befalls good men, and everything is overwhelmed with innumerable sorrows and infinite misery. Morley's pessimism goes so far that he advises his reader 'to accompte yt as a myracle, yf any thinge shall happen well'.[6] Again he says: 'Let vs allways think none other but that we must

[1] MS. Royal 17 D. XIII, f. 15a and b.
[2] Ibid., f. 21a.   [3] Ibid., f. 11a.   [4] Ibid., f. 26a.
[5] Ibid., f. 19b.   [6] Ibid., f. 90b.

be conuersant in evill and not in good thinges, so longe as we shall lyve in this world'[1]—a sentiment repeated, with slight variation, in another passage: 'Who so wilythe to lyve quietlye, let him loke to see none other thinges in this lyff but vanite and vexacion of mynde.'[2] What then is to be done in so gloomy a place of sojourn? First, man must recognize that whatever occurs, does so by divine dispensation, and therefore he must not presume to undertake the work of God by attempting to make all things right and well, for 'our labor ys in vayne, when we swarue frome the will and worde of God'.[3] He must understand that 'thinges be brought to passe, nether by the wisdome of the wyse men, nor yet by the temerite of foles'.[4] Therefore he should be prepared for evil, admitting to himself 'that there ys non other thinge in this liff to be lokid for',[5] and if, contrary to expectation, anything good does happen, if his wife be chaste and his children honest, his lands fertile and his rulers godly, he should give God the praise. He who has been 'trayned in Godes worde'[6] will learn to be content with the present, accepting with gratitude any benefits that may be vouchsafed unto him, for 'yt ys dampnable, where we shall refuse any honeste myrthe or gladnes of mynde offerd vnto vs by God'.[7]

In no case, however, must mankind despair. Morley counsels his reader to go about his task, whatever it may be, in much the same dogged spirit as was afterwards exhibited by Carlyle. Time after time he returns to this point.

'What shall we doo? shall we work no more, shall we leorne no more, because our scolers be not apte to take leornyng, or for because leornid men be in so smale reputacion? No, truly. Do as thou haste don, both in labore and leorning, and loke for the hower which God hath apoynted the to do good in;'[8]

'Yf thou be callid to suche aucthorite in the whiche thou oughtes to be studious about the amendment of other, do as yt lyeth in thy power to do, and God shall at his pleasure performe the same;'[9]

'Do thy office and dutye, and commit the proff therof to God; do well vnto all men, regarde not the windes, nether be thou carefull what shall chaunse.'[10]

[1] Ibid., f. 90b.   [2] Ibid., f. 34a and b.   [3] Ibid., f. 12a and b.
[4] Ibid., f. 22a.   [5] Ibid., f. 46a.   [6] Ibid., f. 15b.
[7] Ibid., f. 16a.   [8] Ibid., f. 34a.   [9] Ibid., f. 34b.
[10] Ibid., f. 96a.

Even if married life be filled with bitterness, man must provide for his family and see to the education of his children—always, however, in such a way as not to force their inclination to suit his own plans but to let them develop the capacities that God has bestowed upon them. On no account must he in a fit of dejection flee from the society of his fellows, but labour diligently at his task.

'Like as the minister of the worde of God doth preche for his parishoners, allthough many do contempne the same, so, yf the scolemaster hath but too scolers, for thoos he must labor, although he hath xx^ti other dulwitted and desparate. Likewise the higher power shuld do, for allthough he cannot kepe all his cytte in good order, yet he shall fynde one or other citesen that shall obserue the same.'

And Morley's advice is clinched with a piece of stoic wisdom, which has almost a Johnsonian ring: 'The discomodites of men are to be sustayned and borne paciently; nether may we be in desperacion of all men, allthough many do perishe.'[1]

Quite apart from such a passage as this, there are numerous indications in the commentary on *Ecclesiastes* that it is not the work of a young man. Thus we find a casual remark that the old 'be redye to ryse at the voyce of euery birde, when as younge men slepe so sowndly that they here nether coke crowynge nor barkinge of dogges, nether yet thunderinges'.[2] But above all there is a hint of age in Morley's disillusionment, his philosophical outlook on life and his practical sagacity in the conduct of human affairs. It is a sage who declares that 'harnes and all other armore are nothinge worthe without wisdom and polyce, and wisdom in warres farre excellyth strenkith and power'.[3] Equally characteristic is his counsel not to oppose those who cannot be overcome, however foolish they may be. Of course, a man should offer sincere advice, in accordance with his duty and office, but to go beyond this, he assures his reader, is to stir up hornets 'and caste thy selff in daunger and perelles nothinge requisite'. He adds: 'This ys a good admonishon for vs that be conuersant in this world so malicius.'[4] And we hear the voice of the skilled

---

[1] MS. Royal 17 D. XIII, f. 79*b*.   [2] Ibid., f. 99*b*.
[3] Ibid., f. 86*b*.   [4] Ibid., f. 87*b*.

navigator who had contrived successfully to ride the stormy seas of Tudor England, when Morley stresses the folly of trying to resist those in power, even if one disagrees with their doings. Rather one must endure patiently, for 'yt ys a gret poynt of wisdom to decemble som tyme and to geve place, for yt puttith down great evilles, as yt ys dayly sene by experiens'.[1] One who had grown thus wary was not likely to advocate extreme courses of action. Indeed, as may be seen from the preface to his translation of the Life of Paulus Aemilius, he admired those who practised moderation and proved that 'the best part . . . is the meane'.[2] Hence his shrewd attitude towards the problems of daily life. Pondering on the evils created by an excessive love of riches, he does not hold that wealth should be cast away, but that it should be used to aid others. And he displays a similar sense of proportion, when he comments on the restless dissatisfaction of mankind:

'No man ys apesid and contentid with his vocacion. He that lokith vppon players thinkyth allways that he can playe better. Yf I heare a nother preche, I think I can do moche better then he. Likwise the servant thinkith, yf I were a kinge, I wolde gouerne and ordre all thinges most wisely.'[3]

In the same way

'the marchaunt man praysith the souldyar, the souldiar nombrith his miseries and praysith the marchaunt. The oulde men prayse youthe. We torne our selffes from our owne thinges which be moste pleasant, and with greate calamite afflicte our selves abowte other. No man can considre his owne goodes, nether lyve contentid with his own fortune and lot, for yf the oulde men wolde pondre the parelles of youthe, they wolde not wishe and desire youth. Contrarye, youthe, seinge so many discomodites of age, wolde gladly sustayne there own discomodites, and not envye al the commodites of age, yf yt hathe anye.'[4]

There was thus something intensely practical about Morley's philosophy of life. He was fully conscious of the dangers and difficulties that man must avoid or conquer, but he never dreamed of turning his back upon them. Far from doing this, he set himself to make the best of the world as he found it. And even though he perceived the frailty of man and described in words

[1] Ibid., ff. 88*b*–89*a*.   [2] MS. Laud Misc. 684, f. 2*a*.
[3] MS. Royal 17 D. XIII, f. 54*a*.   [4] Ibid., ff. 53*b*–54*a*.

of poignant beauty how 'all thinges decaye and perishe; mans
liff, kyngdoms and what so euer appertaynyth vnto men retornith
thether from whens yt came, out of the yerthe into the yerthe,
like as the winde blowith and ceasith blowinge, and as the sonne
ronneth be corse vnto his arisinge',[1] yet he did not ignore the
joy that is to be found by those who are capable of seeing. True,
mankind is far too much absorbed in the pursuit of its desires and
so, striving for the unattainable, fails to grasp what is within
its reach. Thus the covetous man 'lustith after nothinge[2] elles
but money. Evin so the ambicious or desirous of honor beholdith
nothinge but promocions. The lover seyth not his own wiff,
but other mens—that ys to saye, he ys not satisfied with the
present giftes of God. And thus the vngodly beginne there hell
in this lyff.'[3] But Morley was not the man to rush on so blindly,
and though the world appeared to him a vale only too often
obscured by shadows, he was not blind to the joy of common
things. 'Howe swete', he exclaims, 'the sone ys and plesant
light ys,'[4] and again, 'yt ys a most pleasant thinge to see the sone
shine!'[5]

Though the commentary on *Ecclesiastes* is the most compre-
hensive exposition of Morley's views on life, his few poems are
also valuable as a revelation of his personality. From his epitaph
on Sir Thomas West we can deduce what qualities he esteemed
most highly in a man, for he singles out West's virtue, honesty,
liberality, and piety. But it is in his two longer poems that his
ideas are more fully expressed. Both of them are concerned with
the application of philosophy to life, and both of them touch on
themes akin to those discussed in the manuscript presented to
Somerset.

The one poem begins with the line 'All men the do wysshe vnto
them selffe all goode'. Such a desire seems natural enough to
Morley, but, as he perceives, the problem lies in knowing wherein

---

[1] MS. Royal 17 D. XIII, ff. 52*b*–53*a*. One may compare with this a
passage in MS. Add. 12060, f. 1*b*, where he tells Queen Mary that the good
rulers 'remembrith that ther dignytie is no better then a Maye floure,
that to-day shewith fayre and to-morow is withered and drye, and the
beauty therof past'.
[2] MS. nothinges.   [3] MS. Royal 17 D. XIII, f. 52*a*
[4] Ibid., f. 96*b*.   [5] Ibid., f. 52*a*.

goodness consists. Men often long for what is harmful, and the poet admits that he himself often erred in this respect:

> Tyll Reasone rulyde fantasye and my fond wyte dyde charme
> And teld me, yf that good I dyde intende to haue,
> Yt neathar was in dignitye nor in muche gold to saue,
> But to refus both twayne, to hold my selffe contente,
> Not with my fond desyars, but that which Gode hath lente—
> Wysdome and experience to knowe that all delyghte
> Doth pas, as doth the day that passith to the nyght.

Only when he had hearkened to the voice of Reason and realized that in pursuing the unattainable he was throwing the stable good in the mire and losing all chance of enduring happiness, did he learn that content is to be found in the limitation of our aspirations.[1]

Morley once more returns to the question of happiness in the lines which he addressed to his descendants. He describes himself in the seclusion of his room at Great Hallingbury, musing upon this subject:

> Never was I lesse alone then beyng alone;
> Here in this chamber evell thought had I none,
> But allways I thought to brynge the mynd to reste,
> And that thought off all thoughttes I iuge it the beste.
> For yf my coffers hade ben full of perle and golde,
> And Fortune had favorde me even as that I wolde,
> The mynd owt of quyate, so sage Senek sethe,
> Itt hade ben no felicitie, but a paynfull dethe.[2]

Nor does he long for high rank. Other men may do so, if they choose, provided that they regard success and reverses with Stoic calm, ruling Fortune, instead of being ruled by her, but for his part he thrusts all such cravings aside, finding joy in what he has.

It is obvious even to a cursory glance that both of Morley's longer poems are impregnated with Senecan philosophy. But the influence of the famous Stoic is by no means restricted to them; it colours Morley's whole outlook. There is indeed a marked resemblance between the attitude of the two writers to their contemporaries and to life in general, and a survey of Seneca's

---

[1] MS. Ashmole 48, f. 10a.   [2] Ibid., f. 9b.

leading ideas reveals many similarities to the views that have been encountered in Morley's works.

Living under the dominion of Caligula and Nero, Seneca was even more pessimistic than Morley in the age of Henry VIII. At times he was tempted to hate the entire human race. Greed, cruelty, and luxury held sway, crime triumphed, lust prevailed, and baseness was so widespread that his mind was plunged into gloom at such a spectacle. The one certainty seemed to be that matters would become worse rather than better, so that life called not for joy, but tears. In fact, the happiest lot would have been never to enter this world; and the next best was to make an early exit.

Uncongenial though Seneca's environment might be, he recognized, just as Morley recognized in his day, that it was impossible to resist those in power. Hence it was essential to avoid giving offence to the rulers of the State. But by way of compensation the individual is always free to devote himself to his studies and to concentrate on his spiritual development.

Seneca maintains that in this process the difficulties of life have a part to play; only when a man has faced the problems of the everyday world can he know himself. One of the most important of these problems is to assess wealth at its true worth. Seneca admits that riches are a good, and in his opinion no one who has inherited them is under an obligation to cast them away. But wealth is valuable only in moderation, and the owner should never allow it to possess him. To wrangle and struggle for money is foolish, and to strive for power, rank, and high office is equally absurd. At best earthly belongings are given but for a time. The wise man will bear this in mind and limit his wishes. After all, joy is ultimately derived from within.

So, too, the spiritual predominates in Seneca's view of Fortune, of whose mutability the era in which he wrote, no less than that of Morley, supplied many illustrations. Such changes must be treated as inevitable, yet certain restraints can be placed on the sway of Fortune. If we steadily envisage that what she has bestowed may also be withdrawn, adversity can never take us by surprise. Thus our serenity is undisturbed, and the human soul is victorious.

Only the man of philosophic mind attains such strength, and he must subject himself to his own discipline. For this purpose retirement and contemplation are a necessity. Not that a monastic seclusion is essential. Public duties should be performed, but excessive preoccupation even with such business is not to be commended. The ideal mode of regulating life is to observe a happy mean between the ways of a sage and the ways of the world, by seeking the crowd and solitude alternately. In his hours of retirement the wise man will retreat into himself and live within himself. His aim should be to find peace of spirit and lasting tranquillity. If such a state be won, it will be thanks to the subordination of ourselves to reason; in reason is the key to the happy life.

Less characteristic perhaps than these conceptions, which are the very core of Seneca's teaching, is his occasional insistence on the need for submission to the decrees of Fate. Yet he acknowledged that circumstances might arise which would render these counsels of patient acquiescence impracticable. Hence in his system, as a last expedient for those in desperate plight he conceded the right of suicide. When life grows intolerable, it is permissible to make an end, provided that it be done nobly; this privilege he himself claimed.

There are then striking parallels to Senecan philosophy in Morley's writings, and still more remarkable, if allowance be made for the frailties and inconsistencies of human nature, is his attempt to apply the doctrines of the Roman Stoic to the problems of living in Tudor England. Yet, steeped as he was in Senecan ideas, in some respects Morley went his own way. With him determinism looms very large. It is connected with his belief that God's ordinances work for ultimate good, and this faith left in his scheme no place for suicide. For him the only solution of any crisis is to endure, in meek acquiescence bowing to the divine will. His attitude is epitomized in the motto which he appended to his two longer poems and which was written over the door of the chamber where he was wont to lie at Great Hallingbury: 'Si ita Deo placet, ita fiat.'

VII
MORLEY AS A TRANSLATOR

Unlike many other sixteenth-century translators, Morley was well equipped for his various enterprises, in that he possessed a knowledge of foreign tongues and was not limited to the use of French as an intermediary. It is evident that he took pride in his linguistic abilities. Thus with obvious satisfaction he tells how he replied 'after my s[mal] lernyng' to the address delivered to his party in French on behalf of the city of Antwerp,[1] and again he remarks that at Nürnberg he considered diverse questions with a French emissary, 'for asmoche ... that I knewe the speche'.[2] He thought even more of his ability to read Italian, which at that time was no common accomplishment, and he records with manifest gratification the favourable reception of his version of Petrarch's *Tryumphes* by Henry VIII,

'who as he was a Prynce aboue all other mooste excellente, so toke he the worke verye thankefullye, merueylynge muche howe I coulde do it, and thynkynge verelye I hadde not doone it, wythoute helpe of some other, better knowynge the Italyen tounge then I: but when he knewe the verye treweth, that I hadde traunslated the worke my selfe, he was more pleased therewith then he was before'.[3]

In some degree Morley was probably stimulated to undertake the labours of a translator by the example of Caxton, with whose writings he may well have become acquainted during his service in the household of the Lady Margaret.[4] Thus his version of Plutarch's Life of Theseus was prompted by his recollection of the fact that 'all redy the lyfe of the stronge Hercules and of Jason that wan the Golden Flese is in the Inglishe tonge'.[5] Sometimes, too, he was stirred by patriotism to emulate the achievements of other countries such as France and Italy, where the art of translation met with every encouragement.

'I do lamente at my harte,' he told Lord Maltravers, 'consyderynge that aswell in French, as in the Italyan (in the whyche both tongues

[1] *Vide ante,* p. xvi.
[2] MS. Vitell. B. XX, f. 289b. In this connexion it may be noted that in 1531 Morley had in his employment John Gay, a native of Normandy. Cf. *Letters and Papers, Henry VIII,* vol. v, p. 103.
[3] *Vide post,* p. 189.   [4] *Vide ante,* pp. x–xi.   [5] *Vide post,* p. 163.

I haue some lytle knowledge) there is no excellente worke in the latyn, but that strayght wayes they set it forth in the vulgar, moost commonly to their kynges and noble prynces of theyr region and countreys.'

As a case in point he mentions

'one of late dayes that was grome of the chaumber with that renowmed and valyaunte Prynce of hyghe memorye, Fraunces the Frenche kynge, whose name I haue forgotten,[1] that dydde translate these tryumphes to that sayde kynge, whyche he toke so thankefully, that he gaue to hym for hys paynes an hundred crounes, to hym and to his heyres of inheritaunce to enioye to that value in lande for euer, and toke suche pleasure in it, that wheresoeuer he wente amonge hys precyous Iewelles, that booke was alwayes caryed with hym for his pastyme to loke vpon, and as muche estemed by hym, as the rychest Diamonde he hadde'.

On seeing this, Morley goes on to say, 'I thoughte in my mynde, howe I beynge an Englyshe man, myght do aswell as the Frenche man',[2] and so in this spirit of national rivalry his own rendering was begun.

In the main, however, Morley was no doubt animated by a desire to please those to whom he dedicated most of his translations—Henry VIII and the Lady Mary. Quite apart from the light that it throws on his own interests, his choice of themes is significant of the predilections of the recipients. For the Princess he turned into English works of a grave or devotional character; for the King, writings which, though by no means of purely aesthetic value, were of a secular kind. By so doing, he propitiated the one actually in power and gratified the other who was destined to succeed to the throne. Incidentally, he made for himself a reputation as a man of letters. To this he was far from indifferent. Indeed, this is one of the traits that prove how strong was the spirit of the Renaissance in Morley, with its emphasis on the worth of the individual, in contrast to the self-effacing anonymity of the Middle Ages. Thus when he presented to the Lady Mary a medieval commentary on the Psalter, he made an observation characteristic of himself and of his age.

[1] The work in question must have been *Les Triūphes Petrarque traduictes de lāgue Tuscane en Rhime francoyse par le Baron D'opede,* Paris, 1538.
[2] *Vide post*, p. 189.

'And surely', he says, 'I do thynke that he that expounde thys Psalter that to avoyde pryde, he neither wolde wryte hys name, nor yett tell in hys boke what tyme he wrote it, which I do greately meruell at, but that the goode man lokyde to haue laude of Hym for hys trauell that forgettyth noo goode deade vnrewardyde, nor noone euyll deade vnponyshede.'[1]

Such pious reticence was incomprehensible to Morley, who took good care that his achievements should be recognized by his fellow mortals.

But, on the other hand, he had no exaggerated idea of his capacity. On the contrary, he speaks of his work with becoming modesty and readily points out its blemishes. He was well aware that he was no stylist and despaired of doing justice to the grace and eloquence of some of the authors to whose writings he was trying to give an English dress. Thus he remarks that 'yt ys very harde in all things to folowe in ouer naturall tonge the exselent style of this Angelus Pollicianus';[2] and again of Erasmus's paean in praise of the Virgin Mary he says:

'I dar affyrme that emonges dyuers other thynges that he haithe wrytten elegauntly, he neuer wrote with his penne so elegaunte a style as thys, whiche, all thoughe I cannot sett it forthe in Englishe as he hathe doone in the Latten, yet as muche as my wytte can serue me, I haue studyde to sett it furthe in oure tounge.'[3]

As for Cicero, Morley found his meaning as elusive as his style was incomparable. 'I am not ignoraunte,' he confesses, 'but the wordes of Cicero ar so wonderfull and the sense in many places so diffuse that it passeth my learnynge or capacyte to put it in oure speache as it shulde be.'[4] Similarly, he was baffled by the perplexing obscurity in which the Latin version of Plutarch's Life of Theseus was enveloped. And if the Latin prose of his originals was often too much for him, he encountered an even greater obstacle in the rhyme of Petrarch's *Trionfi*: 'I haue not erred moche from the letter, but in the ryme, whiche is not possible for me to folow in the translation, nor touche the least poynt of the elegancy that this elegant Poete hath set forth in his owne maternall tongue.'[5]

Though it is manifest from this and other passages already

[1] See p. 169.   [2] See p. 170.   [3] See p. 172.
[4] See p. 175.   [5] See p. 190.

quoted that Morley was by no means insensitive to aesthetic values, he probably did not seek, and certainly did not achieve, similar qualities in his own writing. For him it was enough to render Cicero, Erasmus, or Plutarch 'rudely, but truly'.[1] The most that he claims is that he has translated 'according to the sens'[2] or that he has 'not moche alteryd from the sence'.[3] The fact is that Morley wrote, not as a scholar for critics, but as a gentleman for royal patrons. On one occasion at least, he was so anxious that the translation should be in the King's hands with all speed that he omitted to revise it carefully. Hence he afterwards admitted frankly to Lord Maltravers: 'I dyd it in suche hast, that doubtles in many places (yf it were agayne in my handes) I thynke I coulde well amende it.'[4] This appears to have been an isolated case of negligence, due to special circumstances, but it indicates that entire precision was not an ideal to which Morley aspired.

A certain measure of inaccuracy was not the only privilege that Morley exercised. When it suited his purpose, he did not hesitate to rearrange the work that he was translating, as is best illustrated by his treatment of the ninety-first and one hundred and twentieth epistles of Seneca.[5] As a rule, however, he does not indulge in such violent alterations, and the changes that he makes are of a minor order. One curious example occurs in his rendering of forty-six lives from *De claris mulieribus*. In describing the undying fame won by Sappho, Boccaccio had written: 'et ipsa inter poetas celebres numerata, quo splendore profecto non clariora sunt regum dyademata, non pontificum infule, nec etiam triumphantium lauree'. The corresponding passage in Morley's rendering is: '... and hyr name sett emongste the moste renomyde poetes, whiche surely is more laude to hyre then the diademe to sum kynges, or the bysshopps myters, or the conquerours lawrell braunches.'[6] Here it will be noted that although the translation is as absolute as the original in speaking of the emblems of bishops and conquerors, a qualification is introduced in the reference to kings. The alteration is slight, but full of significance. Morley was too cautious to run any risk of stirring the wrath of Henry VIII.

[1] See p. 165.   [2] See p. 165.   [3] See p. 170.
[4] See p. 189.   [5] See pp. lviii–lix.   [6] See p. 155, ll. 7–10.

With this exception, there seems to be no guiding principle in Morley's departures from what Boccaccio wrote. Here and there the text before him was undoubtedly corrupt, and one can see how he attempts to make the best of an awkward situation. But elsewhere it is obvious that he has simply failed to grasp the author's meaning. And just as his wayward procedure can be accounted for in this simple fashion, so there is no need to search for any profound explanation of his interruption of his task after finishing the Life of Lucrece. It is unlikely that this was due to any weighty aesthetic considerations. More probably he thought that his version, though incomplete, included the important figures, for it is certain that some of the later biographies treat of minor personages whose introduction was due solely to Boccaccio's desire to bring up his total to one hundred.[1] It is also quite possible that Morley, whose renderings are usually short, grew weary of his labours and resolved to make an end.

As a prose-writer, both in *De claris mulieribus* and elsewhere, Morley is in no wise remarkable. His sentences are sometimes imperfectly constructed, and not infrequently he falls into anacoluthon. Nor does he atone for these defects by grace of style. His verse is, if anything, still more displeasing. Its uncouth air and limping gait repel the reader. Learning Morley certainly had, but none of the qualities of a great writer, and his relations to contemporary personages and problems are a far more interesting object of study than his translations. Consequently, any importance that he may have is purely historical. Nevertheless, the man who perceived the value of Plutarch's *Lives* over twenty years before Thomas Stocker and more than thirty before Sir Thomas North is worthy of some slight tribute, and, with all its shortcomings, his work is a link between Caxton and the later English translators of the sixteenth century.[2] On this score, no

[1] Cf. Henri Hauvette, *Boccace*, Paris, 1914, pp. 399–401, where Boccaccio's final version is considered in relation to the first draft. See also in this connexion Guido Traversari, 'Appunti sulle redazioni del "De claris mulieribus" di Giovanni Boccaccio' in *Miscellanea di studi critici pubblicati in onore di Guido Mazzoni*, Florence, 1907, vol. i, pp. 225–51.

[2] J. P. Collier in *The Poetical Decameron*, London, 1820, vol. i, p. 87, appreciates Morley's historical significance. He argues that Morley ought to be regarded as a predecessor rather than as a contemporary of Wyatt

less than because he was able to discard the French medium on which many of them depended and go direct to his Latin and Italian sources, Morley deserves more consideration than he has hitherto received.[1]

and Surrey, and that in the edition of Edward Phillips's *Theatrum Poetarum* enlarged by Sir Egerton Brydges and published at Canterbury in 1800, his position should have been altered accordingly.

[1] Even so well informed a book as H. B. Lathrop's *Translations from the Classics into English from Caxton to Chapman, 1477–1620*, Madison, 1933, passes over Morley in silence, and C. H. Conley's *The first English translators of the Classics*, New Haven and London, 1927, ignores his renderings of five of Plutarch's *Lives*.

DE CLARIS MULIERIBUS

TO the moste hygh, moste puysaunte, moste exellent and f. 1a
moste Chrysten Kynge, my moste redoubtede souereygne
lorde Henry th'Eighte, by the grace of Gode, of Englonde,
Fraunce *and* Irelonde Kynge, Defender of the Feythe, *and* in
erthe, vndre Gode, suppreme heede of the Churche of Englonde 5
and Irelonde, your moste humble subiecte Henry Parcare,
knyght, Lorde Morley, desyreth thys Newe Yere, with infynyte
of yeres to your imperiall Maieste, helthe, honoure and vyctory.

IN the tyme the hoole worlde was obediente to the Romaynes,
moste victoriouse *and* gr*a*ciouse souereigne lorde, not onely by 10
armes they were renoumede aboue all other naciones, but also
in eloquens and goode lernynge, as it apperethe by thyes oratours
and poetes in the greate Augustus days; that is to saye, Varro,
Tullius Cicero, Virgill, Orace and Ouyde, with diuers others.
And all thoughe that those that ensuyde frome oone emp*e*roure 15
to another were exellently lernede, as bothe the Plynys, Marciall,
Quyntilian *and* Claudian and suche other, yet why it was so that
they coulde neuer attayne to thes afore rehersyde, neither in
prose nor yet in verse, is to me a greate wonder. For asmuche
as they sawe the workes of the other, whiche, as my reasone 20
geuythe me, shulde haue rather causede theym to haue bene
in | science aboue theym then inferiours to theym. For why? If f. 1b
one that gothe aboute to buylde a palace, if he se another whiche
lykethe hym well, it shalbe noo greate mastrie, if he spye a
faulte in his examplar, to amende it in hys worke. And why 25
thys shulde not be, truely, I can geue noo reasone to the contrary.
For soo it was, that euere as the greate empyre of Rome decayde
in deedes of armes, so dyd it in learenynge. In somuche that,
whether it were by the straynge nationes that they were mynglede
with all, or otherwyse, at the laste theimself*es* (that accomptyde 30
all other nationes barbarouse, oonely the Greakes excepte) by
the space of sex or seuene hundrithe yeres were as barbarouse as
the best, thys contynuynge so longe a tyme, that in processe
aboute the yere of our Lorde God, a thousand foure hundrith,

in the tyme of the flowre and hono*ur* of prynces, Kynge Edwarde,
the thyrde of that name, holdynge by ryghte the septre of thys
imperiall realme, as yo*ur* Grace nowe dothe, there sprange in
Italy three excellente clerkes. The fyrst was Dante, for hys greate
5 learnynge in hys mother tunge surnamyde dyuyne Dante. Surely,
not withoute cause. For it is manyfest that it was true, whiche
was grauen on hys tumbe, that hys maternall eloquens touchede
so nyghe the prycke that it semyde a myracle of nature. And
forbecause that one shuldnot thynke I do feyne, I shall sett the
10 wordes in the Italiane tunge, whiche is thys:

Dante Alighieri son, Minerua oscura
D'intelligenza e d'arte, nel cui ingegno
L'eleganza materna aggiunse al segno
Che si tien gran miracol di natura.[1]

15 The next vnto thys Dante was Frauncis Petrak, that not onely
in the Latyne tunge, but also in swete ryme, is so extemyde
that vnto thys present tyme vnnethe is ther any noble prynce
in Italy, nor gentle man, withoute hauynge in hys handes hys
sonnetes *and* hys 'Tryhumphes' or hys other rymes. And he wrote
f. 2a also in the Latyne | tunge certeyn eglogg*es* in versys and another
21 booke namede 'Affrica' *and* 'Of the Remedyes of bothe Fortunes',
with dyuers epistles and other wo*ur*kes whiche I ouer passe.

The last of thies three, moste gratiouse souereigne lorde, was
John Bocas of Certaldo, whiche in lyke wyse as the tother
25 twayne, Dante and Petracha, wer moste exellent in the vulgare
ryme, so thys Bocas was aboue all others in prose, as it apperythe
by his hundrith tayles and many other notable workes. Nor he
was noo lesse elegaunte in the prose of his oune tunge then he was
in the Latyne tunge, wherin, as Petrak dyd wryte clerkly certeyn
30 volumes in the Latyne tunge, so dyd thys clerke. And fyrst 'Of

---

[1] In the MS. these verses read as follows:

Dante alegra son minerua obscura.
De arte & de intelligentia nel cui ingenio.
Le elegantia mat*er*na aio*n*se al scengo.
Que se tient pour miracol de natura.

It is pointed out by P. Toynbee, *Dante in English Literature*, London,
1909, vol. i, p. 34, note 1, that the lines quoted by Morley come, not from
the inscription on Dante's tomb, but from Boccaccio's sonnet on Dante,
written in 1373.

De Claris Mulieribus 3

the Fall of Prynces', 'Of the Geonelogye of the Goddes', and emonge
other thys booke namede 'De preclaris mulieribus', that is, of
the ryght renomyde ladies. Whiche sayde booke, as in the ende
he wrytethe, he dyd dedicate the same to Quene Jane,[1] in hys
tyme Quene of Naples, a pryncesse enduede with all vertues, 5
wysdome and goodenes. And for asmuche as that I thoughte howe
that your Hyghnes, of youre accustomede mekenes and pryncely
herte, woldenot disdayn it, so dyd I imagyne that if by chaunce it
shulde cum to the handes of the ryght renomyde and moste
honorable ladyes of your Highnes moste tryhumphaunte courte, 10
that it shulde be well acceptyde to theym to se and reede the
meruelouse vertue of theyr oune sexe, to the laude perpetuall of
theym. And albeit, as Bocas wrytethe in hys proheme, he
menglyssheth sum not verey chaste emongste the goode, yet hys
honeste excuse declarethe that he dyd it to a goode entent, that 15
all ladyes and gentlewomen, seynge the glorye of the goode, may
be steryde to folowe theym, and seynge the vyce of sum, to flee
theym. Whiche saide worke, my moste noble and gratiouse
souereygne lorde, as farr as it gothe, I haue drawne in to our
maternall tonge, to presente the same vnto your imperiall dignyte 20
thys Newe Yeres Day, praynge to Chryste Jhesu to teche that
right | Christen hande of yours to batell agaynste youre auncyente f. 2b
ennemyes, that they may knowe that He whiche is the way and
the truethe, helpythe your Exellencye in your truethe, so that
they may fall and youe to ryse in honour, victory and fame, aboue 25
all kynges that is, hathe bene, or shalbe. Amen. |

THe preface of th'exellent clerc, John Bocasse, of his booke, f. 3a
intitlede in the Latyne tunge 'De preclaris mulieribus', that
is to say in Englysshe, of the ryghte renoumyde ladyes, wherin
he dothe excuse hymself why, emongste theym that were moste 30
vertuouse and honorable women, he dothe often put in theym
that were vicyouse.

Incipit Prologus Iohannis Bocacij in librum de claris mulieribus.[2]

[1] See *Addenda*, p. 191.
[2] (L *represents the Louvain edition of the Latin original, here printed,*
B *stands for Berne*, S *for Strassburg, and* U *for Ulm.*)

THere be of the olde auncyent wryters, and also of late, of right fam*ou*s clerkes that haue breuely wrytten the lyffes of the illustriouse noble men. Emonge others, the ryght exellent poete Frauncys Petrark, my maister, hathe endytyd and gathrede
5 theyre actes in a compendiouse volume, and well worthy. For, to th'ent*en*t that they myghte be aboue others by theyr notable and hardy act*es*, they not oonely put to theyr study, but also their substaunce *and* their bloode, when the oportunyte of tyme semyde theim so for to do, to noone other entente, but to deserue
10 therby of theyr posteryte a name and fame for euer. Surely, I haue not a litle meruelyde of theym that haue thus wrytten, why they haue not sumwhat touchede the gloriouse actes of women, when it is euydente that dyuers and sundry of theym haue doone ryghte notable thynges. And if men by theyr strength and other
15 worthy ways haue des*er*uede to haue suche prayse and commendation, how muche more ought those women to be praysede, because that they be naturally weike and feble, and theyr wyttes not so quycke as mens wyttes be, if they haue doone suche

SCripsere iam dudum nonnulli veterum sub compendio de viris
20 illustribus libros, et euo nostro, latiori tamen volumine et acutiori stilo, vir insignis et poeta egregius, Franciscus Petrarcha, preceptor noster, scribit et digne. Nam qui, vt ceteros anteierent claris facinoribus, studium omne, substantias, sanguinem et animam exigente oportunitate posuere, profecto, vt eorum nomen
25 in posteros perpetua deducatur memoria, meruere. Sane, miratus sum plurimum adeo modicum apud h[o]sce viros potuisse mulieres, vt nulle memorie gratiam in speciali aliqua descriptione consecute sint, cum liquido amplioribus hystorijs constat quasdam tam strennue egisse nonnulla. Etsi extollendi sunt homines,
30 dum concesso sibi robore magna perfecerint, quanto amplius mulieres, quibus fere omnibus a natura rerum mollicies insita et corpus debile ac tardum ingenium datum est, si in virilem euaserint animum et ingenio celebri atque virtute conspicua audeant

19 Scripsere] iam *add.* BSU.   22 anteierent] anteirant S.   23 sanguinem] sa*n*guine B.   26 huiusce LBSU.   27 nulle] nullam BU.   28 liquido] ex *add.* BU. constat] constet BU.   28-9 quadasm] *om.* B.   29 strennue] quam fortiter *add.* BU.   nonnulla] nonnullas BU.   30 perfecerint] fecerint BU.   32 in] *om.* BU.   33 et] ac BU.   atque] ac BU.

De Claris Mulieribus 5

famouse actes, which shulde be harde | for men to do. And f. 3*b* for that entente they shulde not be defraudyde therof, it came into my mynde that of those that haue deseruyde prayse to put theym in oone volume—not oonely theym that by vertue haue des*er*uede it, but also those that by expresse ande knowne 5 euyll doynge be spoken of vnto thys day. Nor I wyllnot that the reder shall thynke it congruente that I do compare Medea and Sempronia with Lucres and Sulpicia. All thoughe I haue mynglede theym with thies moste chastyste wyfes, my mynde is nothynge that ways. Nor agayne not so strayte that I wolde touche noone 10 other but suche, and in a larger sense, with the patiens of the gentle reder, to put theym with the other. For why? Emonge the Scipions and the Catons and the Fabryciens, moste noble, vertuouse men, is numbrede wyle *and* crafty Hanyball, false and trayterouse Jugurta, the blody and tyra*n*nouse Scilla *and* 15

atque perficiant etiam difficil[l]ima viris, extollende sunt! Et ideo, ne merito fraudentur suo, venit in animum ex hijs, quas memoria referet, in glorie sue decus in vnum deducere eisque addere ex multis quasdam, quas audacia seu vires ingenij et industria aut nature munus vel fortune gratia seu iniuria notabiles fecit, 20 hijsque paucas annectere, que, etsi non memoratu dignum aliquid fecere, causas tamen maximis facinoribus prebuere; nec volo, vt legenti videatur congruum, si Penolopi Lucretie Sulpicieve, pudicissimis matronis, immixtas Medeam, Semproniamque comperiat, quibus pergrande et perniciosum forte fuit ingenium, vel 25 conformes eisdem. Non enim est animus mihi hoc claritatis nomen adeo strictum sumere, vt semper in virtutem videatur exire, quinymo in ampliorem sensum (bona cum pace legentium) trahere et illas intelligere claras, quas quocunque ex facinore orbi vulgato sermone notissimas nouero, cum et inter Scipiones 30 Cathonesque atque Fabricios, viros illustres, sediciosissimos Graccos, versipellem Hanibalem, proditorem Iugurtam, cruentos ciuilis sanguinis Sillam Mariumque et eque diuitem et auarum

18 eisque] eisdem BU.   19 quas] aut *add.* BU.   22 maximis] maximas BU.   vt] *om.* BU.   23 congruum] incongruum BSU.   Sulpicieve] Sulpitiae ut B, sulpicie U.   24 Medeam] Floram *add.* BU; gloriam *add* S.   24–5 comperiat] comperint BU.   25 et] sed BU.   25–6 vel. c. eisdem] *om.* B.   27 strictum] strictim B.   30 inter] Leonidas *add.* BU, Leonardas S.   33 ciuilis sanguinis] a ciuili sanguine B.

Marryus, and the couetouse Crassus, and other whiche I do well
call to mynde that I haue redde of.

But I haue thus sett thei*m*
to gether, to thys entente that, in lokynge and redynge of the
goode, it may stere the reders to goodenes, and to theym that be
5 euyll to gyue theym a bytte, whereby they may withdrawe
theymselff*es* frome so euyll condiciones and ways.

And I haue
so ratyde this my worke that it semythe I haue sumwhat hydde
of the euyll of theym, and emonge the hystoryes and in sum place
put in sum thynges ioyouse and pleasaunte, not withoute geuynge
10 su*m* sharpe prycke to theym, to counseill theim to flye frome
vyce, so that I doo hoope that with thys co*m*myxtion sum vtylyte
and p*r*ofyte shall cum of the same. And for because that men

---

Crassum aliosque tales sepe legisse meminerim. Verum, quoniam
extulisse laudibus memoratu digna et depressisse increpationibus
15 nephanda nonnunquam non solum erit hinc egisse generosos in
gloriam et ignauos habenis ab infaustis paululum retraxisse, sed
il[l]ud restaurasse, quod quarundam turpitudinibus venustatis
opusculo demptum videtur, ratus sum et quandoque hystorijs
inserere nonnulla lepida blandimenta virtutis et in fugam atque
20 detestationem scelerum aculeos addere, et sic fiet, vt immixta
hystoriarum delectationi sacra ment[e]s subintrabit vtilitas; et,
ne more pris[c]o apices tantum rerum tetigisse videar, ex quibus
a fide dignis potuero cognouisse, amplius in longiusculam hystoriam pertraxisse non solum vtile, sed oportunum arbitror,
25 existimans harum facinora non minus mulieribus quam viris
[e]tiam placitura, que, cum vt plurimum hystoriarum ignare sint,
sermone prolixiore indigent et letantur. Attamen visum est, ne
omiserim, excepta matre prima, hijs omnibus fere gentilibus nullas
ex sacris mulieribus, Hebreis Christianisque, miscuisse; non enim
30 satis bene conueniunt nec equo incedere videntur gradu. He

15 nephanda] infanda BU.   hinc egisse] *om*. B.   generosos]
generosis B.   16 gloriam] verum *add*. B.   et] inde *add*. U, etiam in
ignominiam B.   ignauos] ignauis B.   habenis] habenas BU.
16–17 sed i. rest.] et B.   17 il[l]ud] iliud L, id U.   18 opusculo]
om. B.   21 delectationi] delectatione BU.   sacra ment[e]s] sacra-
mentis L, sacra mentis S.   22 pristo LS.   24 pertraxisse]
protraxisse BU.   26 rtiam L.   27 prolixiore] prolixiori BU.

shulde not ymagyne that I shulde but touche suche to breuely,
for theym that knowe not well the hystoryes I haue drawne theyr
lyfes oute in a lengthe, nott doubtynge but to please aswell the
men as the women *ther*by. I wyllnot also forgete to tell youe that
emonge all thies women, whiche were but panymes, our fyrste 5
mother Eue sett asyde, I | . . .¹
[*Desunt nonnulla.*]

¹ Cf. Introduction, p. lxv.

quippe ob eternam et veram gloriam sese fere in aduersam persepe
humanitati tollerantiam coegere, sacrosancta preceptorum tam
iussa quam vestigia ymitantes, vbi ille, seu quodam nature 10
munere vel instinctu, seu potius huius momentanei fulgoris
cupiditate p[e]r[c]ite non absque tamen acri mentis robore
deuenere vel fortune v[r]g[e]ntis impulsu nonnunquam grauissima
pertulere. Preterea he vera et indeficienti luce corusce in [meri]ta
eternitate non solum clarissime viuunt, sed earum virginitatem, 15
castimoniam, sanctitatem, virtutem et in superandis tam con-
cupiscentijs carnis quam supplicijs tyrannorum inuictam constantiam, ipsarum meritis exigentibus, singulis voluminibus a
pijs hominibus sacris litteris et veneranda maiestate conspicuis
descriptas esse cognoscimus, vbi illarum merita nullo in hoc 20
edito volumine speciali, vti iam dictum est, et a nemine demon-
strata describere, quasi aliquale reddituri premium, inchoamus.
Cui quidem pio operi ipse rerum omnium pater, Deus, assit et
laboris sumpti fautor, quod scripsero, in suam veram laudem
scripsisse concedat. 25

FINIT PROLOGUS. INCIPIT LIBER.

9 humanitati] humanitatis B.   sacrosancta] sacrosancti S.   10 ille]
illi S.   12 partite LS.   13 vagantis L, vagentis S.   14 inuicta L,
in munita S, immerita U.   15 earum] eorum BU.   21 dictum] ductum
B.   23 quidem] quidam BSU.

Of Eue, oure fyrste mother.
                            The fyrst Chapitre.

HAuynge intencion to wryte the exellent glory that the noble
women in tyme passyd haue obteyned, it semethe to me that
5 it is not incongruente to begynne at the *commune* mother of vs
all. Eue, than, that moste auncyent mother, as she was the fyrst
of all women, so is she decorate with woundres exellent praysys.
For she was not, as other be, brought forthe into this lac*ri*mable
vale of mysery, in whiche we be borne in to labour and to payne,
10 nor so formyd, nor as we shulde say, shapyn, with that hammar,
nor cryinge and bewaylynge hyr cu*m*mynge into the worlde, as
the maner of al that be borne is, but after that sorte that neuer
syns happned any to be so creatyd as she was. For when that
moste wisest and best worke maister had creatyd Adam of the
15 slyme of the earth with his propre hande, and in the felde, whiche
after was callede Damascene, had translatyd hym into the
gardyn of delycys, bry*n*gynge hym vnto a pleasaunte and soft
slepe, the craft onely to hy*m* knowne, of hym that slept he brought

---

                            De Eua, parente prima.
20   Primum Capitulum.

SCripturus igitur, quibus fulgoribus mulieres claruerunt insignes, a matre omnium sumpsisse exordium non apparebit
indignum. Eua quippe, vetustissima parens, vti prima, sic
magnificis fuit insignis splendoribus. Nam non in hac erumnosa
25 miseriarum valle, in qua ad laborem ceteri mortales nascimur,
producta est nec eodem malleo aut incude etiam fabricata seu
eiulans, nascendi crimen deflens, aut inualida ceterorum ritu
venit in vitam; quinymo, quod nemini vnquam alteri contigisse
auditum est, cum iam ex limo terre rerum omnium faber optimus
30 Adam manu compegisset propria et ex agro, cui postea Dama-
scenus nomen inditum est, in [h]ort[o] deliciarum transtulisset
eumque in soporem soluisset placidum, artificio sibi tantum
cognito ex dormientis latere eduxit eandem sui compotem et

21 claruerunt] claruerint BU.   23 Eua] Ea BU.   24 fuit] et *add.* S.
26 fabricata] fabro facta B, fabre facta U.   31 ortu LS.   32 -que] *om.* BU.

hyr forth rype of age, as well gladde of that mery place she was
in, as also of the sight of hyr husbonde, i*m*mortall, and lady and
quene of all thynges, and of hyr wakynge husbonde felowe and
make, and by hym namede Eue. What more bryghtnes happned
to any that euer was borne? And besydes this, we may right well 5
imagyne that of beauty she was i*n*comporable. And albeit this
gyft exellent of beautie by age or by sum sodeyn feuer in mydle
age gothe soone away, yett for asmuche as emongste women this
is accomptyd for a moste exellent gyft, and many of theim
emongste women haue therby by theyr vnwyse iudgement 10
obteyned fame euerlastynge, as in those that folowe shall to
youe appere, yett thys woman, | aswell by this beauty as by f. 4*b*
hyr wondref̣ull begynnynge, passid theim all. And thus, shee
made cytezyn of Paradyse, whyle she ther had with hyr husbonde
Adam the fruicyon of that pleasaunt place, the vngracyouse 15
ennemy to mankynde, enuyouse of hyr ioye, p*er*suadyd hyr that
in brekynge one thynge to hyre forboden she shulde soone assende

---

maturam viro et loci amenitate atque sui factoris letabundam
intuitu, immortalem et rerum dominam atque vigilantis iam viri
sociam et ab eodem Eua[m] etiam nominatam. Quid maius, quid 20
splendidius potuit vnquam contigisse nascenti? Preterea hanc
existimare possumus corporea formositate mirabilem. Quid enim
dei digito factum est, quod cetera non excedat pulchritudine?
Et, quamuis formositas hec annositate peritura sit aut medio in
etatis flore paruo egritudinis impulsu lapsura, tamen, quia inter 25
precipuas dotes suas mulieres [hanc] numerant et plurimum ex
ea glorie mortalium indiscreto iudicio iam consecute sunt, non
superflue inter claritates earum tanquam fulgor precipuus et
apposita est et in sequentibus apponenda veniet. Hec insuper,
tam iure originis quam incolatus Paradisi ciuis facta et amicta 30
splendore nobis incognito, dum vna cum viro loci delicijs frueretur
auide, inuidus · sue felicitatis hostis nepharia [suasione illius]
ingessit animo, si aduersus vnicam sibi legem a deo impositam

18 sui] *om.* BU.   19 immortalem] in mortalem BU.   20 Eua LS.
22 existimare] *om.* S, arbitrari BU.   25 impulsu] in pulsu SU.   26
[hanc] *om.* LSU.   32 illius suasione LS, illi suasione U, suasione ingessit
illius animo B.

to hygher felicyte and glorye. To whiche persuasione, when shee, by greate lyghtnes more then behouyde hyr for vs, gaue credyte vnto itt, with hyr swete, flatterynge suggestion she drew hyr husbonde to folowe hyr way. And thus they bothe tastynge of
5 the tree of the knowledge of goode and euyll and eatynge of the fructe forboden, they not onely thei*m* self but all theyr posteryte depryuyde frome reste, quyetnes and eternyte into labour and mys*er*able deathe, and frome that delectable country into this dolorouse worlde, full of brears, brembles *and* thornes. For when
10 that bryght light in whiche they went in was goone frome theym, and they clothyde was dep*ar*tyde fro*m* theyr maker, and frome the place of delyte as outelaws expulsed into the vale of Ebron, it folowede that this exellent woman wi*th* thies offenses knowne ouer all was the fyrst, as it is thought, that with hyr husbonde
15 founde the ways to dygge and eare the earth, *and* beynge after experte of the paynes of berynge of children and of the sorowes for the death of hyr children and neuows, sufferynge as well

2 vs] she *add.* MS.

---

iret, in ampliorem gloriam ire posse. Cui dum leuitate feminea magis quam illi nobisque oportuerit, crederet seseque stolide ad
20 altiora conscensuram arbitraretur, ante alia blanda quadam suggestione virum flexibilem in sententiam suam traxit, et, in legem agentes, arboris scientie boni et mali poma dum gustassent temerario ausu, seque genusque suum omne futurum ex quiete et eternitate in labores anxios et miseram mortem et ex delecta-
25 bili patria inter vepres, glebas et scopulos deduxere. Nam, cum lux corusca, qua incedebant amicti, abijsset, a turbato creatore suo obiurgati, perisomatibus cincti, ex deliciarum loco in agros Ebron pulsi exulesque venere. Ibi egregia mulier, his facinoribus clara, cum prima, vt a nonnullis creditum est, vertente terram
30 ligonibus viro colo nere adinuenisset, sepius dolores partus experta est et, quibus ob mortem filiorum et nepotum angustijs angeretur animus, eque misere passa et, vt algores estusque

18 ire] iri BU.   19 nob. oport.] nobis quæ profuerit B.   22 scientie *om.* BU.   24 miseram] miseriam BU.   26 chorusca LS.   28 Ebron] Hebron BU.   29 a] *om.* BU.

heate as colde, and ordeyned at last to dye with thies incon-
ueniencys, lyuyde vnto an extreme age.

Of Semiramis, the Quene of the Assyryens.
The ij^{de} Chapitre.

THe famouse Semiramis was the aunsyent Quene of the 5
Assiryens, but of what kynred she cam of the longe tyme
hathe put it in obliuione. But besydes those olde, | faynede tales, f. 5a
the aunsyent historyens wryteth hyr to be the doughter of
Neptunus, whiche was the sonne of Saturne, and by the errour
of the gentyles accompted to be god of the see. And all thoughe 10
it be not conuenyent to be beleuyde, yet it is an argument that
she was procreate of noble parenttes. This saide lady was
maryede to the ryghte noble Ninus, Kynge of the Assiryens, and
of hy[m] conceyuyde a sonne callede Nynus. Nowe this Nynus,
hauynge conquerede all Asya, ande at the laste the countrye of 15
Bacherys addyd to his domynyone, with the shote of an arrowe
was slayne, leuynge behynde hym hys wyfe but verey yonge and
his onely sonne Nynus afore expressyd. Thynkynge it vnmeate
to put the gouernauns of the hoole Oryent to soo yonge and

---

sinam et incommoda cetera, fessa laboribus moritura deuenit 20
in senium.

De Semiramide, regina Assiriorum. ij.

SEmiramis insignis atque vetustissima Assiriorum regina fuit;
a quibus tamen parentibus genus duxerit, annositas abstulit,
preter id fabulosum [quod] placet antiquis aientibus eam filiam 25
fuisse Neptuni, quem Saturni filium et maris deum erronea
credulitate firmabant, quod, etsi credi non oporteat, argumentum
tamen est eam a nobilibus parentibus genitam. Hec quidem
Nino, Assiriorum reg[i] egregio, nupsit, et ex eo Ninum filium
peperit vnicum. Sane, Nino, omni Asia et postremo Bacheris 30
subactis, sagitte ictu mortuo, cum adhuc hec iuuencula esset, et
filius puer, minime tutum existimans tam grandis et orientis
imperij etati tam tenelle habenas committere, adeo ingentis

25 id] quod BU.   29 rege LS.   29 Ninum] niniam U, paterno nomine
add. B.   30 Bacheris] bacharis U, Bactrianis B.   32 puer] puerum S.

tendre a chylde of age, she was of so highe and noble a hert that
those countreys, that hyr ferse husbounde by armes hadde sub-
dued and coartyd to serue, to take vpon hyr to rule and gouerne
theym all, for as it were with a wyse, subtyle womans craft, she
5 reteyned to hyr the greate hoste of hyr greate husbonde. Now
she was not muche vnlyke to hyr yonge sonne, neither of face,
nor yet of stature, and, to this, theyr speche was not vnlyke the
one of the tother. Whiche beynge a greate forderynge to brynge
to passe hyr pur̃pose, she adournynge aswell hyr oune heede as
10 hyr sones with a bonet, as it were muche lyke to those that the
greate prynces weere in theyr solemme tryhumphes, the Assyryens not beynge acustomyde with suche maner of bonettes,
she so wroughte, to th'entent the nouelte therof shuldnot be noo
meruell, that all the Assyriens shuld were bonettes after that
15 sorte. And thus the wyfe of the sumtyme noble Nynus, faynynge
hyr bothe his wyfe and his chylde, with a meruelouse diligence
maynteyned the kyngly dignyte and the knyghtly cheualry, and
faynynge a contrarye sexe, eschewyde many noble ande wonder-

fuit animi, vt, quas ferus homo armis subegerat nationes coer-
20 cueratque viribus, arte et ingenio regendas femina auderet
assumere. Nam, astu quodam muliebri excogitata fallacia pre-
grandi, mortui viri ante alia decepit exercitus. Erat, nec mirabile, Semiramis liniamentis oris persimilis filio: nude vtrique
gene, nec erat per etatem dissona a puerili feminea vox, et in
25 statura corporis nil vel modicum grandiuscula differebat a nato;
quibus iuuantibus, ne in processu quid fraudem detegere potuisset,
texit caput thiara, brachijs cruribusque velamentis absconditis;
et, quoniam insuetum eousque esset Assirijs, egit, ne afferret
nouitas habitus admirationem accolis, vt ornatu simili omnis
30 vteretur populus, et sic Nyni olim coniunx filium et femina
puerum simulans, mira cum diligentia maiestatem regiam adepta,
eam militaremque disciplinam seruauit et, mentita sexum,
grandia multa et robustissimis viris egregia operata est. Et,

19 fuit] fuerit S.   22 exercitus] exercitum BU.   22–3 nec mirabile]
om B.   23 nude vtrique] vnde vtroque S.   24 erat] erant S.   25 statura]
statuam S.   26 quid] quod BSU. fraudem] fraude S.   detegere]
non *add*. S.   potuisset] obesset *add*. BU.   28 afferret] offerret BSU.

full actes that many a stronge man couldenot haue brought to passe. And thus, nother lettynge for labour, trauell nor payne, nor what enuyouse men saide or dyd agaynste hyr, at last she declared | planely what she was, and that all though she were f. 5*b* a woman, it was not the kynde, but the noble mynde, that 5 was worthy to rule an empyre, and that the more the people woundred at hyr, the more it gaue the occasion to theym to prayse hyr. Thus, as I haue reherside, this lady, takynge to hyr mans hert, not onely defendyd and kept the greate empyre of hyr husbonde deade and goone, but further, in assautynge of other 10 countreys allways victoriouse in batell*es*, she encreascyd on all sydes hyr countrye. For she entred emongste the Indiens, whiche vnnethe noo man afore hyr dyd, and Babilon, the olde, auncyent cyte of Nemrots, whiche he began in the feeld*es* of Se*n*naar, by age decayde, she instoryde agayne and compassyd it with walles 15 of bryke, of hight and greatenes and compas m*er*uelo*us* to se. And breuely, emonge all hir notable and renomede actes, one is

---

dum, nullo labori parcens aut periculo territa, [in]a[u]d[i]tis facinoribus quorumcunque superasset inuidiam, non est verita cunctis aperire, que foret quodve etiam fraude simulasset 20 feminea, quasi vellet ostendere non sexum, sed animum imperio oportunum. Quod, quantum aduertentibus ingessit admirationis, tantum mulieris maiestatem inclitam ampliauit. Hec, vt eius facinora paululum protensius deducamus in medium, sumptis post insigne figmentum virili animo armis, non solum, 25 quod vir suus quesiuerat, tutauit imperium, sed Ethiopiam a se acri lacessitam bello atque superatam iunxit eidem et inde in Yndos vehementia arma euertit, ad quos nondum preter virum quisquam accesserat, Babiloniam insuper, vetustissimum Nembroth opus et ingentem ea etate in campis Sennaar ciuitatem 30 restaurauit murisque ex cocto latere, arena, pice ac b[i]tumine compact[is], altitudine atque grossicie et circuitu longissimo admirandis ambiuit. Et, vt ex multitudine suorum gestorum

18 mandatis LS. 20 etiam] *om.* B, quod uirum *add.* B. 28 euertit] conuertit BU. 29 quisquam] quispiam BU. 30 ingentem] vigentem BU. Sennaar] in *add.* BU. 31 butumine L. 32 compacta LS. et] a *add.* BU.

moste worthy to be had in remembraunce, whiche is thys. Thys
noble woman, beynge in hyr citie, quyete emonge hyr lordes and
gentlewomen, as the facyone was of theym to brayde their heer,
she beynge aboute so to do, it was declared vnto hyr that the
5 cytizens of Babilon were of assent to haue geuen vp the towne
to the Prynce of the Medys, hyr vnkle. The whiche thynge she
toke so greuously that, castynge a way hyr combe, leuynge
womens dressynge a parte, enflammed with ire, [she] toke to hyr
hyr armour, and gatheryng together hyr men of warre, she
10 besegyde the stronge towne and neuer drest hyr heede tyll that
the towne was rendred to hyr agayne, and by fyne force constrayned theym to obey hyr commaundement. Whiche notable
acte was suche that in remembraunce of that same was rasyde
vp in Babilone a greate pyllar of coper with hyr picture, the toone
15 syde of hir heire braydyd and the other not, that longe *and* many
a day was a testimony of the same. To this, she buylded many
townes and cities and dyd many other notable actes, whiche the

---

vnum memoratu dignissimum extollentes dicamus certissimum,
asserunt, ea pacatis rebus et ocio quiescente ac die quodam
20 feminea solertia cum pedissequis crines discriminante ac ritu
patrio in tricas reducente, actum est, cum nondum preter
med[i]os diduxisset, vt illi nunciaretur Babiloniam in ditionem
defecisse preuigni, quod adeo egre tulit, vt proiecto pectine
confestim ab officio muliebri irata consurgens ar[r]iperet arma ac
25 eductis copijs obsideret vrbem preualidam, nec ante, quod
inordinatorum crinium superfuerat, composuit, quam potentissimam ciuitatem nulla obsidione affectam in deditionem cogeret
et suo sub dominio infestis reuocaret armis. Cuius tam animosi
facinoris diu exhibuit testimonium statua ingens ex ere conflata
30 et in Babilonia erecta, feminam solutis ex altero latere crinibus,
ex altero in tricam compositis pretendens. Multas preterea ex
nouo condidit ciuitates et ingentia facta peregit, que adeo

19 ea] eam B.   quiescente] quiescentem *B*.   quodam] quadam
BU.   20 discriminante] disterminantem B, disterminante U.   21 redu-
cente] reducentem B.   22 medos L, medios BSU.   22–3 in dit. def.
preuigni] Babyloniam defecisse B.   23 proiectio L.   24 ariperet L,
coarriperet BU.   26 crinium] criminum U.   27 nulla] longa BU.
28 sub] *om.* BU.   32 condidit] edidit BU.

deuourynge tyme hath now put in obliuyon. Thies actes declarede
here tofore, in a man had been meruelouse, but in a woma*n*
more then | meruelouse, wherby she had deserued eu*er*lastynge f. 6*a*
prayse, but that oone vyse muche blottyde and defacyde all this,
in vsynge hirself moste vnhappely in fleshly lustes. It is saide 5
that she was concubyne to many and vsede hirself more beastly
then womanly in the company of corrupte bawdes, and emongst
other sparede not hyr oune sonne, a yonge prynce of singler
beautie *and* p*er*sonage. O, shamefull and abhomynable fylthe,
whiche, vsed emongeste the wery courtes of prynces, aswell in 10
peace as in warre, aswell in laughynge as in wepynge, this pestilence tryhumphes, ande lytle and litle occupiynge their vnwytty
myndes, drauthe theym headlynge not onely to shame, but
therunto racyse and defacys·frome theym all hono*ur* and glory
away! With this fowll vyce, than, this lady thus shamefully 15
polluted, the better to clooke hyr vng*ra*ciousnes, she made a lawe

---

vetustas absorbsit, vt nil fere superesset preter quod dictum est,
quod ad suam pertinet laudem ad nos vsque deductum. Ceterum
hec omnia, nedum in femina, sed in quocunque viro strennuo
mirabilia atque laudabilia et perpetua memoria celebranda vna 20
obscena mulier fedauit illecebra. Nam, cum inter cetera quasi
assidua libidinis prurigine vreretur infelix, plurimum se miscuisse
concubitui creditum est, et inter mechos—bestiale quid potius
quam humanum—filius Ninus numeratur, vnus prestantissime
forme iuuenis, qui, vti mutasset cum matre sexus, in thalamis 25
marcebat ocio, vbi hec aduersus hostes sudabat in armis. O
scelestum facinus, vt quiete suaui inter anxias regum curas, inter
cruenta certamina et, quod monstro simile est, inter lacrimas et
exilia nulla temporis facta distinctione hec euolat pestis et,
sensim incautas mentes occupans et in precipicium trahens, omne 30
decus turpi nota commaculat. Qua fedata Semiramis, dum putat
astutia abolere, quod lasciuia deturparat, legem illam insignem

17 superesset] super sit BU.   18 pertinet] pertineat BU.   laudem]
et *add.* B.   deductum] est *add.* SU, sit *add.* B.   21 cetera] ceteras U.
22 plurimum] plurium BU.   24 Ninus] nimis S, ninias U.   25 sexus]
sexum BU.   27 quiete suaui] quieta sinam BU.   29 et] *om.* B.   32
deturparat] deturpauerat BU.

that aboute venerall delight*es* hir subiect*es* of bothe sex myght
do what they wolde. And ferynge leste that by other of hir
women she myght be defrauded frome hir fleshly pleasure, she
ordeyned for theim a place separate, wher hir courtyers myght
5 goo to theym who wolde, clothynge theym w*ith* longe garm*entes*,
whiche emonge the Egyptyens and the Assyryens and the
Affricans, as it is saide, is vsyde to thys day. Sum wryteth that
when she fell in the desyre of hyr sonne and had reigned with
hym xxx*ti* yeres, that hyr oune sonne slewe hyr, because she
10 mouede hym to that mat*er*; and other wryteth that those whiche
she pr*o*uokede to vse with hyr, after the dede doone, because she
woldenot the party shulde tell itt, cruelly she made hym to be
put to death. And she, to this, when itt happened hyr to con-
ceyue, to excuse hyr faulte she made that same detestable lawe
15 afore rehercyde. But for all hyr craft, she couldenot so hyr
offences cloke nor hyde, but that she fell in indignacion of hyr
sonne, and ferynge by hyr to be expulsed fro*m* his empyr *and*

---

condidisse aiunt, qua prestabatur subditis, vt circa Venerea
agerent quod liberet, timensque, ne a domesticis feminis concu-
20 bitu fraud[a]retur filij (vt quidam volunt) prima vsum femoralium
excogitauit eisque omnes aulicas subcinxit conclaui, quod, vt
fertur, adhuc apud Egiptios obseruatur et Affros. Alij tamen
scribunt, quod, cum in desiderium incidisset filij eumque iam
etate prouectum in suos prouocasset amplexus, ab eodem, cum
25 annis iam xxx et duobus regnasset, occisam. A quibus dissentiunt
alij, asserentes eam libidini miscuisse seuiciam solitamque, quos
ad explendum sue vredinis [v]otum, aduocasset, vt occultaretur
facinus, continuo post coitum iubere necari. Verum, cum aliquando concepisset, adulteria prodidisse partu, ad que excusanda
30 illam legem egregia[m] cuius paulo ante mentio facta, proditam
aiunt. Tam[en], etsi visum sit pusillum cont[e]gisse ineptum
crimen, filij indignationem abstulisse minime potuit, qui, seu
quod suum tantum cum alijs co[mm]un[ic]atum incestum

20 frauderetur L.   21 aulicas] feminas *add.* BU.   22 Affros] Assirios
BU.   27 fotum LS.   28 iubere] iussisse B.   30 egregia LS.   facta]
est *add.* BU.   31 Tam[en] etsi] Tametsi L, Sed tam etsi B.   pusillum]
pauxillum BU.   contigisse LSU.   ineptum] *om.* B.   32 quin LBU.
33 quod] quem B.   tantum] arbitrabatur *add.* LBSU.   coniunctatum LS.

ashamed to se his mother so vyly to vse hyrself, at the last [he] toke frome hyr hyre lyfe. |

Of Opis, the wyfe to Saturne.
The iij^de Chapitre.

OPis so namede, or otherwyse Rea, yf we shall geue credyte to 5 oure auncyent wryters, aswell in prosperouse fortune as aduerse fortune, shewede hyrself muche honourable. She was the doughter of Vrania, that was of greate auctoryte emongst the Grecyans, muche rude in those days, by his wyfe callede Vesta, and because that she by hyr craft delyuerede Jupiter, 10 Neptune and Pluto frome their deathe that Saturne entendyd to putt theym to, for the conuenaunte and pacte that was betwyxt hym and hys brother Tytan, which saide Jupiter and Pluto by madnes of the people were after taken for goddes, she not onely therefore obteyned to haue the name and dignyte of 15 a Quene, but further, was honourede as a goddesse and mother

---

cerneret minusque equo animo ferret, seu quo[d] in ruborem sue matris luxuriam duceret [aut forsan prolem in successionem] imperij nascituram expauesceret, reginam illecebram i[r]a impulsus absumpsit.   20

De Opi, Saturni coniuge. iij.

OPis seu Ops vel Rhea, si priscis credimus, inter prospera et aduersa plurima claritate emicuit. Nam Vranij, apud rudes adhuc Grecos potentissimi hominis, et Veste coniugis filia fuit. Que, Saturni regis soror pariter et coniunx, nullo, quod ad nos 25 venerit, facinore se egregiam fecerat, [ni] muliebri astucia Iouem, Neptunum atque Plutonem filios a morte cum Saturno a Tytane fratre pacta liberasset. [Q]ui cum inscitia, ymo insania hominum eui illius in claritatem precipue deitatis euasissent homines, hec non solum regine decus adepta est, quinymo errore mortalium dea 30

17 quos LS.   in r. sue] rubori esse B.   sue] suum SU.   18 aut...·
successionem] *om.* LS.   19 illecebram] illecebrem BU.   ita LS.
22 Rhea] quæ & Cybele dicitur *add.* B.   26 in LS.   27 Plutonem]
platonem S.   Tytane] Titano B, Tutone S, Tytone U.   28 Cui LS.

of the goddes and had to hyr dedicate temples and churches, *and*
pristes to serue hyr, by a comune assente of all the people. And
so muche this foull and horrible idolatrye was vsed that the
Romayns labourynge in the ij^de battell with the Cartagines, as
5 it had bene for a holsume helth for theym, thei sent the consuls
to Achila, Kynge of Pargamy, with greate requestes for hyr
image *and* the maner how to worshipp hyr, oute of a cyte of
Asya, beynge noo better then a defourmyde stoone. Yett with
diligens thei brought it to Rome, and with greate reuerence *and*
10 diuers cerymonyes, aswell with the Romaynes as with the
Italiens, she was honourede. It was surely a straynge mokery, or
rather a blyndnes of men, or elles a fraude or craft of the dewyll,
to wourshipp and honour suche a monstruouse thing. But how
it was, this woman lyuynge a longe tyme, hauynge in hir lyfe
15 muche longe laboure, dyede, *and* is turnyde into asshes and
descendid into hell, all thoughe she were, as is saide, by many
yeres taken for a goddesse. |

insignis et deorum mater est habita, eique templa, sacerdotes et
sacra instituto publico constituta sunt. Adeoque enorme malum
20 conualuit, vt laborantibus secundo bello Punico Romanis, quasi
pro salutari auxilio missis consularibus viris, ab Attalo, Pergami
rege, simulacrum eius expetitum precibus est ritusque sacrorum
e Pes[sinun]te, Asie opido, quasi quoddam deforme saxum
sumptum, diligentia Romam delatum atque summa cum reue-
25 rentia susceptum et, postremo insigni locatum loco, tanquam
sublime numen atque reipublice salutare per multa secula
ceremonijs plurimis apud Romanos et Ytalos cultum est. Mirabile profecto fortune ludibrium seu potius cecitas hominum, an
velimus dicere, fraus et decipula demonum, quorum opere actum
30 est, vt femina, longis agitata laboribus, demum anus mortua et
in cinerem versa et apud inferos alligata et dea crederetur et in
tam grande euum fere ab vniuerso orbe diuinis honoraretur
obsequijs.

20 laborantibus] laboribus S.   23 e] et S, et ex U.   spesumate LS,
ephesi monte U.   Asie] phrygiæ B.   opidum SU.   quasi] *om*. B.
24 sumptum] quod incolae matrem deum esse dicebant cum *add*. B,
cum *add*. U.   25 loco] *om*. S, templo BU.   29 velimus] melius BU.
31-2 in tam] vitam U.

Of Juno, the goddesse. f. 7a
The iiijth Chapitre.

JUno, the doughter of Saturne *and* Opis, so muche exaltyd with
the versys of thiese poet*es* aboue all women, emonge the infection of the gentylls was had in reu*er*ence so muche that the 5
gratynge tethe of the tyme, that fretith all thynge away, cannot
so do but that hyr name is yett knowne and spoken of in *our*
dayes. But that fortune onely is more for the grounde of hir
prayse then any other worke that is tolde on hyr. This Juno
was with that same Jupiter of Crete, and the gentyles was so 10
deceiuyde that thei accomptyd this Jupiter god of heuen, and
Juno and he bothe borne at one byrthe. And she conueyde *in*
hir childehode to Samia *and* ther tyll she came to an able age
w*ith* diligence brought vp, at the laste she was geuyne in maryage
to hir brother, as an image whiche was made of hyr in Samia by 15
many yeres bare wittnes of it. For they of Samia, beleuynge that

4 allwomen MS. 9 then] for *add*. MS.

De Iunone, regnorum dea. iiij.

IUno, Saturni [et] Opis filia, poetarum carmine et errore gentilium toto orbi pre ceteris mulieribus gentilitatis infectis labe
celeberrima facta est in tantum, vt nequiuerunt taciti temporum 20
dentes, cum cuncta corrodant, a deo infame erosisse opus, ni
ad etatem vsque nostram notissimum eius non euaserit nomen.
Verum ex hac potius fortuna[m] egregiam recitare possumus
quam opus aliquod memoriale dictu referre. Fuit enim cum Ioue
illo Cretensi, quem decepti veteres celi finxere deum, eodem edita 25
partu et ab infantia transmissa Samum ibique ad pubertatem
vsque cum diligentia educata ; Ioui demum fratri nupta est. quod
per multa secula eidem est statua in templo Sami testata. Nam
existimantes Samij non modicum sibi posterisque suis afferre

18 et 1º] *om*. LS. 19 centeris L. 20 nequiuerunt] nequiuerint BU.
taciti] tacia S. 21 corrodant] corrodent S, corroderent BU. erosisse]
erexisse S, exedisse BU. ni] Hij S, quin BU. 23 fortuna LS. 24
quam] quoniam BU. memoriale] memorabile BU 25 editam L, S *not
clear, but might be read as* editam. 27 nupta est] nupsit B. 28 e idem
eiusdem BU.

itt shulde not be to their litle glory that she was maryede emongst
theym, beynge a quene and a godesse, to th'entent that the
memorye therof shulde neu*er* decay, ther redifiede in hyr hono*ur*
an excedy*ng* greate temple, emonge all the m*er*uells of the worlde
5 meruelous and greate, and all of fyne marble stoone, and in
mydd*es* therof the picture as it were of a mayden goynge to
be maryede, wond*er*ly and moste fynely caruede and wrought.
This greate goddesse at last maryede to this greate kynge, his
empyre farr and neere spredde abrode, she w*ith* hym obteyned
10 no small hono*ur* *and* fame, and to helpe to this the poetes fabills
and the vnwyse idolatry of the gentyles co*m*mytted all women
w*ith* chylde and other that were in ieopa*r*dy and peryll of lyfe
to hyr defense, and other thynges more to be laughede att
then to be beleuyde. Soo that the dewyll*es* p*er*suasion in euery-
15 wher, the madde people reedifyede to hyr temples and churches
and prist*es* and playse after the auncyent facyon, not onely in
f. 7*b* Samia, but in | Aragia and in Cartage, and at laste emonge the

---

glorie, quod se penes apta atque desponsata Iuno, quam illi
reginam arbitrabantur et deam, ne memoria h[e]c dilueretur
20 facile, templum ingens et pre ceteris orbis mirabile estruxere
numinique dicauere suo et ex marmore Pario in habitu nubentis
virginis eiusdem ymaginem sculpi fecere temploque preposuere
suo. Hec tandem, regi magno nupta, excrescente eius in dies
imperio atque fama longe lateque nomen ipsius efferente, non
25 modicum et ipsa splendoris consecuta [est]. Sane, postquam poeticis fictionibus et insana antiquorum liberalitate celi regina facta
est, que mortalis regina fuer[a]t, Olympi regnis eam diuiciisque
prefecere necnon et illi coniugalia iura atque parientium auxilia
commisere et alia longe plura ridenda potius quam credenda,
30 ex quibus, sic humani generis hoste suadente, multa illi vndique
constructa sunt templa, altaria plurima, sacerdotes, ludi et sacra
more veteri instituta; et, vt de reliquis taceam, post Samos
celebri veneratione ab Argiuis, Achaye populis, et a Cartagin[i]en-

18 apta] alta BU.   quam illi] sit quam celi BU.   19 hoc LS.
dilueretur] dilueret BU.   20 estruxere] exstruxere BU.   21 numinique]
eius *add*. B.   Pario] paries S.   22 ymaginem sculpi] imagine sculpti BU.
25 est] *om*. LS.   26 insana] in sanis S.   27 fuerit L.   29 commiscere B.
33 et a] *om*. B.   Cartaginensibus LSU.

Romaynes, lordes of the worlde, by the name of Juno quene, in the Capitall, by the feete of Jupiter, with diuers cerymonyes she was worshippyd many days after that Christe was borne.

Of Seres, the goddesse of corne and Quene of Sicill.

The vᵗʰ Chapitre. 5

SEres, as it is thoughte by diuers auctours, was the moste auncyent Quene of Sicill, and of so hyghe and exellent wytte that she founde the way to eare and ploughe the feeldes and to tame oxen and make theym handsome to the yoke, and with the plowgh and the culter to rayse vp the furrows, and so to sowe 10 the whete, whiche grewe to suche greate habundaunce that after the grounde was well purged frome brears and stoones, it seruyde well the men to eate, that afore hyr days lyuyde but with accornes and apples and other fructes of the wodde. For which dede, all though she were a mortall woman, the people trowede hyr to be 15 a goddesse and gaue to hyr dyuyne honours and beleuyde hyr

---

sibus diu honorata est et postremo, a [V]eijs Romam delata, in Capitolio et in cella Iouis optimi maximi non aliter quam viro iuncta suo locata sub vocabulo Iunonis regine a Romanis, rerum dominis, ceremonijs multis et diu culta est, etiam postquam in 20 terris apparuit deus homo.

De Cerere, dea frugum et regina Siculorum. v.

CEres, vt nonnullis placet, vetustissima Siculorum regina fuit tantoque ingenio valuit, vt, cum agrorum excogitasset culturam, prima apud suos boues domuit et iugo assuefecit et 25 adinuento aratro atque vomere eorum opere terram proscidit sulcisque semina tradidit; que cum in amplissima[m] segetem excreuissent, ea spicis eruere, lapidibus terere, fermenta conficere et cibum deducere homines glandibus et pomis siluestribus assuetos edocuit. Quod ob meritum, cum mortalis esset femina, 30 eam deam frugum arbitrati sunt et diuinis honoribus extulere

---

17 necijs LS.   27 amplissima LS.   28 ea] haec B, eam U.   fermenta] fermento BU.   29 et 1°] in *add.* BU.

to be the doughter of Saturne and Cybele. Besydes thys, they
saye she had but one doughter by Jupiters brother, whiche had
to name Proserpyne. This Proserpyne was rauyshed of Orco,
Kynge of Molose, to the greate sorow of hyr mother, whiche
5 sought for hyr longe. Of this ar many diuers fables and tales.
Ther was also, besydes this Seres, an other Seres at Elusyn, a cyte
of the regyon of Atica, euyn by suche sectes had ther in greate
reputacion, and Tritolomus the Grecian was muche seruysable
vnto hyr. Whiche twayne equally the auncient men gaue
10 dyuyne honours vnto. But it is sufficient as now to putt bothe
theyr names as oone and theyr deedes. Now for trueth, whether
it be best for me to lawde or blame theyr wyttes, I cannot well
tell. For who is he that wyll blame hyr that brought wylde
vagaboundes to dwell in townes, and those that lyuyde afore
f. 8a after the maner of | wylde beastes, into honeste cyuylyte, made
16 theym to eate breade that were wounte to be fedde with accornes,
whereby mens bodyes came to more beautie and strength by that
conuenyent fedynge for mans nature, and the feeldys, purged

---

eamque Saturni et Cybeles credidere filiam. Huic preterea
20 vnicam ex Ioue fratre fuisse filiam, Proserpinam, dicunt; eam
maxima matris turbatione ab Orco, Molossorum rege, raptam et
diu quesitam volunt, multis hinc fabulis occasionem prebentes.
Fuit preterea et Ceres altera apud Eleusim, Attice regionis
ciuitatem, eisdem meritis penes suos clara, cui Triptholomum
25 obsequiosum fuisse volunt. Quas eo quod vetustas deitate et
honoribus eque extulit, sub vno tantum nomine ambarum
ingenia retulisse satis visum est. Harum, edepol, ingenium vtrum
laudem an execrer nescio. Quis enim damnet vagabundos
siluestres: quis eductos in vrbem nemoribus homines? Quis ritu
30 ferarum viuentes in meliorem euocatos frugem? Quis glandes
mutatas in segetem, quibus lucidius, vegetiora membra et
alimenta humano vsui conformiora prestantur? Quis mus[c]o,
vepribus arbustisque incompositis obsitum orbem in cultum, in

20 eam] eamque BU.   21 matris] maris BU.   Orco] orto S.
22 hinc] huic S.   24 eisdem] eiusdem B.   Triptholomum]
Triptolenium B, tripthololonium U.   26 honoribus] hominibus B.
29 eductos in vrbem] vagos siluestresque eductos in vrbes e BU.   31
quibus] corpus *add*. BU.   32 musto LS.   33 in 2°]*om*. BU.

frome brears and brembles, afore foule to loke apon, into beautie
and pr*o*fyte, and the rude worlde to humanyte, and the people
lyuynge in idlenes to move theyr wytt*es* to rusticall labour,
whereby so many cities were founded, so many e*m*pyrs encreascyd, so many goode craftes vsed, and specially, the fyndynge 5
how to sowe this whete? Whiche for asmuche as of theymself
they be passynge goode that I haue here rehersyde, he that wolde
blame thei*m* were well worthy to be accomptyde a foole. Now
contrary to this, who shall laude hyr for thys, that where tofore
the multytude lyuy*ng* separatly emongste the woddes, beynge 10
contentyd with accornes *and* aples, with the mylke of beastes,
w*ith* honye and w*ith* herbys of the grounde, withoute cures,
contentyd onely w*ith* the lawe of nature, sober, chaste, and not
vsynge noo fraude, ennemye onely to the wilde beastes *and* the
byrdes—to haue been brought to more delicyouse meates, in 15
so muche that, excepte we wyll deceiue oureself, this was the redy
way to brynge vs frome all quyetnes and securyte. For by this

---

pulchritudinem et vtilitatem publicam versum? Quis rude
seculum in ciuile? Quis a desidia in contemplationem excitata
ingenia? Quis vires torpentes in speleis in vrbicum seu rusti- 20
canum exercicium tractas, quibus tot ampliate vrbes, tot de
nouo condite, tot aucta imperia, tot mores spectabiles inuenti
cultique sunt frumentarie artis adinuenta noticia? Que cum de
se bona sint, que dicta sunt omnia, reor, iudicio plurium, si quis
faciat, dicetur insipidus. Demum versa vice quis laudet multi- 25
tudinem sparsam, siluas incolentem, glandibus pomisque siluestribus, ferino lacte herbisque atque melle fluente assuetam,
soluta curis habentem pectora, sola nature lege contentam,
sobriam, pudicam et doli nesciam, inimicam feris tantum et
auibus, in molliores atque incognitos euocatam cibos, e quibus, 30
nisi nosipsos decipimus, secutum cernimus, vt in abditis adhuc
latentibus vicijs exitumque timentibus aperiretur iter et pro-

20 vires] viros BU.   21 tractas] tractos B.   23 adinuenta]
inuenta B.   24 sint, que] sit et que BU.   24–5 iudicio . . . laudet] nisi
quis iudicio plurium faciat, merito dicetur, deinde versa uice, quis laudat
B; U *as* L, *substituting* plurimum *for* plurium.   27 melle fluente]
fluento BU.   28 soluta] solutasque B; solutaque U.

the feeldys, that were afore vnclosed and com*un*e to all men, was
dykede, *and* a terme sett by thiese two bitter wordes 'meus' and
'tuus', that is to meane, 'myne' and 'thyne', the names ennemyes
as well to the pryuate welthe as to the com*un*e welth. And vpon
5 this rose pouerty, boundage, stryfe, hate *and* cruell batell, and
burnynge enuy, fleynge all aboute, that so hathe doone that scant
or the syeth were redy to mowe the grasse, it was co*n*ue*r*tyde to
the swerde, and not so in quyete tyll the seese were soughte frome
the este to the west, to brynge the delicate vestures and deynte
10 meetys to farse and fyll the belyes at feastes gay and gloryouse,
whiche brynges euermore with hym idlenes and slouthe. And
f. 8*b* where as afore that Venus wexyde colde, annone | with suche
delycat*es* she beganne to wex warme, to the moste greatest
hurt of the worlde, and that that worste is, the lyf of man
15 shortyde therby by famyne, hungar and battell, whiche afore
that tyme was vnknowne to theym that lyuyde in the wod*es*,
not withoute greate dreade and feare of the ryche. And, to

9 deyntes MS.

---

cedendi prestaretur securitas? Hinc arua eousque communia,
terminis et fossa distingui cepta sunt, agriculationis subiect[a]
20 cure et partiri inter mortales cepere labores. Hinc meum et tuum
venit in medium, nomina quidem inimica pacis publice et priuate.
Hinc pauperies seruitusque necnon et litigia, odia cruentaque
bella et vrens in circuitu euolauit inuidia, que egere, vt vixdum
curuate falces in messem in acutos, rectos in sanguinem gladios
25 verterentur. Hinc sulcata maria et occiduis Eoa cognita et eois
occidua. Hinc mollicies corporum, sagina ventris, ornatus
vestium, accurat[i]ores mense, conuiuia splendida, torpor et
ocium aduenere, et, que in dies vsque illos friguerat, Venus
calefieri cepit maximo orbis incommodo, et, quod deterius forsan
30 est, si minimus eque labentibus annis vt sic celi seu bellorum ira
culta respondeant, subintrat illico annone penuria, et duriora
priscis consurgunt ieiunia, seua fames nunquam siluis cognita
gorgusciolos intrat inopum non absque diuitum persepe periculo.

19 et] *om.* BU.   fossa] fessa S.   subiecte LS, subiere BU.   24 rec-
tos] rectosque BU.   27 ac curator es L, ac curatior es S.   29 quod]
quid B.   30 minimus] minus BSU.   sic] fit BU.   31 subintrant
LS.   33 gorgusciolos] gurgustiola B.

conclude, this delicacy hathe caused the alterynge of mens
complexion, leenes and palenes of face after a deuylyshe colour,
and many other causes to haste mankynde to deathe. Whiche
well called to mynde with other innumerable disconuenyences,
scante I knowe whiche was the better, but well I knowe that in 5
the fyrst golden worlde, all though they were rude, yett they be
more worthy of muche more prayse and commendacion then
thys our harde, brasyn, irone worlde that we nowe ar lyuynge in.

Of Minerua.
The vjth Chapitre.   10

M Inerua the virgyne, surnamede Pallas, with suche clarytude
  was exaltede that the folyshe people beleuyde that hyr
begynnynge was not mortall. Sum say that in the tyme of Ogiges,
the Kynge of [the] lake called Tritonia, not farr frome the place
called Circeum the lesse, that ther she was fyrste seene on earthe 15
and knowne, and forbecause that by processe of tyme she was
seene to make many thynges that were not afore made, not onely
emonge the rude Affricanes but also emonge the Grecians, that

---

Hinc turpis, effera macies, infernus pallor et titubanti incedens
gradu debilitas morborumque et festinate mortis multiplices 20
exoriuntur cause. Quibus inspectis vna cum innumeris alijs vix
scio, ymo scio, quia longe a[ur]ea illa, licet rudia et agrestia
fuerint, his nostris ferreis cunctisque seculis preponenda sint.

De Minerua. vj.

M Inerua, que et Pallas, virgo tanta claritate conspicua fuit, 25
  vt non illi fuisse mortalem originem stolidi arbitrati sunt
homines. Aiunt quidam hanc Ogigij regis tempore apud lacum
Tritonium haud longe a sinu Sircium minori primo visam in
terris et cognitam, et, quoniam tractu temporis multa facientem
vidissent ante non visa, non solum apud rudes Affros, verum 30
apud Grecos, qui tunc tempestate prudentia anteibant ceteros,

19 effera] et effeta BU.   infernus] infernalis B.   22 antea LS.
24 Minerua] que et Pallas dicitur BU.   25 Pallas] dicta *add.* BU.
virgo] *om.* BU.   26 sunt] sint BU.   27 quidam] quidem B.   hanc]
in Attica *add* B.   31 tunc] ea BU.

in those tyme[s] precellyde all other in wisdome, they dyd beleue
that she was procreate, withoute a mother, of Jupiters brayne.
To whiche scornefull opynyon the more faithe was geuen vnto
it, because hyr heade begynnynge was not knowne. Thys aboue
5 all other they affyrme to be a perpetuall virgyne, and to make
f.9a it the better to be beleuyde, they affyrme also that Vulcane |
longe wrestlede with hyr to haue hade hyr uirgynite, but she by
strength vaynquyshede hym. They say further that the way
how to spynne woolle, afore hyr tyme vnknowne, she fyrst
10 inuentyd it, for, lernynge other by what ordre the superfluyte of
the woolle shulde be purgede and how with cardes of yrone it
shulde be dressyd and so be put on the distaf, it folowde that after
that she ymagyned and taught other to weaue it in the lombe.
Wherof that notable fighte betwyxt hyr and Aryagnes is rehersyde.
15 And more, she founde also the vse of oyle, vntyll that tyme to
men vnknowne. Whiche, because it semyde to men to be a

---

absque matre ex Iouis cerebro genitam e celo lapsam creditum
est. Cui ridiculo errori tanto plus fidei auctum est, quanto
occultior eius fuit origo. Hanc ante alia voluere perpetua
20 floruisse virginitate; quod vt pleniori credatur fide, finxere
Vulcanum, ignis deum, in concupiscentie carnis feruorem diu
cum ea luctatum superatumque. Huius insuper incognitum
omnino omnibus ante lanificium inuentum fuisse volunt. Nam
ostenso quo ordine purgata superfluitatibus lana e[a]que dentibus
25 mollita ferreis opponeretur colo atque demum digitis deduceretur
in filum, textrine excogitauit officium eoque docuit, quo pacto
inter[ne]cterentur inuicem fila et tractu pectinis iungerentur et
calce solidarentur in textum. In cuius opificij laudem pugna illa
insignis eiusdem et Ariagnes Colophonie recitatur. Vsum insuper
30 olei eousque mortalibus inauditum hec inuenit docuitque
A[t]tic[o]s bacas mola terere trapetisque pr[e]mere. Quod quia
multum vtilitatis afferre visum sit, ei aduersus Neptu[n]um in

17 e] et BU.   lapsam] sparsam BU.   19 fuit] fuerit BU.
20 vt] et S.   21 in] id est BU.   23 inuentum L.   24 eoque LS.
25 opponeretur] apponeretur BSU.   26 filum] filium S.   eoque] eaque B.
27 intercuterentur LS.   inuicem] *om.* BU.   28 solidarentur] solidaretur
BU.   29 Ariagnes] Arachnes B, aragones S, aragnes U.   30 docuitque]
docuit atque BU.   31 hacticas LS.   primere L.   32 neptuum LS.

thynge muche profitable, in the namynge of the cyte of Athenes,
albeit Neptun*us* straue with hyr for the same, the victory was
geuen to hyr. And besydes all this, they say that she founde first
nu*m*be*r*s and put theym in that ordre whiche be vsed emongst vs
vnto thys day; and, for conclusion, whether it were of the boone 5
of sum byrde, or ells of sum reede, she taught fyrst to men to
pype *and* to blowe in a bagg pype, and that she threw the pype
downe frome heuen to the earthe, because it made theym
defo*u*rmyde *and* to haue greate throtes that blewe in theym.
What more shulde I say? For so diuers p*r*odigiouse meruells bi 10
hyr wytte inuentyde, the olde antiquyte not onely attrybutyde
to hyr the geuer of wisdome, but more, the geuer and graunter
of all godlye thynges. Whereby the Athenes were so drawne,
because theyr cytie was apte to lernynge, the redy way for a man
to cum to prudens, that they toke hyr as the protectres and all 15
craft*es* of scyences dyd onely dedicate to hyr, and made, to this,
to hyr honour a greate and exellent fayre temple. Whiche
accomplisshed and to hyr consecrate, they sett vp an ymage of

nominandis a se Athenis attributa victoria creditur. Volunt etiam
huius fuisse opus, cum iam quadrigarum prima reperisset vsum, 20
ferrum in arma conuertere, armis corpus tegere, aciem bellantium
ordinare et leges omnes, quibus eatur in pugnam, edocere.
Dicunt preterea eam numeros inuenisse et in ordinem deduxisse,
quem in hodiernum vsque seruamus. Ceterum ex osse cruris
alicuius auis, seu ex palustri potius calamo eam tibias seu 25
pastorales fistulas primum composuisse credidere easque in
terras e celo deiecisse, eo quod flantis redderent turgidum guttur
et ora d[e]formia. Quid multa? Ob tot comperta prodigia
deitatum largitrix antiquitas eidem sapientie nomen attribuit.
Quo intuitu tracti Athenienses ab ea nuncupati et eo quod ciuitas 30
apta studijs videretur, per que quisque fit prudens et sapiens,
eam in suam sumpsere tutelam eique ar[c]em dicauere et, ingenti
templo constructo suoque numini consecrato, in eodem illam
effigiauere oculis curuam, eo quod raro noscatur, in quem finem

19 Athenis] hatteis S.   21 arma] arte *add.* BU.   tegere] contegere BU.
23 et] vt S. deduxisse] eduxisse BU.   25 eam] ea S.   26 primum]
primam BU.   28 difformia LS.   29 nomen] numen BU.   32 artem LS.
34 curuam] toruam BU.   noscatur] nascatur B.

hyr, the eyes wherof were sett a sqwynte, because raath or seldome
is knowne to what entent the mynde of a wyseman pretendith.
They wyllyde also that she shulde haue an helmet o[n] hyr heade,
to sygnyfye that the counsells of a wyseman ar cou*erd* and
5 armyde agaynst all thynges, w*ith* a harnes on hyr body, to shewe
that a wyseman is allways armyde agaynste all fortunes and |
f. 9*b* chauncys that cum; hauynge in hyr hande a longe speere to
exp*re*sse therby that a wyse mans counsell stretchys w*ith* hys
strokes afar of. Ouer and besydes this, she had a sheelde of crystall,
10 wherin was paynted the heade of Gorgonius coueryde, meanynge
by that same that wyse men were euer so p*re*uentyde agaynste
all false fraude and deceyte that fooles, that marke it not, semyde
thei wer but harde stoones that they regardyd. And euen afore
hyr thei set an owle, meanynge thereby that a wyse man aswell
15 p*re*uentyth perylls by nyght as by day. At the laste the reuerence
and the fame of this goddesse was so farr spredde abrode that
eu*er*y wher was dedicate to hyr temples and churches, and so
farr spredd this errour that in the Capitall of Rome, nyghe to

3 helment or MS.

sapientis tendat intentum, galeatam, volentes ob id sapientum
20 tecta et armata significari consilia, indutam lorica, eo quod ad
quoscunque fortune ictus semper armatus sit sapiens, longissima
munitam hasta, vt comprehendatur sapientem in longinquo
spicula figere, preterea cristallino egide, et in eo Gorgonis caput
infixum, protectam, pretendentes ob hoc lucida sapienti omnia
25 esse tegumenta, eousque serpentina semper astucia adeo pre-
munitos, vt saxei eorum intuitu videantur ignari, eiusque in
tutelam noctuam posuere firmantes prout in luce, sic et in
tenebris videre prudentes debere. Tandem huius mulieris fama
atque numinis reuerencia se adeo longe lateque diffudit tantumque
30 fauit illi veterum error, vt fere per vniuersum eius in honore
templa construerentur et celebrarentur sacra, eousque con-
scenderet, vt in Capitolio penes Iouem opti[m]um maximum cella

23 eo] Medusae *add.* B.   24 infixum] fixum B.   25 teg. eousque]
tegimenta eosque BU.   27 luce] lucem U.   28 debere] *om.* BU.
30 vt] illi *add.* BU.   vniuersum] orbem *add.* B.   in] *om.* B.   honore]
honorem BU.   32 optinium LS.

the seate of Jupiter, Minerua was sett emonge all the myghty
goddes of the Romay*n*s, next vnto Juno the quene, and she had
in reue*r*ence as a quene w*ith* hyr. But ther be sum helde opynyon
that ther was not onely this Minerua, but also dyuers others of
that name, which gladly I assent to, to make the numbre of noble 5
women the more.

Of Venus, Quene of Ciprys.
The vijth Chapitre.

THere be dyuers that holde opynyon that Venus was a woman
of Ciprys. But of hyr pare*n*tes many doubte. For sum say 10
that she was the doughter of oone Cirus, and sum agayne say
that she was the doughte*r* of this sayde Cyrus, whiche he gatt on
Dion, a woman of Cyprys; and other, to magnyfye hyr bewtie,
affyrme that she was the doughter of Jupiter and of this Dion.
But of what pare*n*tes so eue*r* she was pro*c*reate of, she is put 15
more for hyr exellent *and* inco*m*parable beaute emonge other

---

dedicaretur eidem et inter potissimos Romanorum deos cum
Iunone regina et ipsa pariter regina haberetur. Sunt tamen
nonnulli grauissimi viri asserentes non tam vnius Minerue quam
plurium, que dicta sunt, fuisse comperta; quod ego libenter 20
assentiam, vt clare mulieres ampliores sint numero.

De Venere, Cyprorum regina.

VEnerem Cyprianam fuisse feminam quorundam arbitratur
opinio. De parentibus autem a nonnullis ambigitur. Nam
alij eam Cyri cuiusdam et Syrie volunt filiam, quidam vero Cyri 25
et Dyonis, Cyprie mulieris; nonnulli, reor, ad eius extollendam
pulchritudinis claritatem Iouis et Dyonis predicte genitam
asserunt. Sane, ex quocunque sit patre genita, eam inter claras
mulieres potius ob illustrem eius pulchritudinem quam ob
[de]decorosum inuentum describendam censui. Tanto igitur oris 30

17 et] vt BU.   18 ipsa] dea *add.* BU.   regina 2°] *om.* BU.
19 tam] *om.* BSU.   quam] sed BU.   20 plurium] plurimum B.
21 numero] inumero B, munero U.   27 predicte] predictam BU.
30 decorosum LBU.   inuentum] meritum BU.

noble women in this my wo*u*rke then for any other goode thynge
f.10a in hyr ells to be co*m*mendyd. For ther was [in] | hyr suche
exellent and excedynge beaute that the eyes of thei*m* that
behelde hyr were often tymes deceyuyde. In so muche that diu*er*s
5 sayde that she was that same self starre that nowe is callyde
Venus. And sum calleth hyr a heuenly woman, co*m*men downe
frome the lappe of Jupiter to the earthe, and, brifly, all they,
blyndyd with theyr oune folyshnes, all though they knewe well
ynoughe that she was a mortall woman, yet they affirmede hyr
10 to be an immortall goddesse, and that she onely was the helper
to Cupidos pleasures and the mother therto. Nor she lakte not
hir self the craft of gesturs and counten*au*nces that long*es* to that
ga*m*me, whiche cam so well to hyr wanton purpose, all though
I wyll not wryte all, that she hyrself coulde not resyste suche
15 fylth[y]nes, thoughe she were accomptyd Jupiters doughter and
taken as oone of that moste venerable sorte emonge the best.
Whereby, not onely at Paphos, a wonders auncyent cyte of
Cyprys, they pleasid hyr with fraunkyncens and other ceremonyes,

15 fylthnes MS.

---

decore et totius corporis venustate emicuit, vt sepe intuentium
20 falleretur credulitas. Nam quidam illam ipsum celi sydus, quod
Venerem nuncupamus, dicebant, alij eam celestem feminam in
terras ex Iouis gremio lapsam et breuiter omnes, ceca obfuscati
caligine, quam sciebant a mortali feminam editam, immortalem
asserebant deam eamque infausti Amoris, quem Cupidinem
25 vocitabant, genitricem totis nisibus affirmabant nec illi inter-
cipiendi stultorum intuentium mentes varijs gesticulationibus
deerant artes. Quibus agentibus meritis eousque itum est, vt
nequeuntibus obsistere obscenitatibus multis, quas e vestigio non
tamen omnes scripturus sum, et Iouis filia et ex deabus vna
30 etiam venerandissima habita sit. Nec solum apud Paphos,
vetustissimum Cypriorum opidum, thure solo placata est—nam
mortuam et incestuosam feminam eo existimabant delectari odore,

21 eam] etiam B.　　22 ceca] tetra BU.　　23 feminam] femina BU.
28 multis] mulieris BU.　　　30 Paphum B.　　　32 existimabant]
existimabatur BU.

but after she was deade, the folyshe people thought to please hyr
with those swete sauours that when she was alyue she delytyd
in, when she gaue hyrself to voluptuouse pastymes. To thys,
the Romayns dedicate to hyr a temple, the title wherof was
namede 'the temple of the mother Venus', with many gloriouse 5
thynges therto apperteynynge. What shulde I more say? Thys
Venus was maryede to twayne husbondes, so men beleue, but it
is not certeyn. Albe it they say that she was maryede to Volcan,
the Kynge of Lemmam, sonne to Jupiter, Kynge of Crete, whiche
deade, she maryede Adonay, the sonne of Cynare [and] of Myrra, 10
Kynge of Cyprys. And it is the more easely to be beleuyde that
after she maryede Adonay, because with hym she myght the
more largely vse hyr wanton disportes then with hyr fyrst
husbonde before. But Adonay also deade, she fell into so
detestable venereall delytes that she darked all hyr meruelouse 15
beautie, as one shulde say, not with closyde eyes, but many-
festly, | that all men myght see it. It was not hydde in hyr f. 10b
husbonde Volcan days that she toke to hyr paramoure a knyght

que viuens in prostibulorum voluptabatur spurcici[a]—verum et
apud nationes reliquas et Romanos, qui templum ei sub titulo 20
Veneris genitricis et Verticordie alijsque insignibus olim struxere.
Sed quid multa? Hanc duobus nupsisse viris creditum est; cui
primo, non satis certum. Nupsit ergo, vt placet aliquibus, ante
Vulcano, Lemniorum regi et Iouis Cretensis filio. Quo sublato
nupsit Adoni, filio Cynare atque Mirre, regi Cypriorum; quod 25
verisimilius mihi videtur quam si primum virum Adonem
dixerimus, eo quod seu complexionis sue vicio, seu regionis in-
fectione, in qua plurimum videtur posse lasciuia, seu mentis
corrupte malicia factum sit. Adone iam mortuo in tam grandem
luxurie pruritum lapsa est, vt omnem decoris sui claritatem 30
crebris fornicationibus, non obfuscatis oculis, maculasse videretur,
cum adiacentibus regionibus notum foret eam a Vulcano, viro
primo, cum armiger[o] compertam; ex quo credit[u]m fabulam

19 que] quo B.   spurcicie LBSU.   21 Verticordie] verticorde BU.
22 cui] om. B.   23 primo] nupserit add. B.   24 Lemniorum] lemnorum
BU, leminorum S.   25 Cynare] Cynyrae B.   Mirre] Myrrhae B.
regi] regis B.   31 non obf. oculis] om. B.   32 cum] iam add. BU.
33 armigere LS.   creditam LSU.

of the countrye, wherof is rysune the fable that she playede the
harlote with Mars, the god of battell. At the last, to clooke hyr
vnchaste ways, that the more therby she myght vse hyr waunton
dalyaunces, it is sayde that she was the fyrst that founde thiese
5 comune baudes houses. Which execrable custome many days for
a witnes therof was vsede in Cipris, and other theyr neighbours
had a custome to sende theyr maydyns to Cipris see bankes, that
they myght company with the men that mette theym ther. And
thys abhomynable custome wentt so farr that at the last it flewe
10 into Italy and to the men of Locres and dyuers countres moo.

Of Isidis, Quene and goddesse of the Egyptiens.
The viijth Chapitre.

ISidis, whiche had to name afore Io, not onely to Egyptiens,
but also to the posteryte of diuers regyones was honourable
15 and venerable. But aboute what tyme, or of what parenttes she

---

adulteri[j] Martis et eiusdem sibi comperisse locum. Postremo
autem, vt ab impudica fronte paulum ruboris abstersisse videretur
et lasciuiendi ampliorem sibi con[c]essisse licentiam, infanda
turpitudine excogitata, prima, vt aiunt, meretricia · publica
20 adinuenit et fornices instituit et matronas inire compellit, quod
execranda Cypriorum consuetudo [in] multa pertracta secula
testata est. Seruauere quidem diu mittere virgines suas ad littora,
vt forensium vterentur concubitu et sic future castitatis sue libamenta persoluisse viderentur Veneri et suas in nupcijs quesisse
25 dotes. Que quidem abhominanda stulticia postea penetrauit ad
Ytalos vsque, cum legatur hoc idem aliquando fecisse Lo[c]renses.

De Yside, regina atque dea Egipciorum. viij.

ISis, cui ante nomen Yo, clarissima non solum Egipciorum
regina, sed eorum postremo sanctissimum et venerabile numen
30 fuit. Quibus tamen fuerit temporibus aut ex quibus nata parenti-

16 adulteri LS.   17 paulum] paululum BU.   18 consessisse L.
20 compellit] conpulit BU.   quod] satis add. U.   21 execranda] execran-
dum BU, scelus add. B.   in] so BU, om. L, qui S.   pertracta]
proiecta B.   secula] satis add. B.   24 nupcijs] nuptias BU.   26 hoc]
om. BU.   lotrenses LS (? locrenses L).   28 ante] antea BU.
29 numen] immen S.

descendyd of, emonge the famouse wryters it is in doubte. Ther
be yet that saye that she was the doughter of [In]achys, the fyrst
Kynge of the Argyuys, and the suster to Phoroncus, whiche is
euydent that it was in the tyme of Jacob, the sonne of Israell.
And su*m*, contrary to thys, affyrme that she was gotten of 5
Promothe*us*, then reignynge emonge the Grecyans, whiche
was many days after. And contrary to this, ther be that
holde opynyone that she was in the tyme of Cycropis, Kynge
of the Athenienc*es*; and thiese opinyons dyuerse lack*es* not to
be amonge right famouse wryters. But aboute what tyme 10
that eu*er* she was, it is euydent that for hyr tyme she was
muche worthy to be remembrede. But leuynge a parte the |
wryters discordance, my mynde is to folow the more parte, that f. 11*a*
say hyr to be the doughter of Ynacus, the kynge, which, all
though the poe*t*es fayne, for hyr exellent beautye of Jupiter was 15
belayde and by hym rauysshed, and for to hyde it to haue trans-

2 machys MS.   6–7 and of Phorbantes MS.

---

bus, apud illustres hystoriarum scriptores ambigitur. Sunt
autem, qui dicant illam Ynaci, primi regis Argiuorum, filiam et
Phoronei sororem, quos constat Iacob, filij Ysaac, tempore
superesse. Alij Promethei genitam asserunt regnante apud Argos 20
Phorbante, quod longe post primum tempus effluxit. Nonnulli
eam fuisse temporibus Cycropis, Athenarum regis, [affirmant, et
quidam insuper aiunt Lincei, regis] Argiuorum, [eam floruisse
temporibus]: que quidem inter celebres viros varietates argu-
mento non carent. Hanc inter feminas suo euo egregiam fuisse 25
et memoratu dignissimam [tradunt omnes]. Verum omissis
scriptorum discordancijs, qu[od] plurim[i] arbitrantur, ymitari
mens est, eam s[c]il[icet] Ynaci regis fuisse filiam. Quam etsi
poete veteres fingant ob venustatem forme placuisse Ioui et ab
eo oppressam et ad occultandum crimen in vaccam transformatam 30

18 dicant] dicunt BU.   Ynaci] Inachi B, ynati S, ynaci U.   20 superesse]
imperasse BU.   Promethei] promothei U.   22 Cycropis] Cecropis
B, cytropis U.   22–3 affirmant . . . regis] *so* BU *except* quidem *for* quidam,
om. LS.   23 Argiuorum] Arginorum S.   23–4 eam fl. temporibus] *so* BSU,
om. L.   24 varietates] diuersitates BU.   26 tradunt omnes] *om.* LSU.
27 qui plurimum LS.   28 similem LS.

formyd hir into a kowe and geuyn hyr to the myghty Juno,
which put hyr to Argus that had many eyen, to keepe hyr, tyll
that Mercury the god kyllede hym and conueyde hyr into Egypte,
where she recoue*r*yde hyr fou*r*me agayne, and of hyr name,
5 which was before called Io, was named Isydys. All thys is discrepante from the truethe of the hystory. But the trueth is that
where as she [was] of a meruelouse beautye and at last by Jupit*er*
oppr*e*ssyde, fleynge for feare of hyr father, she toke a shyppe, the
signe wherof was a kowe, *and* in that same shypp fledd into
10 Egypte *and* ther, fyndynge a place mete for hyr to dwell in,
hauynge a noble hert desyrouse to reygne, but how, it is not well
knowne, but she fyndynge there the people rude and barbarouse
and vnnethe vsynge any humanite emonge theym, more lyker
to brute beastes then men, not wi*th*oute greate laboure *and*
15 speciall industry she taught theym to purge the feeldys, to eare
theym and to sowe theym, *and* gathred *and* kepte in tyme, to

1 geuynge MS.   7 was] *om.* MS.

potentique Iunoni concessam et Argum custodem a Mercurio
cesum vacceque a Iunone oestrum suppositum et eam deuectam
cursu rapido in Egiptum ibidemque pristinam a se recuperatam
20 formam et ex Yo Ysidem appellatam, ab hystorie veritate non
discrepant, cum si[n]t qui asserant a Ioue adultero oppressam
virginem eamque, ob perpetratum scelus metu patris repulsam,
cum quibusdam ex suis conscendisse nauim, cui vacca esset
insigne, et ingenio plurimo ac ingenti preditam animo, regnorum
25 cupidine agitatam, secundo vento ad Egipcios transfretasse et
ibidem apta desiderio regione comperta constitisse. Tandem,
cum non habeatur, quo pacto obtinuisset Egiptum, fore certum
creditur, quod ibi reperisset rudes inertesque populos et humana-
rum fere rerum omnium ignaros ac ritu potius brutorum
30 viuentes quam hominum. Non absque labore et industria celebri
illos docuit terras colere, sul[c]is cultis committere semina et
tandem collectas in tempore fruges in cibum deducere, preterea

17 potentique] petentique BU.   20 Ysidem] ysibel S.   21 sicut
LS.   22 repulsam] impulsam BU.   23 nauim] nauem BU.   26 apta]
actam B, acta U.   28 reperisset] comperisset BU.   31 sultis LS, *om.*
BU.

make it mans meate—besydes this, the wylde Egipcians to brynge
theym together and to lyue after a lawe, and shewede theym how
to make carect*es* and letters to wryte, wherby they came to
doctryne to lerne the lawe, and other thynges moo, whiche I
pass ou*er*. In so muche that the barbaryens [Egip]cians thought 5
rather she came oute of heuen then frome the Grekys, and for that
in hyr days they gaue to hyr dyuyne hono*ur*s, [which] godhede
by the craft of the deuyll came after hyr deathe in so greate
veneratione that Rome, the heade of the wo*ur*lde, ordeyned for
hyr a temple of magnyfycence, ther oones a yere hono*ur*ynge 10
hyr after the Egiptiens cerymonyes. And noo doubte .therof
but that to the Occident the people and other barbarouse
nationes thys erro*ur* sprange. | And for Conthucio Apis was thys f. 11*b*
exellent womans husbonde, whome the auncyent men beleuyde
to be co*m*men of Phoronemus, that was descendyd of Jupiter 15
and Neobis, whiche grauntyng hys kyngdome to Archilaus hys

5 grecians MS.

---

vagos et fere siluestres in vnum se redigere et datis legibus ciuili
more viuere, et, quod longe spectabilius in muliere est, coacto in
vires ingenio, litterarum ydiomati incol[a]rum conuenientium
car[a]cteribus adinuentis aptioribus ad doctrinam, qua lege 20
iungerentur, ostendit. Que, vt de reliquis taceam, adeo mirabilia
insuetis hominibus visa sunt, vt arbitrarentur facile non ex
Grecia venisse Ysidem, sed e celo lapsam; et ob id sp[i]ranti
adhuc diuinos honores instituere. Cuius quidem numen fallente
ignaros dyabolo in tam grandem, ea mortua, atque famosam 25
venerationem euasit, vt Rome, iam rerum domine, illi templum
constitueretur pregrande et Egipciaco ritu quotannis solemne
sacrum institueretur. Nec dubium, quin ad Occidentales vsque
ad barbar[a]s nationes hic pene[t]rarit error. Porro huius tam
clare femine vir fuit Apis, quem vetustas erronea Iouis et Neobis, 30
Phoronei filie, filium arbitrata est, quem ayunt Egialio fratri

19 incolorum LS.   20 carecteribus L.   adinuentis aptioribus]
literarum idiomati incolarum conuenirent adinuentis ijsdemque apis B.
23 speranti L.   24 instituere] omnes *add.* BU.   numen] numine BU.
28 Occidentales] occiduas BU.   vsque] et *add.* BU.   29 barbaros L.
penerrarit L, penetraret U.   30 Neobis] Niobes B, Niobis U.   31 Egialio]
Agialeo BU.

brother when he had reigned thyrty and three yeres, where he
went into Egypte with his wyse wyfe, after hys deathe [he was]
taken ther for a god and namede Separasim. Albe it ther be
that say that oone Theologines was hyr husbonde and had of hyr
5 a sonne called Epaphim, that after reigned in Egypte and [was]
taken the sonne of Jupiter, gote*n* by hyr.

Of Europa, Quene of Crete.
The ixth Chapitre.

M Any beleue that Europa was the doughter of a certayne
10 man called Phenysis, but the more parte weene that she
was the doughter of Agenor, Kynge of Phenysis, and of so meruelouse beautie that or he were waare, Jupiter was taken in loue
with hyr. And so the myghty man, lyinge on wayte to ketche
hyr, dyd so muche by a bawde of hys that he made hyr descende

6 taken] by *add.* MS. *This is probably due to anticipation of* gote*n* by.
If it is omitted, the construction is similar to what is used elsewhere by Morley,
cf. pp. 56, l. 19, 76, ll. 7–8 and 179, ll. 28–9.

---

15 Achaie regno concesso, cum Argis trigintaquinque regnasset
annis, secessisse in Egiptum et vna cum Yside imperasse, eque
deum habitum et Osirim seu Serapim nuncupatum. Esto sint,
qui dicant Ysidi Theologonum quemdam fuisse virum et ex ea
suscepisse Epaphum, qui Egipcijs postea prefuit et Iouis ex ea
20 filius ex[is]timatus est.

De Europa, Cretensium regina. ix.

E Uropam arbitrantur quidam filiam fuisse Phenicis; verum
longe plures eam Agenoris, Phenicum regis, genitam dicunt
et tam mirabili formositate valuisse, vt amore inuise Cretensis
25 caperetur Iupiter. Ad cuius rapinam cum moliretur insidias
potens homo, actum voluit lenocinio verborum cuiusdam, vt ex
montibus in litus Phenicum lasciuiens virgo armenta patris

15 Achaie] Actaie B.   17 Serapim] serapium SU.   18 Theologonum]
Thelogonum BSU.   19 Epaphum] epophum U.   20 extimatus
LS.   24 amore] eius *add.* B.   26 voluit] volunt BU.   27 litus]
littusque B.

downe frome a high hyll, where she was, vnto the bounk*es* syde
of Phenycu*m*, lyke a wanton mayden with hyr flok of beastes
that she kept of hyre fathers, and so taken, and shortly putt into
a shyppe, the sygne wherof was a whyte bull, was conueyde into
Crete. Maydens to stray a broode to wantonly and to gyue 5
lyghte eares to suche as speeke fayre to theym, I do little co*m*-
mende it, as by dyuers that I haue knowne, that it hathe hapnede
to, by suche wyldnes to haue runne into greate diffamy and
sclaundre, whiche, all thoughe after they vsede theymselff*es*
chastely, yet coulde they neu*er* clerely put the sclaundre away. 10
Of thys is sprongne the fable that is sayde, that | Marcury f. 12a
compellyd hyr to cum to the see banck*es*, and Jupiter, conuer-
tynge hymself into a bull, to haue taken this Europa. And so,
as it foloweth, from thens she wentt into Egypte, but aboute
what tyme that she was rauysshede, the auctours differ, in that 15
the moste auncyent say that it was in that seasone that Argis
reigned. Sum agayne say, when Ogysius reignede, and sum at the
last write that when Pandio was gouerno*ur* ouer the Athenyens.

---

sequeretur et, exinde rapta confestim atque naui, cuius albus
thaurus erat insigne, imposita, defer[r]etur in Cretam. Vagari 20
licentia nimia virginibus et aures faciles cuiuscunque verbis
prebere minime laudandum reor, cum contigisse sepe legerim sic
agentibus honestati nonnunquam notas turpes imprimi, quas
etiam perpetue demum castitatis decus abstergere non potuit.
Ex his fabulam, que legitur Mercurium impulisse ad litus armenta 25
Fenicum et Iouem, in thaurum versum vacantemque in Cretam
Europam virginem asportasse, causam sumpsisse liquido patet.
Verum in tempore rapine huius prisci discrepant. Nam, qui
antiquiorem ponunt, regnante Argis Danao factam volunt, alij
regnante Ogisio et, [qui] postremi [sunt], Pandione rege Athenien- 30
sibus i perante, que [ma]gis Mynoys, filij Europe, temporibus

20 imposita] imponita BU.   deferetur LS.   22 contigisset L.   sic]
his LSU.   23 nonnunquam] earum B.   quas] quam S.   24 demum]
deinde B.   abstergere] abstersisse LSU.   25 que] qua B.   Mercurium]
per quem eloquenciam lenonis cuiusdam significant *add.* B.   26 vacan]
temque] natantemque BU.   27 liquido] liquide BU.   30 Ogisio-
Acrisio BU, Occisio S.   qui post. sunt] per postremi L; per postremi sunt
S.   Pandione] Plandione B.   31 que] quod BU.   iugis LS.

But how so euer it was, they agree that by Jupiter she was
rauysshede, and after to haue bene maryede to Asterus, Kynge of
Crete, and to haue had by hym Mynos, Radamantus and Sapadon,
albe it that many say she had those children by Jupiter, affirmynge
5 that Asterus and Jupiter were all oone name. Whiche altercasion,
because it touchyth other then me, it sufficyth that the more
parte wolde holde that, to doo hyr the more honour, she was
Jupiters wyfe and the children were by hym gotten, and for
because that she was a womane venerable, to hyr prayse to haue
10 namede the thyrde parte of the worlde after hyr name Europa
for euer. Whiche name, with a generall consent of the hoole
worlde, for hyr noblenes not onely is admytted, but further,
Pictogaras, the illustriouse *and* famouse philosopher, to hyr
honour and remembraunce made an ymage of coper for euermore
15 to endure.

---

conuenire videntur. Hanc aliqui a Ioue oppressam simpliciter
volunt et inde Astero Cretensium nupsisse regi et ex eo Mynoem,
Radamantum et Sapadonem filios peperisse, quos plurimi Iouis
dicunt fuisse filios, asserentibus nonnullis Asterum Iouemque
20 idem. Que disceptatio dum spectet ad alios, claram tanti dei
connubio plures Europam volunt, affirmantes insuper aliqui, seu
quia nobilitatis fuerit egregie—nam Phenices multis agentibus
meritis [suo] euo preceteris scematibus claruere maiorum—seu
dominij et coniugis veneratione seu filiorum regum gratia vel
25 ipsi[us]met Europe virtute precipua, ab eius nomine Europam
partem orbis terciam in perpetuum nuncupatam. Quam profecto
ego insignem mulierem virtutibus non solum ex concesso orbi
nomine [arbitror], sed a spectabili ex ere statua a Pictagora,
illustri philosopho, Ta[r]enti Europe dicata no[min]i.

16 videntur] videtur BU.   17 Astero] Asterio B.   18 Sapadonem]
Sarpedonem BU.   19–20 Ast. Iou. idem] Asterium Iouemque eundem
fuisse B.   20 dum] cum BU.   22 fuerit] fuerat BU.   nam] seu
quod B, seu quia U.   agentibus] *om.* B.   23 suo] *om.* LS.   scematibus]
stemmatibus B, stigmatibus U.   24 dominij et] diuini BU.   regum]
regnum B.   25 ipsimet L, ipsismet S.   26 perpetuum] honorem *add.*
B.   27 ergo L.   28 arbitror] *om.* LS.   statua] statuta U ; ut Varro
refert *add.* B.   Pictagora] Pythagora B, pitagora U.   29 tacenti
L, carenti S.   nomini] noui L.

Of Libia, the Quene of Libia.
The xth Chapitre.

LIbia, as the moste auncyent auctours wyll, was the doughter
of Epaphus, Kynge of the Egiptyens, which he begate of
Cassiop[i]a, his wyfe, and maryede hyr to Neptimo, that is to 5
say, to a myghty man, whose *pro*pre name we knowe not, and
of hyr [he] begate Besiride, after that a terrible tyraunte of
Egypte. Thys ladys exellent womans act*es* the longe tyme of |
yeres hathe putt theym oute of remembraunce. But it semys by f.12*b*
this argument specially that they were greate *and* noble and she 10
of highe auctorite, for asmuche as that greate [parte] of Affryk
is called Libia after hir name vnto this present day.

Off Marpesia and Lampedon, quenes.
The xjth Chapitre.

MArpesia, or otherwyse Narthesia, *and* Lampedo were susters 15
and bothe twayne Quenes of the Amozenes. And [for] the
glory that thei obteyned by their prowes they called theimselff*es*

5 Cassiopa MS.

De Libia, regina Libie. x.

LIbia, vt vetustissimi volunt auctores, Epaphi, Egiptiorum
regis, fuit filia, ex Cassiopia coniuge e[a]que nupsit Neptimo, 20
id est extero atque potenti viro, cuius proprium nomen ad nos
vsque non venit, et ex eo peperit Busiridem immanem, postea
superioris Egipti tyrannum. Huius magnifica opera ab annis
creduntur consumpta; sed ea fuisse permaxima satis argumenti
prestat, eam tante apud suos fuisse auctoritatis, vt eius Affrice 25
pars, cui imperauit Libia, omnis de suo nomine appellata sit.

De Marpesia et Lamp[e]done reginis.
xi. Cap.

MArpesia seu Nartesia et Lampedo sorores fuere Amazonum
inuicem regine et ob illustrem bellorum gloriam sese Martis 30
vocauere filias. Quarum, quoniam peregrina sit, hystoria paulo

20 eque LS.   Neptimo] Neptuuo B, neptuno U.   21 extero] homine
ab Egypto *add*. B.   27 Marpesia] Marthesia B, Marsepia U, Lampo-
done L.   reginis] *add*. Amazonum BU.   29 Marpesia] Marthesia ,B,
Marsepia U.   seu Nartesia] *om*. B.

the doughters of Mars, and because the hystory of theym is
sumwhat straynge, we muste sumwhat strayngely reherse it.
The country of Scithia in those daies beynge all full of woddes,
and so wylde that vnneth any man myght cum to it, stretchynge
5 upon Arthoes vnto the greate Occian, vnto the bosum of Silio
and Scolopia*m*, the men theryn withoute any ordre ledynge
theyr lyfe came at the last to the water of·Thermedonte, nyghe
vnto the confynes of Capadocia, and with spoylynge and robbynge
the Tyryens, began ther to inhabyte. Which sayde Tyryens at
10 length by wysdome and pollicy distressyde and kylled all thes
wylde people, wose wyfes, beynge wonders discontentyd w*ith*
all, mouyde to vengeaunce, with a fewe other men that wer lefft
a lyue, by power and strength put frome their co*n*fynes their
ennemyes and after that to theyr neybourse abowte theym they
15 made warre. And thynkynge at the last that, if they maryede,

altius assumenda est. E Scitia ergo, ea tempestate siluestri et
fere inaccessa exteris regione et sub Arthoo se in occeanum vsque
ab Eusino sinu pretendente, Silios et Scolopicus, vt ayunt, regij
viuentes factione maiorum pulsi, cum parte populorum iuxta
20 Thermodohontem Capadocie amnem deuenere et Tyrijs occupatis
aruis raptu viuere et incolas la†rocinijs infestare cepere. A quibus
tractu temporis per insidias fere omnes trucidati sunt homines,
quod cum egre ferrent viduate coniuges et in ardorem vindicte
deuenissent feruide, cum paucis qui superuixerunt viris in arma
25 prorupere et primo impetu facto hostes a suis demouere finibus,
inde vltro circumstantibus intulere bellum. Demum arbitrantes
seruitutem potius quam coniugium, si exteris adhererent hominibus, et feminas solas posse sufficere bellis et armis, ne mitiores
viderentur habuisse deos ceteris, he quibus viros a cede·finiti-

16–18 Scitia . . . pretendente] Scithya ergo regione quæ in Orientem
porrecta, uno latere Ponto, & ab altero montibus Rypheis, a tergo Asia &
Tanai flumina includit, ut multum in longitudinem latitudinemque protrusa,
Hæc ea tempestate syluestri & fere inaccessa exteris fuerat B.   17
Arthoo] artheo U.   18 Silios] Siliscus U, in hac Plinos & Scholo-
pythus B.   19 viuentes] iuuenes BU.   iuxta] usque ad B.   20 Thermo-
dohontem] Termodoontem B.   deuenere] ibique consedere *add*. B.
Tyrijs] Themiscyrijs B, tirys U.   22 homines] *om*. B.   23 viduate]
eorum *add*. B.   24 superuixerunt] superuixerant B, superuixerint U.
27 adhererent] matrimonio *add*. B.   28 ne] iste *add*. B.   29 ceteris]
quam cætere B.   quibus] quorum B

they shulde be but bounde, and that, contrary, if they lyuyde at
lyberty, they shulde be of power ynough | to kepe and defende f. 13*a*
theimself*fes*, sodeynly those men that were emonge theym
they slewe theym all; and after, with fury runnynge vpon theyr
ennemyes, as it were to reuenge the death of their husbond*es*, 5
so easely vanquysshed the*im* that they were compellyd by forse
to seke to theym for peax, which peax concludyd, to haue succession they drew to their neybours, and when they conceyuyde
with childe, went home to their coun*t*rie. And if it chauncyde
any of theym to bryng men chyldren, streight thei put theym 10
to deathe, *and* the doughte*rs* diligently they norysshed and taught
theym the feat*es* of war, cuttynge a way their ryght pappes, leste
to theym it shulde be a lett, when they came to age, to shote and
to runne with a spere, and the left breste they spayred to geue
sucke to theyr yonge doughters, and thus by this occasion they 15
were called Amozones. Nor in noryshynge of theyr doughters
they vsed not that way that we do, for settynge asyde the distafe
and the spynnynge wheele, they vsede theym to huntynge,
runnynge, chastesynge of horses, shotynge, wrastlynge ande

---

morum fortuna seruasset, communi consilio irruentes in eos 20
omnes interimere, inde in hostes furore conuerso, quasi virorum
neces vlture, illos adeo contriuere, vt ab eis facile pacem impe-
trarent. Qua suscepta ad successionem consequendam vicissim
finitimis adherebant et, cum concepissent, e vestigio reuerte-
bantur in sedes. Tandem qui nascebantur mares occidebantur 25
illico, virgines ad militiam cum diligentia seruabantur, tenellis
igne seu medicamine alio sublato incremento mamille dextre, ne
sagittandi exercicium impediretur adultis, sinistra linquebatur
intacta, vt ex illa nutrimenta porrigerent nascituris, ex quo
Amazonum vocabulum sortite sunt. Nec eis in alendis virginibus 30
fuit ea cura que nostris, nam colo, calat[h]is alijsque muliebribus
abiectis officijs, venationibus, discursionibus, domationibus
equorum, laboribus armorum assiduis, sagittationibus et huiusmodi exercicijs, mat[u]riores puellulas durabant in aptitudinem

---

25 qui] que BU.   28 exercicium] exercitum U.   30 Amazonum]
amasonum U.   vocabulum] quod sine mamma essent *add.* B.
31 calatisve LSU.   34 materiores L.

werynge of harnes, tyll that they haue brought theym vnto a
mannes strength. By which craft not oonely the Tyryens countrye they vaynquyshed, that sumtyme were the lordes of theyr
countrie, but also a greate parte of Europe by armes they gatt
5 to their countrie and also parte of Asya, in suche wise that they
were dradde eu*er*y where. And for because that their power ther
shuldnot lacke a ruler, afore other Marpesia and Lampedo, theyr
husbondes slayne, they made theym their quenes, vndre whose
gouernaunce, as saide is, they largely encreascyd theyr empyre.
10 Thies too ladyes, in deades of armes exellent, depar*tynge
betwyxt theym the prouyncys, defendyd theyr realmes wondersly
well and with the rest of theyr subiec*tes* daily put their neigh-
f. 13*b* bours by forse of armes vnder theyre | obeysaunce, and depar-
tynge the spoyle of theyr ennemyes betwyxt theym, thus rulyde
15 and maynteyned their com*unewelth. But at the last, when
Lampedo had ru*n*ne vppon hyr ennemyes, by a sodeyn inuasion
of theym she hade a greate ouer throwe, and Marpesia, leuynge
of hyr body begotten certeyn doughters, trustynge to muche
of hir strengthe, with a parte of hyr army was distressyde and
20 slayne. What folowede of Lampedo, I do not reme*m*bre that I
haue redde it.

---

et virile robur; quibus artibus non solum Tyrios tenuere campos
a suis olim maioribus occupatos, quinymo Europe ingenti parte
bellorum iure quesita, plurimum Asie occupauere formidabilesque
25 deuenere omnibus. Sane, ne viribus deesset regimen, ante alias
Marpesiam et Lampedonem post cesos viros instituere reginas,
sub quarum auspicijs, vt demonstratum est, suum plurimum
imperium a[u]xere. He quidem, cum militari disciplina insignes
essent, partitis intra se prouincijs, vtputa, cum vna in regni
30 tutelam subsisteret, reliqua parte copiarum sumpta ad subi-
ciendos finitimos earum imperio incedebat, et sic vicissim maximis
partis predis auxerunt aliquandiu rempublicam. Verum, cum
Lampedo ad vltimum in hostes duxisset exercitum, repentino
barbarorum circumadiacentium incursu Marpesia nimium s[ib]i
35 fidens relictis aliquibus filiabus cum parte copiarum cesa est.
Quid autem ex Lampedone secutum sit legisse non memini.

25 deuenere] fuere B.   26 reginas] sibi *add.* BU.   28 anxere L.
He] Haec B.   31 incedebat] intendebat BU.   32 predis] predijs BU.
34 sui LSU.

Off Thisbe, the uirgyne of Babylone.
The xij[th] Chapitre.

THisbe of Babylone, more by the vnhappy fortune that she had in louynge Piram*us* then by any other notable deede, is put here emonge the noble *and* famo*us* women. Nor of this 5 woman we haue noo notable knowlege who, by the auncyent wryters, were hyr parentt*es*. But it is euydent that Piramus and she were nyghe neybours, and their howses io[y]nynge, the oone nyghe the other. By which neybourhed hauynge together continuall company, and bothe passynge goodely and fayre, as they 10 grewe in age, so grewe their loue vnto extreme burnynge fyre, and that by sygnes the tone declarede vnto the tother. And so they bothe c[o]men vnto laufull age, when that Thysbe was mariable, hyr father kept hyr styll at home, to th'entent to mary hyr, wherewi*th* aswell Piram*us* as she were greately displeasede 15 wi*th*all, sekynge busely the way how to co*m*mun and meete together. At the last they founde a clyft in the walle, whiche

13 camen MS.

De Tisbe, Babilonia virgine. xij.

TIsbe, Babilonia virgo, infelicis amoris exitu magis quam opere alio inter mortales celebris facta est. Huius etiam 20 [si] non a maioribus nostris qui parentes fuerint habuimus, intra tamen Babiloniam habuisse cum Pyramo etatis sue puero contiguas domos satis‑creditum est ; quorum, cum esset iure conuicinij quasi conuictus assiduus et inde eis adhuc pueris puerilis affectio, egit [i]ni[qu]a sors vt crescentibus annis, cum ambo formosissimi 25 essent, puerilis amor in maximum augeretur incendium illudque inter se nutibus saltem aperirent aliquando, iam in puberem propinquantes etatem. Sane, cum iam grandiuscula fieret Tisbe, a parentibus in futuros hymeneos domi detineri cepta est ; quod, cum egerrime ferrent ambo quererentque solliciti qua via possent 30 saltem aliquando colloqui, nulli adhuc visam communis parietis inuenere in seposito rimulam, ad quam dum clam conuenissent sepius et consuetudine paululum colloquendo, pariete etiam

19 Tisbes U.   20 etiam] et BU.   21 *om.* LS.   habuimus] habuerimus B, haburimus U.   25 vnica LS.   31 nulli] a nullo B. 32 dum] cum BU.

noo man afore had founde, at which clyfte they mett together,
oft tymes w*ith* syghes and teares *and* lamentationes, in pro-
myttynge peax, embracynge and p*er*petuall loue, whyles theyr
lyues enduryde. And so w*ith* suche enfla*m*mynges they coun-
5 seilled to ru*n* a way the next nyght and how they myght
f. 14*a* beguyle theym of their | fathers houses, and who that fyrst
escapyde, shulde goo to a wodde therby, where was a fayre
fountayne, and not farr fro*m* thens the graue of Kynge Nynus,
and he or she that fyrst came, shulde tary the cu*m*mynge of the
10 tother. Thysbe, that p*er*case more ardently louede, was the fyrst
that deceiuyde hyr gardiens, and w*ith* a clooke cast ouer hyr
heade, in the styll of the nyght, all aloone gatt oute of hyr fathers
house, and, the moone gyuynge lyght to hyr way, all hastely
wentt onwarde and came at the last to the well, tremblyng for
15 eu*er*y lyght noyse she herde, [and] seynge cu*m*mynge to the
welle a lyones, all affrayde, leuynge behynde hyr hyr vayle and
hyr clooke, fledde vnto the wodde. The lyones, when she hadde
well fedde, fyndynge ther the clooke and the vayle, w*ith* hyr

obice, quo minus erubescebant, ampliassent exprimendi affec-
20 tiones suas licentiam, sepe suspiria, lacrimas, feruores, desideria
et passiones omnes aperiebant suas, nonnunquam etiam orare
inuicem pacem animorum, amplexus et oscula, pietatem, fidem
dilectionemque perpetuam. Tandem excrescente incendio de
fuga iniere consilium, statuentes [vt] nocte sequenti quam
25 primum quis posset suos fallere, domos exiret, et se inuicem, si
quis primus euaderet, in nemus ciuitati proximum abiens, penes
fontem, Nini regis busto proximum, tardiorem operiretur.
Ardentior forte Tisbes, prima suos fefellit, et amicta pallio intempesta nocte sola patriam domum exiuit, et luna monstrante
30 viam in nemus trepida abijt, et dum secus fontem expectaret et
ad quemcunque rei motum sollicita caput extolleret, leenam venientem aduertens, relicto inaduertent[e]r pallio aufugit in bustum.
Leena autem pasta, siti posita, comperto pallio et aliquandiu ad
illud cruentato ore de more exfricato atque exterso vnguibus,

24 iniere] iniuere BU. *om.* LS.   26 primus] prior B.   27 busto]
bustui U.   operiretur] expectaret B.   30 trepida] intrepida BU.
dum] cum BU.   32 aduertens] animaduertens B.   inaduertentur L.
33 pasta] sua *add.* BU.   posita] ponita U.   34 cruentato] cru-
ento BU.   exfricato] fricato B.

blody mouthe taare it *in* pecys *and* after drynkynge of the welle
wentt hyr way. Piram*us*, that had taryd sumwhat to longe
leuynge hys fathers house, in the styll of the nyght came into the
wodde, and fyndynge the clooke and the vayle of Thisbe torne
and all foullyd with blody spot*tes* here *and* ther, thy*n*kynge 5
verely that sum wylde beste had deuoured hyr, fyllyde all the
place aboute hym with clam*our* and crye, accusynge hy*m*self
that he was the cause of the deathe of that moste swete, louynge
virgyne, and dispysynge for that hys lyue, hauynge his swerde
aboute hym, toke the poynte therof *and* thrust it to hys hert and 10
soo fell downe deade in the place. What more? Thisbe, extemynge
the lyones to be goone, and ferynge leste Piramus shulde thynke
she shulde tary to longe, by that way she wentt vnto the wodde,
she ca*m* agayne to the fountayne, and seynge ther Piramus, not
all dede, but pantynge toward*es* death, for feare it had bene the 15
lyones she drewe backe. But when by the lyght of the moone
[she] p*er*ceyuyde it was hyr Piramus, and wenynge to haue
enbrasyd hym, sawe the bloode gushe oute frome hys hert and
[hym] at the poynte to dye, fyrst astonyde, and next cryenge
oute, she assayde with speky*n*g, with kyssynge, and w*ith* 20

---

laceratum liquit et abijt. Interim tardior Pyramus eque relicta
domo deuenit in siluam, dumque per silentia noctis intentus
comperisset laceratum cruentumque pallium Tisbis, ratus eam
a belua deuoratam, plangore plurimo locum compleuit, se miserum
incusans, quoniam dilectissime virgini seue mortis causam ipse 25
dedisset, et aspernans de cetero vitam, exempto quem gesserat
gladio, moribundus secus fontem pectori impegit suo. Nec mora
Tisbes potatam leenam abijsse rata, ne decepisse videretur
amantem aut diu expectatione suspensum teneret, pedetentim
ad fontem regredi cepit. Cui iam propinqua palpitantem adhuc 30
Pyramum sentiens, pauefacta fere iterum abijt; tandem lune
lumine percepit qui[a] iacens suus esset Pyramus, et dum in
amplexus festina iret, eum sanguini per vulnus effuso incu-
bantem atque iam omnem effundentem animam comperit. Que,
cum aspectu obstupuisset, primo mesta, tandem ingenti cum 35

32 qui L, quoniam BSU.   dum] eius *add.* BU.   33 sanguine U.

f. 14*b* wepynge, to haue callyde hym in vayne | to lyf agayne; but
when she couldnot haue noo worde on hym, thynkynge, as the
trueth was, that he demyde hyr to haue bene deuourede and
for that had slayne hymself, with syghes, and with the greatest
5 lamentation that euer creature made, she prayde Piram*us* at the
leste, yf ther were any sparke of lyf in hym, he shuld either speke
or looke vpon hyr. A meruellouse thynge, all though he were
euyn at the poynte to gyue vpp hys gooste, he lyft vpp hys heuy
eyes vppon hys Thisbe! Whiche when Thisbe saw, w*it*houte more
10 delay, with that same self weypon that Piram*us* hadd slayne
hymself, she thrust hyrself to the stomake, and so wher *tha*t
enuyouse fortune woldnot the tone shulde not enbrase the tother
alyue, [she] coulde not forbed but that the bloode of the tone
shulde be mengled w*ith* the tother. Who shallnot haue pyte of
15 thies two yonge folkes, or who is he that cannot lamente the hard
cha*u*nnce of twayne so true louers? Surely, he hath a stony herte

fletu, frustra prestare subsidia et animam retinere osculis et
amplexu aliquandiu conata est. Verum, cum nec verbum audire
posset, quin nihilpendi tam feruenti pridie desiderio optata basia
20 et amantem in mortem festinare videret, rata quoniam eam non
comperisset occisum, in acerbum fatum cum dilecto a se puero
amore pariter et dolore suadentibus ire disposuit; et arrepto
capulotenus ex vulnere gladio cum gemitu ploratuque maximo
nomen inuocauit Pyrami orauitque vt Tisbem suam saltem
25 morientem aspiceret et exeuntem expectaret animam, vt inuicem
in quascunque sedes incederent. Mirum dictu, sensit morientis
deficiens intellectus amate virginis nomen, nec extremum negare
postulatum passus, oculos in morte grauatos aperuit et inuocan-
tem aspexit, que confestim pectori adolescentis cultroque super-
30 incubuit et effuso sanguine secuta est anima[m] iam defuncti.
Et sic quos amplexu placido inuida fortuna iungi minime passa
est, infelicem amborum sanguinem misceri prohibuisse non
potuit. Qui non compatietur iuuenibus, qui tam infelici exitui
lacrimulam saltem vnam non concedet, saxeus erit. Amarunt

18 audire] haurire BU.   19 quin] sensissetque BU, que S, *evidently
having omitted* sensisset *after* posset, *which occurs at the end of a line.*
nihilpendi] vilipendi BU.   21 occisum] occisam BU.   25 inuicem]
simul B.   30 anima L.   31 inuida] ex inuidia B, inuidia U.   33 Qui] Quis
BSU.   qui] quis BSU.   34 concedet] concedit BU.   Amarunt] se *add.* BU.

that cannot do it. They louyde, yonge children, and by that dyd
not des*er*ue so blody an ende. I willnot say but loue in youthe is
an offense, but not verey greate in single persones. Theyr offense
myght well haue turnede into matrymony. The vngraciouse lote
or chaunce offendyde, or ells p*er*case their sorowfull fathers and 5
mothers. Lytle *and* lytle the hote loue of youthe shulde be
refraynyde, leste, if we assay with to muche haste to drawe theym
frome it, we leede theym by desperatione into p*er*ditione. The
passione of Cupido is of immoderate power, and to yonge men
wellnere a pestilence, and a co*m*une euyll which neades we muste 10
suffre, for nature hathe so wyllyde that in o*ur* youthe we shulde
be styrrede to it, leste that in age we shulde not be of power to
encreasce mankynde.

Off Ip*er*mystra, Quene of the Argyuys.

The xiijth Chapitre. | 15

I Permystra, aswell of kynne as of dignyte honorabyll, was the f. 15*a*
doughter of Danaus, Kynge of the Argyuys, and of Lynsey,
his wyfe. It is gatheryde oute of the olde, auncyent hystoryes

---

pueri. Non enim ob hoc infortunium meruere cruentum; florentis
etatis amor crimen est, nec horrendum solutis crimen. In con- 20
iugium ire poterat; peccauit sors pessima et forsan miseri
peccauere parentes. Sensim quippe frenandi sunt iuuenum
impetus, ne dum repentino obice illis obsistere volumus, despe-
rantes in precipicium impellamus. Immoderati vigoris est cupidinis passio et adolescentium fere pestis est, commune flagicium, in 25
quibus edepol pacienti animo tolleranda est, quoniam sic rerum
volente natura fit, vt dum etate valemus vltro inclinemur, ne
humanum genus in defectum corruat, si coitus differantur in
senium.

De Ypermestra, Argiuorum regina. xiij.   30

Y Permestra genere et dignitate clara, Danai, Argiuorum regis,
filia et Lincei coniunx fuit. Colligitur autem ex historijs
antiquorum duos quondam in Egipto fuisse fratres, Beli prisci

21 poterat] poterant BU.   22 quippe] quidem BU.   25 est, com.
flag.] et come flagitium BU.   27 inclinemur] in prolem *add.* BU.   30 Yper-
mestra] Hypermnestra B.   regina] et sacerdote Iouis *add.* BU.   32 Lincei]
seu ut quidam uolunt Lini B.

that sumtyme ther were twayne brethren in Egypte. Danaus was the tone, and the tother was namede Egistus. Neither fortune gaue theym not chyldre alyke, all thoughe theyr numbre was lyke, for Danaus had fyfty doughters, and Egistus had as many 5 sonnes. But when Danaus had bene warnede by an orakyll that by the hande of hys neuowe, that is to say, by his brothers chylde, that he shulde be slayne, and pryuely was vexyde in hys mynde therwyth, for asmuche as of so greate a numbre of brethren he knewe not whome he shulde suspecte, it chauncyde that when 10 bothe their children were comen to rype age, that Egistus askede of his brother Danaus that all his sonnes myght be maryede to his doughters. Which saide Danaus, ymagenynge therby to haue murdre[d] theym all, grauntede vnto it, and when the day of maryage came, commaundyde all his doughters, as they wolde 15 his welth and their oune profyte, that when their husboundes after the bankett were faste a sleepe, with sharpe knyffes to kyll theym, which, accordynge to their fathers precepte, pryuyly hydynge their knyffes, when they were a sleepe, cruelly murdrede theym

2 Egistius MS.   9 suspecte] And *add.* MS.

---

filios, spectabili preeminentes imperio, quorum Danaus vnus, 20 alter autem Egistus nuncupatus est; nec prolis ambobus fuit equa fortuna, esto numerus esset equus. Nam Danao quinquaginta fuere filie: filij totidem Egisto. Sane, cum habuisset oraculo Danaus, quoniam manu nepotis ex fratre occideretur et clam angeretur timore plurimo, cum ex tam ingenti multitudine 25 nesciret cuius suspectas deberet habere manus, contigit vt iam pubescentibus vtriusque filijs peteret Egistus, vt Danai filie omnes filijs suis iungerentur coniugio. Quod Danaus seue excogitato facinore vltro concessit, desponsatisque filiabus nepotibus, cum nupciale sacrum pararetur, eas omnes su[m]mopere 30 premonuit, vt si salutem suam vellent, vnaqueque virum suum nocte prima, dum vino epulisque madentem somnoque illigatum graui cognosceret, ferro perimeret. Que omnes cultris clam cubiculis suis illatis, marcentes hesterna crapula iuuenes, iussu

20 Egistus] Ægyptus B.   22 oraculo] in oraculis B.   23 et clam] clamque BU.   26 filijs] liberis B.   27 seue] seuo BU.   29 sumopere LS.   32 Que omnes] Quæ omnis B. Quod omnis U.

all. Onely Ipermestra absteyned frome so detestable a deede.
She had so fast and sure sett hyre hert vpon hyr husbonde, whose
name was Lynus, after a maydenly facyon to loue hym, and for
that hauynge pyte in hyr herte, to hyr greate laude, to do so
fowlle a deede, she dyd not as hyr other susters dyd, but per- 5
suadede hyr husbonde to flee away to sum sure place to saue
hymself. Nowe the cruell father beynge wounders gladd with hys
doughters for th'accomplyshment of hys commaundement, onely
gentle and pytefull Ipermestra was brawlede and chydden. And
because she hadnot doone as hyr susters hade doone, he putt 10
hyr into a foule prysone. O, we moste myserable mortall men,
how often do we desyre that whiche is cause of oure perdicyon,
ande | not lokynge to the ende of that we couett, feare not f. 15b
by all detestable facyones to brynge to passe oure myndes,
thynkynge that, as it were, we myghte with euyll doynge cause 15
slypper fortune to stande and abyde with vs! And that whiche
is moste scornefull, this breue and shorte lyfe of ours, we not
onely goo aboute to prolonge it, but as it were to make itt
perpetuall, albe it we see dayly afore oure eyes on all sydes men
to goo to deathe. And besydes thys, with how many abhomyn- 20

interficere parentis. Ast Ypermestra sola abstinuit; apposuerat
quippe virgo iam animum suum in Linum seu Linteum, virum
suum, vt moris est puellarum e vestigio viso sponso illum diligere
et ob id ei compassa, ingenti cum laude sua, a nefanda cede
abstinuit, suasitque iuueni fugam qua tutus esset. Verum, cum 25
ceteris mane ob patratum scelus trux pater applausisset, Ypermestra sola obiurgata et carcere clausa pium aliquandiu fleuit
opus. Heu, miseri mortales, quam cupido animo quamque
feruenti peritura concupiscimus et occasum intueri aspernantes,
quam execrandis vijs, si prestetur, celsa conscendimus; quibus 30
sceleribus conscensa seruamus, quasi obscenis operibus arbitremur
volubilem firmari posse fortunam; et, quod ridiculum est, quibus
criminibus, quam scelestis facinoribus volatilem fragilemque vite
huius dieculam, non dicam longare, sed perpetuare conamur, cum
in mortem ire ceteros cursu volucri videamus; quibus detestandis 35

21 parentis] parentes U.

able counseills, w*ith* howe many vngracyouse workes, do we
moue the iudgemente of Gode agaynste vs! Leuynge other a
parte, what a myscheuouse deede was thys of Danaus, that
soughte the way w*ith* the bloode of his neuows to prolonge hys
5 olde, tremblynge yeres [and] weykyde hymselfe fro*m* the helpe
and ayde of so goodely and stronge a felysshypp, w*ith* hys p*er*-
petuall shame *and* dishono*ur*! The cursyde olde wretche yma-
gynede a fewe of his crokyde yeres to be put afore the lyfe of so
many of hys yonge sonnes, which p*er*auenture myght haue turnede
10 to goode, if he had not murdred thei*m*. But by the bloode of the
yonge men to haue prolonged hys lyfe, what dyd it seme other
but to shamefull and abhomynable an acte? And to hys more
rebuke, he armyde not hys men agaynste theym, but the handes
of hys doughters to myschef to brynge in another, to make theyr
15 wyffes to be pollutyde with p*er*petuall diffamy, whiche, if thei
had bene pyteouse, had des*er*uyde laude for euer. And thus,
whiles he studyede to p*r*eserue his oune lyfe, he dyd litle remembre
how muche boldenes and how an euyll example he left to vngraciouse women, by the examples of hys doughters, to accom-

---

20 consilijs, quibus nefandis operibus, dei irritamus iudicium! Vt
alios sinam, testis infandus sit Danaus, qui, dum plurimo nepotum
sanguine suos iam tremulos annos ampliare nititur, robust[a] se
ac splendida nepotum nudauit acie et perhenni labefactauit infamia. Arbitratus est homo nequam, paucos frigidosque annos
25 senectutis sue, floridis adolescentie nepotum suorum preponendos
fore, quod forsan tanquam vtili[u]s existimasset alius, dummodo
seruasset honeste. Verum per vulnera iuuenum filiorum quesisse
suum prolongasse senium, immane facinus iure videri potest et,
qu:od plurimum ignominie superaddit, non satellitum manus sed
30 filias armauit, vt non tantum nepotes auferret, sed vt scelere
filias funestas haberet, quas habere pietate potuisset honestas;
et dum vitam seruare hoc crimine cupit, non aduertit quantum
audacie, quantum fraudis, quantumque detestande enormitatis
futuris perniciosis mulieribus infausti relicturus esset exempli.

22 robusto LS.   23 et] *om.* U.   26 vtiliores LSU.   28 suum]
suumque B.   29 superaddit] semper addit BU.   30 armauit] in scelus
add. BU.   34 futuris] futurus U.   mulieribus] & *add.* B.

plyshe agaynste theyre husbound*es*. The faythe of maryage, he
caused it to be dispysede, and hys children to breeke it. And
wher as he shulde lyke a meeke father haue brought emonge theym
blessyng*es*, he brought emongste theym blody knyffes. And
where hys parte was to exhorte theym to loue the toone the 5
tother, he taughte theym how to kyll and murdre the toone the
tother. And that whiche he durste not doo in the day, he causede
it to be doone by nyght. And that which he feryde to doo in
the feelde, | he dyd it in hys chambre, not aduertesynge that as f. 16*a*
many lyf*es* as he toke away frome the freshe, yonge gentle men, 10
soo many diffamyes and shames he brought to hym and his for
euer. And thoughe he trustyd sure to haue sauyde hymself
therby, yet oon was ordeynede of God to deuoure hym, frome
whose hande the olde caytyfe couldnot escape, but hys hurtfull
and tyrann*us* bloode shulde be aswell shedde, as he had shedde 15
the bloode of hys innocent neuouse. But to reuerte to thys
history. Linus, fledde to the kyngdo*m* of Argyuys emonge the
Grecyans, with wisdome and manlihode was ther made kynge.

Fidem coniugij calcari fecit perfidia ; vbi sacras inferri faces thalamis pius iussisse parens debuerat, ne[f]ast[o]s gladios imperauit ; 20
vbi in coniugalem dilectionem natas hortari consueuimus, is in
odium animauit et cedem ; et quod in omnes ausus non fuisset,
in singul[o]s natas immisit ; quod die non attemptasset, nocte
perfici voluit ; quod non presumpsisset in castris, thalamis
mandauit impleri, non aduertens, quia quot annos viridi iuuentuti 25
nepotum auferret per scelus et fraudem, tot sibi fedata igno-
miniosi sui facinoris secula reseruabat, et [qui] quinquaginta iure
generos habere poterat, hostis male merito seruatur vnus. Cuius
tandem manus, dei iusto volente iudicio, truculentus senex
euadere non potuit, quin ille noc[uu]s effunderetur sanguis quem 30
tam multo nepotum sanguine redemisset ; qui tandem, seu
pulsus, seu profugus, seu vocatus, transfretauit in Greciam et
Argiuorum regnum ingenio et viribus occupatum tenuit. Sunt

20 nephaustus L, ne phastus S, nephaustos U, infaustos B.   21 vbi] nos
add. B.   22 et 1º] *om*. U.   cedem] certe *add*. U. et 2º] atque B.   23 singulas
LS. att. nocte] attentasset nocti BU.   26 auferret] aufferebat U.   26–7
ignominiosi] ignominosi BSU.   27 reseruabat] reseruaret B. qui *om*. L.   28
merito] meritus B. seruatur] seruatus est BU. vnus] vnico Nepoti B.   30 eua-
dere] euasisse BU. nociuis LS.   31 tandem] *om*. B.   33 tenuit] Quo *add*. LSU.

And how it was, callynge to remembraunce the crueltie of
Danaus, made warr vpon hym *and* slewe hym, *and* reigned hymself for hym, and toke oute hys deare wyfe oute of prysone, *and*
not oonely made hyr Quene of Argyuys, but further, namede hyr
5 as the felowe to Juno, to hyr double hono*ur*. And thus, hyr
susters by vngraciouse tyranny hauynge des*er*uyde euerlastynge
shame, she for hyr wyfely pyte hathe obtaynede eternall fame
vnto this present day.

Off Nyobe, Quene of Thebes.
10   The xiiij^th Chapitre.

NYobe wellnere emongste all the vulgar people is knowne
a notable woman, for asmuche as she was the doughter of
the myghty *and* famouse Tantalus, Kynge of the Frygyens, and
suster to Pelopis. She was maryede to Amphyon, that tyme
15 Kynge of Thebes, of grete fame, as well because he was the sonne
of Jupiter, as also because he was a man of synglar eloquens.

---

qui velint predictum facinus a Danao perpetratum, sed a quocunque factum sit, a Lino truculent[i]e memore occisus occubuit
et pro eo Linus ipse regnauit Argiuis, eductaque e carcere Yper-
20 mestra, e[a]que melior[e] omine sibi iuncta coniugio regni parti-
cipem fecit; que non solum regina refulsit sed Iunonis Argiue
sacerdos effecta, candore splendoris duplicis ornata apparuit et
cum sorores in turpem abijssent infamiam, ipsa ob commenda-
bilem pietatem nomen suum laude dignum ad nos vsque dimisit
25 insigne.

De Nyobe, regina Thebanorum. xiiij.

NIobes fere vulgo inter egregias notissima mulier, cum
vetustissimi atque famosissimi Frigiorum regis, Tantali,
nata fuisset, et Pelopis soror, nupsit Amphioni, Thebarum regi,
30 ea tempestate clarissimo, tam quia Iouis proles quam quia

17 Danao] ibi *add*. B.   a 2°] *om*. S.   17–18 quocunque] ubicunque B,
quomodocunque U.   18 truculente LS.   memore] memorie LS.
20 eque LS, atque B.   meliori LS, melior U.   22 apparuit] comparuit
BU.   24 dimisit] transmisit B.   27 Niobe B. mulier] mulierum BU.
29 Thebarum] Thebanorum BU.   30 clarissimo] clarissimi BU.

And beynge accompanede with hyr, in tyme he had of hys wyfe
Nyobe seuen sonnes and as many doughters. And that whiche
shulde haue bene to a wyse womane | cause to haue laudyde f. 16*b*
God was to hyr by pryde a destructione, for as well elatyde
for hauynge of so many children, as by the greate stock she 5
was descendyd of, she was not aferde to speke against goddes.
It so chauncyde by the commaundement of [M]a[n]tona, the
prophet of Teresia, that hyr children wer busyde in doynge
sacrifyce aboute the ceremonyes of Apollo and the superstitiones
of Diana. Which Nyobe perceyuynge, as it were all in a rage, 10
with a greate company of seruaunttes aboute hyr and hire children
after a pryncelyke facyon, [she] approchyd to the place, saynge
vnto theym: 'What madnes haue the Thebans to goo aboute
suche ioly sacryfyce with a woman of a straynge countrie, and
to suffre hyr twane children, the baster[d]s of Tytan, beynge no 15
more in numbre, that they shulde do to the goddes sacryfyce,
when I, beynge a quene and doughter to Tantalus, hauynge so
many fayre children as fourtene in numbre, shulde haue doone

7 Namtona MS.

precipua valeret facundia, et ex eo perseuerante regni gloria
septem peperit filios et filias totidem. Sane, quod sapienti 20
profuisse debuerat, superbienti fuit exicium, nam tam splendore
conspicue prolis quam maiorum suorum fulgore elata, etiam in
numina obloqui ausa est. Erant equidem iussu Mantonis,
Thiresie vatis filie, soliciti dierum vna Thebani circa sacra
Latone, matris Appollinis et Diane, veteri superstitione veneran- 25
dis [n]u[min]ibus, cum, quasi agitata furijs, circumsepta natorum
acie et regijs insignita notis, prosilijt in medium Niobes clamitans
quenam illa esset Thebanorum dementia, Latone sacra disponere
et exteram feminam seu Titanis genitam duos tantum adulterio
conceptos connixam filios sibi eorum regine preponere, rege 30
Tantalo nate, et que quatuordecim eis videntibus illis ex coniuge

19 precipua] precipue BU.   23 iussu] cuiusdam *add*. U.   24 Thiresie]
thirosie S, Tiresiæ cuiusdam B. sacram LS.   25 veteri] veterum BU,
veterl S.   26 muneribus LS. cum] tum BU.   27 prosilijt] prosiliuit
BU.   28 que nam LSU, quæ nam B.   Thebanorum] Tebanorum BU.
sacra] sacrum B.   29 seu] cui B, Cei U.   30 connixam] enixam BU.
31 illis] *om*. B.

myself the ceremonyes.' By thies proude wordes, how it was
that not longe after she sawe it with hyr oune eyes, hyr children
with a strange pestilence were deuourede all. And Amphion,
hyr husbonde, beynge orbate or voyde of so many swete children,
5 for pure sorowe with his oune swerde slewe hymself, the Thebans
thynkynge noone other but thys chaunce came to theym oonely
by the dyuyne hande *and* strooke of Gode. Thus Nyobe, viduate,
and heuy of the lost*es* of hyr husbounde *and* of so many fayre
children, became at the laste so muete, and spake so fewe wordes
10 that it semyde hyr to be more a stoone that cannot be remouede
then a woman. For whiche cause the poet*es* feyne that at
Siphilum, where hyr children were buryede, that ther she was
conuertyde into a stoone. It is a harde thynge to beere those
proude folkes *and* be in company with theym. But a womans
15 pryde to susteyne is intollerable, for asmuche as of theyr oune
nature they be inclynede to pryde, and those that be otherwyse,
allways ar more apte to vertue then to rule. It is therfore noo

peperisset genitos, sibique tanquam digniori cerimonias illas deberi.
Tandem paruo temporis tractu factum est, vt ea vidente letali
20 peste nati omnes pulchra iuuentute florentes infra breue spacium
absumerentur vsque ad vnum, et Amphyon, qui ex pa[tr]e quatuordecim filiorum repente orbus effectus esset, dolore impellente
manu propria gladio transfoderetur, existimantibus Thebanis
hec superum vi vlciscentium numinis iniuriam contigisse. Nyobes
25 autem tot funeribus superstes vidua mestaque in tam grandem
atque obstinatam taciturnitatem deuenit, vt potius immobile
saxum videretur quàm femina. Quam ob causam a poetis postea
factum est eam apud Syphilum, vbi sepult[i] fuerant filij, in
lapid[ea]m statuam fuisse conuersam. Durum est et odiosum
30 plurimum superbos, non dicam tollerare sed spectare homines:
mulieres autem fastidiosum et importabile, cum illos feruentis
animi atque elati, vt plurimum, natura produxerit: has vero
mitis ingenij et remisse virtutis, lauticijs potius quam imperijs

18 peperisset] peperisse BU.   21 absummerentur LS.   et] *om.* B.
parte L.   22 orbus] orbem S.   effectus] factus BU.   24 hec . . .
vlcisc.] hæc iure superis ulciscentibus B, hec iura superum vlciscentium U.
vi] *om.* S.   numinis] innuminis S.   28 factum] fictum BU.   Syphilum]
Sipylum B.   sepulte LS.   29 lapidum LS.

me*r*uell thoughe the strooke of Gode light vppon suche prowde women, when they cannot | keepe theym withyn the terme f. 17*a* of humylyte, as this folishe Nyobe dyd—scornyd wi*th* the vnstedfaste gyft*es* of fortune ande, wenynge *tha*t it came of the gyft*es* of nature and not of Gode, the fayre fructe of children, she 5 loste theym all. It hade been mete for hyr to haue geuyn laude for suche thynges to the geuer of all goode. And because she neclecte it, she not onely in hyr tyme bewayled it, but nowe after many worldes hyr foly is spoken and comonde of.

Off Ysiphile, Quene of Leumi. 10
The xvth Chapitre.

YSiphile was a right honorable woman, aswell for the pyte she shewde to hyr father, as also for hyr infortunate exyle and [the] deathe of Arthemor, to whome she was guydo*ur* and rular. Thys

---

aptas produxit. Quamobrem mirabile minus, si in elat[a]s dei 15 procliuior ira sit et iudicium eius, quotiens eas sue debilitatis contingat excedere terminos, vt insipiens Nyobes fecit, fortune lusa fallacia et ignara quoniam ample prolis parentem fore non virtutem parientis sed nature opus esse, in se celi benignitatem flectentis. Satis igitur illi ymo debitum erat, deo ex concessis 20 egisse gratias, quam sibi diuinos qualescunque honores quesisse, tanquam sui fuisset operis tam numerosam prolem atque conspicuam peperisse; que, dum superbe potius quam prudenter operata est, egit vt infortunium viua fleret et post multa secula suum nomen posteritati foret exosum. 25

De Ysiphile, regina Leumi. xv.

YSiphiles insignis fuit femina, tam pietate in patrem quam ĩnfelici exilio et Arthemori alumni morte atque subsidio natorum oportuno in tempore repertorum. Fuit etenim hec

15 elatis LS.   16 eius] seuius BU.   19 se] eos B.   22 numerosum]
numero suam B.   26 Leumi] Lemni BU.   27 Ysiphiles] Hypsipyle B.
28 Arthemori] Archemori B, archemoni U.

sayde lady was doughter of Thoant*es*, Kynge of Leumi, reignynge
in those days when that the vngraciouse woodenes was in the
myndes of the women to withdrawe theym frome the obeysance
that wom*en* shulde haue to theyr husbondes, for, despysynge the
5 alegaunse that they oughte to theyr olde Kynge, Isyphile beynge
emonge the other women one of the conspiracy, with a mutuall
consent they concludyde that, the next nyght after, euery wyfe
shulde murdre theyr husbond*es*. Now the reste agreynge lyke
ragyde beast*es* ther vnto, onely Isyphile was mouede to a moore
10 meeke way[e], for, remembreynge that it was against nature to
fyle hyr handes w*ith* hyr fathers bloode, declarynge to hyre
father the counsell of the other women, [she] wyllyde hym in all
haste to take a shyppe and flie a way to an ile callyde C[h]yu*m*,
thereby to advoyde the co*m*une furye of the reste. And to clooke
15 the matere the bett*er*, she causide to be made a co*m*une fun*er*all,
as thoughe it hade bene in verey deede for the buryinge of hyr
f. 17*b* father. Whiche beleuyde of all the wome*n* | as it had bene a
thynge of truthe, she anone was sett in hyre fathers throone and
takyne emonge the vngraciouse women verey quene in deede.
20 It is a moste holy thynge, the pyte that children haue toward*es*
their parent*tes*. For what thynge is more syttynge, what more

10 ways MS.   13 Clymu*m* MS.

Thoantis, Lemniadum regis, filia, eo euo regnantis, quo rabies
illa subiuit mulierum insule mentes subtrahendi omnino indomita
colla virorum iugo. Nam paruipenso senis regis imperio, adhibita
25 secum Ysiphile, vnanimes in [id] deuenere consilium, vt sequenti
nocte gladijs seuiretur in quoscunque masculos; nec defuit opus
proposito. Sane, seuientibus reliquis, consilium mitius menti
Ysiphilis occurrit; nam rata fedari paterno sanguine inhumanum
fore, genitori detecto reliquarum facinore eoque in nauym
30 demisso, vt Chium effugeret publicam iram, e vestigio ingenti
constructo rogo, se patri postremum exhibere finxit officium;
quod cum crederetur a cunctis, patrio imposita throno loco regis,
impijs mulieribus regina suffecta est. Sanctissima quippe filiorum
pietas in parentes est. Quid enim decentius, quid iustius, quid

22 Lemniadum] leminadum S.   23 insule] solens U, *om.* B.   25 id]
eum LS.   33 suffecta] prefecta B.

ryghtuouse, what more prayse-wo*ur*thely then to quyte with all
humanyte and honour theim that, when we were not able to
helpe ourselfe, kept vs and w*it*h ferue*nt* loue noryshede vs, tyll
we came in poynte and state to helpe o*ur*selff*es*, made vs to be
taught goode man*ers*, goode instructione and lerny*ng*, and studyd 5
as well to gyue vs worldly goodes as knowlege of ve*r*tuouse
thynges? Which sayde Isyphyle hauynge doone so well to hyr
father, not withoute goode, iuste cause she is well worthy to be
emongste the numbre of noble women. She, than, thus reignyng,
were it by chaunce or by forse of contrary wyndes, Jasone, 10
goyng into Colcos, all thoughe the women wolde haue wi[th]stonde
hym, he toke londe in hyr countrie, where at the laste he was well
receyuyde of the Quene, aswell at bedde as at borde. And when
he wente hys waye after he had had by hyr too children, by the
lawe that was made emonge the women, wylde she, nylde she, 15
she was compellyde to sende theym oute of hyr londe, as sum say
to Chyum, to hyr vnkles, to norishe. And at the last, when it
was knowne that agaynst the lawe she had sauyde hyr fathers
lyfe, the women sett vppon hyr all in a rage, in somuche she had

---

laudabilius quam his humanitate atque honore vices reddere, 20
quorum labore inualidi alimenta sumpsimus, solertia tutati
sumus et amore incessabili in prouectiorem etatem deducti et
instructi moribus et doctrina, necnon honoribus atque facultatibus
aucti et ingenio valemus et moribus? Nil, equidem! Que cum
ab Ysiphile impensa sint cum cura parenti, non immerito 25
illustribus addita mulieribus est. Ea igitur regnante, seu vi
ventorum impulsus seu ex proposito deuectus, cum Argonautis
in Colcon redeuntibus Iason frustra prohibentibus feminis
occupato litore, a regina hospicio atque lecto susceptus est. Ex
quo abeunte cum geminos in tempore peperisset filios eosque 30
Le[m]niadum lege cogeretur emittere, vt placet aliquibus, in
Chium ad auum nutriendos iussit efferri. Ex quo cognito quod
seruato patre decepisset reliquas, in eam concursum est, vt vix

24 Nil, equidem] *om.* B.   Que] atque B.   25 Ysiphile] omnia officia
add. B.   28 Colcon] Colchon B, cholchon U.   redeuntibus] tendenti-
bus BU.   31 leuinia dum LS.   32 efferri] offerri BU.   33 vt] et BU.

muche wo*u*rke to do to entre a shyppe and saue hyrself. And as
she saylyde in sekynge hyr father and chyldren, sodeynly by
pyrates of the see she was taken and trobled, *and* tost here ande
ther, [and] at the last delyu*e*ryde to Lygurgus, the Kynge of
5 [N]e[m]eus, for a greate gyfte, by whom she receyuyde the
custody of the Kynges sonne, called Opheltis. And as she was
attendynge of hym and had desyre to drynke, leuynge the litle
chylde playnge emonge the flowres, it hapnede by hyr passyde
Adrastius, goynge toward*es* Thebes, and he questionde with hyr
f. 18*a* of hyr fortune. She declaryde and tolde hym all | [and] the
11 Kynge so confortyd hyr, saynge that she shulde shortly to-
cum to better chaunce. But when she was returnyde to hir yong
chylde, in hyr absence a serpent had slayne hym, for whiche she
made suche sorowe and lamentatione that well nere she troblede
15 all Ad[r]ascus hoste. And at the last the thynge knowne to
Lygurgus, she half madde and more was res*e*ruyde to a straynge
deathe. But what deathe I cannot tell.

5 Meneus MS.   15 Adascus MS.

---

conscensa naui a furore seruata publico, dum patrem natosque
quereret, a pyratis capta et in seruitutem deducta est varijsque
20 exanelata laboribus Lygurgo, Nemeo regi, dono data, curam
Opheltis, paruuli et vnici Lygurgi filij, suscepit. Cui dum vacaret
obsequio, transeunti atque propter es[t]um siti periclitanti
Ad[r]asti, Argiuorum regis, exercitui in Thebas eunti rogata,
Longiam ostendit, relicto in pratis inter flores alumno. Verum,
25 dum percunctanti Ad[r]asto preteritos exponeret casus, ab
Eunoe et Thoante adultis filijs et sub rege militantibus cognita
atque in spem fortune melioris erepta, ludentem inter herbas
alumnum cum verbere caude serpentis comperisset occisum,
fere plangoribus totum turbauit exercitum, a quo n[a]tisque
30 furenti ob dolorem Lygurgo subtracta, incognito mihi euentui
mortique, seruata est.

19 quereret] et *add.* BU.   20 exanelata] exantlatis B, exanelatis U.
Lyg. Nem.] Lycurgo Nemeæ que in Arcadia B.   22 esum LS.   23
Adiasti LS.   24 Longiam] Langiam fontem B, langiam U.   25
Adiasto LS.   27 erepta] erecta B.   29 exercitum] exercitium U.
notisque LS.   30 subtracta] subacta B.

Off Medea, Quene of Colchos.
The xvjth Chapitre.

MEdea, the verey techer of the auncyent cruelty, was the doughter of the noble Oetes by Perse his wyfe, and metely fayre, but in wytche crafte moste cunynge of all women. For 5 what maister so euer she had, suche knowledge was in hyr to knowe the vertue of herbes that neuer noone knewe theym better. She coulde by hyr arte and enchauntmente troble the skye and make the wyndes to blowe, to cause tempest*es*, the ryuers to stande and, to thys, mengle poysones together, and to smyte 10 fyre *and* make it borne where she wolde, *and* many myscheuouse moo actes whiche I ouer passe. Neyther hyr vngraciouse mynde was not muche discrepant frome hyr craft, for where that faylede, she coulde well vse the swerde. Now it fortuned in those dayes that Jasone beynge a yonge gentle man, that Pelias hys vncle 15 lyinge in wayte, vndre the pretense to sende the sayde Jasone to wynne in Colcos the Golden Flees, to haue had hym destroyede,

---

De Medea, regina Colcorum. xvi.

MEdea, seuissimum veteris perfidie documentum, Oete, clarissimi regis Colcorum, et Perse coniugis filia fuit, 20 formosa satis et maleficiorum longe doctissima. Nam, a quocunque magistro instructa sit, adeo herbarum vires familiares habuit, vt nemo melius, nouitque plane cantato carmine turbare celum, ventos ex antris ciere, tempestates mouere, flumina sistere, venena conficere, elaborantes ignes ad quodcunque incendium 25 componere et huiusmodi perficere omnia. Nec illi, quod longe peius, ab artibus fuit dissonus animus; nam deficientibus eis ferro vti arbitrabatur leuissimum. Hec Iasonem Thesalum, eo seculo conspicuum virtute iuuenem, a Pelia patruo, sue probitati insidianti, sub pretextu gloriosissime expeditionis missum in 30 Colcos ad aureum surripiendum vellus, eiusdem capta prestancia

18 Colcorum] Colchorum BU.   19 Oete] filij Persæ *add.* B.   20 Perse] Hypsee B.   23 plane] plene U, *om.* B.   25 elaborantes] elaboratos BU. 27 nam] his *add.* B.   eis] *om.* B.   29 sue] *om.* B.   probitati] Iasonis *add.* B.   31 surripiendum] suscipiendum BU.

whiche Jason, aryuynge at Colchos, was ardently belouede of
Medea. And she, to gett his fauo*ur*, caused a rumor to ryse
emonge hyr father subiect*es*, in suche wyse *tha*t whyles they
straue and foughte togethre, Jason, hyr loue, had space *and*
5 tyme to haue hys entent. What a deede that was, lett a wyse
f. 18*b* ma*n* well | considre that with oones lokynge on Jasone she
was so taken in loue that it folowede to be the ruyne of hyr
oune naturall father! This vngratiouse pagente playde, when
therby she hade obteyned to lye in Jasones armes, takynge with
10 hyr all hyr fathers s*u*bsta*u*nce, pryuylie with hym she went
a waye. And besydes thys, not so contentyd, she myndyde more
myschife. Castynge in hyr fantasye that Oetes wolde folowe
theym that fledde, to stay hym, in an ile callede Tomitania, by
which neades Oetes shulde passe in folowynge thei*m*, hauynge
15 with hyr hyr yonge brother callede Absoetes, she caused hym to
be cutt in pecys and the partes therof to be throwne here and
ther by the feldes, to that entent that when hyr sorowfull father
shulde goo aboute to gather theym together, Jasone and she
myghte the better escape away. Nor he was not deceyuyde of
20 hyr entent, for after that sorte it chauncyde. At the laste,

dilexit ardenter egitque ad eius promerendam gratiam, vt [orta]
inter incolas seditione patri suscitaretur bellum et consequendi
votum Iasoni spacium prestaretur. Quis hoc etiam sensatus
arbitraretur homo, quod ex vno oculorum intuitu opulentissimi
25 regis exterminium sequeretur? Eo igitur patrato scelere, cum
dilecti iuuenis meruisset amplexus, cum eodem secum patriam
substantiam omnem trahens, clam fugam arripuit nec tam grandi
facinore contenta in peius trucem diuertit animum: arbitrata
quidem Oetam secuturum profugos, ad eum sistendum in Thomi-
30 tania, Ph[a]sidis insula, per quam secuturo transitus futurus
erat, Absirtum seu Egialeum puerum, fratrem suum, quem in
hoc secum fuge comitem traxerat, obtruncari et eius membra
passim per arua dispergi iussit, vt, dum sparsa miserabilis recolli-
geret genitor et eis lacrimas tumulumque daret, fugientibus etiam
35 fuge spacium commodaret. Nec eam fefellerat opinio; sic enim

21 *om.* LS.   29 quidem] quidam S.   30 phisidis LS.   31 Absirtium
LS, absirtim U.   34 et] vt U, *om.* B.   tumulumque] cumulumque U.
etiam] interim B.

suffreynge muche troble, she aryuyde with Jason into Thessaly.
Now Eson, beynge wonders olde, was so gladd of the cumynge
home of his sonne and of hyr *that* it semyde he was for ioy made
a yonge man agayne. Whiche when Medea p*er*ceyuyde, w*ith* all
haste she coulde, she sowde debate betwyxt Eson and his children, 5
and dyd so muche that shee armyde the children agaynst the
father to make hyr husbonde Jason kynge. But at the laste,
Jason, abhorry*n*g hyr by thiese ways, in the place of hyr toke to
hys wyfe Crewsa, the doughter of C[r]eon, Kynge of Corynthe,
whereat Medea was so impacient that by hyr wytche crafte, in 10
the syght of Jasone, with fyre she burnte not oonely Crewsa, but
also the children that Jasone had had by hyr, and so fledd to
Athenes, and ther was maryede to the Kynge, by whome she had
a sonne, *and* wolde haue slayne with poysone Thesius, to th'entent
to haue made hir sonne heyre, but Thesius p*r*euentyd with goode 15
remedy and, hyr myschyfe knowne, yet agayne she fledde.
And at the laste, | hauynge obteynede the fauo*ur* of Jasone, f. 19*a*

factum est. Tandem, cum post errores plurimos in Thesaliam cum
Iasone deuenisset suo, Esonemque socerum tam ex reditu nati
quam ex parta victoria predaque et illustri coniugio tanta 20
replesset leticia, vt reuocatus in floridam videretur etatem,
Iasoni paratura regnum arte sua zizaniam inter nat[o]s et Peliam
seuit e[o]sque misere armauit in patrem. Ceterum, labentibus
annis exosa Iasoni facta et ab eodem loco eius Creusa, filia
Creontis, Chorinthiorum regis, assumpta, impaciens fremensque, 25
cum multa in Iasonem excogitasset, eo prorupit, vt ingenio suo
Creusam Creontisque regiam omnem absumeret igne volatili et
spectante Iasone, quos ex eo susceperat filios, trucidaret et
aufugeret in Athenas, vbi, Egeo nupta regi, cum Medum a se
[denomina]tum iam filium suscepisset ex eo et frustra Theseum 30
redeuntem temptasset occidere veneno, tercio fugam arripuit et,

20 parta] aperta BU.   21 replesset] replebat B.   22 natas LS.
Peliam] Thessalis fratrem Æsonis *add*. B.   23 easque LS.   24
Creusa] Glauca B.   25 Chorinthiorum] Corinthiorum BU.   27 Creusam
. . . absumeret] creusam creontisque filiam regina omnem assumeret U,
Glaucam Creontis filiam & Creontem cum regia omne absumeret B.   30
tum L, demonia tum S.   et] cum *add*. BU.   31 temptasset] tentasset
B, temtasset U.   occidere] occideret BU.

she wentt with hym agayne to Colchos and restorede hyr father
to hys kyngedome. What she dyd after, or whether she wentt,
or where she dyede, I do not remembre that I haue redde it.
But because it shulde not seeme that I shulde forgett, I say it is
5 not con̄uenyente to let our eyes to largely go aboute to beholde
womene. In lokynge on theym, what do we but drawe our hert*es*
to all con̄cupiscencys, that moue vs to couetouse, that maketh
vs to prayse theyr beauty and often to blowe theyr deformyte
vnaduysedly? And by that meanes, not beynge rightfull iudges,
10 we condempne often goodenes *and* saue that which is noughte,
with blottynge *and* infectynge o*ur* myndes with to shamefull
cogitationes. Suche then as be thus taken w*ith* thys dishonest
beautie, the cause of theyr takynge is noo other but wanton
lookes, wanton gestures, wherby Cupyde bloweth the fyre, tyll

12 w*ith*] that *add*. MS.

---

15 cum Iasonis in gratiam redijsset, vna cum eo, omni Thesalia ab
Agialeo, Pelie filio, pulsi, repatriauit in Colchos senemque atque
exulem patrem regno restituit. Quid tandem egerit quoue sub
celo seu mortis genere diem clausit, nec legisse memini nec
audisse. Sed, ne obmiserim, non omnis oculis prestanda licentia
20 est. Eis enim spectantibus splendores cognoscimus, inuidiam
introducimus, concupiscentias attrahimus omnes; eis agentibus
excitatur auaricia, laudatur formositas, damnatur squalor et
pauperitas indigne, et, cum indocti sint iudices et superficiebus
rerum tantummodo credant, sacris ignominiosa, ficta veris et
25 anxia [letis] persepe preficiunt et, dum abicienda commendant et
breui blandientia tractu, inficiunt nonnunquam animos turpissima labe. Hij nescij a formositate etiam inhonesta, a lasciuis
gesticulationibus, a petulantia iuuenili mordacibus vncis
capiuntur, trahuntur, rapiuntur tenenturque, et, cum pectoris
30 ianua sint [oculi], per eos menti nuncios mittit libido, per eos
Cupido insufflat suspiria: et totos incendit ignes, per eos emittit

15 redijsset] redisset BU.   16 atque *om*. BU.   21 con-
cupiscentias] concubinas B, concupinas U.   omnes] omnis B.
22 auaricia] audacia BU.   23 superficiebus] superficietatibus S.
24 ignominiosa] ignominosa BU.   25 *om*. LS.   28 vicijs BU.
30 *om*. LBSU.   31 totos] cæcos B, cecos U.

the verey trueth, howe it is, be opp*r*essyde. If the*n* men were wyse, other they wolde looke vpp w*ith* their eyes to heuen, or ell*es* shett theim and looke downward*es* to the earthe; betwyxt bothe is noo sure way. And therefore we shulde with a sharpe bytt, as it were, to rule our eyes frome beholdynge suche folyes. 5 And if Medea had bene soo circumspecte as so to haue doone, whe*n* she fyrst behelde Jasone, hyr fathers kyngedome had stonde longare in hono*ur*, hyr brother had bene alyue, and hyr maydenhode vncorrupte, which all perysshede by suche regardes and vnhoneste lookes. 10

Off Aragne, a woman of Colophone.
The xvij[th] Chapitre.

ARagne of Asia was a woman of the country, that is to meane, of noo greate stocke borne, *and* she was doughter to Colophonia, a dyare of woole; *and* | albe it she was descendyd of a basse f. 19*b* stocke, yet is she by dyuers notable vertewes in hyr worthy 16 to be co*m*mendyde. Su*m* auncye*n*t wryters thynke she was the

---

cor gemitus et affectus suos ostendit illecebres. Quos, si quis recte saperet, aut clauderet aut in celum erigeret aut in terram demergeret; n[u]llum illis inter vtrumque tutum iter est; quod si 20 omnino peragendum sit, acri sunt prohibendi, ne lasciuiant, freno. Apposuit illis natura fores, non vt in somnum clauderentur solum, sed vt obsisterent noxijs. Eos quippe si potens clausisset Medea aut aliorsum flexisset, dum erexit auida in Iasonem, stetisset diutius potentia patris, vita fratris et sue virginitatis 25 decus infractum, que omnia horum impudicicia periere.

De Aragne, Colophonia muliere. xvij.

ARagnes, Asiatica atque plebeia femina, Ydomonij, Colophonij lanarum tinctoris, fuit filia, que, quamquam origine minus clara fuerit, nonnullis tamen meritis extollenda est. Asserunt 30 quidam veteres lini vsum eius fuisse [industria] inuentum eamque

fyrste that founde the vse to weife lynnyne clothe, and to make
and knytt net*tes* to catche fyshe *and* fowlle. And when hyr
sonne, whose name was Closter, was comen to age, she taught
hym so to dye and stayne coloures *that* noo peynture coulde haue
5 amendyd it. Whereby it is thoughte, as I haue sayde, she was
the fynder of that crafte; and surely, this in a woman is not to
be despysede. Now she had not oonely the exercyse of weyuynge
in Epheis where she dwelte, but eu*ery* wher aboute hyr hyr scyens
was praysede so muche that she fell in so greate pryde that she
10 comparede with the goddesse Pallas with hyr cunnynge. And
when she coulde not well susteyne to be ouercomen by Pallas,
by desperation she toke a halter *and* hangde hyrself, whiche gaue
place to thiese poe*tes* to feyne. For as the name of Aragne dothe
goo nyghe the name of that worme callyde a spy*n*nar, whiche
15 allways is weuynge wondersly the coppewebb*es*, they say that
Aragne by the pyte of the goddes was conuertid into a spynnar
and styll occupyede aboute the arte or craft of spynnynge. And
sum say, all thoughe she put the halter aboute hyr necke, yet

---

primam recia excogitasse, aucupatoria seu piscatoria fuerint in-
20 certum. Et cum eius filius, cui nomen Closter fuit, fusos lanificio
aptos reperisset, arbitrantur quidam hanc texture artis principa-
tum suo euo tenuisse, ta[m]qu[e] circa hanc grandis ingenij, vt
digitis filisque et spatula et alijs tali officio oportunis id egisse[t]
quod pictor peregisset peniculo. Non equidem in muliere spernen-
25 dum officium. Sane, dum non solum Ypheis cohabitans textrinam
habebat, sed vbique se fama celebrem audiret, adeo elata est,
vt ausa sit aduersus Palladem huius artis repertricem certamen
inire, et cum se superari equo animo ferre non posset, induto
laqueo vitam finiuit. Ex quo locus fingentibus datus est, nam,
30 cum nomine exercicio[que] aranea vermis cum Aragne conueniat
et filo pendeat et ipsa pependit laqueo, Aragnem miseratione
deorum in araneam versam dixere et assidua cura pristino vacare
seruicio. Alij vero dicunt quod esto laqueum induerit moritura,

19–20 fuerint incertum] fundere in terram LS.   22 tamque]
tanquam L, tamquam S.   23 filisque] filijsque S.   egisse LS.
24 penniculo LS, penicillo B, pinniculo U.   25 Ypheis] Colophonijs
B.   30 exercicio LS.   31 et 2°] vt BU.   pependit] pendebat BU.

by the helpynge of other she was lett to hange hyr self *and* constraynede allways to weeue, as it is sayde nowe. If ther be any so insolent to weene hymself to *p*recelle all other in any craft, lett Aragnes aunswer therunto whether that she myght by pryde tor[n]e the heuyn and so drawe all sciences to hyrselfe, or whether 5 God was so benygne to hyre prayers that, as who shulde say, he shuldnot take cure of noo more but vppon hyr oonely, to make hyr moste cunnynge in hyr crafte. Surely, so to beleue is to [beleue] an exedynge foly, for that eternall wysdome not alonely to one wytte, but to dyuers hathe and dothe geue variete of 10 sciences, as hym semythe best, in suche wyse that those, that do | flee idlenes by exercyse of naturall mouynge, do cum to f. 20*a* wounders knowledge, not after one fortune nor sorte, but by diuers. And if this be true, as it is in deede, what can lett but that science oone hathe, another may haue; and for oone to 15 thynke hymself more cunnyng then he is, in deede is sygne of a verey folyshe and vnwytty wytte. I wolde to God we hadd no more to laughe at then thys Aragne. But ther be many in suche

5 tore MS.

non tamen mortuam adiutorio interueniente suorum, sed artificio posito dolore vacasse. Nunc autem, si quis est, obsecro, qui se 20 credat in aliquo anteire ceteros, dicat, si libet Aragnes ipsa, an celum vertere et in se dignitates omnes trahere potuisse arbitretur, aut potius ipsum deum, rerum satorem omnium, precibus et meritis sic in se benignum fecisse potuerit, vt adaperto munificentie sue sinu in illam gratias effundere cunctas coegerit 25 omissis ceteris. Sed quid quero, sicut hec arbitrata videtur? Stultissimum, Hercle! vertit eterna lege natura celum et apta rebus varijs ingenia cunctis prebet. Hec prout ocio atque desidia torpentia fiunt, sic studijs et exercicio luculenta et maximarum rerum capacia, et eadem impellente natura in rerum omnium 30 noticiam desiderio vehuntur: esto non eadem solercia vel fortuna. Et si sic est, quid obstat quin multi possint eadem in re pares effici? Et ob id quemquam se solum existimare inter tam innumerabilem mortalium multitudinem cursu preualere ceteris ad gloriam stolide mentis est. Optarem quippe vt Aragnes vnica 35

19 suorum] seruorum BU.   artificioso LS.   23 satorem] factorem BU.
24 potuerit] *om*. B.   26 sicut] sic et BU.   29 fiunt] *om*. B.
30 capacia] fiunt *add*. B.   31 vehuntur] vehimur BU.   32 eadem
in re] eodem iure B.

madnesse that, whyles they be in pryde, they enhaunce theymselfe aboue other *and* make that Aragnes is the lesse to be
laughte at, hauynge so many felowes.

Off Orithia and Anthiobe, Quenes of the Amozanes.

5   The xviijth Chapitre.

ORithia was the doughter of Marpesia, which was Quene of
the Amazones. And after hyr mothers death, with Anthiobe,
whiche many wryte to be hyr suster, they twayne reynede ther
as qwenes. Now this Orithia was a ryght exellente virgyne and
10 dyd [in] batells w*i*th hyr suster Anthiobe, that reygnede with hyr,
so many notable actes that, to hyr highe hono*ur*, she greately
encreasced hyr empyre. In so muche that Euristeus, the Kynge
of Mesena, all thoughe he were wonders myghty, thought it
hardd to wynne frome hyr a gerdle, whiche she waare, of a greate
15 pryce, and for that desyrede Hercules, as they say, to haue
spoyled that same ensyne fro*m* hyr. It was a verey hyghe glorye

---

in hoc nobis esset ridiculum, cum sint innumeri tanta illaqueati
dementia, qui, dum se in precipicium stolide presumptionis
efferunt, Aragnem minus ridendam faciunt.

20   De Orithia et Anthiobe, reginis Amazonum. xviij.

ORithia Marpesie fuit filia, et vna cum Anthiobe, quam
quid[a]m sororem existimant suam, post Marpesiam Amazonum regina fuit et ante alia virginitate insignis et commendanda
plurimum, tantum cum consorte regni Anthiobe bellis valuit, vt
25 multis Amazonum imperium honoribus ampliarit et adeo mili-
taris discipline suas laudes extulit, vt arbitraretur Euristeus,
Micenarum rex, durum posse bello eius obtineri baltheum et ob
id aiunt debitori Herculi tanquam maximum iniunctum, vt illud
a⌊u⌋ferret eidem. Eximia quippe mulieri gloria est, sibi ob

17 in hoc] huius vanitatis nobis ridiculum præberet B, in hec U.   19
ridendam] irridendam BU.   20 Anthiobe] Anthiope B.   21 Marpesie]
marsepie U, Marthesiæ B.   Anthiobe] anthiope S.   22 quidem L.   22–3
Amazonum] amasonum U.   24 Anthiobe] anthiope S.   25 ampliarit]
ampliauerit B, ampliauit U.   26 Euristeus] mnesteus U.   29 afferret LS.

to hyr that Hercules, which was conquero*ur* of all thynges,
shulde make warr vppon hyre; which, when he made expedicyon
ꞏand had entrede with nyene greate shyppes and occupiede their
fronters, in the absence of Orithia it was noo greate wonders
thoughe easely they were ouerco*m*men, | beynge so fewe as they f. 20*b*
were. Thus was taken the noble Menalyppe and Ipolite, susters, 6
wherby Anthiobe was co*n*strayned to geue vpp Orithias gerdle,
but after the gerdle restoryde agayne to Menalippe. And so
when Orithya was reuertyd and herde that Theseus had taken
with hym Ipolite, thys vallyaunte lady was not aferde with hyr 10
army to inuade Grece, but, forsaken of theym that shulde haue
comen to hyr ayde, and oue*r*comen by the Athenyens, she was
compellyd to reuerte agayne into hyr kyngdome. Nor what she
dyd afterwarde I do not remembre that I haue herde it.

Off Erithrea Sibilla. 15
The xixth Chapitre.

SIbilla Erithrea was a muche noble woman, and ther was ten
of thies Sibills, as the moste p*ar*te wryteth, and they gyue to

---

splendidam armorum virtutem obiectum Herculem cuncta super-
antem. Cuius cum expeditionem intrasset et nouem longis nauibus 20
Amazonum occupasset litus, absente Orithia in tumultuantes,
Amazones ob paucitatem et incuriam de se facile victoriam prebuere capteque Mena[li]p[p]e et Ypolite, sorores, Anthiobe, dato
regine baltheo, Menalippe restituta est. Verum, cum asportasse
Ypolitem Theseum expeditionis socium audisset Orithia, in 25
Greciam omnium conuocatis auxilijs bellum mouere ausa est:
sed ob dissensionem ab auxilijs derelicta, ab Atheniensibus
s[u]parata in regnum redijt, nec quid egerit vlte[r]ius inuenisse
recordor.

[De Erithrea Sibylla.] 30

ERithrea seu Eriphila mulier ex Sibillis vna et insignis plurimum fuit. Quas quidem Sibillas decem fuisse numero
quidam putant easque proprijs designant nominibus et, quoniam

20 nouem] nomen S.   23 menapelle LS.   Ypolite] Hyppolite B.
anthiope S.   26 omnium] omnem BU.   27 derelicta] relicta BU.
28 separata LS.

eche one of theym sundry names. And for because they were all
pr*o*phett*es*, they were surnamede Sibills, for this worde 'Sios' in
the Greke signifyeth 'God' and in the Laten 'God', and 'Bilos',
as it were, 'the mynde of God', or 'berynge Gode in their myndes'.
5 Of which ten Sibills this aboue all other was the moste venerable.
And hir beynge was in Babilone, sumwhat afore the battell of
Troy, albeit that ther be sum that weene that it was she that
prophesyde, whe*n* Romulus was Kynge of the Romaynes. The
name of thys woma*n*, as I haue sayde, was Erith[r]ea, and it is
10 thought that she was so called, because that she longe dwellyd
in an ile called Erith[r]ea, wher were founde diuers of hyr pr*o*-
phecyse. Ther was in thys woman so muche wytte and so muche
deuocyone toward*es* God that not wit*h*oute a speciall grace of
f. 21*a* God she des*er*uyde, if it be true, the which is writte*n* | of hyr,
15 with so greate clerenesse to declare the thynges to cum that
it semyde better the Gospell then a pr*o*phecy. And when the
Grek*es* demaundyd o[f] hyr how they shulde pr*o*spere goynge to

plurimum vaticinio valuere omnes, Sibillas cognominant. Nam
'syos' Celico sermone 'deus' Latine sonat, 'biles' autem 'mentem'
20 dici dixere, et ideo Sibille, quasi 'ment[is] diuine' seu 'mente deum
gerentes'. Ex quibus venerabilibus omnibus hanc fuisse celeberri-
mam referunt et eius apud Babilonios aliquandiu ante Troyanum
bellum fuisse originem, esto nonnulli eam Romuli, Romanorum
regis, tempor[e] vaticinatam putent. Huius, vt quidam dicunt,
25 nomen fuit Eriphila seu Erithrea, ideo nominata, quia apud
Erithream insulam diu morata sit et ibidem plurima eius carmina
sint comperta. Fuit igitur tantum eius ingenij aut orationis aut
deuotionis meritum in conspectu dei, vt vigili studio, non absque
diuino munere, meruit (si verum sit ab ea dictum, quod legitur)
30 futura tanta claritate describere, vt euangelium potius quam
vaticinium videatur. Hec quidem percunctantibus Grecis tam
prelucide suos labores et Ylionis excidium descripsit carmine, vt

18 omnes] et quod diuina consilia nossent *add.* B.   Sibillas] sic illas
BSU.   18–20 Nam . . . dixere] Nam Aeoli οἴους deos uocant, & βουλή
consilium deorum Latine sonat B.   19 Celico] eolico U.   mentem]
mente U.   20 mentis] mente LSU.   23 esto] ast BU.   24 temporis
LS.   putent] putant BU.   25 seu] sed BU.   27 tantum] tanta vis
BU.   29 meruit] meruerit B.   32 Ylionis] Ilij B.

besege Troy, she tolde the c[o]u[r]se of it so planely that it coulde
not be no better telde. So dyd she of the empyre of Rome with
fewe versys tell their chauncys so planely that the declarynge
semyde a thynge past, rather then that for to cum. And that
which by my iudgement is muche more, the secrete, dyuyne 5
thynges inuoluyde in the prophetes of the Incarnatione of Christe,
by the grace of the Holy Gooste, she planely declarede it all. The
lyfe of the Son of God and His wourkes *and* how [He] was
betrayede, mockede and scornede, *and* suffrede death, *and* after
rose agayne—all thies mysteries were by hyr openede *and* tolde; 10
by which merytes I thynke vereyly that God louede hyr, and for
that she oughte to be aboue all the gentyles laudyd *and* to be
credyde. And ther be that affyrme that she lyuyde a perpetuall
virgyne, whiche I beleue right well, for asmuche as it was not
possible so muche holynes to remayne but onely in a chaste 15
breste, nor so muche ly[ght]e therto. But in what houre or when
she decessyd, it is oute of mynde.

1 cause MS.　　　16 lyethe MS.

nil post factum quam ante nosceretur clarius. Sic et Romanorum
imperium casusque varios paucis versibus complexa est longe
ante eius inicium, vt nostro seculo breue[m] potius epytoma[m] 20
scripsisse videatur quam predixisse futurum et, quod longe maius
meo iudicio est, archanum diuine mentis, non nisi per figuras
rerum et implicata prophetarum, ymo sancti spiritus per pro-
phecie verba predictum aperuit incarnandi verbi misterium, iam
nati vitam et opera, proditionem, capturam, illusiones et in- 25
honestam mortem resurrectionisque triumphum et ascensionem
et ad extremum iudicium reditum, vt hystoriam dictasse, non
venturos predixisse actus ap[p]areat. Quibus meritis et dilectissimam deo fuisse arbitror et pre ceteris gentilium mulieribus
venerandam. Sunt qui asserant insuper eam virginitate perpetua 30
floruisse, quod ego facile credam; non enim in contagioso pectore
tanta futurorum lux effulsisse potuisset. Quo tempore seu qua
in parte decesserit, abolitum est.

20 breue LSU.　　epythoma LS, epithoma U, Epitomē B.　　21 et]
homo *add*. B, huius U.　　22 non nisi] necnon B.　　23 rerum] veterum
BU, verum S.　　27 reditum] rediturum LS.　　28 apareat LS
30 asserant] asserunt BU.　　32 effulsisse] euulsisse S.

Off Medusa, the doughter of Phorci.
The xx^ti Chapitre.

MEdusa was the doughter and heyre of the ryche Kynge
Phorcis, and hyr kyngdome was neere the see called
5 Athlanticu*m*, whiche many beleue to be the ilis of Hesperyde.
Thys woman, if we shall geue credyte to the olde, auncyent
wryters, was of so an excedynge beautie that not onely she sur-
mountyde all others, but, to thys, she semyde a creature in
fayrenes aboue nature, that she mouyde dyuers that dwelte
f. 21*b* farr fro*m* | hyr onely to trauell to beholde hyr. For she had a
11 heere lyke the golden wyere, and a face of beautye meruelouse,
and a body of shappe and stature so equall in all feturs that it
myght nott be amendyde; but aboue all thynges she had so
swete and delicate eyes that whome she gentlely and pleasauntly
15 regardyd, she made theym, as one shulde say, vnmouable, and
as thoughe they had forgotten theymsel*ff*es. Besydes thys, sum
affyrme hyr to be moste cunnynge in knowynge the tyllynge and
planty[nge] of trees and of all suche thynges that belonges therto,

18 plantys MS.

De Medusa, filia Phorci.
20 ### xx. Cap.

MEdusa Phorci, ditissimi regis, heres fuit et filia, eique
opulentissimum regnum extitit in Athlantico mari, quod
Hesperidas fuisse insulas nonnulli credidere. Hec, si fidem
vetustati prestare possumus, tam admirande fuit pulchritudinis,
25 vt non solum excederet ceteros sed quasi quoddam preter
naturam mirabile quam plurimos ad se videndam excitaret
homines. Fuit quidem illi capillicium aureum et [nu]m[e]rosum,
faciei decus precipuum et digna proceritate corpus elatum; sed
inter cetera tam grandis ac placidus oculorum illi fuit vigor, vt
30 quos benigne respiceret, fere immobiles et sui nescios redderet.
Preterea nonnulli eam agricolationis fuisse peritissimam asserunt

19 Phorcys B.   21 Phorcys B.   22 in] *om.* BU.   Athlantico]
a thlantico U, Atlantico B, athlautiaco S.   24 possumus] possimus BU.
25 ceteros] ceteras BU.   27 mirosum LS.   31 agricolationis] agriculationis BU.

and for that to haue obteynede the surname of Gorgonis. By
whiche worke, with a wou*nder*s wytty facyon, not onely she
sauyde and kepte hyr fathers su*bsta*nce, but therto belongynge
greatly encreascede it, in so muche that i*n* ryches she passyde
all the prynces of the Occident. And thus, what with hyr beautie 5
and what wi*th* hyr ryches, frome a farr emongste straynge
naciones she was so renomed that, emonge the other cou*n*treys,
her name came to the Argyuys, where that Persyus, beyng a
yonge, lusty gentleman, herynge of hyr fame, was soore desyrous
to see hyr p*er*sone and to occupye hyr threasure, and hauynge a 10
shypp namede Pegasus of wounders swyftnes, w*it*h a meruelouse
celerite saylede thyder, and ther so wysely wentt to wo*ur*ke that
he not oonely by armys vaynquisshede the quene, but toke also
hyr treasoure, and lodyne, as it were, with ryches, wentt to hys
countrey agayne. Of thys the poet*es* haue founde place howe to 15
feyne. To that, it is redde that Medusa conuertyde theym into
stoones whome she behelde, and that hyr fayre heere was
turnyde into serpent*es*, for asmuche as that she hade a*n*greade
Mynerua with pollutynge in fleshly pleasure hyr temple w*it*h
Neptun*us*, and that for to punyshe hyr offence, Pegasius, syttynge 20

eamque inde Gorgonis consecutam cognomen, cuius opere mira
cum sagacitate non solum patrias seruauit diuicias sed in immen-
sum auxit, adeo vt qui [n]ouere crederent eam occiduos quoscunque reges anteire thesauris. Et sic tam pulchritudine eximia
quam etiam opulentia et sagacitate in amplissimam famam apud 25
remotas etiam nationes euasit. Verum, inter alios celebri rumore
ad Argiuos delata est, quos inter Perseus, iuuentutis Achiue
florentissimus, audito talium relatu in desiderium incidit et
videndi speciosissimam feminam et occupandi thesauros, et sic
naui conscensa, cui Pegasus equus erat insigne, in occasum celeri- 30
tate mirabili deuectus est ibique prudentia vsus et armis reginam
occupauit et auro et opima onustus preda remeauit ad suos. Ex
his locum sibi poetica adinuenit fictio, qua legimus Medusam
Gorgonem assuetam saxeos facere quos inspiceret eiusque crines
versos in angues ira Minerue, eo quod templum eius Neptuni 35
concubitu viciasset peperissetque Pegasum et Perseum equo

22 patrias] proprias BU.   in] *om.* BU.   23 voluere L, vouere S.   eam]
iam B.   26 inter alios] *om.* B.   32 honustus LS.   35 eo quod] eoque S.

vppon a flyeng hors, entrede hyr countrye and spoyled hyr treasure frome hyr. It is an vngraciouse possessione to haue golde *and* treasure, and they be not well vsyde to noo profyte to the
f. 22a haver. And all though golde shyne | fayre, yet of it cumeth
5 all mysery. For he that possessythe the golde, ferythe a thowsande maner of ways to be spoyled of it, so that hys reste is taken away and hys sleepe, feare enters the mynde, and trust is mynyshede, and suspectione doth encreas; and breuely, all the honeste vse of lyfe by couetouse is lettyde. And if by sum
10 infortunate chaunce hys goode be lost, taken, or spoylede, he is deuourede and torne in pecys with cures to be made of a couetouse man a poore man. Then laugheth at hym the liberall man, the enuyouse scornythe hym, and his mysery emonge the vulgar people is noo better but a fable.

15 Off Yole, the doughter of the Kynge [of] Ethioll.
The xxjᵗⁱ Chapitre.

YOle, the doughter of the Kynge of Ethioll, emonge the other virgynes of that regione was of exellente beaute. Ther be

---

ins[i]dentem alato eius in regnum euolasse et Pallanthei egidis
20 vsu superasse. Infelix auri possessio est, quod, si lateat, possessori nullius est commodi: [si] fulgeat, mille concupiscentium nascuntur insidie: etsi stent violentorum manus, non cessant possidentis anxie cure; fugatur enim quies animi, subtrahitur somnus, timor ingreditur, fides minuitur, augetur suspicio et
25 omnis breuiter vite vsus impeditur misero. Si vero casu quocunque pereat, anxietatibus excarnificatur pauper factus, auarus laudat, liberalis ridet, inuidus consolatur, inops et omne vulgus dolentis canit in fabulam.

De Yole, Etholorum regis, filia.
30 [V]i[c]esimumprimum Capitulum.

YOlem Eurici, regis Etholie, filiam speciosissimam inter ceteras regionis illius virginem, sunt qui asserant amatam ab Hercule

19 insedentem LS, insidentes U   et Pallanthei] Pallanteique BU.   20 est] *om.* B.   21 *om.* LS.   22 etsi stent] et sistent B.   24 ingreditur] ingeritur BU.   30 Uisesimumprimum L.   31 Eurici] Euryti B, euriti U.

that say she was belouyd of Hercules, the conquero*ur* of the
wo*ur*lde. Whiche sayde Hercules hade fyrst the graunte of hyr
father to mary hyr, and after by the p*er*suasio*n* of hys sonne,
[he] denyede that Hercules shulde wedde hyr. Wherfore Hercules,
beynge wondres angry, mouede a cruell warr agaynst hym *and* 5
slewe hym. And when he had takyn hys prouynce, he toke also
hys deare belouyde Yole; whiche sayde Yole, berynge more at
hyr hertt the deathe of hyr father then she dyd the loue of Hercules, desyro*us* to be reuengyde, with a m*er*uelouse dissemylynge
loue and with other toyes she drew Hercules into so feruent a 10
fantasy with hyr that she assuryde hyrself that, what so euer
she desyred hym to do, he wolde not say 'Nay'. And so, as
though she dyd abhorre so rughe a | garmente as Hercules was f. 22b
wonte to weere, fyrst she made hym to sett asyde hys clubbe,
wherewith he was wonte to tame monsters, and aftre to caste 15
asyde the lyons skynne, whiche was a token of hys fortitude and
strength, and to sett also asyde hys shelde, hys bowe and hys
arrowes. Whiche doone, as thoughe she were not well co*n*tentid
with all, she made hym, besyds thys, to spynne of the dystafe,

orbis domitore. Cuius nupcias cum illi Euricus spopondisset, 20
ayunt, pos[c]enti, suasione filij postea denegasse. Quamobrem
iratus Hercules acre bellum mouit eidem eumque interemit
prouincia capta, et dilectissimam sibi Yolem surripuit. Que
quidem magis paterne cedis [dolore] affecta quam sponsi dilectione, vindicte auida mirabili atque constanti astucia, quem 25
gereret animum ficto amore contexit et blandicijs atque artificiosa quadam petulantia in tam feruentem sui dilectionem
Herculem traxit, vt satis aduerteret nil eum negaturum quod
posceret. Ac inde quasi horreret tam hispidum habitu amantem,
acri viro ante alia ponere clauam, qua monstra domuerat, im- 30
perauit: ponere leonis Nemei spolium, sue fortitudinis insigne,
ponere populeum sertum, pharetras sagittasque fecit. Que, cum
non satis animo sufficerent suo, audacius inermem precogitatis
telis insiluit, et primo digitos anulis orna[r]i precepit, caput

20 dormitore L.   21 possenti L.   24 *om.* LBSU.   29 Ac] At BU.
31 ponere] *om.* BU.   32 ponere] *add. comma or virgula* BU.   33
audacius] in hostem *add.* BU.   34 anulis] annulis BU.   ornati L.

to combe hys rughe heyr, to put rynges on hys fyngars, to washe
hys bearde with swete balme, and, breuely, to put a delycate
cappe on hys heade, and to clothe hys body with fyne and softe
garment*es*—thynkynge planely that to a maydyn armyde with
5 fraude *and* deceite that it was muche more to hyr hono*ur* w*ith*
suche pleasures to ouercu*m* Hercules then other with the swerde
or the malle. Ouer and besydes thys, not thynkynge to haue
reuengyde hyrself ynoughe, she soo wrought that Hercules,
geuyne to thies pleasures, satt clothyd emo*n*ge the wome*n*, as
10 he had bene a verey woman in dede, and weuynge and spynnynge
emonge the other with those fyngars that he hade in hys cradle
stranglede the serpent*es* with all. Surely, a verey sure argumente
of mans imbecillyte and of the crafte and the deceyte of women!
With thies craft*es* thys woman, reuengynge hyr fathers deathe,
15 not with strengthe but with wantonnes deceyuyde Hercules and
gatt hyr by it a fame for euer. And as many vyctoryes as
Hercules had obteyned by subduynge the monsters thoroughoute

asperum vng[u]entis c[i]pricis deliniri, et hirsutos discrim[in]ari
crines, ac hispidam vngi nardo barbam, et puellaribus cor[o]llis
20 et Meonia etiam insigniri mitra. Inde purpureos amictus molles-
que vestes precepit induere, existimans iuuencula fraudibus
armata longe plus decoris tam robustum hominem effeminasse
lasciuijs quam gladio vel aconitis occidisse. Porro, cum nec his
satis sue indignationi satisfactum arbitraretur, in id egit molliciei
25 deditum, vt etiam inter mulierculas, femineo ritu sedens, fabellas
laborum suorum narraret, et pensis a se susceptis lanam colo
neret, digitosque quos ad extinguendos in cunis adhuc infans
angues durauerat, in valida iam ymo prouecta etate [ad] extenu-
anda fila molliret. Equidem humane imbecillitatis et muliebrium
30 astuciarum non minimum intueri volentibus argumentum est.
Hac igitur animaduersione artificiosa iuuenis cum perpetua in
Herculem ignominie nota patris mortem non armis sed dolis et
lasciuia vlta est et se eterno dignam nomine fecit. Nam quotquot
ex quibuscunque monstris Euristeo triumphos victoriosus egit

18 asperum] aspersum BU.   vngentis capricis LS. hirsutos] pectine *add.*
BU. discrimari L.   19 corallis LS.   20 Inde] In B.   23 aconitis]
achonicis U.   25 vt] et S.   28 in v.] inualida BU.   prouecta] profecta
BU. ad] *om.* LS.   34 victoriosus] victoriosos BU.

the worlde, so muche the more glory it was to Yole to tryhumphe
of hym. Thys pestiferus passyon is wonte often to assaute the
delycate yonge maydyns and also the wanton and idle yonge
men, for asmuche as Cupyde allwais is a dispyser of grauyte
and of delycatnes an exellent maynteyner. And thus false 5
Cupyde dyd penetrate the harde brest of Hercules and broughte
into hym a farr more greate monster then euer he conquerede
in hys tyme, which, if he had well remembrede hym self, he
wolde not so soone haue left vertuouse laboure and | taken f. 23a
hymself to idlenes, seynge so greate an ennemye as Cupyde is, 10
dyd so assaute hym. Let vs then awaake and arme our mynd*es*
and our hertt*es*, for ther is noo man that neades agaynste hys
wyll to be vaynquysshed of hym, so that he do wythstonde the
fyrste inuasyone and begynnynge of hym, in refraynynge his
eyes frome lokynge of vanytes, and in stoppynge hys eares, as 15
the serpent dothe, frome herynge of his incantationes, and with
continuall study to suppresse wantonnes. For Loue at the fyrst
offerithe hymselfe to those that be not ware of hym gentlely and
smylyngly, and if he be receyuyde with a gladd hoope, he dothe
p*er*suade to vse gay garmentt*es*, new facyones *and* new dalyaunsys, 20

Hercules Alcides, ex tot victrix ipsius Yoles gloriosius triumphauit.
Consueuit pestifera hec passio deliciosas subire puellas et lasciuos
ocios[os]que persepe occupare iuuenes, cum grauitatis Cupido
sit spretor [et] molliciei cultor eximius, et ob id intrasse predurum
Herculis ¦pectus, longe maius monstrum est, quam que sepe 25
domuerat ipse, fuerint. Quod non modicum salutis sue sollicitis
debet iniecisse timoris et torporis etiam excu[ss]isse, cum pateat
quam validus, quam potens hostis immineat. Vigilandum igitur
est et robore plurimo nobis armanda sunt corda, non enim inuitis
incumbet. Obstandum est igitur principijs, frenandi sunt oculi, 30
ne videant vanitates, obturande sunt more aspidis aures, laboribus
assiduis est premenda lasciuia, blandus quippe incautis se offert,
et placidus intuitu primo, etsi recipiatur spe leta primo delectat
ingressu, suadet ornatus corporum, mores compositos, facecias

21 Hercules] *om.* BU.   toto LS.   23 ociosque L.   24 *om.*
LS.   26 fuerint] fuerunt BU.   27 torporis] corporis BS.   excucisse
L.   30 igitur] ergo BU.   31 obturande] obstruende BU, obscu-
rande S.

songes, dauncys, versys and playse, with deynty bankett*es* contynually. But afterwards, when by proue he hathe all ocupyede
the man, he dothe, as who shulde say, chayne or bynde the mynde
frome all libertye, bryngynge in syghes and lamentationes, and
5 oppressithe all scyences and wytte and reasone, makynge noo
differense betwyxte vyces and vertues, so that he may obteyne
that thyng that he dothe couete, takynge all hys ennemyes
that doo wit*h*stande hym. And so, the fla*m*me burnynge hys
vnhappy brest, he gothe and cu*m*methe aboute, neu*er* seasynge
10 tyll he do fynde the thynge that he sowghte; and ofte, after the
syghte, sekynge to se agayne a begynnynge to kyndle a newe
fyer. And when ther is noo place of penytence, then weepe they,
then speke they faire, flatterynge wordes; then do they enstructe
theire bawdes; then promysse they gyftes; and in verey deede
15 bothe gyue *and* take, and often deceyue theyr kepars, not
sparynge for noo watche, till at the laste they cum to pleasures
and enbrasynges. Then the ennemy to chastyte and the p*er*sua-
do*ur* to suche myschyfe dryuethe shamefastnes and honeste
cleene a way; euen as a hogge tumblynge in the myre, so is he apte

---

20 vrbicas, choreas, cantus et carmina, ludos et commessationes
atque similia. Postquam vero approbatione totum occupauerit
hominem et libertate subacta mentibus cathenis iniectis et
vinculis, differentibus preter spem votis suspiria excitat, premit
in artes ingenia, nullum discrimen faciens inter virtutes et vicia,
25 dummodo consequatur optatum, in numero ponens hostium
quecunque obstantia, hinc exurentibus flammis infelicium pectora
itur rediturque, et ambitu indefesso res amata perquiritur, et
ex iterato sepius visu semper noua contrahuntur incendia, et
cum non sit penitentie locus, itur in lachrimas, dictantur preces
30 mellitis delinite blandicijs, instruuntur lene, promittuntur
munera, donatur, proicitur, nonnunquam falluntur custodes, et
septa vigilijs capiuntur corda, et in concupitos quandoque
deuenitur amplexus. Tunc pudoris hostis et sceleris suasor rubore
et honestate fugatis, parato volutabro porcis grunnientes effundit

21 approbatione] stolida *add.* BU.   28 ex it.] exiterato BU.   31
proicitur] et *add.* BU.   32 concupitos] concubitos U.   34
grunnientes] grannientes S, grinnientes U.

to all carnall actes; then sobriete is sett asyde; Ceres and Bacchus
called, tryhumphes Venus, in suche wyse that all the nyght thorowe
they attende to noone other but to that shamefull play. Nor for
that the fury is not quenchyde, but for the more parte augmen-
tide. | Whereby the greate Hercules shall fall into that detest- f.23b
able seruytude, honour shalbe forgotten, substaunce shalbe 6
waystede, and hate shalbe armyde, often tymes to the greate
parelle of our lyfe. Nor thies thynges ar not withoute sorowse,
for nowe is stryfe, forwythe slypper peax, nowe hoope and
strayght agayne suspicione, wherby the zele of our sowlle and 10
oure body is consumede. But if a man cannot cum to that he
couettes, then loue, voyde frome all reasone, puttith, as who
shulde say, the spurres to the horse. Then is ther nothyng but
wepynges and complayntes, in so muche that sumtyme by deathe
they heele theyr malady. But fyrste they assay with wichecrafte 15
to speede; they counseile with the Caldeys, they make louynge
drynkynges with flaterynge; and streyght they turne that to
stryfe. In somuche that thys vngraciouse scoole maister bryngeth

---

illecebres coitus. Tunc sobrietate reiecta, Cerere et Bacho feruens
aduocatur Venus, noctesque tot[e] spurcido consumuntur in luxu. 20
Nec ob id semper furor extinguitur iste, quinymo persepe in
ampliorem insaniam augetur. Ex quo fit vt in obedientiam illam
detestabilem Alcides corruat, obliuiscantur honores, effundantur
substantie, armentur odia, et vite sepissime subeantur pericula.
Nec carent ista doloribus, interueniunt rixe et paces tenues, 25
rursum suspiciones et [z]elus, animarum consumptor et corporum.
Ast si minus deuenitur in votum, tunc amor rationis inops
addit[is] virge calcaribus exaggerat curas, desideria cumulat,
dolores fere intollerabiles infert, nullo nisi lacrimis et querelis et
morte nonnunquam curand[o]s remedio. Adhibentur a[n]icule, 30
consuluntur Caldei, herbarum, carminum et maleficiorum ex-
periuntur vires, blandicie vertuntur in minas, par[a]tur violentia,
damnatur frustrata dilectio. Nec deest quin aliquando tantum

19 illecebres] illecebras BU.   20 toto L.   22 augetur] augeretur B.
26 scelus L.   animarum] animorum BU.   27 tunc] tum BU.
28 addite LS, additus B.   30 curandas LS.   auicule LS.
31 herbarum] atque add. BU. maleficiorum] maleficorum B, malefactorum
U.   32 parcitur LS.

theym into [so] muche fury that they be redy to ende theyr days
with halter or with sworde, they care not whether. O, howe swete
and pleasaunt is suche loue that, in that he geuythe vs cause to
hate hym, we extolle hym so muche and exalte hym and make of
5 hym a gode; we pray to hym and w*i*th wepynge teares co*m*mytte
aduoultery and other detestable thynges not honeste to tell!

Off Dianira, Hercules wife.
The xxij^{ti} Chapitre.

Dianira was the doughter, as sum wryte, of Oenei, Kyngè of
10   the Etholiens, and suster to Melleager—so swete and so
fayre a virgyne that to haue hyr to wife Hercules and Achelaus
straue whiche shulde haue hyr. But when the victory fell to
Hercules, she was belouyde of the Centaure called Nessus. And
when Hercules dyd conuey hyr frome Calidon to hys countrey,
15 at Ebnio, a ryuer of Calidon, it fortunede Hercules to meete
f.24a with Nessus, and forbecause he was a Centaure, | that is to

---

furoris ingerat malorum artifex iste, vt miseros in laqueos
impingat et gladios. O quam dulcis, quam suauis hic amor, quem,
cum horrere ac fugere debeamus, in deum extollimus, illum
20 colimus, illum supplices oramus, et sacrum ex suspirijs lacrimisque
conficimus, stupra adulteria incestusque offerimus, et obscenita-
tum nostrarum coronas immittimus!

De Deyanira, Herculis coniuge. xxij.

Deyanira Oenei, Etholorum regis, vt quidam asserunt, fuit
25   filia et Meleagri soror, tanta insignis formositate virgo, vt ob
eius nupcias consequendas certamen inter Atheolum et Herculem
oriretur. Que, cum victori cessisset Herculi, a Nesso Centauro
adamata est, et cum illam Hercules e Calidonia transferret in
patriam, ab Ebeno, Calidonie fluuio, [imbrium pridianarum tur-
30 gido moratus], obuiam habuit amantem Nessum, se, quia eques

19 extollimus] & *add.* B.   20 oramus] exoramus BU.   23 Herculis
coniuge] Oenei Ætholorum regis filia B, U *the same, but* cenei etholorum.
24 Oenei] cenei U.   26 Atheolum] Acheloum B.   27 Centhauro
LS.   29–30 *So* U, *om.* LS, ab imbre pridiano turgido moratus B.
30 obuiam] obuium BU.

say, half a man and half a horse, Hercules requyrede hym to carye Dianira ouer the water. Nessus, gladd therof as thoughe he had wonne that pray whiche he desyrede, caryinge Dianira ouer the ryuer, as faste as he myghte, fledde away. Whiche seynge Hercules and that he coulde not ouertake hym on foote, [he] toke hys bowe 5 and a[n] arrowe inueni*m*yde and shott so directly to Nessus that he strooke hym to the deathe. Nessus, felynge hys deathe wounde, deliueryde to Dianira a shert inuenymede, *pr*omysynge Dianira that if Hercules myght put it vpon hym, he shulde neu*er* after with-drawe hys loue from hir, neither loue any other but hyr. 10 Whiche Dianira, geuynge more credyt to hym then was hyr parte, with thankes to Nessus, for a litle tyme she kept it secrete. Now Hercules fallynge in loue with Yole, Dianira by Licaon, hyr s*er*ua*un*tte, sent to Hercules the sherte, and Hercules put on the shert. At the laste, with the poysone of it so entrede hys fleshe, 15 it made Hercules stark madde, so that wylfully he entrede to a fyer and was burnte. And Dianira, viduate frome so greate a man, wenynge to saue hym, lost hym, and for sorow *ther*of, slewe hyrself.

15 fleshe] that *add.* MS.

esset, ad transportand[a]m Deyaniram vltro Herculi obsequiosum prebentem. Cui cum concessisset Hercules naturus 20 post coniugem, ipse quasi voto potitus, cum transuadasset fluuium cum dilecta, fugam arripuit, quem cum non posset pedi[b]us Hercules consequi, sagitta Lernea infecta tabe fugientem attigit. Id sentiens Nessus seque mortuum arbitratus, vestem sanguine suo infectam confestim Deyanire tradidit, asserens, sic 25 cruentam t[u]n[ica]m si induat, posse Herculem ab omni extero in suum amorem retrahere. Quam Deyanira credula loco pregrandis muneris sumens, clam aliquandiu seruatam Herculi O[m]phalem seu Yolem amanti per Lycam seruulum caute transmisit. Ipse autem, cum sudore cruorem cum veneno infec- 30 tum resoluisset porisque bibisset, versus in rabiem se igni comburendum vltro concessit. Et sic Dyanira tanto viduata viro, dum retrahere speraret, perdidit et Nesso etiam vindictam expiauit.

19 transportandum LS. 23 peditus LS. Lernea] lerna U.
24 Id] quod BU. mortuum] moriturum B. 26 tunicam] tenentem
LS, *om.* BU. induat] eam Herculi, ipsam *add.* B. Herculem] eum B.
extero] alieno amore B. 29 oniphalem LSU. Lycam] Lycham B.

Of Yocasta, the Quene of Thebes.

The xxiij^{ti} Chapitre.

YOcasta, the Quene of Thebes, is knowne more by vnfortunate chauncys then by any thynge ell*es*. Thys Yocasta descendyd
5 frome the fyrste noble founders of Thebes and, beynge a mayden, was maryede vnto Layus, the Kynge of Thebes, of whome she conceyuede a sonne. And because Layus had aunswere of the goddes that hys son shulde sley hym, he co*m*maunded hyr, all
24*b* thoughe it were soore agaynste | hyr mynde, to caste the chylde
10 to the wylde beastes, for to be deuourede; and Layus thynkynge in verey deede it hade bene so, yet it chaunsid that the chylde was kepte and noryshede with the Kynge of Corynthe, whiche toke hym as hys oune pr*o*pre sonne. And so, cu*m*ynge to age, at a place called Phosenses he slewe in battell hys father Layus *and*
15 ther, not knowynge that Yocasta was hys mother, toke hyr to hys wyffe and begate on hyr too sonnes, Ethocles and Polynyces, *and* too dought*er*s, the oone namede Ysmena and the other Anthygona. And thus she semynge as well by the children she had as by hyr kyngdome to be moste happy, she had aunswere of the
20 goddes that hym that she thoughte to be hyr husbonde was hyr sonne, and albe it that she toke it wond*er*s heuely, yet hyr sonne

---

De Yocasta, Thebarum regina. xxiij.

YOcasta, Thebarum regina, fuit magis infortunio suo clara quam meritis aut regno. Hec quidem, cum a primis Thebarum
25 conditoribus originem duceret splendidam, virgo, nupsit Layo, Thebanorum regi, ex quo cum concepisset filium, ob aduersum Layo responsum e[x] oraculo sumptum, natum iussa feris obiciendum egra tradidit. Que[m] cum e vestigio deuoratum existimasset, apud Corinthiorum regem pro filio educatum atque
30 iam etate prouectum, occiso ab eodem apud Phocenses Layo, vidua incognitum sumpsit in coniugem et ex eo Ethioclem et Polinicem filios et totidem feminas Ysmenam et Anthigonam peperit filias. Et cum iam tam regno quam prole videretur felix, deorum responso quem legittimum arbitrabatur virum, eum esse
35 filium nouit. Quod etsi ipsa ferret egerrime, egrius tamen ille:

27 et L.   28 Que LS.   30 prouectum] profectum BU.   32 Ysmenam] scilicet *add*. BU. Anthigonam] Antigonam B.   34 legittimum] legitimum BU.

toke it more heuely, in so muche that he for verey shame that he
had for hys mysdeede, he put oute not onely hys propre eies, but
also forsooke hys kyngdome. And hys too sonnes fallynge at
debate who shulde succede in the realme, after many dredefull
encountres and battells the tone slewe the tother, for sorowe 5
wherof the myserable mother and aunte to bothe theym, wery
to see suche infortunate chauncyse fall to hyr sonnes and doughters, to make shorte processe slewe hyrselfe. Sum wryte, she
deferryde not hir deathe so longe, but seynge hyr husbonde to
haue put oute bothe hys eyes, as I haue sayde, made an ende with 10
hyr oune hande of hyr infortunate yeres.

Of Almachea Sibilla.

The xxiiij^{ti} Chapitre.

ALmachea Sibilla, a mayden, whiche sum call Deiphebe, was
the doughter of Gla[u]cus, of Cu[m]is, an olde towne of 15

15 Glancus MS.   Cunis MS.

---

adeo vt dum ob ruborem patrati sceleris eternam cuperet mortem,
oculos abiecit et regnum. Quod discordes assumentes filij in bellum
fractis federibus venere, etsi grandi [Iocaste] tristicia sepe
aduersum se in certamen descenderent, maximo eos decertantes
duello mutuis vulneribus occisos accepit. Cuius doloris impatiens 20
misera mater et auia, esto Creontem fratrem iam [regem] cerneret
et orbum filium, virumque captiuum, et Ysmenam Anthigonam-
que filias labenti fortune implicatas, reluctantem fessamque
malis animam ferro iam anus expulit et anxietates cum vita
finiuit. Sunt tamen qui velint eam tamdiu noxios errores suos 25
ferre non potuisse, quinymo cum vidisset E[d]i[p]um oculos
eicientem illico in se seuisse.

De Amalchea seu de Deiphebe Sibilla. xxiiij.

ALmachea virgo, quam quidam Deiphebem, Glauci filiam,
vocant, ex Cumis, Calchidiensi Campanie veteri opido, 30

16 ob] *om.* B.   mortem] noctem BU.   17 oculos] effossos *add.* B.
abiecit] obiecit SU.   18 *om.* LS.   19 aduersum] aduersus BU.
21 *om.* LS.   22–3 Anthigonamque] Antigonamque BU.   23 implicatas]
implicitas BU.   26 Epidum LS.   28 Amalchea] Amalthea B,
Almathea U.   Deiphebe] Deiphobe B.   30 Calchidiensi] Calcidensium
B, calchidiensium U.

Campana, had hyr begynnynge, and for as muche as thys was oone
of the Sibills, when the destruction of Troy was, yet it is sayde
f. 25a that she lyuede vnto Tarquin*us*, the | Kynge of Romaynes tyme.
Nor thys woman neuer suffrede hyr body to be pollutede with
5 noo man. And albeit the poet*es* feyne that she was belouyde
of Phebus, and by hys rewarde had grauntyde to lyue so longe
a lyfe, and besydes that, to haue a dyuyne spyryte, yett I beleue
she had not that gyfte of Phebus, but of that sonne that lyghtethe
all men that cu*m*s into thys worlde, whereby she dyd bothe wryte
10 and tell many thynges to cum. Thys woman also, as it is sayde,
dwelte nere vnto that noble lake of Baians, where was a meruelouse exellente oracle, the whiche I myselfe haue seene, and haue
also herde that it berythe hyr name vnto thys present day. And
thoughe by exedynge yeres it be decayede, yet it kepythe styll the
15 man*er* and fo*ur*me of the auncyent mageste, and gyuethe admiratione to those that beholde it, because of the magnitude or

7 spyryte] And *add*. MS.

---

originem duxisse creditur; et, cum ex Sibillis extiterit vna,
Troiane desolationis tempore floruisse atque in tam longum
deuenisse euum, vt ad Prisci Tarquinij, Romanorum regis, vsque
20 tempus deuenerit, arbitrantur aliqui. [Fuit] h[ui]c [antiquorum
testimonio tanta virginitas, vt tot seculorum spacio nulla] viri
contagione fedari passa sit; et, quanquam poetarum testentur
fabule hanc a Phebo dilectam et eius munere et longeuos annos
et diuinitatem obtinuisse, ego quidem reor virginitatis merito
25 eam ab ipso vero sole, qui illuminat omnem hominem venientem
in hunc mundum, vaticinij suscepisse lumen, quo multa predixit
scripsitque futura. Huic insuper in Baiano litore secus Auerni
lacum dicunt insigne fuisse oraculum, quod quidem et ego vidi
audiuique, quod seruet ab ea cognomen vsque in hodier-
30 num. Quod etsi corrosum sit vetustate plurima et incuria
semirutum, etiam si[c] [in] [r]uinis maiestatem seruat veterem
et admirationem prestat adhuc intuenti magnitudinis sue. Sunt

20 neque hinc L.   20–1 antiq. . . . . nulla] *om*. LS.   22–3 test. fab.]
litere testentur BU.   27 scripsitque] scripsissetque U.   Huic] Hinc
BU.   in] *om*. B.   Baiano] baione U.   29 in] diem *add*. BU.   31
sit numinis LS.

greatenes of it. And there be also that affyrme that thys was she
that wentt with Eneas to hell, whiche I beleue not, and therfore
I let it passe. But those that do say that she lyuyde so many
yeres, do tell that she came to Rome and brought to Tarquyne
nyne bookes, whyche bookes, because Tarquyne wolde not gyue 5
to hyr for theym the pryce that she demaundyde, that in the
Kynges presence she threwe three of theym in the fyer, and the
next day agayne folowynge offrede to Tarquyne the reste,
[saynge] that oneles he wolde gyue hyr the pryce that she de-
maundid, she wolde burne theym also. Tarquyne therby was so 10
mouede that he boughte theym. Whiche sayde bookes he causede
diligently to be kepte, *and* the Romaynes longe aftre sett so muche
store by theym that in all theyre greate daungiers they toke the
saynges of those bookes as an oracle. It is herd for me to beleue
that thys woman was with Deiphebe, but yet we rede that she 15
dyede in Scecill and that ther hyr tumbe is shewede by the inhabi-
taunt*es*. And, for conclusion, with studye and the dyuyne grace
withall we be made noble, whiche is denyede to suche as wyll do

---

preterea, qui dicant hanc Enee profugo ducatum ad inferos
prestitisse, quod ego non credo; sed de hoc alias. Qui autem 20
illam plura vidisse secula volunt, asserunt eam venisse Romam
et Tarquinio Prisco nouem attulisse libros, ex quibus, cum
negaretur a Tarquinio precium postulatum, tres eo vidente
combussit; et, cum die sequenti ex sex reliquis illud idem
precium, quod ante ex nouem petiuerat, postulasset asseruisset- 25
que, ni daretur, tres e vestigio exusturam, [quod cum fecisset]
die sequenti [pro] reliqu[i]s a Tarquinio petitum suscepit. Quos
cum seruasset, a posteris compertum est eos Romanorum facta
omnia continere; quam ob causam maxima cum diligentia post
hec Romani seruauere et iuxta oportunitatum exigentiam de 30
futuris consulturi ad eosdem quasi ad oraculum recurrebant.
Mihi quidem durum est credere hanc eandem extitisse cum
Deiphebe; eam tamen apud Siculos clausisse diem legimus et
ibidem diu eius tumulum ab incolis demonstratum est. Studijs
igitur et diuina gratia illustres efficimur, que nemini se dignum 35

19 hanc] eam BU.   26 quod cum fec.] et LSU.   27 pro
reliquis] reliquos LSU.   petitum] pret um *add.* B.

noo goode. And if we do well beholde suche as dreme in idlenes by
losynge of the tyme, all thoughe they lyue to extreme age, they
be noo better then he *tha*t frome hys mothers bely gothe [and]
f. 25*b* is borne to hys graue. And for the reste, | yf that a woman
5 wakynge in vertue do preuayle in wytte and in dyuine knowledge,
what may be thoughte to vs mys*er*able men any other but,
gyuynge o*ur*self in lernynge and vertue, we shulde be co*n*uertyde
vnto the dyuyne knowledge of the deite? Lett theym then
lamente and weepe, that lese so greate a gyfte by idlenes and
10 exteme theymselff*es* no bett*er* emonge men but verey stoones.

Of Nycostrata, or otherwyse Carmenta, doughter to
Kynge Yonius.
The xxv^th Chapitre.

15 **N**Ycostrata, whiche was surnamede Carme*n*ta emongste the
Italianes, was doughter of Yonius, the Kynge of Arcadia, as
sum wryte, and was maryede to Palla*n*tes, which lady not onely

---

facienti denegata sunt. Quod si spectaremus desidia torpentes,
sentiremus plane, quod tempore perdito ab vtero etiam annosi
morientes deferamur in tumulum. Demum, si ingenio et deitate
20 peruigiles valent femine [ad tantam diuinitatem sanctitatemque
prouenire,] quid hominibus miseris arbitrandum est, quibus ad
omnia promptior [est] aptitudo? Si pellatur ignauia, in ipsam
quippe euaderent deitatem. Fleant igitur et tabescant, quibus
tam grande donum inertia sublatum est, et se inter homines
25 animatos fateantur lapides! Quod fiet, dum suum crimen con-
fitebuntur elingues.

De Nicostrata seu Carmenta, Yonij regis filia. xxv.

NIcostrata, cui postea Carmenta apud Ytalos nomen, fuit
Yonij, regis Arcadum, filia. Secundum quosdam Pallanti
30 Arcado nupsit, secundum alios nurus fuit eiusdem. Nec regni

17 spectaremus] iam non, ut fit *add.* B.   18 perd. ab vtero] siue
frugi ab utero perdito B.   19 deferamur] absque omni decore
deferantur B.   deitate] dei gratia B.   20-1 *om.* LSU.   21 hominibus miseris] viris B.   22 *om.* LS.   23 tabescant] omnes uiri
add. B.   27 Yonij] yoni S.   29 Arcadum] archadum U.

was decorate with the name of a quene, but also she was moste cunnyng in the Greke letters. So exellente a wytte had she in lernynge, and she was so vigilant in study theron, that she became a notable prophete. And sumtyme to thos that demaundyd questiones of hyr she tolde theym thynges to cum and wrote also 5 true thynges that folowed many yeres after, and for that the Latyns, abolyshyng hyr fyrste name, callede hyr Carmenta. Thys woman was mother to Euander, the Kynge of Archadia, whiche the olde tales affyrme, because he was eloquent, to be sonne of Mercurye. But as sume saye, yet it fortunede by chaunce he slewe 10 hys oune father, and sum other wryteth that it was by the sedicione of the people. Whether it wer the tone or the tother, he was expulsyde owte of hys realme and by the counsell and prophecying of hys mother toke shyppynge and saylede so longe that at the last he arryuyde at the mouthe of Tyber, | and f. 26a by hyr counsell, by the hyll called Pallantes, whiche had *that* 16 name by hys sonne Pallas, he reedyfyede ther a towne, where

---

solum fulgore fuit insignis, quinymo, Grecarum litterarum doctissima, adeo versatilis fuit ingenij, vt ad vaticinium vsque vigilanti penetraret studio et vates efficeretur notissima. Que, 20 cum querentibus et a se ipsa nonnunquam expromeret futura carmine, a Latinis quasi primo Nicostrate abolito nomine Carmenta nuncupata est. Hec autem mater fuit E[u]andri, Arcadum regis, quem fabule veterum, seu quia eloquens atque facundus homo, seu quia astutus fuerit, ex Mercurio volunt fuisse 25 conceptum. Qui, vt quidam dicunt, cum casu eum, qui verus erat pater, occidisset, seu, vt alijs placet, seditione ciuium suorum alia ex causa orta e regno pulsus a[ui]to, suadente Carmenta matre et magna vaticinio promittente, si has peteret, quas ostenderet, sedes, facta perigrinationis socia, conscensis nauibus, cum pa[rt]e 30 populorum secundo vento ad ostia Tyberis ex Peloponeso deueniens, eadem matre duce in Palatino monte, quem a Pallante patre seu a P[a]llante filio nominauit, vbi postea Roma ingens

21 expromeret] exprimeret BU.   23 enandri LS.   28 pulsus] expulsus BU.   aiuto L.   30 patre L.   31 ostia] hostia LSU. Peloponeso] peloponenso SU.   33 pellante L.

aft*er* the greate Rome was buyldyd, and namede the towne after
the hyll Pallantes. Now when Carment[a] was comen thyther,
she founde the people ther all rude and barbarouse and muche
lyke to wylde men. All thoughe that Saturne a lytle tofore had
5 taught theym how to sowe and to eare, yet they knewe noo
lett*er*s as the Grekys dyd. Wherfore thys lady, p*er*s[eyu]ynge in
hyr mynde the pleasure of the grownde *and* forseynge what a cyte
that sumtyme shulde be made ther, she taughte *and* deuysed
emonge theym carecters and letters discrepant frome other
10 nationes. To whiche godly purpose Goddes helpe lackyde not, soo
that by Hys grace she sett forth onely sexten lettres, as Cadm*us*,
the buylder of Thebes, had doone to the Grecians, whiche we call
vnto thys present tyme the Latyn lettres. Whiche inuentione
semyde to be suche to the Latyns that they beleuyde hyr rather

2 Carmentys MS.   6 p*er*suadynge MS.

---

15 condita est, cum suis et matre consedit construxitque oppidum
Pallanteum. Sane, Carmenta, cum indigenas fere siluestres
comperisset homines—esto iam dudum Saturni profugi munere
segetes didicissent serere—eosque nullo litterarum vsui seu
modico et hoc Greco assuetos, a longe diuina mente prospiciens,
20 quanta loco regionique celebritas seruaretur imposterum, indignum rata, vt adminiculo exterarum litterarum futuris seculis
sua monstrarentur magnalia, in id studium iuit totis ingenij
viribus, vt proprias et omnino a ceteris nationibus diuersas
litteras exhiberet populis, cui [in]ceptui nec defuit deus. Sua enim
25 gratia factum est, vt nouis ab ea adinuentis caracteribus secundum Ytalicum ydeoma harum coniunctiones edoceret, contenta
sexdecim tantum excudisse figuras, vti diu ante Cadmus,
Thebarum conditor, adinuenerat Grecis, quas nos in hodiernum
vsque Latinas dicimus eiusque tenemus munere dato; aliquas
30 et oportune quidam sapientes addider[u]nt, nulla ex veteribus

16 fere] fore BU.   17 munere] numem BU.   19 et] ex BU.
22 id] eum S, *om.* BU.   23 vt] *om.* BU.   24 inceptui] ceptui BLSU.
nec] non BU.   26 ydeoma] et *add.* LS.   harum] earum BU.   27 tantum]
om. B.   excudisse] exduxisse U, duxisse B.   29 Latinas] literas BU.
dato] datas sed B, *add.* quibus U.   30 quidam] quidem BU.   addiderint LSU, *add.* sed B.   nulla] nullam U.

to be a goddesse then a mortall woman ande for a p*er*petuall
memorye buyldyde vndre the Capitoll an oratory, callede Carmenta. And Rome, when he was moste greateste, woldnot
chaynge it, but the gate of the cytie, whiche by necessite then
buyldyde they namede it Carme*n*ta, of the name of thys woma*n* 5
Carme*n*ta. Italy in olde tyme aboue other regyones florysshede
in hono*ur* *and* ve*r*tue, shynynge as a celestiall lyghte. Nor soo
renomyde a countrye hath not bene vndre the heuen. For f*r*ome
Asya came ryches *and* su*m*ptuousnes of howsholde, mete for
kynges, *and* nobilyte of bloode p*r*ocedynge frome the Grecians, 10
fyrste had of Troyanes. The Egyptiens gaue vs arsmetryke *and*
geometry; and philozophy and eloquens *and* wellnere a]l mecani-
call craft*es* descendyd frome the Grek*es*; Saturn*us* the outelawe
founde fyrste husbondrye, knowne but to a few me*n*; co*m*une

---

amota. Cuius in litteris vaticinium etsi plurimum mirati sint 15
Latini, hoc tamen inuentum adeo mirabile visum, vt profecto
crediderint rudes non hominem, sed potius deam esse Carmentam.
Quamobrem, cum viuentem diuinis celebrassent honoribus,
mortue sub infima Capitolini montis parte, vbi vitam duxerat,
sacellum suo condidere nomini et ad eius perpetuam memoriam 20
a suo nomine loca adiacentia Carmentalia vocauere. Quod
quidem nec Roma iam grandis abolesse passa est, quinymo
ianuam ciuitatis, quam ibi exigente necessitate ciues construx-
erant, Carmentalem per multa secula de Carmente nomine
vocauere. Multis olim dotibus Ytalia pre ceteris orbis regionibus 25
florida fuit et fere celesti luce corusca. Nec tantum suo sub celo
tam splendidus quesitus est fulgor. Nam ab Asya opulentia venit
et supellectilis regia, sanguinis claritas, etsi multa addiderint
Greci, a Troyanis habita primo. Arismetricam et geometriam artes
dedere Egipcij; philosophia et eloquentia ac mechanicum fere opus 30
omne ab eisdem Grecis sumptum est; agriculturam paucis adhuc
cognitam Saturnus intulit exul; deorum infaustus cultus ab

15 Cuius] Huius B.   in litteris] mulieris BU.   16 Latini] latij BU.
visum] est *add*. BU.   22 abolesse] abolere B.   23 ianuam]
portam B.   28 supellectilis] supellex B.   multa] multum BSU.
29 Arismetricam] Arithmeticam B.   30 ac] et BU.   30–1 fere
opus omne] opus omne fere BU.   31 agriculturam] agricultura U.

lawes descendyde frome the Athenens, and the Cesars stableysshede
the scenates; Simon Petrus was the fyrst that brought and
f. 26b stablyshede the true feyth frome Jherusalem, but | the knyghtly
prowyse the noble Romayns taught, so that with theyr valyaunte
5 deades they subduede the hoole worlde. The Latyn fygures,
it appeareth by that afore rehersyde that it came frome
Carmenta, whiche, cumynge frome Archadia into Italy, it is to be
beleuyde that she taught fyrst the gramer rules—a fortunate
seede, to growe in tyme to cum to rype corne. Wherevnto God
10 was so fauorable that the glory therby, aswell of the Grekes tunge
as of the Hebrewe tunge, in parte is abaytede, for the moste parte
of Europe vse oone tunge. Whereby the gestes and actes of
prynces and the workes of God with a perpetuall memory be
seruyde, in so muche that the thynges we neuer sawe with oure
15 eyes, by the wrytynges we knowe theym; by thys we sende oure

---

Etruscis et Numa Pompilio habitus; leges publicas Athene primo,
inde senatus consultus et Cesares prebuere; sacerdotium summum
religionemque sinceram a Hierusolimis attulit Symon Petrus;
disciplinam autem militarem veteres excogitauere Romani, qua
20 et armorum atque corporum robore et in rempublicam caritate
integra orbis totius sibi quesiuere imperium; litterarum caracteres
satis ex dictis patet, quoniam maioribus nostris Carmenta con-
cesserit, cum iam ex Archadia deuenisset Ytaliam; sic et grama-
tice facultatis prima dedisse semina creditum, que in ampliorem
25 segetem successu temporum prisci traxere, quibus adeo propicius
fuit deus, [v]t Hebraicis Grecisque litteris parte maxima
glorie dempta omnis quasi Europa amplo terrarum tractu nostris
vtatur, quibus delinita facultatum omnium [infi]nita splen-
dent volumina, hominum gesta deique magnalia perpetua ser-
30 uantur memoria, vt, que vidisse nequiuimus ipsi, eis opitulantibus
cognoscamus. His vota nostra transmittimus et aliena cum
fide suscipimus, his amicicias in longinquo iungimus et mutuis
responsionibus conseruamus; he deum, prout fieri potest, nobis

16 Etruscis] Hetrustis B, etrustis U.   18 Hierusolimis] Hierosolymis
B, ierosolimis U.   20 et armorum] ac morum B.   22 quoniam]
quando B.   23 Ytaliam] ytalica S, italica U.   24 creditum] creditur
BU.   25–8 quibus . . . vtatur *om.* B.   26 et LS.   28 munita LS.

myndes frome afarr to oure freandes and haue frome oure freandes
aunswere agayne. Nor ther is nothynge possible to be sowght, but
that by thys we may fynde it, and breuely, what so eu*er* the mynde
cannot kepe, by wrytynge may be surely fownde *and* kepte. And
thys is so muche to the Italian hono*ur* that nother the rapyne of 5
the Germaynes, nor the Frenshe fury, nor the pollicy of the
Englishe men, nor the Spanyshe rage, nor noone other barbarouse
countrey coulde let but that they theimselff*es* ar glad to lerne
thies oure letters and neu*er* durste take the glory of this tunge a
way frome the Latyns, but allways in other greate wrytynges 10
they sett the carrect*es* of that exellent tunge in all causys. Wherby the further the tonge is admytted, the more glorye is it to the

---

describunt; he celum terrasque et maria et animantia cuncta
designant; nec est, quod queras possibile quod ab his vigilans
non possis percipere; harum breuiter opere, quicquid amplitudine 15
mentis complecti atque teneri non potest, fidissime commendatur
custodie. Que tamen etsi alijs ex his nonnulla contingant, nil
tamen nostris commendabile aufertur. Ceterum ex tam egregijs
dotibus quedam perdidimus, quedam dedimus et nonnulla adhuc
solo nomine potius quam effectu tenemus. Verum, quomodo- 20
cunque de ceteris nostro aut crimine aut fortuna actum sit, nec
Germana rapacitas nec Gallicus furor nec astucia Anglica nec
Yspanica ferocitas nec alicuius alterius nationis inculta barbaries
vel insultus hanc tam grandem, tam spectabilem, tam oportunam
Latino nomini gloriam surripuisse potuit vnquam, vt suis prima 25
litterarum possent aut auderent dicere elementa et longe minus
suum compertum fuisse gramaticam, quas, vti comperimus ipsi,
sic etiam dedimus vltro, nostro tamen semper insignita vocabulo.
Vnde fit, vt, quanto longius feruntur, tanto magis Latini nominis
ampliantur laudes et honores clarius[que] vetustissimi decoris, 30
nobilitatis et ingenij testimonium deferunt et incorruptum nostre

---

13 et 1°] *om.* BU.   15 quicquid] quicquam S.   16 mentis] menti S.
atque] ac BU.   17 alijs] literis & linguis *add.* B.   18 tam] tot BU.
19 dedimus] addidimus BU.   20 solo] fere BU.   21 aut 1°] an BU.
23 Yspanica] Hispana BU, yspania S.   25 vnquam] nunquam S,
suis] sui scilicet iuris BU.   27 compertum] et inuentum *add.* B.
30 clarius LS.   31 deferunt] referunt B.

speche, and for that we wyllnot be accountyde so ingrate nor
vnkynde, but that, asmuche as in vs is, we wyll make it to be
prased and laudyde for euer.

Of Procrys, the wyfe to Zephalus.

5   The xxvjth Chapitre. |

f. 27*a* PRocris, the doughter of Pandion, Kynge of Athenes, was
maryede to Zephalus, the sonne of Kynge Eolus. Thys Procris,
as she is dispysed for hyr couetuousnes of the wyffes and matrones,
so muche the more is she well exeptyde to men, for by hyr the
10 vyce of wome*n* is the bett*er* knowne. For as he and she, bothe
yonge, lyuyde togedre with muche ioy *and* pleasur, to theyr bothe
myshappe it fortunede that a fayre mayden namede Arua, or
sum wryetethe Aurora, fell in loue with Zephalus, a wondre fayre
wenshe, and labo*ur*ynge all in vayne, she assayde to haue had hir
15 desyres with Zephalus. But when she sawe that it woldenot be,

---

perspicacitatis seruant etiam indignante barbarie argumentum.
Cuius tam eximij fulgoris, etsi deo datori gratias agere debeamus, multum tamen laudis, caritatis et fidei Carmente debemus.
Quamobrem, ne a quoquam tanquam ingrati iure redargui
20 possimus, vt illud pro viribus in eternam memoriam efferamus,
pijssimum est.

De Procri, Zephali coniuge. xxvi.

PRocris Pandionis, Athenarum regis, nata et Zephalo, Eoli regis
filio, nupta, vti auaricia sua pudicis matronis exosa est, sic
25 et viris accepta, quoniam per eam ceterarum mulierum vicium
adapertum sit. Nam cum leto pioque amore vir et vxor iuuenes
gauderent, eorum infortunio factum est, vt desiderio Zephali
caperetur Arua seu potius Aurora quedam, vt placet aliquibus,
spectande pulcritudinis mulier, quem cupidine Procris sue deten-
30 tum aliquandiu frustra in suam sententiam precibus trahere

16 indignante] nobis *add.* BU.   18 laudis] et *add.* BU.   20
efferamus] offeramus BU.   22 Zephali] Cephali BU.   23 Eoli] Æoli
B.   24 filio] filia BU..   vti] quemadmodum B.   sua] *om.* B
26 adapertum] apertum B.   iuuenes] viuentes BU.   28 Arua] Aura
BU.   30 precibus] *om.* BU.

all dysdaynously she spake to Zephalus and sayde: 'What ayles
the, so feruently to loue thy wyfe Procris? Thow shalt, yf thow
wylte proue it, fynde that for golde and syluer she wyll loue
another better then the.' Zephalus, herynge hyr so say, and
desyrouse to proue hys wyfe in deede, feynede to goo into a farr 5
countrie and, strongely dysguysynge hymselfe, returnyde backe
agayne and assayde *with* gyfftes to moue his wyffes chastyte.
But all thoughe he promysede many greate gyft*es*, yett coulde he
not cum to hys purpose at the fyrst; but styll gyuynge hyr
iewell*es* apon iewell*es*, so longe he [f]ol[ow]de hyr that at the last 10
he bowed downe hyr doubtefull mynde to folowe hys desyre, and
[she] promysede sum nyght, geuynge hyr golde therfore, to be
enbrasyde in hys armes. Zephalus, wonders sorowfull, opnede to
hys wyfe what he was and howe by fraude he had tempted hyr to
lye with hym, whiche as soone as Procrys herde, ashamede and 15
desperate for sorowe, [she] fledde desolate, alone, vnto the wodd*es*.
But Zephalus, louynge hyr hartely, promysynge to forgyue hyr,
dyd what he coulde to haue callede hyr agayne, but she despysed
so for to do; wherby it may be well sayde, ther is noo forgeunes

10 solarde MS. 12 and promysede that sum MS.

---

conata est. Ex quo inquit indignans: 'Penitebit te, Zephale, adeo 20
feruide dilexisse Procrim: comperies, faxo, si sit qui temptet eam,
aurum amori preposuisse tuo.' Quod audiens iuuenis, experiri
auidus, perigrinationem longinquam fingens abijt, flexoque in
patriam gradu, per intermedium muneribus constantiam temp-
tauit vxoris. Que, quantumcunque grandia sponderentur, impetu 25
primo mouisse nequiuere: eo tandem perseuerante et yocalia
augente ad vltimum hesitantem flexit animum, illique nox
optatique amplexus, si detur sponsum aurum, promissi sunt.
Tunc Zephalus merore consternatus aperuit quonam dolo
friuolum Procris amorem intercepisset, que rubore conspersa et 30
conscientia impulsa facinoris, confestim in siluas abijt et se
solitudini dedit. Iuuenis autem amoris impatiens vltro venia
data, precibus aspernantem reuocauit in gratiam. Sed quid refert?

20 Ex quo] propter quod B. Zephale] Cephale BSU. 27 augente]
agente BU. 29 Zephalus] Cephalus BSU. consternatus] con-
tristatus BU. aperuit] BS apparuit. quonam] BLS. quoniam, U qm̄.

can helpe agaynste the bytte of oones conscience. Procrys,
fery*n*ge and castynge in hyr mynde that allways hyr Zephalus
f. 27*b* wolde | ley to hyr charge hyr couetouse, ra*n*ne frome the woddes
to the rockes here and there at auenture. And soo it fortunede
5 hyr husbonde on a certayne day dyd ryde a huntynge, and
Procrys lay becky*n*ge emongste a sorte of reedys, and as the reedys
mouede here *and* ther wi*th* the mouynge of Procrys, Zephalus,
thynkynge it hadd bene sum wylde beaste, shotte at aduenture in
to the reedys and hytt hys vnfortunate wyfe with an arrowe to the
10 herte. And soo she peryshede. I haue forgotten to say that ther is
nothynge hathe moore powere on erthe then golde, whiche thys
woma*n* sekynge to obteyne, at the last therby soughte hyr oune
deathe. Now by my iudgement thys immoderate loue of golde
cumethe of a folyshe, fonde appetyte, *and* specially for thys, that
15 all thoughe we see oone hauynge noo vertue in hym at all, yet
hauynge plentye of golde and syluer, we thynke hym aboue all
other to be honourede and exaltede.

Nulle sunt indulgentie vires aduersus conscientie morsus ; agebatur
Procris in varios animi motus et zelo percita, ne forte id in se
20 blandicijs A[ur]ore vir ageret, quod ipsa in illum auro mercata
fuerat, clam per scopulos et abrupta montium iuga valliumque
secreta venatorem consequi cepit, quod peragens, contigit, dum
inter vallium herbida calamosque palustres latitans moraretur
Procris, credita a viro belua, sagitta confossa perijt. Ignoro, quid
25 dixerim potius, an nil esset potentius auro in terris aut stollidius
querere quod comperisse non velis. Quorum dum vtrumque
insipiens mulier approbat, sibi indelibilem notam et mortem
inuenit, quam minime inquirebat. Sed, vt auri immoderatum
desiderium sinam, quo stolidi fere trahimur omnes, queso [quid]
30 tam obstinato zelo correpti dicant, quid inde sibi emolimenti
sentiant, quid decoris, quid laudis aut glorie consequantur ? Meo
quippe iudicio hec ridicula mentis est egritudo a pusillanimitate
patientis originem ducens, cum non alibi viderimus quam hos
penes, qui se adeo deiecte virtutis existimant, vt facile sibi
35 quoscunque preponend[o]s fore concedant.

19 percita] partita BSU.   20 amore LS.   22 consequi]
persequi B.   23 moraretur] moueretur BSU.   29 trahimur] trahuntur
BU.   quid *om.* LSU.   35 preponendas LS.

Of Argia, the wyfe of Poli[n]ices, and doughter of the Kynge Adrastus.
The xxvijth Chapiter.

ARgia, a woman of Grece, descendynge of the noble kynges of
Grece, [was] doughter of Kynge Adrastus, and as she was 5
a louynge *and* desyrouse spectacle to beholde for hyr exellentnes,
so was she a ryght reuerente and honorable wytnes of true, wyfely
feythe to hyr husbonde. Whereby not oonely in hyr days she had
prayse *and* lawde, but further, hyr name and fame is commendable in our tyme and shalbe for euer. Thys woman was maryede 10
to Poly[n]ises, the sonne of Edippus, Kynge of Thebes, then
beynge an outelawe; whe*n* then she had broughte hym forthe
a chylde that was callede Tessander, now she well aduertysynge
hyr husbonde to be won-|dersly troblede for the fraude of hys f.28*a*
brother, whiche studyede to destroy hym, beynge a pertaker 15
of hyr husbond*es* sorowe, she not onely with wepynge teares
prayde hyr father, then beynge an olde man, to helpe hyr husbonde, but at lengthe so wroughte that in verey deede she armyde
hyr father agaynste hyr husbo*n*d*es* brother, whiche, besydes the

1 Polimices MS.   11 Polymises MS.

De Argia, Polliniti[s] coniuge, et Adrasti regis filia. xxvij. 20

ARgia, Greca mulier, ab antiquis Argiuorum regibus generosam
ducens originem, Adrasti regis filia fuit et spectabili pulcri-
tudine sua, vti de se contemporaneis letum spectaculum prebuit,
sic et posteris integerrimum atque preclarum coniugalis amoris
testimonium perhenne reliquit: ob quod in nostros vsque dies 25
nomen eius fulgidum precipua coruscatione deuenit. Hec igitur,
nupta Polliniti, filio Edipi, Thebarum regis, et exuli, cum iam ex
illo Tessandrum peperisset filium, aduertens eum ob fratris
fraudem mordacibus agitari curis, facta anxietatum particeps,
patrem iam senem non solum exorauit lachrimis precibusque, 30
verum et armauit in Ethyo[cl]em preter pactionum leges cum

20 Polliniti L, pollicinis S.   Poll. . . . et] *om*. BU.   23 contem-
poraneis] cum temporaneis BU.   25 perhenne] perenne B.   27 Pol-
liniti] Pollicinio S.   28 Tessandrum] Thessandrum BU.   eum] patrem
B.   30 solum] consolata et *add*. B.   31 verumque LS.   et]
etiam BU.   ethyodem LS

pacte that was betwyxte theym, occupyede the kyngedome of
Thebes by tyranny. And leste p*er*auenture that the fatale
prophecy shulde be a let, she dyd so muche liberally rewarde the
wyfe of Amphiorax that she causede hyr to tell wher hyr husbonde
5 was hydden secretly, for because he pr*o*phecyede that aswell
hymself as those that went to Thebes shulde be destroyede. So
that Amphyorax with Ad[r]astus and Polynyses went to the seege
of Thebes, but to theyr mysfortune. For after many batells
betwyxte the Thebans, *and* the dukes of bothe p*ar*ties slayne, *and*
10 Adraustus depryuyde frome helpe and for that dryuyn away,
when Argia had herde that the body of hyr husbonde lay deede,
vnburyde emonge an infynyte numbre of other that were slayne,
streightways puttynge of hyr ryche apparell, with a fewe w*it*h hyr,
she toke hyr way into the campe. Neither those that lay robbynge
15 by the passage, nor the blody handes of the Thebans, nor the
wylde beastes, nor yet the byrdes that folow the caryen of deede
bodyes, nor the cruell co*m*maundement of Kynge Creon that

7 Audastus MS.   10 dryuynge MS.

---

fratre Thebanum regnum occupantem tyrannice, et ne fatale
responsum detrimentum susciperet, Euridici, Amphiorai vatis
20 coniugi, preter naturam femineam liberalis effecta, preciosum
illud monile, matronis olim Thebanis infaustum, vltro contulit.
Ex quo latitans patefactus Amphioraus in Thebas itum est, sed
infelici omine. Nam post plurimam certaminum stragem ceteris
interfectis ducibus et Adrasto auxilijs nudato atque fugato, cum
25 inter cetera sordidi vulgi cesique cadauera Polliniti[s] corpus in-
sepultum iacere anxia coniunx audisset, e[x]templo regio abiecto
splendore et mollicie thalami atque debilitate feminei sexus
seposita, paucis comitantibus, arripuit iter in castra. Nec eam
terruere insidentium itinera manus impie, non fere, non aues
30 occisorum hominum sequentes corpora, non circumuolantes, vt
arbitrantur stolidi, cesorum manes nec, quod terribilius videbatur,
Creontis imperantis edictum, quo cauebatur pena capitalis sup-
plicij, ne quis cuiquam occisorum funebre prestaret officium, quin

24 Adrasto] Adrastro L, Adrasco S.   fugato] semifugato BU.   25
polliniti LS.   26 e templo LS.   29 insidentium] insidiantium BU,
insidencium S.   33 quin] quando B.

charged, peyne of deathe, noone shulde bury theym that lay
deade in the feelde, couldenot lett hyr but that at mydnyght,
with a heuy hert, she went emonge the stynkynge, deade men and
neu*er* left tyll she founde hyr husbonde. O, me*r*uelouse true,
louynge hert of a true, noble wy[ff]e! All thoughe the face of hyr 5
husbonde were defo*ur*myd w*ith* duste and bloode, yet it coulde
not so blynde hyr but that she knewe hym, and, enbrasynge hym
in hyr armes *and* kyssynge hym and w*ith* salte terys wypynge
hys deformyde visage, she neu*er* left hym tyll she had made a
greate fyre, as the vsage was i*n* those | dayes to burne the bodyes, f. 28*b*
[and] tyll she had w*ith* greate lame*n*tatione and teares co*n*sumede 11
hym to ashys. I deny not but many goode wyfes haue often wept
to see theyr husbond*es* syke, to se thei*m* in pryson, to se theym
suffre other harde chauncys, but yet all that is nothynge to be
accomptyde to the loue of thys goode, chaste Argia. For thys 15
fearyde not to seeke hyr husbonde emonge hyr ennemyes; thys

ardenti mestoque animo nocte media certaminis aream intrans,
cesorum atque tetro odore redolentia corpora, nunc hec, nunc illa
deuolueret, vt parue facis auxilio, ora tabentia dilectissimi viri
cognosceret. Nec ante desistit quam quod querebat inuenerit. O 20
mirum! semesa iam facies armorum rubigine, squalore completa
puluereo, et marcido iam cruore respersa, nulli iam edepol cogno-
scenda amantissime coniugi occultari non potuit, nec infecti vultus
sordes vxoris amouere potuerunt oscula, non voces, non lacrimas,
non ingens Creontis imperium. Nam, cum sepe vitalem spiritum 25
per oris oscula exquisisset, lauisset lacrimis fetidos artus et sepe
vocibus in suos amplexus reuocasset exanimem, flammis iam
f[l]agrantibus, ne quid pij officij obmissum linqueret, tradidit,
consumptumque vrna condidit: nec igne pa[t]efact[o] p[i]o facinore
seueri regis subire gladium et cathenas expauit. Fleuere persepe 30
plurime virorum egritudines, carceres, paupertatem et infortunia
multa, stante tamen spe mitioris fortune et amoto seuerioris
pauore, quod etsi laudabile videatur, extremum tamen dilectionis
i[n]dicium dici non potest, vt Argie dici obsequia potuere. Hec
hostiles petijt agros, dum flere posset in patria: fetidum tractauit 35

20 desistit] destitit BU.   21 completa] oppleta BU.   24
potuerunt] potuerit B.   28 fragrantibus LS.   29 patefacto pio]
pauefacta pro LS.   30 expauit] expiauit BU.   34 iudicium LSU.

handlede the stynkynge caryone of hyr husbonde; and though
she was in daungyer of hyr lyfe and myght by other haue doone
those ceremonyes, she dyd theym hyrself; and fynally, [she] not
onely dyd exequyes of hyr husbonde pryncelyke, but manyfestly
5 bewaylede hys deathe, whiche she myght haue doone in hyr
chambre. Thus the true loue of a true, louynge woma*n*, thus the
holy bounde of matrymonye, thus the vndefyled chastite may doo
in a goode woma*n*, as thys goode Argia dyd, wherby she hathe
well dese*r*uyde a cleere, hono*u*rable name for euer.

10   Of Mantone, the dought*er* of Ter[i]sia.
                 The xxviij[th] Chapitre.

MAntone, the doughter of Terisia, the greate prophete of
Thebes, was in the Kynge Edippus tyme and in hys sonnes
tyme. Thys woma*n*, beynge vndre hir father whiche taughte hyr,
15 was of so p*r*egnante a wytte that the scyence of perema*n*si,
founde of the Caldes, or, as sum wryteth, of Nembrothe, she so

                 10 Thersia MS.

---

cadauer, quod iniunxisse poterat alijs: flammis regium impendit
honorem, dum clam infodisse qualitate temporis inspecta satis
erat. Vlulatus emisit femineos, vbi poterat pertransire tacita: nec
20 quod speraret habebat ex occiso exule, cum quo[d] timeret adesset
ab hoste. Sic verus amor, sic fides integra, sic coniugij sanctitas
et illibata castitas suasisse potuere: quo merito laudanda, colenda
et splendido extollenda preconio venit Argia.

              De Manthone, Tyresie filia. xxviij.

25 MAnto, Tyresie maximi Thebanorum vatis filia, tempore Edipi
regis filiorumque fuit insignis. Hec quidem sub patre magistro
tam prompti atque capacis fuit ingenij, vt piromanciam, vetustissimum Caldeorum seu, vt volunt alij, Nembroth inuentum, adeo

19 pertransire] transire BU.   20 quo L, quid BSU.   25 Manto]
Mantho BU.   Tyresie] Thiresiæ B, thiresie U.   Edipi] Oedipi B.
28 Caldeorum] Chaldeorum B.

exellent was learnyde in it that in hyr tyme noone knewe better
the mouynge of the heuenly flammes, the colours and the mur-
merynge of the ayre (I cannot tell by what dewylyshe worke) to
dyuyne of thynges to cum. Besydes that, with the lyghtes
and longes of beastes she coulde well dyuyne what | shulde f. 29a
happen after, soo that she drewe, as it is thought, by hyr craft 6
vnclene spyrytes and dewyles to hyr and compellyd theym to gyue
aunswers of those thynges that shulde happen after. Now when
the prynces of Grece that besegyde Thebes were vaynquysshed,
and Creon occupyinge the kyngdome of Thebes, [she], fleynge 10
frome the newe kynge, went into Asya and after ordeynede ther
the famouse temple of Apollo, and ther was delyuerede of the
exellent poete Mopses, whose father was nott, nor yett is not yet
knowne. But sum thynke contrary to thys and saye that with a
certeyn numbre of hyres she wonderyde, after the battell of 15
Thebes, here and ther so longe, tyll she arryuyde in Italy and ther
conceyuyd a chylde, whiche was callede Cytheon, and of sum

9 Thebes] and *add.* MS.

---

egregie disceret, vt euo suo nemo melius flammarum motus,
colores et murmura, quibus, nescio quo dyabolico opere, futurorum dicunt demonstrationes inesse, cognosceret. Preterea fibras 20
pecudum et thaurorum iocinora [et] quorumcunque animalium
exta perspicaci cognouit intuitu traxitque sepissime, vt creditum
est, suis artibus spiritus immundos et inferorum manes coegit in
voces et responsa dare querentibus. Sane, cum iam bello cecidis-
sent Argiui reges, qui Thebas obsiderant, occupassetque Creon 25
ciuitatis imperium, hec, vt placet aliquibus, regem nouum fugiens
secessit in Asiam ibique Clarij Appollinis fanum, postea celeberri-
mum diuinitate, instituit et Mopsum, inclitum seculi vatem—
esto, ex quo conceptum, non prodat antiquitas—peperit. Alij vero
aliter sentiunt dicuntque eam cum complicibus quibusdam suis 30
post Thebanum bellum errasse diu et tandem in Ytaliam deuenisse
ibique Tiberino iunctam cuidam concepisse ex eo et peperisse

18 vt] et S.   21 thaurorum] taurorum BU.   iocinora] iecinora B.
[et] *om.* LS.   27 Clarij] Darij BU; *Morley understood* Clarij *to be* clari.
28 inclitum] *add.* sui BU.   29 vero] *om.* BU.   32 Tiberino] Thyberino B,
thiberino U.

callede Bianor, and frome thens, takynge hyr sonne w*ith* hyr,
went vnto Cisalpina Gall[i]a, where, fyndynge a platt nyghe to
Benacho, enuyroned w*ith* water *and* lakes, of verey nature wonders
stronge, in that place to th'entent she withoute dreade the better
5 myght vse hyr crafte of enchauntment, ther to haue stablyshed
hyr dwellynge place. And of hyr name after hyr decesse the
towne was callede Mantua. And sum say, contrary to thys, that
to hyr deathe constantly she p*er*seuerede a virgyne. Surely, it
is a thynge, if she so dyd, co*m*mendable, all thoughe she vsede
10 suche sorcery, to co*m*mende hyr v*ir*ginyte to Gode.

Of the wyffes of Mennon.
The xxix^th Chapitre.

THe names of the wyffes of Mennia *and* how many they were
in numbre, by the slaknes of wryters is not had in mynde.
15 Surely, agaynste goode reason, for as muche as they be worthy

2 gallea MS.

---

filium quem Citheonum dixere, a quibusdam Byanorem etiam
vocitatum, et inde cum prole in Cisalpinam Galliam transiecisse,
vbi cum p[al]ustria loca, Benaco contermina lacui, comperisset sui
natura munita, seu vt suis incantationibus posset vacare liberius,
20 seu vite residuum securius ducere, media in palude in supere-
minente aquis solo posuisse sedem et ibidem post tempus mortuam
atque sepultam. Circa cuius tumulum aiunt Citheonum ciuitatem
suis constituisse eamque de matris nomine Manthuam vocitasse.
Quidam vero arbitrati sunt eam in mortem vsque constanti pro-
25 posito virginitatem seruasse, floridum quippe atque sanctissimum
opus et laudabile plurimum, [ni] illud nephastis suis [labefactasset]
artibus deoque vero, cui dicanda est, virginitatem seruasset.

De coniugibus Meniarum. xxix.

MEniarum vxorum numerus ac nomina, seu coeuorum scri-
30 bentium desidia, seu animositatis vicio, nobis subtracta

17 transiecisse] transiuisse BU.   18 plaustria L, plaustra S.   Benaco]
venato S.   19 incantationibus] cantationibus B, cantacionibus U.
20–1 in supereminente] insuper eminente BSU.   21 solio LS.
26 in L.   labefactasset *om.* LS.   27 vero] vota BU.   30 animosi-
tatis] annositatis BU.

to be hade in laude *and* memory, albeit enuyouse fortune so wolde not. Yet in all we can or may, we shall cause theym to be had in mynde w*ith* oure posteryte.

Thies men of | Mennany were of the felowshyppe of Jason, verey f. 29*b* towarde yonge men, whiche after the expedycione of Jason 5 into Colchos had reuertyde agayne into theyr countrie. Leuynge theyr oune naturall countrye, they chose theym a place to dwell emongste the Lacedemoniens, which not oonely of theym was freely grauntyde the*ir* dwellynge in their cyte, but, to that, they receyuyde theym emongste the fathers *and* presydent*es* of theyr 10 com*u*ne welthe. Of whiche sayde greate beneuolence *and* gentlenes they litle reme*m*brynge, they conspyrede emongest theymself to haue not onely brought the towne in seruytude, but to haue take frome theym quyte and cleene their lybertye. Ther was then emo*n*ge thies a sorte of ryche yonge gentlemen, aswell by theym- 15 self*es* as also by the affynyte that they had w*ith* the Lacede- monyens, in syngulare reputatione. And aboue other they had

6 Colchos] and *add.* MS.

---

sunt. Equidem indigne, cum non vulgari facinore meruerint in precipuam efferri gloriam. Sed postquam inuidenti fortune sic visum est, qua poterimus arte, ornabimus innominatas digno 20 preconio easque pro viribus in memoriam posteritatis educere tanquam meritas bene conabimur. Menie igitur fuere ex Iasonis atque Argonautarum socijs non minime nobilitatis splendidissimi iuuenes, qui cum peracta expeditione Colchida redissent in Greciam, veteri relicto solo apud Lacedemones sibi elegere sedes. 25 Quibus non solum a Lacedemonijs amicabiliter concessa ciuitas est, verum inter patres et reipublice presidentes assumpti sunt, cuius tam splendide magnificentie successor[e]s minus memores, libertatem publicam ignominiose seruituti velle subigere ausi sunt. Erant enim ea tempestate opulenti iuuenes: nec solum suo fulgore 30 perlucidi, verum et generosorum Lacedemoniorum affinitatibus septi gemina fulgebant luce. Nam inter alia erant eis speciosissime

18 indigne] indignæ silentio præteriri B. 22 mer. bene] bene meritas BU. 24 Colchida] Colchica B. 28 magnificentie] munificentiæ B, munificentie U. successoris LS. 29 ignominiose] ignominose BU. 30 ea] a BS. 31 generosorum] generosum BU.

fayre women to theyr wyfes, beynge descendyde of the moste
nobleste bloode of the cytesens—of truthe, noo small gyfte of thys
mundayne glorye, and a greate numbre adherenttes to theym for
the same. For whiche causes eleuate in their myndes, they toke
5 it not as thoughe it had bene geuyn theym thys felicyte by the
comune assente of the cyte, but by theyr oune merytes. And for
that folyshly they caste theyr myndes to occupye at theyr wyll
the comune welthe and to haue put the reste in to seruytude;
whose vngracious myndes knowne, withoute more styrrynge they
10 were taken and caste, as the deseruyde, into a stronge prysone.
Now the guyse was that those that shulde suffre deathe that
allways the nyght before, the hangemen shulde be sent to theym
to gyue theym monycyone that the next day folowynge they
shulde suffre deathe. Thyes Mennons wyffes, heryng of thys,
15 lamentyde oute of measure and caste emongest theym a way to
delyuer theym that hathe not been herde of before that tyme.
Thei put on theyr backes vyle vestementes, and with wepynge
and waylynge, when the day was paste and the nyght comen, they
dyd entreate somuche the kepars of the castles that they myghte

20 coniuges a nobilissimis ciuibus ducentes originem, non edepol pars
vltima mundani decoris, cui et clientele addebantur ingentes, ex
quibus non gratiam publice patrie felicitati sensere, sed suis
ascribentes meritis, eo se fatuitatis euehi permisere, vt ceteris se
preferendos fore existimarent: ex quo in cupidinem corruere
25 imperij, et hinc ad occupandam rempublicam temere conatus
exposuere suos. Quam ob causam, detecto crimine, capti carceri-
que traditi et capitali supplicio tanquam patrie hostes damnati
sunt auctoritate publica. Et cum nocte sequenti Lacedemonum
veteri more deberet illis a carnificibus mors inferri, meste flentes-
30 que coniuges pro liberatione dampnatorum inauditum iniuere
consilium, nec cogitato distulere operam dare. Squalidis igitur
vestimentis, velato ore, opplete lacrimis, cum iam in noctem
occumberet dies, quoniam nobiles essent femine, intrandi carcerem

22 gratiam] modo *add.* B.　　patrie] permisere *add.* S.　　sensere]
referre neglexere B.　　23 fatuitatis] fatuitati SU.　　permisere *om.* S.
28 cum] dum BU.　　30 liberatione] deliberatione BU.　　32 velato]
velatoque BU.　　33 quoniam] quam B.

haue libertie that nyghte to be with theym in the prysone. And
so, when they were entred, | they dyd not consume the tyme f. 30a
in wepynge, but with deliberate aduyse put theyr garmentes
on theyr husbondes backes and their husbondes on theyrs; and so
clothede in theyr wyffes habyttes, feyny[ng]e to weepe and bewail, 5
with theyr heedys coueryde [they] went their way, theyr wyfes
remaynynge prysoners in theyr steedes. Nor the fraude was not
spyede tyll in the mornynge, when they were callede to execu-
tione, in the place or steede of the men ther they founde women.
Surely, thys was a greate feythe of the women and a ryght laud- 10
able loue. Lett vs then passe ouer what the Senate dyd to the
kepars that were deceyuyde and what ordre the Senate toke, after
they were escapped. I wyll say by the olde institution that the
indissoluble bounde of maryage gothe to thys naturall poynte
that, where as betwyxte too that loue not, ther can be noo greater 15
hatered, soo in lykewyse, where ther is true loue betwyxt man
and wyfe, ther can be no greater loue. For that fyre, kyndled

5 feynyde MS.

perituros visure viros facile a custodibus obtinuere licentiam. Ad
quos cum venissent, non tempus consumpsere lacrimis et ploratu
sed repente explicato consilio cum [viris] mutatis vestibus velatis- 20
que illis femineo ritu faciebus, flentes deiectis in terram oculis
fingentesque mesticiam, noctis etiam suffragantibus tenebris et
reuerentia nobilibus feminis debita, deceptis custodibus morituros
emiserunt, ipsis damnatorum loco remanentibus. Nec ante fraus
comperta est quam venientibus suppliciorum ministris, vt dam- 25
natos in mortem educerent, pro viris femine comperte sunt.
Grandis profecto mulierum fides et egregius amor! Sed sinamus
fraudis in custodes ludibrium, salutem damnatis exhibitam,
qu[i]d patribus visum sit et qu[i]d inde secutum; sacri coniugalis
amoris vires et audaciam mulierum paululum contemplemur. 30
Instituto nature, veteri indissolubili nexu firmato, nonnulli volunt
dissidentium coniugum nullum fore perniciosius odium, sic et
conuenientium amorem excedere ceteros. Nam rationis igne suc-

19 venissent] deuenissent BU.   20 *om.* LS.   26 sunt] sint BU.
29 quod LS.   33 amorem] amori B.   excedere] concedere BU.

w*ith* reason, burnethe not, as we shulde say, to madnes, but
warmeth into pleasynge of the tone parte to the tother, and w*ith*
so greate charyte couples the*im* together that equally, wyll they,
nyll they, ones vnyte with so pleasaunt a co*n*formyte, that to theyr
5 contynuac*i*on therin ther is nothynge of neither parte forgotten,
so that theyr fortunes and labours be all oone, *and* agaynst all
myschyff*es* the toone to the tother either w*ith* counseill or with
deede can fynde a remedy agaynst it. With thies swete boundes
the wyffes of Mennya deceyuyde the kepars, poyntyde the tyme
10 and the place how to do it, demynge assuredly that ther is
nothynge more honeste for theym then to delyuer by theyr oune

census non vrit ad insaniam sed in complacentiam calefacit et
tanta caritate corda copulat, vt eque se*m*per cuncta nolint velint-
que, et tam placide assuetus vnitati ad continuationem sui nil
15 omittit, nil agit tepide vel remisse, etsi hostis fortuna sit, vltro
labores et pericula subit, et vigilantibus in salutem meditatur
consilia, remedia comperit, et excudit fallacias, si exigit indigentia.
Hic suauissimus et iam placido conuictu firmatus coniugum
Meniarum tanto feruore impulit animos, vt qu[a]s nequissent
20 ante vidisse, periclitantibus viris, ingenij pressis viribus, decipulas
inuenirent, instrumenta pararent, rerum ordinem, tempus ratio-
nemque agendorum, vt oculatos seuerosque custodes deciperent,
et sublata sensualitatis nebula aduertentes quoniam nil honestum
pro salute amici omittendum sit, ex intimis cordis latebris excitata
25 pietate, vt viros periculo exi[m]erent, temerario ausu in id irent,
vt quos publica damnauerat auctoritas, pudicus coniugalis amor
absolueret, quos carceri mancipauerat, emitteret, quos iam tenere
dirum videbatur et capitale supplicium, e carnificum manu sub-
tractos securitati viteque donaret. Et, quod permaximum visum
30 est, delusa legum potestate, decreto publico ac patrum auctoritate
et totius ciuitatis voto frustrato, vt quod optabant impleretur,
non expau[e]re loco damnatorum sub deceptorum custodum im-

16 vigilantibus] vigilantissimus BU.   17 exigit] exigat BU.   19
quos LS.   21–2 rationemque] rationesque BU.   25 exinierent LS.
26 auctoritas] autoritas BU.   27 mancipauerat] manciparat BU.
28 e] et LS.   29 donarent LS.   30 delusa] lusa BU.   auct.]
autoritate BU.   31 impleretur] implerent B, implerentur U.   32 ex
pauore LS.   imperio] imperium B.

parelles theyr husbondes frome deathe. Surely, I cannot to muche
meruell nor laude nor commende so true a feythe, soo perfyte a
bounde, and I thynke surely that if their loue had not ben bownde
so true and so iuste, they wolde rather haue slepte at home at
theyr ease then to haue doone so honourable and wyfely an 5
acte. | And, for to conclude in fewe wordes, I dare well say they f. 30b
were verey men that dissymylede theymselfes to be women, and
they true wyfes and goode wyfes that dissymyled the contrary.

Of Panthasilea, the Quene of the Amozenes.
The xxxti Chapitre.   10

PAnthasilea, a virgyne, was Quene of the Amozenes, and she
succedede the too quenes Orithea and Antiopi, but of what
parentes she was procreate I haue not redde it. They say this
woman, dispysynge all womans apparell, put harnes on hyr, well
as hyr elders had doone, so that she coueryde hyr golden heere 15
with a helmett and hyr syde with a queuer of arowes, and after
a vallyaunte knyghtes facyone mountyd vpon goode horses and

11 Pantathasilea MS.

---

perio sese claudere. Non edepol tam sinceram fidem, amorem tam
integrum admirari sufficio, et ob id ratum habeo, si remisse
amassent, si tenui fuissent astricte v[in]culo, cum illis per ocium 20
domi torpere fas esset, hec tam grandia non fecissent. Attamen,
vt multa paucis concludam, has asserere audeo veros certosque
fuisse viros Meniasque iuuenes quas simulabant feminas extitisse.

De Penthesilea, regina Amazonum. xxx.

PEnthesilea virgo Amazonum regina fuit et successit Orithie et 25
Antiopi reginis; quibus tamen procreata parentibus non legi.
Hanc aiunt oris incliti spreto decore et superata mollicie feminei
corporis, arma induere maiorum suarum aggressam, et auream
cesariem tegere galea, et latus munire pharetra, et militari non
muliebri ritu currus et equos ascendere seque pre ceteris reginis 30

20 vmculo L.   22 vt] et S.   concludam] claudam BU.   25 Penthesilea]
Pentesilea BU.   26 Anthiope B.   27 oris] omnis BU.   29 cesariem]
cesariam U.   29–30 non muliebri] om. BU.

charyotes, in suche wyse that aboue all quenes she dyd with goode
ryghte preferre hyrselfe. And she lacked not, to thys, an exellent
wytte, in so muche that she was the fyrste that inuentyde thiese
battell axes, afore hyr tyme not knowne. Thys Panthasilea,
5 herynge of the vallyauntnes of the worthy Hector, louyde hym
moste hertely and, desyrouse to haue hade by hym a chylde to
haue bene an enherytour of hyr realme after hyr, in that greate
oportunyte she descendyd frome hyr countrie to the Troians
helppe, with a greate numbre of hyr maydens. Nor the greate
10 fame of the Grekys made not hyr so affrayde but that sume tyme,
more desyrouse by hyr vallyauntnes to please Hector then w*ith*
hyr beautie, often she ranne emongest the thyckest of the Grecianes
and with hyr speere ouerthrewe sumtyme oone, sumtyme another.
f. 31a And now | *and* then with hyr swerde she made way afore
15 hyr and furthwithe with hyr bowe shotte at theym that fledde,
in suche wyse that Hector hymself was meruelede at hyr deedes.
But at the last this valli*a*unt virago, preasynge emonge the moste
valliaunt*es* of the Grekes, to the entente to shewe to hyr loue what

---

mirabilem exhibere viribus et disciplina ausa est. Cui nec ingenium
20 validum defuisse constat, cum legatur securis vsum in seculum
vsque suum incognitum fuisse compertum. Hec, vt placet aliquibus, audita Troyani Hectoris virtute inuisum ardenter amauit
et cupidine in successionem regni inclite prolis ex eo suscipiende,
in tam grandem oportunitatem cum maxima suorum copia eius
25 in auxilium aduersus Grecos facile prouocata descendit. Nec eam
clara Grecorum principum perterruit fama, quin Hectori armis et
virtute cupiens potius quam formositate placere, sepissime certamina frequentium armatorum intraret, et nonnunquam hasta
prosternere, quandoque obsistentes gladio aperire et persepe arcu
30 versas in fugam turmas pellere et tot ta[m]qu[e] grandia viriliter
agere, vt ipsum spectantem aliquando Hectorem in admirationem
sui deduceret. Tandem, dum in fortissimos hostes virago hec die
preliaretur vna, seque vltra solitum tanto amasio dignam
ostenderet, multis ex suis iam cesis letali suscepto vulnere mise-

19 exhibere] exhibuere B.   22 inuisum] nondum uisum B.   23
suscipiende] suscipiendi BU.   24 suorum] suarum BU.   25 Grecos] Gra-
ios BU.   27 potius] *om.* BU.   30 fugam] *add.* in LS.   tanquam LS.
32 die] *om.* BU.

a noble hert she had, not withoute greate slaughter of theym was
slayne.   I deny not but sum say that or she came to Troy, Hector
was deade, and s[he] in a sharppe conflycte was woundede to the
deathe.   But whether it be the tone or the tother, it may be
meruelede at to see a woman to runne emongst armede men, but   5
that vse often chaungeth in to a nother nature *and* that thies
women were muche more vallyaunte then sum men be, whiche
by idlenes and voluptuousnes be turnede to be lyke women,
euen as an hare that weryth an helmet on hys heede.

Of Polixene, Kynge Priamus doughter.   10
The xxxj^{ti} Chapitre.

POlixene the virgyne was the doughter of Ky*n*ge Priamus by hys
wyfe Eccuba, of so exellent a beautie, and so goodely a thynge
that the feerse breste of Achilles was persyde therwyth, in so
muche that by the p*er*suasyon of Eccuba hyr mother he was 15
brought, in hoope to haue hyr, into the temple withyn Troy of
Apollo and ther by Parrys murdrede and slayne. O, that it was

3 so MS.

---

randa, medios inter Grecos a se stratos occubuit. Alij vero volunt
eam, Hectore iam mortuo, applicuisse Troyam et ibidem, vt
scribitur, acri in pugna cesam. Essent qui possent mirari mulieres 20
quantumcunque armatas in viros vnquam incurrere ausas, ni
admirationem subtraheret, quoniam vsus in naturam vertitur
alteram, quo hec et huiusmodi longe magis in armis homines
facte sunt quam sint quos sexu masculos natura fecit et ociositas
et voluptas vertit in feminas seu lepores galeatos.   25

De Polixena, Priami regis, filia. xxxi.

POlixena virgo, Priami, regis Troianorum, ex Hecuba fuit filia,
tam floride pulcritudinis adolescentula, vt seuero pectori
Achillis Peliadis flammas immittere potuerit cupidinis eumque
matris Hecube fraude in suam necem nocte solum in templum 30
vsque Appollinis [T]imbrei deducere. O, quam minus debito lapsis

20 in] *om*. BU.   22 quoniam] quod B.   vertitur] vertatur BU.
31 cimbrei LS.   O] ob BU.   minus debito] *om*. B.

agaynste all goode ordre, when the Troyans were vaynquyshede
and Ilion burnte *and* destroyede, that so swete a mayden shulde
be deuowred by the hande of Pyrrus for to satisfye for another
woma*n*s offe*n*ce! But if we shall gyue credyte to the wrytynge
5 of our elders, when she was broughte to Achilles tumbe, seynge
f. 31*b* the feerse | yonge man Pyrrus with hys swerde redye to smyte
of hyre heede, albeit those that stoode aboute hyr wepte and
lamentyde hyr deathe, the poore, innocente vi*r*gyne with so
constante a hert strechyde forthe hyr necke that the Grekes noo
10 lesse meruelede therwythe then they were mouede w*ith* pyte at
hyr. It is doubtles a thynge worthy to be had in reme*m*braunce
to se in that sex, after so dyuers mutation of fortune, a mayden
so constant, when often suche sodeyn mutationes, vnder the
swerde of the victore, ryght noble and hardy hertes haue bene
15 abashede there at. I can right well beleue that the worke
procedyde of hyr gentle herte, to shue to other how lytle
deathe is to be extemyde and all the false variete of mutable
fortune.

Troyanis viribus et Ylione deiecto a Neptholemo in piaculum
20 man[i]um patris et ad eius tumulum deducta est ibique, si
maiorum litteris fides vlla prestari potest, videns acrem iuuenem
expedisse gladium, flentibus ceteris circumstantibus, innocens
adeo constanti pectore et intrepido vultu iugulum prebuit, vt non
minus admiratio fortitudinis eius quam pietas parentis moueret
25 animos. Magnum quippe et memoratu dignum nequiuisse tenella,
etas, sexus femineus, mollicies regia, mutata fortuna, grandem
pressisse virginis animum, et potissime sub victoris et hostis
gladio, sub quo nonnunquam egregiorum virorum nutant et
persepe deficiunt animosa pectora. Crediderim facile hoc
30 generose nature opus, vt ostenderet hac mortis paruipensione
quam feminam produxisset, [ni] tam cito hostis surripuisset
fortuna.

19 Ylione] Ilio B.   Neptholemo] neptholomeo S, neoptholemo U,
Neoptolemo B.   20 manum L.   patris] sui *add.* B.   22 gladium]
gaudium U.   24 pietas] pietatis BS.   parentis] filij Neoptomi erga
patrem Achillem B.   25 nequiuisse] quod B.   26 fortuna] *add.*
potuit B.   28 nutant] mutant S.   30 hac] ac U.   31 in LS.

Of Heccuba, the Quene of the Troyanes.
The xxxij^{ti} Chapitre.

HEccuba was the moste noble Quene of the Troyanes, and of
a woman ordeynede to so hard fortune a bryghtnes moste
exellent, and, to thys, a verey playne example of o*ur* wrechidnes. 5
This Quene, as sum tell, was the doughter of Diama*n*tis, and, as
sum say, of Cipseus, Kynge of Trace, to whiche opynyone I gladly
condescende, for because the more parte so say. Thys, beynge
a mayden, was maryde to the noble Priam*us* and had by hym as
well sonnes as doughters. Emonge other, she had that clere and 10
bryghte lyghte of knyghtly prowes, Hector, which had in hym so
many noble condiciones that not oonly he hym self hathe de-
s*er*ued fame eu*er*lastynge, but also by hym hys father, hys mother
and hys countrie hathe gotten | eternall glorye. Thys woma*n* f. 32*a*
then that I haue spoken of had by thys not onely greate fame, 15
but also by hyr waywerde fortune, [was] notable to all the worlde.
For thys noble Hector and yonge, valyaunte Troylus, she sawe
theym bothe slayne, the twayne fyrme pyllars of the Troyans.

De Hecuba, regina Troyanorum. xxxij.

HEcuba, Troyanorum preclarissima regina, fuit eque perituri 20
splendoris fulgor eximius et miseriarum certissimum documentum. Hec secundum quosdam Dyamantis Aonis filia extitit.
Alij vero Cipsei, regis Tracie, volunt, quod quid[e]m et ipse
arbitror, cum sic opinetur a pluribus. Nupsit hec virgo Priamo,
regi Troyanorum illustri, et ex eo mixtim vtriusque sexus concepit 25
peperitque filios decem et nouem, inter quos iubar illud eximium
Frigie probitatis Hector, cuius tantus fuit militie fulgor, vt non
se tantum eterna fama splendidum faceret, quinymo et parentes
patriamque perhenni nobilitaret gloria. Verum, non tantum
felicis regni decore ac multiplicis prolis serenitate fulgida facta est, 30
quin vrgente aduersa fortuna orbi toto long[e] deueniret cognita.
Hectorem nempe dilectissimum sibi et Troylum adolescentem et
iam maiora viribus audentem manu Achillis cesos, et ea cede regni

22 Dyamantis] Dimantis BU.   23 Cipsei] Ciphæi B.   quidam LS.
29 perhenni] perenni BU.   31 longo LS.

She sawe also Parys slayne of Pyrr*us* and Deyphebus deformydly
deade, Troy brunte, and Polices, hir yonge son, in hys fathers
lappe oppressyd, and hyr olde husbo*n*d Pryam*us* afore hys
domesticall goddes deuowrede, Ilion to be brunte and Cassandra
5 *and* Andromaca, hyr doughter in lawe, *and* hyrselfe to be compellyd by forse to go in to exyle, and, last of all, Polidorus hyr
sonne, by the fraude of Polinestor, by the see syde put to deathe.
With thyes sorowes *and* harde fortunes su*m* say that she fell
madde and ranne in the feeldys of the Traciens, howlynge as a
10 dogge, and ther dyede and was buryede at Hellespont. And sum
say, contrary, that she was ledde in seruytude wyth the other in
to Grece, and to th'entent that ther shulde not lacke noo parte of
mysfortune to hyr, that at the laste she sawe hyr doughter Cassandra afore hyr eyes, by the co*m*maunde[me]nt of Clytemystra,
15 Agamenons wyfe, to be put to deathe.

14 cōmaundent MS.

---

solidam basem fere euersam mestissime fleuit. Sic et a Pyrro
Paridem trucidatum, inde auribus naribusque truncatum Deiphe-
bum atque fede exa[n]i[m]atum, Ylionem igne cremari Danao,
Policem patris in gremio confodi, Priamum ipsum senem secus
20 domesticas aras exenterari, Cassandram filiam, Andromacam
nurum, seque captiuam ab hostibus trahi, Polixenam ante Achillis
tumulum obtruncari, Astianactem nepotem ex latebris surreptum
saxo illidi, miseranda aspexit. Et postremo Tratio in litore tumu-
latum adolescentulum Polidorum, Polimestoris fraude occisum,
25 comperit atque fleuit. Quibus tot tamque immanibus oppressam
doloribus in rabiem versam volunt aliqui, Tratiosque per agros
ritu vlulasse canum et sic mortuam et in tumulo Hellespon[t]ia[c]i
litoris cui nomen a se Cynose[m]a sepultam. Nonnulli dicunt in
seruitutem ab hostibus cum reliquis tractam et, ne miseriarum illi
30 particula deesset vlla, vidisse vltimo Cassandram occiso iam
Agamenone Clitemestre iugulari iussu.

18 examinatum L, exaiatum S.   20 Andr.] Adromatam S, Andro-
machen BU.   21 Polix.] poliesenam S, polisenam U.   22 Ast.]
Astyonactem B, astionactem U.   23 aspexit] conspexit BU.
Tratio] taceo B, tacio U.   23–4 tumulantum L.   24 Polim.] Polymnes-
toris B.   25 comperit] operit BU.   26 Tratiosque] Thraciosque B,
traciosque U.   27 hellesponciati LS.   28 Cynosenia BLSU.
31 Clit.] Clytemnestræ B.   iugulari] iugulata est B.

Of Cassandra, the doughter of Pryam*us*, Kynge of Troye.
The xxxiij^{ti} Chapitre.

CAssandra was the doughter of Priam*us*, Kynge of Troye. And thys woma*n* had, either by hyr study, or ells by the gyfte of God, or by sum diabolicall craft, the spyryte of p*r*ophecye. 5 Ande thys is affyrmede to be true, that longe or Helene was rauyshed by Parys, and or the cyte was besegyde, she tolde aswell that | as the ruyne of Pryamus and the burnynge of Ilion and f. 32*b* the fynall destruction of hyr fathers kyngedome. And because that neither hyr father nor hyr brother dyd gyue credyte to it, 10 she was oft tymes betyne and chastysede for so tellynge; and of this is risyne the fable that she was belouyde of the god Apollo, and that she grauntyde to be at hys co*m*maundeme*n*t, so that by hym she myght haue the knowlege of thynges to cum. Whiche when Apollo had grauntyde, she denyinge hyr promysse, Apollo 15 coulde not take frome hyr that ones he had frely geuyne hyr, and for that cause, beynge soore displeased, wyllyde that noo man

11 betnyne MS.

De Cassandra, Priami, Troianorum regis, filia. xxxiij.

CAssandra Priami fuit, Troianorum regis, filia. Huic quidem, vt vetustas asserit, vaticinij mens fuit, seu quesita studijs, 20 seu dei dono, seu potius dyabolica fraude, non satis certum est. Hoc tamen affirmatur a multis eam longe ante rapinam Helene, audaciam Paridis et aduentum Tyndaridis et longam ciuitatis obsidionem et postremam Priami atque Ylionis desolationem persepe et clara cecinisse voce. Et ob hoc, cum nulla dictis suis 25 prestaretur fides, a patre et fratribus verberibus castigatam volunt: ac etiam fabulam inde confictam eam scilicet ab Appolline dilectam et in eius concubitum requisitam; quem se prestaturam promisisse dicunt, si ab eodem ante eidem futurorum noticia prestaretur. Quod cum suscepisset negassetque promissum, nec 30 Appollo posset auferre concessum, aiunt illum muneri adiecisse

19 Huic] Huc B, hunc U.   22 rapinam] raptum B, rapi U.
23 audaciam] audaciamque BU.   24 postremam] postremum BU.
27 confictam] confectam B.   28 quem] cui B.

shulde beleue hyr saynges, were they true or false, and for that, what so euer she prophecyede, no man gaue therto credyte. Thys woma*n* was maryde to a yonge man callede Corebus, whiche was slayne, or he couplede with hyr, in the batell. And at the last,
5 Troy wastyde *and* perysshed, she fell emonge the other captyues into Agamenons handes, to whom she tolde that by hys wyfe Clytemestra hys deathe was co*n*spyrede. To whose wordes when ther was noo feythe geuyn to it, after many perylls she arryuyde with Agamenon at Misenas, where by the co*m*maundement of
10 Clytemestra she was put to deathe.

Of Clytemestra, the wyfe to the Kynge Agamenon.
The xxxiiij[th] Chapitre.

CLytemestra was the doughter of Kynge Tyndar*us*, of Leda hys wyfe, whiche was suster to Castor *and* Polinyx and to the
15 fayre Helene. And all though she be by hyr auncyent stocke ryght famouse, yet by hyr vngracyouse deede doone to hyr
f. 33*a* husbonde she is more | spoken of. For hyr husbonde Agamenon

10 putto MS.

---

neminem quod diceret crediturum. Et sic factum est, vt quod diceret tanquam fatue dictum crederetur a cunctis. Hec autem
20 nobili cuidam Corebo desponsata iuueni, prius illum in bello perdidit quam ab eo susciperetur in thalamum, et demum pereuntibus rebus captiua Agamenoni cessit in sortem. A quo cum Micenas traheretur, eidem cecinit a Clitemestra preparatas insidias atque mortem. Cuius verbis cum fides daretur nulla, post mille
25 maris pericula Micenas cum Agamenone deuenit, vbi eo Clitemestre fraude ceso, et ipsa eiusdem Clitemestre iussu iugulata est.

De Clitemestra, Micenarum regina. xxxiiij.

CLitemestra Tindari, regis Oebalie, filia fuit ex Leda, et Castoris atque Pollucis et Helene soror, virgoque nupsit Aga-
30 menoni, Micenarum regi. Que, etsi genere satis e[t] coniugio clara esset, nephario tamen ausu clarior facta est. Nam imperante

23 cecinit] *add.* sibi BU.   28 Oebalie] cebalie U.   29 Pollucis]
polluas S.   30 ex LS.

beynge chosen emper*our* emonge the Grekes at the seege of
Troy and [she] ha[uynge] had afore that by hym many chyldren,
it so chauncyde that Egistus, whiche was a yonge man all geuen to
idlenes, and because he was electe to presthode, he dyd not goo
to the warres, whereby at length he fell in concupyscence with 5
thys Clytemestra and, breuely, vsed hyr at hys pleasure. The
whiche vngracyouse deede accomplisshed, ferynge the cumynge
home of Agamenon with Cassandra, by the p*er*suasion of hyr
darlynge thys valyaunte virago w*ith* fraude *and* folish boldnes
conspyrede the deathe of hyr husbonde. And, as sum say, as he 10
satte at sopper, tryhumphantly arayde, hauynge garment*es* that
he had wonne at the spoyle of Troy, hys honeste wyfe prayde
hy*m* to put on a garmente after the Grekes facyon, which saide
garmente she affirmede to haue made hyrself. And soo hade she

2 and had had MS.   3 that] by *add*. MS.

Agamenone viro Grecorum copijs apud Troyam, cum ex eo iam 15
plurimos filios peperisset, ociosi atque desidis iuuenis Egisti, olim
Tiestis ex Pelopia filij, qui ob sacerdotium abstinebat ab armis, in
concupiscentiam incidit et, vt placet aliquibus, Nauplij senis
Palamedis olim patris suasionibus, eius in amplexus et concubitum
venit. Ex quo scelere secutum est vt, seu timore ob patratum 20
facinus redeuntis Agamenonis, seu amasij suasione et regni
cupidine, seu indignationis contexte ob Cassandram, que ab
Agamenone deducebatur Micenas, animosa mulier armato animo
et fraudibus temerario ausu surrexit in virum eumque victorem
Ylij redeuntem et maris tempestatibus fessum, ficta oris leticia 25
suscepit in regiam. Et, vt quibusdam placet, cenantem et vino
iam forte madentem percuti iussit ab adultero ex insidijs pro-
deunte. Alij autem dicunt, cum recumberet vestimentis victoria
quesitis implicitus, quasi Grecanicis festum clarius esset futurum,
placida adultera coniunx illi suasit vt patrias indueret vestes et 30
quas ipsa in hoc ante confecerat easque exitu capitis carentes,

16 plurimos] plures BU.   17 Tiestis] Thyestis BU.   22 contexte]
conceptæ B, concepte U.   23 deducebatur] ducebatur BU.   27–8
prodeunte] prodeuntem BU.   28 recumberet] recubaret BU.
29 Grecanicis] grecanijs U.   clarius] darius S.   30 placida]
placide BU.   31 capitis] capiti U.   carentes] carentis S.

doone in dede—in suche wyse that when [he] shulde haue put
it on hys heede, ther was noo place oppen for it, and in the meane
tyme that he gropyde here and ther, by the monytion of thys
worthy harlott, Egistus, hyr p*ar*amour, slewe hym; and that
5 doone, with Egistus she reignede seuen yeres. Now in the meane
season Ho[r]estes, hyr sone gotten by Agamenon, cumen to mans
age, whyche was kept frome hyr fury by the freandes of hyr
fyrste husbonde, berynge sore at hys hert hys fathers deathe and
desyrouse to be reuengyde, slewe bothe the harlott *and* the
10 aduoulterer. Whome of thies twayne shall I more blame, either
the myschyfe of the mother or the boldnes of the son. For the
noble, yonge man was not affrayde to do a greate euyll, that is,
to kyll hys oune mother; but how muche more was the harlote
to blame, to murdre hyr oune husbonde! Now when eu*er*y man
15 hathe sayde hys fantasy, thys is myne—that is, to lawde the
vertue of Horestes that suffrede not longe vnpunyshed the fowle

6 Honestes MS.

---

audax porrexit eidem. Et cum iam brachia manicis iniecisset vir,
quereretque circumuolutus vnde posset emittere caput, semi-
ligatus adultero percussori ab e[a]dem suadente concessus est et
20 sic eo neminem vidente percussus est. Quo facto regnum occupauit omne et cum adultero Egisto per septennium imperauit.
Sane, cum excreuisset interim Horestes, Agamenonis ex ea filius,
quem clam seruauerant a furore matris amici, animumque in
necem patris vlciscendam sumpsisset, tempore sumpto eam cum
25 adultero interemit. Quid incusem magis nescio, scelus an audacia[m]. Primum pregrande malum non metuerat vir inclitus.
Secundum quantominus decebat perfidam mulierem, tanto ab-
hominabile magis. Habeo tamen qu[o]d laudem, Horestis scilicet
virtutem, que diu sustinere passa non est a pietate inceste matris
30 retrahi, quin in immeritam patris necem animosus vltor irrueret
et in male meritam matrem filius ageret quod minus meritus

19 eodem LS.   20 neminem] nemine BU.   22 Horestes]
Orestes B.   23 animumque] animum BU.   25-6 audacia L.
26 metuerat] meruerat BU.   28 quid LBSU.   29 sustinere]
substinere U, abstinere B.   30 vltor] vltro BU.

aduoultry of his mother, but, as hys fathers bloode vndes*er*uyde
was shedd, so in lykewyse to shedde in recompe*n*s the | bloode f. 33*b*
of Egistus th'aduoulterer and of the cursyde ladye virago, hys
mother.

Of Helene, the wyfe of Kynge Menelaus. 5
The xxxvth Chapitre.

HElene, aswell by hyr wantonnes as for the cruell batells that
ensuede therby, is a woma*n* spoken of thorow oute the
worlde. She was the doughter to Tyndarus, the Kynge of Oebalie,
whiche he had by Leda hys wyfe of synguler beautie, and maryede 10
to Menelaus, the Kynge of the Lacedemoniens. Thys Helene, as all
hystoryens wryte, aswell Grekes as Latynes, was of so exellent a
shappe that she passyd all others. For the dyuyne poete Homer
it weryde hym in man*er* to descryue hyr in hys poecye. And
besydes thys, peynters *and* keruers of ymages, they dyd all they 15
coulde to peynte and kerue hyr excedy*ng* beautefull pycture, to

---

genitor ab adultero sacerdote, incesta imperante femina, passus
fuerat et eorum quorum imperio et opere paternus sanguis effusus
fuerat, [v]t in auctores verteretur scelus, et effuso sanguine
piaretur. 20

De Helena, Menelai regis, coniuge. xxxv.

HElena tam ob seruatam lasciuiam, vt multis visum est, quam
ob diuturnum bellum ex ea consecutum, toti orbi notissima
femina, filia fuit Tyndari, Oebalie regis, et Lede form[os]issime
mulieris et Menelai, Lacedemonum regis, coniunx. Huius, vt omnes 25
aiunt veteres Greci Latinique post eos, tam celebris pulchritudo
fuit, vt preponatur facile ceteris. Fatigauit enim, vt reliquos
sinam, diuini ingenij virum Homerum, antequam [illam] posset
secundum precepta satis conuenienter describere carmine. Preterea pictores et sculptores multiplices egregij omnes eundem 30
sumpsere laborem, vt tam eximij decoris saltem effigiem, si pos-

19 et LS.   auctores] autores BU.   et] *om.* BSU.   21 Menelaij
LS, Menelay U.   22 seruatam] suam BU.   23 bellum] belli BU.
24 Oebalie] Cibalie B, cebalie U.   formissime LS.   25 Menelaij LS.
28 illam *om.* LS.

leue it to theyr posteryte. Emonge other, Zewcis Era[cl]eotes, in hys
tyme the moste famouse peynter, was hyrede of theym of Croty-
ensis for muche money with hys cunyng pensyll to drawe hyr.
Where vnto he put all the science and crafte he had, and hauynge
5 noone other exemplar but onely the verses of Homer *and* the
greate fame that went on hyr, he dyd ymagy*n* in hys mynde by
thys meanes to drawe hyr. Fyrste he behelde all the fayreste
chyldren that were in Grece, next all the fayre wyffes *and* maydens,
that of all the heepe pe*r*fytly notede he myght make oone Helene.
10 And scante he thought, for all that, to peynte hyr so fayre as she
was. And I do not meruell at it. For who coulde with pensell
f. 34*a* or wit*h* toole or wit*h* colou*r* drawe the gladnes of | hyr eyes,
the pleasaunte effabilite of hyr redolente mouthe, the heuenly

1 Eradotes MS.

---

sent, posteritati relinquerent. Quos inter summa conductus a
15 Crotoniensibus pecunia, Zensis Eracleotes, illius seculi famosis-
simus pictor et prepositus ceteris, ad illam p[in]niculo formandam
ingenium omne artisque vires exposuit. Et cum preter Homeri
carmen et magnam vndique famam nullum aliud haberet exemplum, vt per hec duo de facie et cetero persone statu potuerat
20 mente concipere, excogitauit se e[x] alijs plurimum pulcherrimis
formis diuinam illam Helene effigiem posse percipere, et alijs
poscentibus designatam ostendere et ostens[am] posteritati relin-
quere. Primo ex formosissimis pueris et inde sororibus formosio-
ribus quinque precipue decore spectabiles selegit, et collecta
25 secum ex pulchritudine omnium forma vna, totis ex ingenio celebri
emunctis viribus, vix creditum est satis plene quod optabat arte
potuisse perficere. Nec ego miror. Quis enim picture vel statue
peniculo aut colore poterit inscribere leticiam oculorum, totius oris
placidam [a]ffabilitatem, celestem risum motusque faciei varios,

15 Crot.] Cotoniensibus BU.   Zensis] Zeuxis B, censis U.   Erac.]
Heracleotes BU.   16 puniculo L.   20 et LS.   plurimum] plurium
U.   pulcherrimis] pulchris B.   22 et ostensam] *om.* B, et ostensis
LS.   23 ex] *om.* BSU.   sororibus] et *add.* LS, ex *add.* BU.   24
precipue] præcipuo B, precipuo U.   selegit] elegit BU.   26
emunctis] depromptis B.   27 vel] aut U.   27-8 vel . . . colore]
penicillo aut statuæ scalpro uel ullo colore B.   28 penniculo LS,
pinniculo U.   poterit] potuit BU.   29 effabilitatem LS.

smylynge, the variable mouynge of hyr delycate face *and* other
innumerable qualytes in hyr, when it apperteyneth oonely to
nature so to do? He dyd then what he myght do and, as oone that
was moste cu*n*nynge, left hyr pycture ther, to be seene of his
posterite. Of this is feynede a fable—because of the bryghtnes of 5
hyr swete eies, rutylant as the star, of the swetnes of hyr face, hyr
golden heere hangynge vnto hyr feete, hyr wellfauo*ur*de forhede,
hyr iuorye throote, of hyr swete sounde of hyr voyce, hyr speciall
goode grace and gesture, that Jupiter, conuertyde into a swanne,
dyd forme hir hymselfe, so that whiche hyr parentes coulde not 10
geue hyr, she had it geuene of God, and for that she coulde not
be peyntyde to hyr perfectione. Thys Helene then, for hyr beautie
hauynge far and neere greate fame, mouede Theseus to cum where
she was, and [he], fyndynge hyr playnge emongest other maydens,
by force toke hyr a way, albeit he dyd nothynge to hyr, but oonely 15
kysse hyr and beholde hyr, because she was so yonge, all though

---

et decores secundum verborum et actuum qualitates, cum solius
hoc nature officium sit? Fecit ergo quod potuit et quod pinxerat
tanquam celeste si,nulacri decus posteritati reliquit. Hinc acu-
tiores finxere fabula₁a eamque ob sidereum oculorum fulgorem, ob 20
inuisam mortalibus l ucem, ob insignem faciei candorem aueam-
que come volatilis copiam, hinc inde per humeros petulantibus
recidentem cincinnulis et lepidam sonoramque vocis suauitatem,
necnon et gestus quosdam tam ameni roseique oris quam splendide
frontis et eburnei gutturis, ac ex inuisis delicijs pectoris assurgentis, 25
non nisi ex aspirantis concipiendis aspectu Iouis in cignum versi
descripsere filiam, vt preter quam a matre suscepisse poterat,
formositatem intelligeretur ex infuso numine quod peniculis
coloribusque ingenio suo imprimere nequibant artifices. Ab hac
tam spectanda pulchritudine in [L]aconas Theseus ab Athenis 30
euocatus ante alios virginem et etate tenellam in palestra patrio
ludentem more audax rapuit, etsi preter oscula pauca eidem

17 decores] decoros BU.   21 inuisam] a nullis ante uisam B.
22 humeros] humores U.   23 cincinnulis] cincinnis B, cincinulis U,
tintinullis S.   24 ameni] cinamei S, cynamomi B, cinamomi U.   25
inuisis] nunquam uisis B.   26–7 ex aspirantis concipiendis . . . filiam]
ex conceptu Ledæ et Iouis in cignum uersi procreatam B.   28 numine]
datum *add.* B.   penniculis LS, pinniculisU, pennicillo B.   30 iaconas
L.   31 patrio] primo B.

this was a begy*n*nynge of the losse of hyr virgynyte. But so it
was that whether it were by Theseus mother, or, as sum say, by
Protheus, Kynge of Egypte, Theseus beynge absent and Helenes
freandes demaundynge to haue hyr agayne, she was r*e*storede
5 home to hyr countrie and shortly after, comen to womans yeres,
was maryede to Menelaus, Kynge of the Lacedemonyens, and
[he] had by hyr oone doughter callede Herimonia. Now it was
so that Parys, Kynge Priam*us* sonne, callynge to mynde the
promysse that Venus had made hym for iudgeynge of hyr to be
10 the fayreste of the too goddessys Juno and Pallas, declared vnto
hys father Priamus, if he wolde lett hym goo to Grece, he wolde
brynge home agayne Exion, whiche had bene rauysshed long
before by theym, or ells sum other in her steede, to reuenge hyr |
f. 34*b* takynge. Wherunto, all thoughe the noble Hector sayde
15 'Nay', yet Pryamus agreade with a goodely nauy, as to a
kynges sonne ap*er*teynede, to sende hys sunne in to Grece. And,
breuely, all thynge made redy, he toke shyppynge and saylede so
longe that he arryuyde into Grece; and ther, seynge Helene of

---

auferre nequiuerit, aliqualem labefactate virginitatis iniecit
20 notam. Que fratribus ab Electhra, Thesei matre, seu, vt volunt
alij, a Protheo, rege Egiptio, absente Theseo repetentibus restituta, et tandem matura viro Menelao, Lacedemonum regi, con-.
iugio iuncta est, cui Hermionam filiam peperit vnicam. Post hec
fluentibus annis cum redisset Ylionem Pari[s], qui ob somnum
25 pregnantis matris in Yda fuit expositus et in lucta Hectorem
fratrem superasset non cognitus, mortem[que] crepundijs ostensis
et a matre cognitus euitasset, memor sponsionis speciosissime
coniugis sibi a Venere ob lat[am] a se apud Ydam s[ententi]am;
seu, vt alij volunt, postulaturus Hesionam fabrefactis ex Yda
30 nauibus regio comitatu sociatus transfretauit in Greciam et a
Menelao fuit susceptus hospicio. Ibi, cum vidisset Helenam celesti
decore conspicuam atque regio in cultu lasciuientem seque intueri

19 nequiuerit] nequiuerat BU.   labefactate] labefactæ B, labefacte
U.   20 Electhra] elethra S, Alethia BU.   24 redisset] redijsset
BU.   patri L.   somnum] sompnum S, somnium BU.   25 Yda]
Idam B, ydam U.   fuit] fuerat BU.   26 mortem LS.   28 oblate LS.
Ydam] inter tres deas *add.* B.   siluam LS.

a heuenly beautye *and* full of dalyaunce, taken with hyr loue and
she agayne with his, often castynge theyr wanton eyes the tone
of the tother, she agreade to goo w*ith* hym to Troy. And fortune
lackede not to helpe to their purpose, for Menelaus was goone into
Crete. And sum say, contrary to thys, that she beynge in the 5
temple, he rauysshed hir by force and caryede hyr w*ith* hym to hys
shyppes and so saylede to Troy. Of whose cu*m*mynge hys father
was wondres gladde, supposynge to haue well reuengyde the
takynge of Exione, hys sustre. By thys takynge of thys wanton
woma*n* all Grece was vpp on a rore, and, demyng more faulte in 10
Parys then in Helene, gatherynge together a thowsande shyppes,
they sailed to Troy and, occupiynge the port*es* therof, besegyde
the towne. Now to what ende that Helens fayre beautie came to,

cupientem, captus illico, et ex moribus spe sumpta captatis temporibus s[cint]illantibus feruore oculis, furtim impudico pectori 15
ignem sue dilectionis ingessit, ceptisque fortuna fauit, nam exigente oportunitate eo relicto Cretam Menelaus perrexerat. Quamobrem placet aliquibus eis equis flammis vrentibus ex composito
factum esse, vt Paris ignem per quietem ab Hecuba visum
portaret in patriam et vaticinia adimpleret maxima cum parte 20
thezaurorum Menelai noctu ex Latonico litore, seu, vt alijs placet,
ex Citharea ibidem vicina insula, dum in templo quodam patrio
ritu ob sacrum conficiendum Helenam vigilantem raperet parate-
que classi imponeret, et cum ea post multa pericula deueniret in
Troyam, vbi cum precipuo honore a Pryamo suscepta est, eo existi- 25
mante potius notam iniurie abstersisse ob detentam a Thelamone
Hesionam quam postremo regni sui desolationem suscepisse in
patria. Hac huius illecebra mulieris vniuersa Grecia commota est.
Et cum Graij principes omnes Paridis potius iniuɩ,ɑm ponderarent
quam Helene lasciuiam, ea frustra repetita sepius, in Troye exci- 30
dium coniurarunt vnanimes collectisque viribus cum mille vel
amplius nauibus armatorum onustis, littus inter Sygeum et
Retheum, promonthoria Frigie, occupauere et Ylionem obsede-
runt, frustra obsistentibus Frigijs. Helena quidem quanti foret

15 stillantibus LS.   17 perrexerat] perexerat B, prexerat SU.
22 patrio] primo BU.   25–6 existimante] extimante BU.   27
postremo] postremam BU.   33 promonthoria] promuntoria BU.
Frigie] phrygiæ B.   34 Frigijs] phrygijs B.

it was easy for hyr to see—fyrst Troy besegyde, the countrye all
aboute fyrede, the Troyans and the Grekes oone kyllynge another,
and all the feeldes full of bloode and deade bodyes. But the seege
so contynuynge and Hector slayne of Achyles, and Parys of
5 Pyrrus, she thoughte she hadnot synnyde enowghe before, but
puttynge oone synne to another, she maryede the yonge Dei-
ph[eb]us. Now for conclusione, the Grekes assaynge by treasone
to gett that whiche they coulde not doo by force, they feynede
theym to flye, and the Troyanes, gladd therof, eatynge and
10 drynkynge and makynge greate feaste, sodanly in the nyght the
Grekes reuertyde and, fyndynge noo defense, toke the cite and
burnte Ilion and all the rest. And the xx^{ti} yere of hyr rauyshynge

6–7 Deiphus MS.

sua formositas ex muris obsesse ciuitatis vidisse potuit, cernens
litus omne completum hostibus et igne ferroque circum desolari
15 omnia, populos inire certamina ac per mutua vulnera in mortem
iri, et tam Troyano quam Greco sanguine cuncta fedari. Que
quidem tam pertinaci proposito repetita est atque detenta, vt dum
redderetur, per decennium cede multorum nobilium cruenta per-
seueraret obsidio. Qua stante Hectore iam mortuo ab Achille
20 atque a Pyrro acerrimo iuuene trucidato Paride, quasi parum sibi
visum sit peccasse semel, Helena secundas iniuit nupcias nup-
sitque Deiphebo iuniori. Tandem cum proditione temptaretur quod
armis obtineri non posse videbatur, hec que obsidioni causam
dederat, vt opus daret excidio et ad viri primi gratiam promer-
25 endam, in eandem volens sciensque deuenit, et cum dolo simulassent Greci discessum, Troyanis perterritis, fessis laboribus, et noua
leticia festisque epulis victis somnoque sepultis, Helena choream
simulans accensa face in tempore ex arce reuocauit intentos. Qui
redeuntes cum tacite semisopitam vrbem reseratis ianuis intras-
30 sent, ea incensa et Deiphebo fede ceso, Helenam post vigesimum

17 quidem] quidam U.   dum] non *add.* BU.   19 Qua] quia S.
ab] et BU.   20 parum] paruum BU.   22 temptaretur] a Grecis *add.* B.
24 opus] operam B.   25–6 in . . . discessum] Quicquid poterat contra
Troianos moliebatur, tandemque ex constituto cum per dolium Græci
simulassent discessum.   26 fessis] fessisque B.   27 Helenam B.   28
reuocauit] Græcos *add.* B.   29 semisospitam LS.   30 incensa] censa B,

she was deliuerede agayne to hir husbond Menelaus. Sum excuse
and say, because she was rauysshede | agaynste hyr wyll, hyr hus- f. 35*a*
bonde toke hyr agayne, whiche sayde Menelaus, goynge home,
by tempeste was dryuen into Egypte, where of Kynge Polibyus
he was well receyuede, and after saylynge in to Lacedemony the 5
eight yere after Troy was burnte, ther with hys wyfe taryede. But
how longe Helene lyuede after, or what she dyd, or where she
was buryede I do not remembre to haue redde it.

Of Circes, the doughter of the sonne.
The xxxvj\ti Chapitre.   10

CIrces, for the knowledge that she had, as the poetes wryte, in
enchauntmentes, is vnto this day famus. She was doughter
to Solis, which he had by Perse hys wyfe, that was doughter to
Oceanus, the suster to Oethes, Kynge of Colchos. I thynke she is
sayde to be the doughter of Solis, because that she floryshede in 15
excessyue beautie, or because that she had moste perfyte knowledge in the vertue of herbes, or ells for asmuche that she coulde

---

a raptu annum Menelao restituere coniugi. Alij vero asserunt
Helenam non sponte sua a Paride raptam et ob id a viro meruisse
suscipi, qui cum ea Greciam repetens a tempestate et aduerso 20
vento agitatus plurimum in Egiptum cursum vertere coactus, a
Polibo rege susceptus est. Post hec sedatis procellis in Lacede-
mona cum requisita coniuge fere post octauum annum a desolato
Ylione susceptus est. Ipsa autem quamdiu post hec vixerit, aut
quid egerit, seu quo sub celo mortua sit, nusquam legisse recordor. 25

De Circe, Solis filia. xxxvi.

CIrce cantationibus suis in hodiernum vsque famosissima
mulier, vt poetarum testantur carmina, filia fuit Solis et Perse
nymphe, Occeani filie, sororque Oethe, Colcorum regis; Solis, vt
arbitror, ideo filia dicta, quia singulari floruit pulchritudine, seu 30
quia [circa] noticiam herbarum fuit eruditissima vel potius quia

23 requisita] reacquisita B, reaquisita U.   24 Ipsa] est *add*. U.
25 nusquam] nunquam BU.   27 Circe] Circes BU.   29 Colcorum]
Colchorum BU.   31 *om*. L.   fuit] fuerit BU.

so well worke with theym, whiche the son by dyuerse respectes
dothe gyue to all thynges that growe, as those that haue the
science mathematicall dothe affirme. But how she came frome
hyr oune countrye of Colchos in to Italy I haue not, as I remembre,
5 redd it. But that hyll, that emonge the V[o]l[s]cos is called
Etheus, berythe vnto thys present day, as all the inhabitantes
affyrme, Circeus of hyr name. And forbecause that the parte that
is spoken of hyr is taken oute frome the poetes, we wyllnot charge
the redar longe therwythe, but breuely tell hyr lyfe. Thiese
10 poetes say that as many shipmen as dyd arryue by chaunce of
f. 35b the wyndes or by tempeste at | thys Circes, that whether it
were by enchauntement or by sum meruelouse doynge, that she
alteryde theym into dyuers formes, lyke vnto beastes. And
emonge other, the wauerynge company of Vlixes were so seruyde,
15 but by the helpe of Marcurye they were delyuerede, so that Vlixes,
hauynge a nakyde sworde in hys hande, threte to kyll hyr, oneles
she conuertyde theym into mans lyknes agayne. Whyche doone,
Vlixes taryede with hyr oone hoole yere and begate on hyr

5 valcos MS.   10 poetes] that *add.* MS.

---

prudentissima in agendis, que omnia Solem diuersis habitis
20 respectibus dare nascentibus mathematici arbitrantur. Quo autem
pacto relictis Colcis Ytaliam pecierit, minime legisse memini. Eam
Etheum, Volscorum montem, quem de suo nomine dicimus in
hodiernum vsque Cyrceum, incoluisse omnes testantur. Et, cum
nil preter poeticum legatur ex hac tam celebri muliere, recitatis
25 succincte poeticis, quo prestabitur ingenio, mentem excuciemus
credentium. Volunt igitur ante alia quoscunque nautas, seu ex
proposito seu tempestatis impulsu ad dicti montis, olim insule,
litora applicantes, huius artibus c[a]n[t]atis carminibus seu infectis veneno poculis in feras diuersarum specierum fuisse con-
30 uersos et hos inter vagi Vlixis fuisse socios, eo Mercurij mediante
consilio seruato. Qui cum euaginato gladio mortem minaretur
venefice, socios reassumpsisse in formam redactos pristinam et,
per annum contubernio vsu[m] eiusdem, ex ea Thelegonum

21 Colcis] Colchis BU.   pecierit] me *add* BU.   23 testantur]
historiæ *add.* B, historie *add.* U.   cum] eum B.   28 artibus] arte
et B, artis U.   conatis LS.   30 Vlixis] Vlyssis B.   33 vsus LBSU.
Thel.] Theologonum BU.

Thelogonus and lernede of hyr muche what, vndre what crafte
she dyd suche straynge thynges.   And other wryte that not far
frome the towne of Gayeta, beynge in Campania, she was ther a
woman of greate ryches and power and of a verey fayre speche,
sparynge to fullfyll the pleasure of no man, so that she myghte fare 5
the better by it.   In soo muche that to suche as came to hyr porte,
with fayre wordes she not oonely drewe theym to fullfyll hyr
pleasure, but, to thys, vsede hyr men to be pyrates and robbers
on the see, all honeste sett a syde, and to vse false byinge *and*
sellynge of ware.   And su*m* say she causede many men, for the 10
fauo*ur* she shewde theym, to fall into pryde, and so those that by
suche vngraciousnes she drewe to suche myschife, for asmuche
as theyr reason was past theym, that they comparede theym vnto
beastes.   Whereby we may well comp*r*ehende, aswell by men and
women, seynge theyr wanton condiciones, that ther is many 15
Circes in the worlde, and by theyr vyle lyuynge conuertes theymselff*es* into brutyshe beastes.   Now where it is sayde that Vlixes by
the counseill of Mercurye ouercame hir, it is asmuche to say that

---

suscepisse filium dicunt et ab ea plenum consili[j] discessisse, quo
sub cortice hos existimo latere sensus.   Sunt qui dicunt hanc 20
feminam haud longe a Gayeta, Campanie o[p]pido, potentissimam
fuisse viribus et sermone nec magni facientem, dummodo aliquid
consequeretur optatum, a nota illesam seruasse pudici[ci]am et
sic multos ex applicantibus suo littori blandicijs et ornato sermone
non solum in suas illecebras traxisse, verum alios in rapinam et 25
piraticam impulisse, nonnullos omni honestate postposita ad
exercenda negocia et mercimonia dolis incitasse et plures ob sui
singularem dilectionem in superbiam extulisse, et sic hi, quibus
infauste mulieris opera humana subtracta videbatur ratio, eos ab
eadem in sui facinoris feras merito crederetur fuisse conuersos. 30
Ex quibus satis comprehendere possumus hominum mulierumque
conspectis moribus multas vbique Circes esse et longe plures
homines lasciuia et crimine suo versos in beluas; Vlixes autem
Mercurij consilio predoctus prudentem virum satis euidenter

19 consilium LS.   20 dicunt] dicant BU.   21 Gayeta] Caieta BU.
Campanie] campani S.   22 magni fac.] magnifacientem SU, mag-
nificantem B.   23 pudiciam LS.   25 et] *om.* BU.   33 suo
versos] subuersos B.   Vlixes] Vlysses B.   34 predoctus] perdoctus B.

a wyse man wyllnot easeyly be vaynquyshede with no flaterynge
wordes, but hys wytte *and* counseill dothe often delyuer theym
that be wrappyde in suche vnwyttye boundes. For the rest is
euydent, that the hystory affyrmythe, Vlixes to haue arryuede
5 ther and to haue taryede a space with hyr. It is sayde further
of sum, that thys woma*n* was maryede to Pycus, the Kynge
f. 36*a* of the Latyns sonne, and that she enstructed | hym in hyr
scyens of wyche crafte, and because that he louyde besyde hyr
Pononia, the fayre nymp[h]e, she co*n*uertyde hym in to a pye.
10 But the truethe is, she had a tame pye in hir house, wherewyth
she made men beleue that she dyuynede of thynges to cum. But
where, or how, or in what maner this woma*n* dyede is to me
vnknowne.

Of Camylla, the Quene of the Volscus.
15   The xxxvij[th] Chapitre.

CAmilla, the noble and renomyde quene, was gotten of the
moste aunsyent Kynge of Volscus on Casmylla, hys wyfe.

3 bewrappyde MS.

---

ostendit, quem adulantium nequeunt laqueare decipule, quinymo
et documentis suis laqueatos persepe soluit a vinculo. Reliquum
20 satis patet ad hystoriam pertinere, quo constat Vlixem aliquandiu
permansisse cum Circe. Fertur preterea hanc eandem feminam
Pici, Saturni filij, Latinorum regis, fuisse coniugem eumque augurandi docuisse scientiam et ob [z]elum, quia Ponionam Nympham
adamaret, eum in auem sui transformasse nominis. Erat enim illi
25 domesticus picus auis, ex cantu cuius et motibus sumebat de
futuris augurium, et, quia secundum actus pici vitam duceret, in
picum versus Picus dictus est. Quando seu quo mortis genere aut
vbi hec defuncta sit Circe, compertum non habeo.

De Camilla, Volscorum regina. xxxvij.

30 CAmilla insignis et memoratu dignissima virgo fuit. Ex Volscorum reg[e] antiquissimo et Casmilla coniuge genita, nascens

20 quo] qua BU.   constat] constant S.   21 Fertur] Refertur BU.
23 scelum L.   Ponionam] Pomonam BU.   24 illi] ille B.   25
motibus] moribus B.   27 Picus] *om*. BSU.   dictus] dictum BU.
30-1 ex Volscorum] et Volscorum regina, hæc ex Metabo (methabo U)
Volscorum BU.   30 Ex] et S.   31 regi LS.

Hyr byrthe was the deathe of hyr mother. For when she was
broughte to bedde on hyr and sawe that she muste neades dye,
she prayde hyr father Methabo that, one lettre put away of hir
oune, p*ro*pre name, the wenche myght be callyde, to hir solas,
Camilla. Thys mayden, frome the day of hyr byrthe tyll hir 5
death had euer hard happe and fortune. For shortly after the
deathe of hyr mother, hyr father by the sedicione of hys people
was put oute of hys realme, and toke nothynge with hym, goynge
into exyle, but onely thys, hys litle doughter, whiche he loued
moste hartely. And so, goynge alone on hys feete *and* litle Camilla 10
in his armes, it chauncyde hym to cum to a ryuer called Emasyn,
with rayne the day before rysyn wonders hyghe, and seynge that
with the chylde he couldnot swyme ouer, at the laste, God
helpynge therto, fownde thys way, whiche woldenot so renomyde
a virgyne shulde peryshe that tyme. He toke the barcke of a 15
greate tree and wrapte Camylla theryn *and* tyede | it to a speere, f. 36*b*
whiche he had in hys hande, and swy*m*mynge ouer the ryuer,

---

matri mortis causa fuit, nam, cum enixa paruulam moreretur, a
Methabo patre vna tantum ex materno nomine dempta littera
Camillam filiam nuncupauit in sui solacium. Huius quidem 20
virginis a natali suo die seuera fortuna fuit. Nam paululum post
matris f[un]us Methabus, Priuernatum, ciuium suorum, repentina
seditione regno pulsus, nil [per] fugam arripiens preter paruulam
hanc filiam suam sibi pre ceteris rebus dilectam 'asportasse in
exilium potuit. In quod cum solus pedesque miser effugeret et in 25
vlnis sociam deportaret Camillam, ad Emasenum fluuium pridiano
ymbre tumentem deuenit, nec cum onere infantule prepeditus
posset enatare, in oportunum deuenit consilium porrigente deo,
qui celebrem futuram virginem ignobili absumi fato nolebat.
Illam igitur suberis cortice inuolutam iaculo, quod forte ferebat, 30
alligauit atque Dyane deuouit, si seruasset incolumem, et vibrato
totis viribus brachio iaculum cum filia in ripam transiecit aduersam, quam e vestigio nando secutus est et, cum illam dei munere

18 paruulam] paruula BU.   19 vna] vnica BU.   littera] s *add.* BU.
22 fimus L.   Priuernatum] primatorum BU.   23 *om.* LSU.   25
effugeret] fugeret BU.   26 sociam] filiam BU.   Emasenum]
Damascenum BU.   29 absummi LS, assūmi U.   31 alligauit]
allegauit S.   incolumem] incolumen U.   32 filia] filiam B.

when he came on the other syde, he drewe the speere quycklye
to hym, and so withoute harme sauyde hys deare doughter. And
so when by the syghte of hys eye [he] perceyuyde she had noo
hurte, all though he were in mysery, yett merely he went vnto
5 the woddes. Nor it was not withoute hys greate laboure to
noryshe hyr, for asmuche as that he coulde gett no mylke but of
the wylde beastes. And euer as she grewe in yeres, so dyd hyr
father clothe hyr in wylde beastes skynnes and taughte hyr to
proue hyr strengthe and shote with a bowe, to weere a queuer,
10 to runne after hartes *and* wylde gootes *and* to ouercu*m* theym,
and to despyse all femynyne labo*ur*es, and aboue all thynges to
loue uirgynyte, to laughe at yonge mens wanto*n* desyres, and
vtterly despyse maryage w*it*h any man, were he neu*er* so greate.
With thys exercyse at the laste callede agayne to hyr kyngdome,
15 she had so noble a herte that she neuer wolde chaunge hyr purpose.
At the laste Eneas came fro Troy, and for Lauynya hauynge greate
debate with Turnus, Camylla, fauorynge the party of Turnus,
came to hys ayde with a greate company of hyr subiectes. Ande

13 despysynge MS. *Probably the scribe has omitted something after* greate,
as may be seen from the Latin original.

---

comperisset illesam, in miseria letus siluarum pecijt latebras nec
20 absque labore plurimo paruulam educauit lacte ferino. Que cum
in validiorem euasisset etatem, tegere ferarum corpus cepit
exuuijs et tela vibrare lacertis fundasque circumagere, arcus
tendere, gestare pharetras, cursu ceruos capreasque siluestres
insequi atque superare, labores femineos omnes despicere, virgini-
25 tatem pre ceteris inuiolatam seruare, iuuenum amores ludere et
connubia potentum procerum omnino respuere ac sese totam
Dyane obsequio, cui pater deuouerat, exhibere. Quibus exercicijs
durata virgo, in patrium reuocata regnum, seruauit robore inflexo
propositum. Tandem, cum a Troya Eneas veniens Lauin[i]am
30 sumpsisset coniugem et ob id bellum inter eum Turnumque
Rutulum esset exortum, congregantibus eis vndique copias,
Camilla, Turni partibus fauens, cum grandi Volscorum agmine

24 labores] labors U.　　25 ceteris] omnibus *add.* BU.　　27
deuouerat] deuorauerat U.　　29 Lauinam LS.　　30 sumpsisset] in
add. BU.

so, often runnynge valiauntly emonge the Troyanes *and*, emonge
other, ha[uynge] slayne Corebus the priste, whiche had wonder
goodely harnes, and couetynge to spoyle theym, of oone of Eneas
knyghtes, called Aruns, with an arrowe vndre the lyft pappe she
was wounded to the deathe, and so, to the greate hurte of the 5
Rutylyans, emongste the thyckeste of the armyde men she
exspyrede. I wolde the maydynes in our tyme shulde looke on
thys virgyne well and, or thei be maryede, beholde thys maydyn,
beynge emonge the woddes wi*th* a queuer of arrowes gyrdyd
aboute hyr, with co*n*tynuall labour chastesynge all vncleene 10
desyres, settynge a syde all deyntines, all caruyde cuppes, and
with a constant mynde, not onely denyinge all enbrasynge,
but further, vtterly stoppynge hyr eares frome all wa*n*ton
co*m*munication and dalyaunce. Let theym se, warnede, what |

2 had MS.   4 Arnus MS.

---

venit auxiliatrix eidem et, cum sepius armata irruisset in Frigios 15
et die vna acriter pugnans multos occidisset ex eis, [et] nouissime
Corebum quemdam, Cibelis sacerdotem, armorum eius auida
sequeretur, ab Arunce quodam ex hostibus sagitta sub papilla
letaliter percussa, maximo Rutilorum damno moribunda collapsa
est et inter armata exercitia expirauit. Hanc intueantur, velim, 20
puellule hodierne et, dum sui iuris virginem adultam et pro libito
nunc latos agros, nunc siluas et lustra ferarum accinctam pharetra
discurrentem, labore assiduo lasciuias, illecebres appetitus pre-
mentem, delicias atque molliciem, accuratas offas et elaborata
pocula fugientem et constantissimo animo coeuorum iuuenum, 25
non dicam amplexus, sed verba etiam respuentem viderint, monite
discant, quid eas in domo patria, quid in templis, quid in theatris,
in quibus spectantium multitudo et seuerissimi morum censores
conueniunt, deceat, minus quidem honestis negare aures, os
taciturnitate frenare, oculos grauitate compescere et gestus omnes 30

15 Frigios] Phrygios B.   16 die] de B.   pugnans] pungnans BU.
[et] *om*. LS.   17 Cibelis] Cybeles B.   18 sequeretur] insequeretur BU.
Arunce] Arunte B, arrunte U.   19 Rutilorum] Rutulorum BU.   20
et] sic *add*. BU.   25 iuuenum] *om*. B.   26 sed] scilicet B.
respuentem] respuente U.   29 aures] apres U.   30 compescere]
mores componere *add*. BU.   omnes] omnis B.

f. 37a | they oughte to do in the temple, in theyr fathers howses, and
remembre further, that it is not honeste to do that they may do,
but thys there onely honeste is to loue chastite, vntyll they be
apte to cum to the holy bounde of matrymonye.

5 Of Penolepe, Vlixes wyfe.
The xxxviij[th] Chapitre.

PEnolepe was the doughter of Ycarus *and* wyfe vnto the ryght
hardy knyghte Vlixes, of chastite *and* vndefylede wyfely
honeste a moste holy example, for euer to remayne. This womanly
10 wyfes chastite was assayde all in vayne for to haue bene broken,
but it wolde not be. For when thys yonge, swete damosell, because
of hyr beautie *and* hyr synglar goodnes, was dearely belouyde of
hyr father, and that he hade gyuen hyr in maryage to Vlixes, she
hauynge by hym oone son called Thelemacus, fortune so wolde

---

15 suos honestatis mole comprimere, ocia, commessationes, lauticias
nimias, choreas et iuuenum vitare consortia, sentiantque, quoniam
nec optare quod libet nec, quod licet, agere sanctum sit aut
castitati conforme, vt prudentiores facte et laudabili virginitate
florentes in sacras nupcias mature m[ai]oribus obtemperantes suis
20 deueniant.

De Penelope, Vlixis coniuge. xxxviij.

PEnelope Ycari regis filia fuit et Vlixis strenuissimi vir
coniunx, illibati decoris atque intemerate pudicicie matronis
exemplum sanctissimum et eternum. Huius quidem pudoris vires
25 a fortuna acriter agitate sed frustra sunt, nam cum iuuencula
virgo et ob venustatem forme plurimum diligenda a patre iuncta
fuisset Vlixi, peperissetque ex eo Thelemacum et ecce in expeditionem Troyani belli vocatus, ymo vi fere tractus Vlixes, ab eo

17 sanctum] factum BU.   aut] *om.* BU.   18 castitati] castitate B.
prudentiores] prudenciore S.   19 moribus LS.   21 Penelope]
Penolope U. Vlixis] Vlyssis B *here and also elsewhere in this life. Other
cases show a similar spelling.*   22 stren.] strennuissimi L, seuerissimi
BU.   27 eo] ea BU.   Thelemacum] thelematum S, Thelemachum
U, Telemachum B.

that by force he was compellyde with the other Grekes to goo to
the seage of Troy, leuynge noo more company with hys wyfe but
Laertes, a man of greate age, and Anti[cl]ia hys mother, and hys
litle towardes sonne. Now the seage ther durynge ten yeres, and
at the laste Illion destroyde, ther was noone of the rest of the 5
noble Grekes wyfes that lay as wydowes but for that tyme, saue
oonely Penolepe, for Vlixes with tempestes and with wonder
chauncys tossyde here and there, so wanderynge aboute the
wourlde that noo man knewe where he was nor in what coste.
Wherfore, hys cummynge lokede for dayly into hys countrye 10
and not seene, nor of noo man it was thoughte no nother but
for a truthe he was | deade, for sorowe wherof hys myserable f. 37b
mother Anti[cl]ia honge hyrself. Penolepe then, all thoughe she
moste heuyly bewayled hys absence, yet the feare that she had,
leste he shulde be deade, greuede hyr muche more, so that [after] 15
many lamentationes, teares, and callynge in vayne Vlixes hyr
husbonde, with a chaste purpose she determyned to lyue with
Laertes and hyr litle sonne as a wydowe for euer. But hir

3 Antidia MS.

---

cum Laerte iam sene et Anticlia iam matre et paruo filio relicta
est. Sane, perseuerante bello nullam preter decemnalem vidui- 20
tatis iniuriam passa est. Attamen, Ylione deiecto, cum in scopulos
tempestate maris illisos aut repetentes domum proceres aut in
peregrinum litus impulsos, aut vndis absorptos, seu paucos in
patriam receptos fama monstraret, solius Vlixis erat incertum quo
cursum tenuissent naues. Quamobrem cum expectatus diu non 25
reuerteretur in patriam, nec appareret ab vllo visus, mortuus
existimatus est, qua credulitate Anticlia, genitrix miseranda, ad
leuandum dolorem vitam terminauit laqueo. Penelope autem, etsi
egre plurimum ferret viri absentiam, longe tulit egrius sinistram
mortis eius suspicionem. Sed post multas lacrimas et Vlixem 30
frustra vocatum sepissime, inter senem Laertem et Thelemacum

19 Laerte] patre *add.* BU.   et 1°] *om.* B.   Anticlia] *might easily be read*
Antidia L, Anthiclia BU.   iam] *om.* BU.   21–2 in scopulos . . .
proceres] repetentes domum proceres atque in scopulos tempestate maris
illisos BU.   22 in] *om.* B.   26 visus] vsquam visum BU, vsuque
visus S.   28 leuandum] leuiandum S, liniendum B, leniendum U.

beautie *and* hir ryghte honest facyon and hyr exellente *and* noble
bloode were in suche exteme thorow Grece that many noble men
burnynge in hyr concupiscence, specially of Ytar[chi]a *and*
Thephala[n]ia and of Eth[o]lia, thiese wolde neu*er* suffre hyr to be
5 in quyete but allways stery[d]e hyr to take an other husbonde.
And it helpte well to theyr appetytes, the longe taryenge of
Vlixes, whiche daily was lokte for and yet not herde of, wherfore
it was thoughte of all men that he was deade. And, to thys, it
chauncyde that poore Laertes goynge oute vppon a tyme into the
10 countrye, that those that burnede in hyr concupiscence entrede
hyr palace and aswell by force as by p*er*suasion mouede hyr to
maryage. But the goode Penolepe, ferynge leste that the holy
chastite of hyr honeste shulde be broken, sey*ng* that noo 'nay'
myghte haue place, lyghtnede with the dyuyne helpe, imagynede
15 for a tyme w*ith* craft to prolonge their rage. She requyrede that
she myghte make an ende, or they wolde enforce hyr, of a certeyne
garmente whiche she was weuynge for hir husbonde, and that

3 Ytharea MS.   4 Thephalamia MS.   Eothelia MS.
5 sterynge MS.

---

puerum in castissimam et perpetu[am] viduitatem senescere
firmato animo disposuit. Verum et cum forma decens moresque
20 probabiles et egregium genus ad se diligendam atque concupis-
cendam quorundam nobilium ex Ytarchia atque Thephalania et
Etholia prouocasset animos, plurimum instigationibus eorum
vexata est. Nam cum in dies spes vite Vlixis aut reditus eiusdem
continue videretur minui, eo ventum est vt abeunte rus ob fasti-
25 dium procatorum Laerte, procatores ipsi Vlixis occuparent regiam
et Penelopem precibus atque suasionibus pro viribus et sepissime
in suum prouocarent coniugium. Ast mulier, metuens ne forte
sacri pectoris violaretur propositum, cum iam cerneret viam
negationibus auferri, diuino profecto illustrata lumine, terminis
30 et astucia infestos saltem ad tempus fallendos esse arbitrata est,
pecijtque [ab] instantibus sibi tamdiu liceret expectare virum,
donec telam, quam more regalium mulierum ceperat, perfecisse

18 perpetuitatem L.   21 Ytarchia] ytharchia S, ytachia U, Ithaca
B.   Thephalania] Cephalania BU.   25 procatorum] procorum
B.   procatores] proci B.   26 atque] ac BU.   31 *om.* LBSU.

fynyshede, if he came not, or it were endyd, then she wolde agree
to theyr requestes. They easely grauntynge to hyr desyre, thiese
worshipfull prouokers were mockyde *in* this maner, that is, what
so euer Penolepe weuyde on the daye, at nyght she defacyde it
cleene. But thys wyle p*er*ceyuyde, and the poynte co*m*men that 5
ther was no more excuse to be founde, by the wyll of God, the
twenty yere after Vlixes hade goone frome hys goode wyfe, alone
and vnknowne he arryuyd from | Phe[n]ycu*m* to Itarchia, and f. 38*a*
by chaunce co*m*mynynge w*ith* certeyn shepehyrdes, he herde in
what state hys wyfe and his realme was. Wherfore, disguysynge 10
hymself lyke a poore man, he ca*m* to Sybot, hys porter, whiche,
knowynge hym to be hys lorde *and* wonders glad of hys returne,
he tolde hym all how his wife was handlede with euyll p*r*ouocars.
Vlixes than, emonge other maters, demaundyd hym of hys son,
and Sybot sayde that at that poynte he was returnynge frome 15
Menelaus to cu*m* to the ayde of hys mother. Vlixes well conforted
with those goode newes, it came so to passe that Thelemacus,
hauynge greate trust in Sib[o]t, arryuyde at hys house, hys father
beynge ther, whiche, anoone knowynge hym to be hys father,

8 Phemycu*m* MS.   18 Sibit MS.

posset. Quod cum facile concessissent competitores egregij, ipsa 20
femineo astu quicquid in die solerti studio texens videbatur operi
iungere, clam reuocatis filis subtrahebat in nocte. Qua arte, cum
eos in regia Vlixis bona assiduis conuiuijs consumentes aliquandiu
lusisset, nec iam amplius videretur locum fraudi posse prestari,
dei pietate factum est, vt ex Phenicum regno nauigans post vige- 25
simum sui discessus annum solus et incognitus Vlixes Ytachiam
veniret, pastoresque suos scis[c]itaturus rerum suarum status
adiret, et cum ex astucia pauper incessisset habitu a Sybote iam
sene portario suo comiter susceptus ab eodem referente fere
omnem rerum suarum comprehendit seriem, et Thelemacum a 30
Menelao redeuntem vidit, seque clam illi cognitum fecit, et consilium suum aperuit omne, factumque est vt a Sybote incognitus
deduceretur in patriam. Qui cum vidisset quo pacto rem suam

22 iungere] coniungere BU.   23 consumentes] consummentes U.
26 Ytachiam] Ithacam B.   27 scissitaturus LS, est *add*. U.   status]
statum BU.   32 apperuit LS.

made the greatest ioy of the wo*u*rlde and breuely concludyde to
be reuengyde of the outrage doone to his mother. What shulde
I tary lengar? Vlixes, takynge wi*th* hym Sibot and hys son with
dyuers others, shettynge the palace gates, streight wentt to the
5 chambre where thiese brokers of hys chaste wyfe were eatynge
and drynkynge and makynge good cheere, *and* with theyr swordes
in theyr handes slewe Eur[i]ma[c]us, the sonne of Polybyus, *and*
Anthmeu*m*, Amphion, Crisyppum *and* Agelau*m* wyth dyuers
others askynge mercy in vayne, and with those, certeyn wome*n*
10 that were agreade of the treason, and that doone, takynge hys
deare, chaste wyfe in hys armes, declarynge what he was, the ioy
that she made therof noo tunge can tell. But ther hathe bene of late
emo*n*ge the Grekys poetes oone Lycophron, that saythe noone
of the Grekys ladyes, theyr husbondes beynge at Troy, but they all
15 brake theyre matrymonye. And emonge all other he sclaundred
goode Penolepe, that she shulde do as the reste dyd. But God

distraherent procatores atque pudicam Penelopem eorum renuen-
tem coniugium, irritatus cum Sybote subulco et Phylitia opil[i]one
suo atque Thelemaco filio clausis regie ianuis in procatores
20 conu[i]uantes insurgens, Eurimacum, Polibi filium, et Anthmeum
Amphinonis atque Crisippum Samium, Agelaum aliosque frustra
veniam exorantes vna cum Melantheo caprario suo hostibus arma
ministrante atque mulieribus domesticis, quas nouerat cum procatoribus contubernium habuisse, occidit suamque Penelopem ab
25 insidijs procancium liberauit, que tandem cum vix eum recognos-
cere potuisset, summo perfusa gaudio diu desideratum suscepit.
Vult tamen Lycophron quidam nouissimus poetarum ex Grecis hanc
suasionibus Nauplij senis ob vindictam occisi Palamidis, filij sui, fere
omnes Grecorum coniuges lenocinio in meretricium deducent[i]s
30 Penelopem cum aliquo ex procatoribus in amplexus et concu-

17 distraherent] retraherent SU.   procatores] proci B.   17–18 ren-
nuentem LS, reuerentem B.   18 opilone LS.   20 coniuuantes L.   et] *om.* B.
Anthmeum] anthinoum BU.   21 Amphinonis] Amphinones S.   Crisippum]
Chrysippum B.   23 mulieribus] uirisque *add.* B.   25–6 recognosceret
L.   26 perfusa] perfuso BU.   27 Lycophron] Lycophion B, licophion
U.   28 Nauplij] Naupli BU.   occisi *om.* BU.   Palamidis]
Paliemedis B, palimedis U.   29 omnes] omnis B.   deducentes L.
30 Penelopem] Penelopen B, penolopen U.

forbede I shulde beleue it, that so goode and chaste a wyfe,
laudyd of so many greate clerkes shulde be of that sorte, the vertue
of whome so muche more is it to be commendable, that she
allways abode in a constante mynde, all though she were temptyde
to the contrary neuer so muche. | 5

Of Lauina, the Quene of Laurentum.   i. 38b
The xxxixth Chapitre.

LAuina, the Quene of Laurentum, descendyd of Saturne, Kynge
of Crete, and she was onely doughter to Kynge Latyne by
Annata, hys wyfe, and at the laste geuyne to wyfe to Eneas, the 10
vallyaunte Troyane knyghte. Thys woman is more spoken of for
the greate battells that ensuede for hyr betwyxte the sayde Eneas
and Tornus then for any other thynge ells that she dyd. She was
of exellent beautie, and for because she was also an heredytour
to the Kynge hyr father, Tornus, then a yonge prynce of a greate 15
towardnes, often demaundyd hyr of hym. But Latinus, that

bitum venisse. Quod absit, vt credam celebrem castimonia
multorum auctorum literis mulierem [vni]us in contrarium asse-
rent[i]s Penelopem preter castissimam extitisse. Cuius quidem
virtus tanto clarior atque commendabilior est, quanto rarior 20
inuenitur, et maiori impulsa certamine perseuerauit constantior
inconcussa.

De Lauinia, Laurentum regina. xxxix.

LAuinia, Laurentum regina, genus a Saturno Cretensi ducens,
Latini regis et Amate, coniugis eius, filia fuit vnica et tandem 25
Enee, strenuissimi Troyanorum ducis, coniunx, magis belli Enee
Turnique Rutuli tam clara quam alio facinore suo. Hec quidem
ob insigne formositatis sue decus et patrium regnum, cui succes-
sura videbatur, a Turno, Rutulorum rege, ardentissimo iuuene
instantissime in coniugium petebatur eique ex eo spem fecerat 30
Amata mater que auia desiderio nepotis fauebat impense. Sane,
Latinus augurandi peritus, cum ab oraculo suscepisset filiam

18 minus LS.   18–19 asserentes LS.   19 Pen.] Penelopen B,
penolopen U.   25 adamate LS.   26 stren.] strennuissimi L.
28 patrium] paternum BU.   30 petebatur] petita est BU.

knewe thynges to cum, wolde neuer graunte to it, for asmuche as
that he knewe a straynger of a nother countrye and regyone
shulde marye hyr. Now Eneas cumynge frome Troy, and he also
askynge Lauina to wyfe, the father, aswell for the greate bloode
5 he was of, as also for that it was the goddes pleasure it shulde so
be, grauntyde gladly to it, wherfore betwyxt Tornus and Eneas
beganne mortall warr. And soo, after muche bloode shedynge *and*
deathe of many noble men on bothe parties, Eneas obteynede the
victorye at the laste and maryede Lauina, and for that Annata,
10 Latinus wife, hangede hyrself. And sum say that thies batells
beganne after Eneas had maryede hyr. But whether it be the
tone or the tother, it is euident that Lauina conceyuyde by the
noble Eneas a sonne, and that or hys wyfe were delyuerede, he
dyede at a ryuer called Numacum, *and* she, ferynge Ascanyus, hyr
15 sonnes halfe brother, hydde hyr emongst the woddes and ther was
delyuerede of a sonne, and, as many wryte, namede hym Julius
Siluyus. Nowe Ascanyus, beynge of a gentle nature, after that
he hade buyldyte Alban the cytie, restorede Lauyna and hyr
f. 39a son to theyr paternall kyngdome, whiche Lauina, | receyuynge

20 extero duci tradendam, coniugis tardius ibat in votum, quinymo
cum a Troya profugus aduenisset Eneas, Latinus, tam ob generis
claritatem quam ob oraculi m[o]n[it]us eidem poscenti amiciciam
spopondit et filiam. Quamobrem inter Eneam Turnumque bellum
suscitatum est et post multa certamina obtinentibus Troyanis per
25 vulnera, sanguinem mortesque plurium nobilium, ab Enea in
Lauinie nupcias itum est, mortua ob indignationem Amata laqueo.
Sunt tamen qui velint bellum post nupcias exortum, sed qualiter-
cunque gestum sit, constat Lauiniam ex Enea clarissimo principe
concepisse filium et eo ante diem partus apud Numicum fluuium
30 rebus humanis subtracto, cum Ascanium priuignum regnantem
timeret, secessisse in siluas et ibi peperisse atque, vt volunt
aliqul, Iulum nominasse Siluium. Sane, cum mitior creditus
esset in nouercam Ascanius, et sibi Albam ciuitatem condidisset,
vltro secedens Lauinie regnum patrium liquit, quod Lauinia

22 munus L, munitus S.   23 et] *om.* BU.   25 sanguinemque U.   26
mortua] iam *add.* BU.   29 Numicum] inimicum S.   31 ibi] Posthumium
add. B, postumium *add.* U.   32 iulium SU, Iulium B.   34 Lauinia] patriam
add. BU.

De Claris Mulieribus 133

it of Ascanius and well callynge to mynde hys gentylnes, all hyr
lyfe tyme not onely wysely maynteyned it, but further, lyuede
chastely, withoute to take a nother husbonde, tyll she dyede, and
in hyr tyme, when hyr son came to age, re[s]y[gn]yde the realme
to Siluyus. And sum say that Ascanyus noryshede hy*m* and 5
maryede hym to Melapondy by hys gentlenes *and* frat*er*nall loue.

Of Dido, or otherwyse Elissa, the Quene of Cartage.

The xlᵗⁱ Chapitre.

Dido, whiche afore hade to name Elissa, was bothe the buylder
and Quene of Cartage. I haue ententione sumwhat at large 10
to speke of hyr prayse, if percase with my poore penne I may wype
a way the obprobry that sum haue obiectyde agaynste hyr withoute deserte touchynge hyr hono*ur*able wydowhede. And that I
may sumwhat the more ascende so to do, it is knowne well inowghe
that the people of Phenyses came frome the farthest parte of 15
Egypte, nyghe vnto Siria, and by theyr hyghe wyttes there
reedifyede many fayre tounes *and* cytes. Emonge the other

4 Receyuyde MS.

---

veterem pectori generositatem gerens, honeste atque pudice viuens,
summa cum diligentia tenuit, illudque tamdiu seruauit, donec
Siluio pubescenti resignaret in nihilo diminutum. Volunt tamen 20
aliqui eam a siluis reuocatam Melampodi cuidam nupsisse et
Siluium ab Ascanio fraterna beniuolentia educatum.

De Dydone seu Elyssa, Tyria Carthagin[i]ensium regina. xl.

Ydo, cui prius Elissa nomen, Carthaginis eque conditrix et
regina fuit. Huius quidem in veras laudes paululum am- 25
pliatis fimbrijs ire libet, si forte paucis literulis meis saltem pro
parte notam indigne obiectam decori sue viduitatis abstergere
queam. Et vt altius in suam gloriam aliquantisper assumam,
Phenices, vt satis vulgatum est, populi industria preclarissimi ab
extrema fere Egipti plaga in Syrium venientes litus, plurimas et 30
preclaras ibidem condidere vrbes. Quibus inter alios rex fuit

20 Siluio] scilicet filio *add.* BU. 23 Carthaginensium LB, carta-
ginensium U, Carthagniensium S.

Agenor was their kynge, a prynce of a ryght renomyde fame, of
whose genealogye it is beleuyde that thys Dido descendyd, whose
father was Belus, Kynge of Phenyses, whiche, after that he had
subduede the ile of Cipres, ther dyede, leuynge thys yonge, to-
5 warde virgyne Dido with Pigmalion, his brother, and therwythe
hys treasure and hys realme; which saide Pigmalion, puttynge
Dido in hyr kyngedome, as ryght was, [she] was maryede to
f. 39*b* Acerbus, or, as sum call hym, Sikkarius, the | pryste of Hercules,
whiche sayde offyce with the Tyryens was moste honorable, next
10 vnto the Kynge. Thiese too lyuyde together moste honorably
and louyde moste hartely. Nowe thys Pigmalion was the moste
couetouse man to haue golde that then lyuyde, and thys Acerbus
moste ryche, all thoughe by hys wysdome he so bestowede it that
it was not well knowne in what place it lay, but the fame woldnot
15 haue it kept sec*r*ete. Pigmalion, fallen into ragynge purpose to
haue it, slewe at vnwayres by treason Acerbus, whiche when Dido
knew, she toke it [so] vnpatiently that scante she escapede for
sorowe the deathe. And so, after she had lamentably a longe

14 fame] that *add.* MS.

Agenor, nostro nedum suo euo prefulgidus fama, a quo genus
20 Dydonis inclitum manasse creditum est. Cuius pater Belus,
Phenicum rex, cum Cypro insula subacta clausisset diem, eam
virgunculam cum Pigmalione fratre grandiusculo Phenicum reliquit fidei. Qui Pigmalionem constituentes genitoris in solium
Elyssam puellulam et forma eximiam Acerbe seu Syceo vel
25 Sycarie, vt dicunt alij, Herculis sacerdoti, qui primus erat post
regem apud Tyrios honore, coniugio iunxere. Hi autem inuicem
sanctissime se amarunt. Erat pre ceteris mortalibus cupidissimus
et inexplebilis Pig[m]alion auri, sic et Acerba ditissimus. Esto
regis auaricia cognita illud occultasset latebris. Verum, cum
30 fama[m] occultasse nequiuerit, in auiditatem tractus Pigmalion
spe pociundi per fraudem occidit incautum. Quod cum cognouis-
set Elyssa, adeo impatienter tulit, vt vix abstineret a morte. Sane,

19 nedum] sed *add.* LS.   23 Pigm.] Pygmaleone B.   *Other cases are spelt*
accordingly in this life.   24 Acerbe] Aterbe BU.   Syceo] Sychæo B,
sicheo U.   25 Sycarie] Sicario BU.   qui] cui BU.   26 honore]
honor BU.   28 pignalion LS.   Acerba] Aterba BU.   30 fama LS.

tyme wept and wailede and in vayne called hyr deare husbonde,
cursynge hyr vnhappye brother Pigmalion, of hyr oune mynde
she determynede to flee a way. And sum say she was warnyde so
to do in hyr sleepe, leste hyr couetouse brother wolde slay hyr, as
he had doone hir husbonde. She than, takynge to hyr a mans 5
wytte and herte, after as hir name porporteth, for Phenicum in
Laten signyfyethe a virago, whiche as in Englishe we may say
'a woman reysyde of a man', she so wrought that dyuers of the
prynces, suspectynge the murdre of Acerbus, drew to hyr, and
she makynge redy preuely as many shyppes as she had, in the 10
nyght with those that were of hyr opynyon toke all hyr husbondes
treasure and conueyde it into hyr shyppes, and vsyde with so
doynge a meruelouse pollecy. She toke certeyne vesselles and
fylled theym aswell with hyr treasure as also with that she myght
get of hyr brothers, and toke other vessells and fylled theym with 15
grauell. And when she was entrede the shipps and those that were
of hyr consent with hyr well entrede the hyghe sees, they all
meruelynge what she ment, she toke then the barrells fyllyde with

cum multum temporis consumpsisset in lacrimis et frustra sepius
dilectissimum sibi vocasset Acerbam atque in fratrem diras omnes 20
execrationes expetisset, seu in sompnis monita, vt placet aliquibus,
seu ex proprio mentis sue consilio fugam capes[s]ere deliberauit,
ne forsan et ipsa auaricia fratris traheretur in necem. Et pos[i]ta
feminea mollicie et firmato in virile robur animo, ex quo postea
Dydonis nomen meruit, Phenicum lingua sonans quod 'virago' 25
Latine, ante alia nonnullos ex principibus ciuitatum, quibus varijs
ex causis Pigmaleonem sciebat exosum, in suam deduxit sententiam. Et sumpta fratris c[l]asse, seu ad eam transferendam, seu
in aliud preparata, confestim naualibus compleri socijs iussit, et
nocte sumptis thezauris omnibus quos viri nouerat et quos fratri 30
subtraxisse potuit, clam nauibus imponi fecit et excogitata astucia
pluribus inuolutis harena repletis sub figmento thezaurorum Sicei
videntibus omnibus easdem onerauit. Et cum iam altum teneret
pelagi, mirantibus ignaris in mari proici inuoluta iussit, et lach·
rimis se mortem quam diu desiderauerat thezaurorum Acerbe 35

grauell and threw theym in to the see, saynge that with wepynge
teares the deathe *tha*t she had desyrede to haue by the deathe
f. 40*a* of hyr husbonde, she by | the drownynge of the treasure hade
fownde it, but that, she sayde, she had compassion of those
5 whiche was with hyr, knowy*n*g for certeyn, if they returnede
backe agayne, that the cruell Pigmalion wolde put theym to a
terryble deathe, and for that, yf they with hyr wolde flee at
auenture, that whyles she lyuyde, she wolde in goode and ill take
that parte that they dyd. Now the poore maryners, herynge hyr
10 say thus, all thoughe it greuyde theym to forsake theyr naturall
countrye, yet for feare to dye they consentyde to goo in to exyle
and, raysynge theyr sa[y]les, arryuyde at last in Cyprys, where,
after the custome fyndynge by the see syde certeyn v*i*rgynes
goynge to do sacryfyce to Venus, she toke theym with hyr by
15 force and with theym also Jupiters highe p*r*este, which prophecyede goode of hyr viage. And so, leuynge Crete at hyr backe and
Cycyll of hyr ryght hande, she saylede towardes Affryke and,
goynge by the shoores of Mesilia, entrede to a rode after well
knowne; and thus with muche troble and saylynge by the sees,

12 saales MS.

---

20 submersione adinuenisse testata est. Sed socijs compati quos non
dubitabat, si ad Pigmalionem irent diris supplicijs vna secum ab
auarissimo atque truci rege carnificari, sane, si secum fugam
arripere vellent, non se illis et eorum oportunitatibus defuturam
asseruit. Quod miseri audientes naute, etsi egre natale solum
25 patriosque penates linquerent, timore tamen seue mortis exterriti
in consensum exilij venere faciles, et flexis proris ea duce in
Cyprum ventum est, vbi virgines Veneri in litore libamenta
suorum more soluentes, ad solacium iuuentutis et prolem pro-
creandam rapuit et Iouis antistitem cum omni familia premonitum
30 et magna huic fuge subsecutura vaticinantem socium peregrina-
tionis suscepit. Et iam Creta post tergum et Sycilia a dextris
relicta, litus flexit in Afrum et Messaliorum oram radens, sinum
intrauit postea satis notum, quo tutam nauibus stationem arbi-

23 defuturam] defunctam B.   25 linquerent] liquiuerent S, liquerent
U.   32 radens] vadens BU.

there she determynede to rest hyrself and hyr wery maryners.
Nowe those that dwellyd nyghe there aboutes, desyrouse to se
what strayngers they were, bryngynge, as custome is, marchaun-
dyse to ent*er*medle with theym, anone with suche facyone Didos
company grewe day by day in fauoure with theym; in somuche 5
that, seynge the ryght honest facyo*n* of Dido, [they] began
wondersly to fauo*ur* hyr, soo that they wyllede verey gladly to
haue hyr and hyr trayne to dwell emonge theym. And all thoughe
she hade herde ryght well that hyr brother thrett to make warr
agaynst hyr, yet, settynge all feare a parte and kepynge secrete 10
what hyr entencione was to do, she desyrede to bye noo more
grou*n*de of the inhabitantes then she coulde compasse with an
oxe hyde, which to hyr gladly grauntyde (O, wond*er*full womans
wytte!), she cutt the hyde in small lasys, and so by that
was compassede aboute a greate peece of grounde, and thus 15
by hyr wysdome deceyuyde theym all. And by thys meanes
that ther was founde a horse heede as they dyggedde | for the f. 40*b*
fundatione, they deuynyde the cite to be a ryght renomyde,
cheualerouse cite, whiche she namede Cartage; and the castell

---

trata dare pauxillum quietis fatigatis remigio statuit; vbi adueni- 20
entibus vicinis desiderio visendi forenses et alijs commeatus et
mercimonia portantibus, vt moris est, collocutiones et amicicie
iniri cepere. Et cum gratum appareret incolis eos ibidem mansuros
esse et ab Vticensibus olim a Tyro eque profectis legatio suasisset
sedes, confestim esto audisset fratrem bella minantem null[o] 25
territa metu, ne iniuria[m] inferre cuiquam videretur, et ne quis
eam magnum aliquid suspicaretur facturam, non amplius quam
quantum quis posset bouis occupare corio ad sedem sibi consti-
tuendam ab a[c]colis telluris in litore mercata est. O, mulieris
astucia! In frusta iussu suo conscissum bouis corium scissurisque 30
iunctis, longe amplius quam arbitrari potuerint venditores am-
plexa est! Et auspicio equini capitis bellicosam ciuitatem condidit
quam Carthaginem nuncupauit, et arcem a corio bouis Birsam;

---

21 visendi] visendit U.   alijs] alij B.   23 cepere] cœptæ B, cepte
U.   25 nulla LS.   26 iniuria LS.   29 acolis LS.   30 In frusta]
om. BU, frustra S.   scissurisque] facturisque S, fracturisque BU.   31
potuerint] potuerunt BU

therof she namede 'Byrsam', that sowndythe in that langage 'an
oxe sky*n*ne' or 'hyde'. And that done, shewynge hyr treasure,
whiche they had thoughte hade bene loste, she put theym in so
goode conforte and hoope that furthwythe the walles and the
5 towres of that noble cytie of Cartage were redifyede, to the whiche
thys worthy wydowe gaue lawes, in shewynge how and in what
maner they shulde lyue. Wherby, aswell for hyr hyghe, exellente
wytte as also for hyr famouse cytie and ryches that she had, the
nobylite and worthynes of hir was spredd a broode thorow oute
10 all Affryke. And nowe, the Affrycanes beynge wonderly geuyne
to the voluptuousnes of the body, it came so to passe that the
Kynge of Musitana burned in hyr concupiscens and sent vnto
suche as were the greateste prynces abowte, oneles he myght
haue hyr to hys wyfe, he wolde vtt*er*ly destroy hyr new redyfyede
15 citie. The prynces than, knowy*n*g hyr moste constante mynde
and purpose, as concernynge to keepe hyr chastyte, vnnethe durste
breake it vnto hyr, but w*it*h circu*m*location and by meanes p*er*-
swadyde hyr to marye hym, saynge that in so doynge she shulde
brynge the barbarouse prynce to an honest facyon of lyue and

---

20 et cum quos fraude texerat, ostendisset thezauros et ingenti spe
fuge animasset socios surrexere illico menia, templa, forum et
edificia publica et priuata. Ipsa autem datis populo legibus et
norma viuendi, cum repente ciuitas euasisset egregia, et ipsa
inclita fama pulchritudinis inuise et inaudite virtutis atque casti-
25 monie per omnem Affricam delata est. Quamobrem, cum in
libidinem promptissimi homines Afri sint, factum est, vt Musi-
tanorum rex in concupiscentiam veniret eiusdem, eamque quibusdam ex principibus ciuitatis [su]b belli atque desolationis surgentis
ciuitatis denunciatione, ni daretur, in coniugium postulauit. Qui
30 cum inuenissent vidue regine sacrum atque inflexibile castitatis
propositum, et sibi timerent plurimum ne petitoris frustrato
desiderio bello absorberentur, non ausi Dydoni interroganti quod
poscebatur exponere, verbis reginam fallere et in optatum deducere sua sententia cogitauerunt, eique dixere regem cupere eorum

20 quos] cum *add.* BU.   26–7 Musit.] Musicanorum BU.   28 ob
LS.   atque] et BU.   desolationis] desolationes B.   30 inuenissent]
nouissent BU, venissent S.   33 exponere . . . fallere] verbis exponere,
reginam fallere BU.   34 dixere] dixerunt BU.

cause aswell hyrselfe as hyr subiectes to lyue in a quiet; and to
clooke theyr purpose the better, they desyrede hyr to shew hir
pleasure who shulde goo to suche a fearefull and terryble prynce
to declare the message. And all thoughe they thoughte the Quene
had not perceyuyde where aboute they wentt, yet she knewe it 5
ryght well, and after a sadd, wyse pause she aunswerde to theym,
saynge: 'My deare subiectes, I am not ignoraunte but that, as I
am borne and gotten of my father, so am I to my countrye, so that
I do accompte hym noo goode cytezen that for the comune
wealthe, if neade shall so requyre, is not contentyd to dye. Goo 10
your ways, therfore, and with a lytle vastynge and burnynge of
me put a way a greate peryll | frome your countrey.' By thies f. 41a
wordes it semyde to the prynces to haue obteynede what they
wolde, and so, they geuynge the feith of the Kynge to hyr
and she promysynge with hyr ryght hande the same, she de- 15
partyde, not beynge so bolde as to agayne say their desyres, but
within hyrself assuredly concludede by deathe to kepe hyr
chastite. And herynge that Eneas of Troy was arryuyde to cum

---

doctrina efferatam barbariem suam in mores humaniores redigere,
et ob id sub belli interminatione preceptores ex eis poscere; verum, 20
eos ambigere quisnam ex eis tam grande vellet onus assumere, vt
relicta patria apud tam immanem regem moraturus iret. Non
sensit regina dolos, quinymo in eos versa: 'Egregij ciues', inquit,
'que segnicies hec, que socordia! An ignoratis quia patri nascamur
et patrie, nec eum rite ciuem dici posse qui pro salute publica 25
mortem, si casus postulet, nedum incommodum aliud renuat. Ite
igitur alacres et paruo periculo nostro a patria ingens belli incendium remouete.' His regine redargutionibus visum est principibus
obtinuisse quod vellent, et vera regis dete[xe]re iussa. Quibus
auditis satis regine visum est se sua sententia petitum approbasse 30
coniugium, inge[m]uitque secum non ausa suorum aduersari dolo.
Stante tamen proposito repente in consilium iuit quod sue pru-
dentie oportunum visum est dixitque se, si terminus adeundi
virum detur ituram, quo concesso atque adueniente Enea Troyano

21 quis nam LS.   tam grande] *om.* BU.   24 socordia] secordia U,
sordidia S.   26 aliud] aliquod BU. rennuat LS, renuit BU.   27 nostro]
vestro BU. a patria] *om.* BU.   29 dextere LS.   31 ingenuitque L.
32–3 prudentie] pudicitie BU.

to hyr citie, she incontynent, feynynge as thoughe she wolde
make a solempne sacryfyce to the godd*es*, causede to be made an
excedynge greate fyre; and so, kyllynge certeyn beastes, as the
vse was, she hyrselfe ascendyd on the heepe of wodde, redy to
5 kyndle, hydyng vnder hyr vesture a sharpe knyfe, and, the people
co*m*maundyde to assemble aboute hyr, the chaste lady sayde vnto
theym: 'My deare cytezens, ye woll tha‡ I goo to take a husbonde,
and as ye wyll, so to my husbonde I wyll goo,' and saynge thies
wordes, toke the sharpe knyfe and thrust hyrselfe therwyth to
10 the hert. They that stode about hyr assayde to haue holpen hyr,
but all in vayne, for thus the example of chastyte ther exspyrede.
O, the cleere and venerable lyghte of wydowhode! I‿wolde to
Gode all women, wydowes and wyffes, moste specially those that
be chrystened, myght beholde the, and if they myghte, I wolde
15 also they considrede that same innocente bloode of thyne, shedd
to preserue thy chastyte! Suche, emo*n*ge other, that not oonely
mary twys, but thrys, or fowre tymes, and thynke it but a tryfyll,

---

nunquam viso, mori potius quam infringendam fore castimoniam
rata, in sublimiori patrie parte opinione ciuium manes placatura
20 Siccei rogum construxit ingentem et puella tecta veste et ceremonijs seruatis varijs ac hostijs cesis plurimis illum conscendit,
ciuibus frequenti multitudine spectantibus quidnam factura esset.
Que cum omnia pro votis egisset, cultro quem sub vestibus
gesserat exerto ac castissimo apposito pectori vocatoque Syceo,
25 inquit: 'Prout vultis, ciues optimi, ad virum vado.' Et vix verbis
tam paucis finitis, summa omnium intuentium mesticia in cultrum
sese precipitem dedit, et auxilijs frustra admotis, cum perfodisset
vitalia pudicissimum effundens sanguinem, iuit in mortem. O
pudicicie inuiolatum decus! O viduitatis infracte venerandum
30 eternumque specimen, Dydo! In te, velim, ingerant oculos vidue
mulieres et potissime Christiane tuum robur inspiciant! Te, si
possunt, castissimum effundentem sanguinem tota mente con-
siderent et he potissime quibus fuit, ne ad secunda solum dicam
sed ad tercia et vlteriora etiam vota transuolasse leuissimum!

18 fore] *om.* BU.   21 seruatis] paratis BU.   24 exerto] exacto BU.
33 secunda] secundam BU.   34 tercia] tertiam B, terciam U. et] *add.* ad BU.

what wyll ye say, ye women markyde with the marke of Chryste,
if that a pagane woma*n*, to whome Chryste was vnknowne, to gett
hyr an honeste name, all though it were not for the glorye eternall,
with suche p*er*seuerante ande constante a mynde to go willfully
to the deathe with hir oune hande rather then with a nother, or 5
she wolde breake hyr fyrst feythe or violate hyr holy-purposed
chastite? Sum women percase wyll aunswer me, specially suche
as be redy to excuse their faultes, and say: 'I muste do so. I was
destitute of helpe; my fa-|ther and mother were deade. I coulde f. 41*b*
not be in rest, but allways oone or other prouyde me to fullfyll 10
theyr appetyte. I am a woman of fleshe, bloode and boone,
and not of the harde yron.' O, wanton and scornefull excuse!
To whome, I pray youe, dyd Dido put hyr trust, she beynge
an outelawe and banysshed and persecutyde by hyr vnkynde
brother? Thynke youe not but that Dido had dyuers procurers 15
to breake hyr wydowhode, as well as others? Yes, I put youe
oute of doubte. And she hirselfe was neither yron nor stoone,
but as ye ar, of fleshe, bloode and boone. But that the body
couldenot do, the mynde coulde do, that is, rather to dye then to

---

Quid inquient, queso, spectantes Christi insignite caractere, si 20
exteram mulierem gentilem, cui omnino Christus incognitus, ad
conseq[u]endam perituram laudem tam perseueranti animo, tam
forti pectore in mortem vsque pergere, non aliena sed sua illatam
manu antequam in secundas nupcias iret, antequam venerandis-
simum obseruancie propositum violari permitteret. Dicet, arbi- 25
tror, aliqua, cum perspicacissime ad excusationes nostre sint
femine: 'Sic faciendum fuit; destituta eram, in mortem parentes
et fratres abierant, instabant blandicijs procatores, nequibam
obsistere, carnea non ferrea sum.' O ridiculum! Dido quorum
subsidio confidebat, cui exuli frater vnicus erat hostis? Nonne 30
Dydoni procatores fuere plurimi? Ymo et ipsa Dydo erat nec
saxea aut lignea magis quam hodierne sint. Non equidem. Ergo
mente saltem valens, cuius non arbitrabatur posse viribus euitare
illecebras, moriens ea via qua potuit euitauit. Sed nobis, qui nos

21 gentilem] infidelem *add.* BU.   22 conseqnendam L.   perituram]
parituramque B.   27 eram] eam S.   28 abierant] obierant BU.   29 Dido]
sub *add.* BU.   31 nec] ne BU.   32 aut] ac B.

violate hyr holy chastyte. But ye that be Chrysten, haue Chryste
to your helpe, and surely our meeke Redemptor euer sauethe
theym that puttes theyr trust in hym. May it not be that he that
delyuerede the three children frome the flammynge forneys and
5 Susan frome the false cryme obiectyd agaynst hyr, [can] delyuer
the frome those that ly in wayte to deuoure thyne honeste?
Doubtles. Thow mayste, and thow wyll, bowe thyne eyes downwarde and looke vppon the grounde, whereto thow shall goo, and
stoppe thyne eares lyke vnto the rocke, and by that way repell the
10 bettynge of the water of temptation frome the, and so saue thy
chastite. But agayne sum wyll aunswere to thys and say: 'I am
a lady that hathe fayre landes and possessiones, a goodely house
and well trymmyde, stuffe of householde pryncely lyke, and large
ryches of golde, syluer and plate, and I was desyrouse to be a
15 mother, to the entente this greate substaunce shulde not fall into
strayngers handes.' O, madde and vnwytty desyre! Was not
Dido a quene of a greate kyngedome withoute chyldren? And
why dyd she refuse to be a mother? For she, lyke a noble woman,
perceyuyde ryght well that it is a madnesse for a woman to make

5 obiectydyt MS.   6 honeste] is *add*. MS.   *The construction is
confused.*

---

20 tam desertos dicimus, nonne Christus refugium est? Ipse quidem
redemptor pius in se sperantibus semper adest. An putas qui
pueros de camino ignis eripuit, qui Suzannam de falso crimine
liberauit, te de manibus aduersantium non possit auferre? Si
velis, flecte in terram oculos et aures obsera atque ad instar
25 scopuli vndas venientes expelle et immota ventos afflare sine;
saluaberis. Insurget forsan et altera dicens: 'Erat mihi longe
lateque protensus ager, domus splendida, suppellectilis regia et
diuiciarum ampla possessio: cupiebam effici mater, ne tam grandis
substantia ad exteros deferretur.' O, insanum desiderium! Nonne
30 et Dydoni absque filijs regnum erat? Non diuicie regie? Erant
equidem. Quid et ipsa mater effici recusauit? Quia sapientissime
arbitrata est nil stolidius fore quam tibi destruere, vt edifices

20 nonne] si *add*. BU.   23–4 Si velis] B *adds question-mark, and* U *virgula,
thus linking these words to the preceding sentence.* S, *on the other hand, agrees
with* L.   26 Erat] erant U.   30 Non] nonne BU.   31 Quid] quod BU.

another and vndo hyrself. And I say to the further, if thow
haue greate ryches, doste thow not se the poore people of
Chryste, which thow maiste | with mesure bestowe it to theym, f. 42a
and buylde therby a palace in eternall glorye, and so wyth a
double vertue adorne thy chastyte? Besydes thys, thow haste 5
freandes whiche prouyde to be to the kynde, true and louynge.
Ther can be no more apte eyares then theym, for so it may be that
thow maiste haue chyldren, but thow shalte not haue theym as
thowe thynkest to haue, but as nature wyll, so shall they be.
Now cumethe the thyrde, and she wyll say: 'Ther was no remedy 10
but that I shulde mary. My father commaundyde me to it, my
kynsmen enforsede me to do it, and my neyghbours wilnot suffre
me to be in quyete, vntyll I mary.' A, goode lady, as who shulde
say ye were so ignoraunte that in resistynge the fyre of concupiscence, all theyr wordes shulde be vastyde in vayne. May yowe not 15
see Dido that coulde not lyue, because she wolde not be vnchaste?
Myght she not a lyuyde, trow ye, *and* yet bene chaste? Now
another, that is wylyer then the rest, wyll say to thys: 'Dothe not

17 alyuyde MS.

alteri. Ergo castimoniam maculabo, vt agris, vt splendide domui,
vt suppellectili pariam possessorem si[ue], quod contigit sepissime, 20
destructorem. Nonne et tibi diuicie ingentes, que profecto expen-
dende, non abiciende sunt, et Christi pauperes multi sunt, quibus
dum exhibes, tibi eterna palacia construis, quibus dum exhibes,
castimoniam alio fulgore illustres? Preterea et amici sunt,
quorum nulli aptiores heredes cum tales habeas quales ipsa 25
quesitos probaueris, filios autem non quales volueris, sed quales
natura concedit, habebis. Veniet et tercia, asserens quia sic illi
fuerit agendum, cum parentes iusserint, consanguinei coegerint, et
affines suaserint, quasi ignoremus ni quod sua concupiscentia
suasisset, ymo effrenata iussisset, predicta omnia frustrata esset 30
negatione vnica. Potuit mori Dydo, ne viueret impudica: hec vt
pudica viueret, connubium negare non potuit. Aderit suo iudicio
astutior ceteris vna que dicat: 'Iuuenis eram; feruet, vt nosti,

19 castimoniam] castimonia BU.   20 sino LS.   21 et] etsi BU.
27 concedet BU.   30 frustrata esset] frustrasset BU.   31 BU *connect*
negatione vnica *with the following sentence.*   Potuit] voluit BU.

the doctour of the gentyll*e*s, Saincte Poule, teche that it is better
to mary then to burne?' O, verey well spoken, as thoughe I had
spoken onely to olde matrones, for that Dido dyd so fyrme and
sett hyr hert that thys rage in hyr had noo place! O, vngraciouse
5 myndes that [say] thys goode counseill well geuyne of Sayncte
Paule! How many tymes do yow aleage hym to thynges dishoneste! I tell youe, the strength of a man sore wastyde may be
restoryde, but chastite wastyde, neuer. If a panyme woma*n* for
a lytle vayne glory, withoute [to] haue other mede, myghte
10 refrayne hyr lust, may not a Christen woman so do as she dyd?
Alas the whyle, wyll we do ymagyne with suche excusys to beguyle
God, that wyll not be beguyled, not onely we leese oure goode
fame in thys worlde, but ru*n*ne into eternall peyne in the tother!
Let the matrones then be asshamede therfore to see the body of
f. 42*b* Dido deade and wi*th*oute spyryte, and when they call to | mynde
16 the cause of hyr deathe, let theym looke downwarde to the
grounde, that a membre of the dewell, a paynyme, shulde wi*th*

---

iuuentus; continere non poteram; doctoris gentium aientis "Melius
est nubere quam vri" sum secuta consilium.' O, quam bene
20 dictum, quasi ego aniculis imperem castitatem, vel non fuerit dum
firmauit animo castimoniam iuuencula Dydo! O, scelestum
facinus! Non a Paulo tam sancte consilium illud datur, quin in
defensionem facinoris persepe turpius all[e]getur. Exhaustas
vires sensim cibis restaurare possumus, superfluas abstinentia
25 minorare non possumus. Gentilis femina ob inanem gloriam
feruori suo imperare potuit et leges imponere; Christiana,
vt consequatur eternam, imperare non potest. Heu mihi! dum
fallere deum talibus arbitramur, nosipsos et honori caduco, vt
eternum sinam, subtrahimus et in precipicium eterne dampna-
30 tionis impellimus. Erubescant igitur intuentes Dydonis cadauer
exa[n]i[m]e, et dum causam mortis eius excogitant, vultus
deiciant, dolentes quod a membro dyaboli Cristicole pudicicia

19 suum LS. 20 aniculis] anniculis BSU. 21 scelestum] cœleste
B, celeste U. 22 sancto BU. 23 alligetur LS. 26 Christiana]
Christina B. 27 consequatur] consequeretur BU. eternam] eterna B.
29 eternum] eternam U. 30 igitur] ergo BU. 31 examine L, exanire
U, exinanire B. et] vt BU.

hyr chastyte passe a Crysten womans chastyte. Let not then the
wydowes think with theyre teares, nor with theyr black gownes,
to haue doone all they shulde do to theyr husbondes, when they
be deade, but keepe to oone theyr loue for euer, yf they wyll
fullfyll the offyce of a chaste wydowe. What the dewyll is it, oone 5
other for to take so many husbondes then for to folowe Valaria
and Messalyna in corners where rat*tes* and myse haue theyr
cauerns? But I wyll touche thys in another place. And I confesse
in deede sumwhat to haue passyde the boundes of my tale. But
who is so well aduysed but that in suche a graue mater [he] dothe 10
not, as it were with a forse, speeke in it? But now to [r]euerte to
the hystory. Dido thys wyse extyncte, hyr cytezens with teares,
wit*h* cryes and lamentationes toke hyr chaste body and with
dyuyne honours buryde it, and not onely gaue hyr the name of the
mother of the countrye, but further, as longe as Cartage stoode, 15
buyldyt in hyr honoure temples and aulters, to hyr per̄petuall
fame and laude for euer.

11 deuerte MS.

---

superentur. Ne putent, dum lacrimas dederint et pullas assum-
pserint vestes, defuncto peregisse omnia. In finem vsque seruandus
est amor, si adimplere velint viduitatis officium. Nec existiment 20
ad vlteriora vota transire, quod nonnulle persepe faciunt, potius vt
sue prurigini sub ficto coniugij nomine satisfaciant, quam vt sacro
obsequantur connubio [et] impudicicie labe careant. Quid enim
aliud est tot hominum amplexus exposcere et tot inire quam post
Valeriam Messalinam caueas et fornices intrare? Sed de hoc alias. 25
Fateor tamen laboris incepti nimium excessisse terminos. Sed
quis adeo sui compos est, quin aliquando vltra propositum effera-
tur ab impetu? Cognoscant, queso, qui legerint et nos vnde
diuertimus reuertamur. Dydonem igitur exanguem cum lacrimis
publicis et merore ciues, non solum humanis sed diuinis etiam 30
honoribus funus exercentes magnificum, extulere pro viribus.
Nec tantum publice matris et regine loco sed deitatis inclite eique
fauentes assidue dum stetit Carthago, aris templisque et excogitatis
sacrificijs coluere.

18 Ne] Nec BU.   pullas] pulcas B.   21 transire] transiere U.
23 *om.* LS.   27 quin] quoniam S.   28 Cognoscant] ignoscant BSU.
32 eique] eisque BSU.

Of Nicaula, the Quene of Ethyope.
The xli Chapitre.

THe extreme barbarouse countrye of Ethyope broughte furthe
Nicaula, whiche is so muche the more to be commendyd
5 that, beynge borne in so rude and barbarouse a countrye, [she]
had in hyr so exellent vertues. For it is euydent, if we shall
gyue credyte to the auncyenty, that after the names of the
f. 43a Pharaose and | theyr succession faylede, that thys woman was not
oonely Quene of Ethyope, but also of Egypte and of Arraby, and
10 by the greate ile of Meroe ther to be inhabytede, hauynge so
infenyte of golde and syluer and ryches that it is thoughte theryn
she passed all other creatures in thys present lyfe. She dyd not
wantonly vse hyr substaunce in pleasures and playse as other
do, but vnto suche knowledge of the thynges naturall that, all
15 thoughe we knowe not hyr maister that taughte hyr, that it was
a woundre to se it. And, to thys, Holy Scryptur berythe wytnes
that thys is that woman whiche the Bybble nameth Saba. Herynge

---

De Nicaula, Ethiopum regina. xli.

NIcaulam extrema, vt percipi potest, Ethyopum produxit
20 barbaries, que quidem tanto memoratu dignior est, quanto
inter incultiores exorta moribus effulsit splendidior. Constat
enim, si fides datur antiquis, hanc deficientibus Pharaonibus, seu
eorum prolem seu alteram, Ethyopum atque Egiptiorum et, vt
nonnulli asserunt, Arabum reginam fuisse clarissimam et in Meroe,
25 insula Nyli permaxima, habuisse regimina: ibique tam grandi
diuiciarum abundasse copia, vt credatur in hac vita fere mortales
excessisse ceteros. Quam inter diuiciarum delicias non ocio et
molliciei feminee deditam legimus, quinymo, etsi preceptorem
ignoraremus, tanta eam rerum periturarum scientia preditam
30 sensimus, vt mirabile visum sit ; quod etiam sacre testari videntur
litere qu[a]rum auctoritate monstratur. Hanc quam Sabam

24 in] ni S.   Meroe] Menonoere S.   25 regimina] regna BU.   26
habundasse LSU.   29 ignoraremus] ignoremus BU.   eam] earum BU.
perit.] peritarum BU.   scientiam B.   31 quorum LS.

the wysdome of Salomon, in hyr tyme of so greate a fame that
he was spoken of thorow the worlde, thys woman dyd not, as
fooles do, sett lyghte by wysdome, but, meruelynge at it, leuynge
hyr kyngedome of Meroe, sett in an angle of the worlde, and
goynge by Ethyopia and by the Egyptiens vnto the Reede See, 5
with a greate and a tryhumphaunte company of lordes *and* seruaunt*es* came to Jherusalem, to se and to lerne of Salomon knowledge and cu*n*nynge, to hys greate meruell also to beholde the
womans magnyficence and ordre. Whiche, hono*ur*ably receyuyde,
and she puttynge c*er*teyn questiones to Salomon, and he assoy- 10
lynge theym to the verey truethe, she confessyde playnely that
hys wysdome was more then the fame that wentt of it, farr
excedynge mans capacyte, oonely geuyne to hym of Gode. And
then, gyuynge hym many ryche gyftes, speciall certeyn gryftes
whiche berythe the p*er*fyte bawme (Salomon, p*er*ceyuyng the 15
greate vertue therof, causede theym to be graftyde not farr frome
Assaltys and diligently to be kepte), and he of hys parte gyuynge

2 worlde] that *add*. MS.

---

nominant audita scientie Salomonis suo euo florentis fama, que
celebris totum iam compleuerat orbem, dicunt fuisse miratam,
cum consueuerunt stolidi seu ignari floccifacere talia, non mirari. 20
Et, quod longe maius, non solum mirata est, quinymo Meroe fere
altero orbis angulo insigni relicto regno, per Ethyopes, Egipcios et
Rubri Maris littora atque Arabum solitudines tam splendidc
comitatu tamque magnifico sumptu, regioque permaximo famu-
latu, venit illum auditura Hierusalem, vt ipse Salomon, regum 25
omnium ditissimus, mulieris magnificentiam miratus sit. Que
summo cum honore ab eo suscepta, cum enigmata exposuisset
quedam et eorum solutiones cum diligentia audiuisset, vltro con-
fessa est, Salomonis sapientiam longe famam atque humanorum
ingeniorum capacitatem excedere: nec dubium dei dono, non 30
studio quesitam fuisse. Inde dona exhibuit illi magnifica, inter
que fuisse creduntur balsama sudantes arbustule, quas post-
modum Salomon haud longe ab Assaltidis lacu plantari iussit et

18 scientie] scientia BU.   20 consu.] consueuerint BU.   21
solum] sola B.   Meroe] menonoere S, a maiore BU.   22 orbis] ex *add*.
BU.   Egipcios] Ægyptiosque B, egiptiosque U.   28 audiuisset]
audisset BU.

to hyr iewell*es* of an infynyte pryce, with greate ioy she returnyde
home into hyr countrye. Sum do beleue thys to be that high
quene callede Candase, that in lyke wyse as the Kynges of Egypte
were callede Pharaose, after hyr, many yeres they were callede of
5 hyr name Candases. |

f. 43*b*   Of Pamphile, the doughter to Platre.
                              The xlij Chapitre.

I Fynde that Pamphile was a Grekyshe woman, but of what
   countrye ther, tyme hathe put it oute of remembraunce. But
10 hyr fathers name is knowne, for it is sayde that oone Platre was
hyr father. Whiche Pamphile, all thoughe she may not, because
of hyr so meane progenyto*ur*es, be to hyghely exaltede, yet, for
that she addyde to the com*m*une wealthe goode, it is not reason that
she be defraudyde of hyr laude and prayse. Ther is noo goode
15 thynge newe founde by any creature, but *tha*t it is an argument
of a greate wytt of the persone that fyndeth it, and for the qualyte
of the thynge to be com*m*endyde for it. The olde auctours wyll,

---

coli; demum versa vice susceptis muneribus, summa cum laude
in patriam abijt. Sunt et qui credunt hanc eandem illam celsam
20 meridiei reginam fuisse Candacem, a qua imposterum, vt Phara-
ones ante, sic Egipcij reges diu cognominati Candaces sunt.

                  De Pamphile, Platre filia. xlij.

P Amphilem quandam Grecam fuisse feminam comperio, et cum
   ex qua patria vetustas abstulerit, patris tamen nomen benigna
25 reliquit, nam cuiusdam Platre fuisse filiam reperitur. Que etsi
amplissimis titulis decorari non possit, quoniam aliquid reipublice
addidit boni, sua laudis portione taciturnitate fraudari non debet.
Nil enim noui, quantumcunque post factum videatur facile, ab
aliquo compertum est, quod non sit ingentis ingenij argumentum
30 et pro rei qualitate aliquali gloria numerandum. Hanc igitur

19 abijt] redijt BU.   credunt] credant BU.   20 meridiei]
Meroe BU.   vt] vti BU.   24 ex] ea *add*. B.   abs-
tulerit] abstulit BU.

to whome of reasone we shulde gyue su*m* credite, that this Pamphile fyrste founde the sylke worme and fyrst gathrede theym of frome trees, and after taught howe to purge theym, and consequently to put theym to the dystafe to spynne and then to weeue theym. And so, tyl hyr tyme the way vnknow*n*, she was the 5 fyrst inuento*ur* of it. Wherby reasone dothe well tell what a wytt she had that coulde fynde suche a p*r*ofytable crafte.

Of Rehea Ilia, a virgyne of Vesta.
The xliij Chapitre. |

REhea Ilia descendyd of an honorable *and* speciall famouse f 44*a* bloode and was sumtyme of an exellente beautie emonge the 11 Italiens, for she was of the bloode of the Siluyens, reygny*n*ge successyuely oone after another, frome the descent of the valyaunte Troyan Eneas. Now Numytor beynge Kynge of the Albonoys, and Rehea a verey yonge, tender virgyne, Amylyus that was the 15 brother to Numytor, couetouse for to reigne, settynge a syde the lawe, that is, that the elder ought to be the heyre, put hys brother

---

volunt auctores, quibus fides prestatur aliqua, primam et ex arbustulis volitantem bombicem collegisse et illam a superfluis purgasse pectine, et purgatam apposuisse colo, ac etiam ex ea 20 filum trahere, et inde texere docuisse, et sic eius vsum eo vsque [in]cognitum induxisse. Cuius rei excogitata ratio ostendet facile quantum in reliquis agendis debuerit Pamphiles valuisse.

De Rhea Ylia, Vestali virgine. xliij.

RHea Ylia generosi sanguinis precipua clari[t]ate inter Ytalos 25 emicuit olim, nam per Siluios, Albanorum reges, successiue regnantes atque descendentes ab Enea, inclito Troyanorum duce, traxit originem, Numitore ex dictis Albanorum rege prestante. Ea quippe adhuc existente virguncula factum est vt Amulius, Numitoris frater iunior, impulsus regni cupidine, iure gentium paruipenso, 30 Numitorem vi regno priuaret. In quem ne seuiret, fraterna inter-

---

18 auctores] autores BU.   prima B.   et] *om.* BU.   22 cognitum LS.
24 Ylia] vlia S.   25 clarirate L.   28 Numitore] munitore S.   *Similarly in other cases of the name.*

frome hys kyngedome. But, remembry*n*g sumwhat hemself that
it shulde be abhomynable to shede hys brothers bloode, he wolde
not put hym to deathe, but suffrede hym to lyue pryuely emongst
the poore paysans of the country. But yonge Lausus, that was
5 [N]u[m]ytor sonne, to th'entente he wolde remoue suche an
ennemye, he causede hym to be putt to deathe, and hys suster
Rehea, as sayde is, verey yonge, he sparede hyr, but to the entent
that he wolde vtterly ordeyn that she shulde neuer haue chylde,
he put hyr emonge the virgynes of Vesta and compellyde hyr to
10 vowe pe*r*petuall virgynyte. Whiche sayde Rehea comen to pe*r*fyte
age, by what meanes or by whome it is not knowne, but hyr
swollne bely declarede that she was wyth chylde, and soo,
broughte abedde, [she] had at oone byrthe Romulus and Remus,
the fyrst founders of the cytie of Rome, for whiche offense, all
15 thoughe she were descendyd of the bloode royall, yet by the olde
ordynauncys and by the Kynges co*m*maundemente, she was
buryede quycke. But thoughe hyr body were ouerwhelmyde wyth
earthe, yet hyr chyldren haue causede hyr to haue fame perpetuall, whiche the tyraunte, hyr vncle, dyd what he coulde to

5 Munytor MS.   13 and MS.

---

20 cessit pietas, contentus vt ruri rel[e]gatus priuato vacaret ocio. In
Lausum vero adolescentulum, Numitoris filium, vt regni amoueret
emulum, animo truci deseuit eoque ceso Yliam, Lausi sororem,
adhuc puellulam seruauit. Verum, vt illi auferretur connubij spes
omnis et prolis, Vestalibus virginibus addi[di]t eamque perpetuam
25 virginitatem profiteri coegit. Que cum in pleniorem deuenisset
etatem, stimulis acta Venereis, quo pacto nescitur, eam tamen in
amplexus deuenisse viri, turgidus patefecit vterus, nam pregnans
effecta Romulum Remumque, Romane vrbis parentes, ex vno
eodem[que] partu enixa est. Quod ob crimen, quantumcunque
30 regia fuerit femina, instituto veteri regioque iussu expositi sunt
filij et ipsa viua infossa est. Sane, etsi corpus eius terra obrutum
sit, natorum opus egregium in sublime culmen ipsius nomen
euexit egitque, vt id posteritati venerabile foret, quod tyrannus
lege sacra abolesse conatus est. Hanc dum mente intueor, video-

20 religatus LS.   24 addit LS.   eamque] eam quam B.   25 in] ad B.
29 eodem LS.   34 abolesse] abolere BU.

haue defacyte it. I cannot but laughe, callynge vnto mynde those
that we calle cloysterars or nunnes, how often tymes pryuyly they
clooke their veneriall pastymes and how thyes couetous men,
to the entente | they wolde not do the coste to marye theyr f. 44^b
doughters, as it were by a pretens of deuotione compell the poore 5
maydens by force to entre the cloyster, or, more planely, to shett
theym into perdycyone, saynge that they haue dedycate theyr
chyldren to Gode, not doubtynge but therby they and theyres
shall haue the better happe and by theyre prayers after theyr
deathe go to the place of quyete. O, greate mokery and fonde, 10
folyshe doynge! Ar ye so ignoraunte that ye knownot a womans
lyuynge in idlenes muste neades serue Venus ande in maner to enuy
vnhoneste women, because they may not do as they do, and to
laude more theyr dwellynge places then theyre oune propre
sellys? And in beholdynge the maryages of the seculare yonge 15
men, theyr feastes, theyr tryhumphes, thynke youe not but they
lamente that they may not be maryede, also in cursynge theyr
freandes that clothyde theym with those blacke cowlles and
roobes, and seeke all ways possible how they may breake oute of

---

que sacras vestes et sanctimonialium velamenta Veneris ali- 20
quandiu tegere furta, quin quorundam insaniam rideam continere
nequeo. Sunt quidam qui, vt auari porciunculam dotis natis
subtrahant, sub pretextu deuotionis paruulas filias aut quandoque
puberes sed coactas monasticis claustris, nescio vtrum dicam
claudunt aut perdunt; aientes se deo dicasse virginem que intenta 25
precibus rem suam deducet in melius morientique piorum lucra-
bitur sedes. O, ridiculum stolidumque! Ignorant ociosam
feminam Veneri militare et summe publicis inuidere meretriculis
earumque cellulas suis preponere claustris, et dum secularia
coniugia spectant, vestes ornatusque varios, choreas et festos dies, 30
se nulla coniugij habita experientia, vere et ab ipso vite huius
ingressu viduas, deflent fortunam suam, parentum animas, vittas
et claustra tota execrantur mente, nec alibi solature mesta pre-
cordia recurrunt quam in meditationem, quo pacto in fugam
carcerem erumpere possint aut saltem intromittere mechos, 35

22 porc.] portiunculam BU.   26 morientique] morientemque B.

that obscure cloyster, or, if that cannot be, study how to brynge in
yonge men dayly with all, because theyr freandes wolde nott suffre
theym to haue husbondes? Yes, surely. Beholde, thies be the
prayers of theym, whiche they weene, that so inclose theym, to cum
5 to heuen therby. O, ye vnwytty parentes, that make theym to do
that whiche yourselffes cannot do, that often geuythe youe cause
to lamente theyr vnlaufull doynge, in commyttynge oppression, in
hauynge chyldren not laufully procreate, and, in conclusion, compellyd to fynde basterdes, that myght, if ye had maryede theym,
10 haue founde ryght heyres! See wherto that your couetouse exten-
dith and beholde, vnwyse as ye be, that not by constraynte, but
when they be of laufull yeres and haue reasone and [be] well
broughte vpp in vertue, that then ye shulde dedicate theym to
God, and not afore. And of that sorte I do thynke ther is now but
verey fewe; and it is muche more necessary to haue feware then so
15 many to breke and violate the holy vowe they take vppon theym. |

<hr>

1 cloysters MS.   12 of] *add.* a MS.

incestum querentes agere furtim, quod palam illis sublatum
est fecisse coniugio. He sunt, non dicam omnium sed plurimarum,
contemplationes in deum precesque transcendentes ethera, quibus
aucti saluique fient, qui illas intrusere carceri. Heu, miseri
20 parentes et necessarij quicunque alij, dum [putant] alias posse
perpeti quod ipsi nequirent et fugiunt miseri; persepe flentur
stupra turpissima, infames partus, nepotes expositi aut infanda
morte necati, exclusiones ignominiose, fugeque, et postremo de-
honesta[ta]s oportet alere, quas honestas potuisset auarus coniu-
25 gibus iungere! Sentiant ergo dementes, si alienas vires suis metiri
non volunt, quoniam non inscie, non paruule, non coacte, deo
dicande sunt virgines, quinymo persancte ab infantia patria in
domo nutrite, honestate et probandis moribus imbute, etate
prouecte, et quod agant integra mente noscentes, sponte sua, non
30 coacte, iugum subeuntes virginitatis perpetue; quas rarissimas in-
ueniri arbitror, sed longe melius est talium paruum esse numerum
quam multitudine illecebri dei sanctuarium prophanari.

20 *om.* LBSU.   23 ignom.] ignominose SU, ignominosæ B.   23–4
dehonestas L.   24 auarus] varijs BU.   25 iungere] coniungere BU.
27 persancte] perfectæ B, perfecte U.   29 quod] quid S.
32 prophanari] prophanare BSU.

Of Gaya Cirylla, the wyfe to Kynge Tarquin*us* Priscus.   f. 45*a*
The xliiij^{ti} Chapitre.

ALbeit I do not well knowe nor fynde of whome Gaia Cirylla descendyd, yet I do thynke that either she was a Romane or a Tuscane woma*n* borne, *and* the ryght deare belouyde wyffe of 5 Tarquin*us* Priscus. Thys noble woman, all thoughe she were a kynges wyfe, norishede in pastymes and pleasures, yet she wolde not lyue in idlenes, but, geuynge hyrselfe to spy*n*nynge of woole, whiche then emonge the Italyens was thoughte to be honorable, she was so exellent in it that vnto thys present day she hathe by 10 the same renoume and fame. Nor thys lackyde not in hyr dayes, for, beynge aswell reputyde honorable as profitable to the Romaynes, or euer they hade brought in the delyc*es* of Asia, it was a lawe emonge theym that when any newe maryde woma*n* shulde entre the house of hyr husbonde, that she shulde be demaundyd 15 what was hyr name, and the bryde shulde aunswere and say that hyr name was Gaya Cirylla, the whiche was taken as a goode

---

De Gaya Cirilla, Tarquini[j] Prisci regis [coniuge]. xliiij.

GAya Cirilla, etsi eius originis nullam stare memoriam compererim, Romanam tamen aut Etruscam fuisse mulierem reor, 20 et veterum constat auctoritate quoniam Tarquini[j] Prisci, Romanorum regis, fuerit gratissima coniunx. Hec cum esset prestantissimi ingenij femina, quantumcunque regia coniunx et in regia esset domo, ocio torpere passa non est, quinymo cum se lanificio dedisset (quod credam eo tempore apud Latinos honora- 25 bile), adeo erga illud egregiam opificem atque solertem fecit, vt in hodiernum vsque nominis sui fama protensa sit. Nec euo suo publico caruit munere, nam cum apud Romanos mirabilis et amantissima femina haberetur, nondum eis marcentibus delicijs Asiaticis, instituto publico cautum est, vt ab intrantibus nouis 30 nupcijs primitus sponsorum suorum domos vnaqueque rogaretur, quo vocaretur nomine rogataque se e vestigio Gayam vocari profiteretur, quasi ex hoc sumpture essent future frugalitatis

18 Tarquini LS.   filia LS.   20 aut Etr.] ab Hetruscam B.   21 Tarquini LS.   28 mirabilis et] *om.* B.   29 eis] *om.* BU.   33 sumpt. essent] sumptura esset B.

sygne or token that the wyfe shuld be suche a oone as Gaya was. Whiche custome, thoughe now a days men thynke it but a tryfyll, yet emonge the aunsyente it was an euydente iudgement of the wytte and goodenes of this honorable woman.

5   Of Sapho, a mayden of Lesbia, and a poete.
The xlv^ti Chapitre. |

f. 45*b* SApho was a mayden of Lesbia and of Mitelena, and ther is noo more knowne wherof she came. But, and we noote well hyr study and goode lerny*n*g, we shall well iudge that she descendyd 10 of ryghte hono*u*rable parentt*es*. A vyle and, as it were, a rusticall mynde scante shulde haue desyrede suche scyences. But all thoughe it is not knowne in what tyme she was, yet aswell hyr yonge age as also hyre competente shappe of body and hyr study in poese, whereby she ascendyde the harde pathe of Parnaso with 15 dilygente labour, the Musys not agayne sayng therto, at the last

---

omen. Quod quantumcunque apud insolentes modernorum animos videatur perrarum, non dubitem quin apud prudentiores illius seculi simplicitate pensata optime et plurimum laudande mulieris videatur i[n]dicium.

20   De Sapho, puella Lesbia et poeta. xlv.

SAphos Lesbia ex Mitelena vrbe puella fuit, nec amplius sue originis posteritati relictum est. Sane, si studium inspexerimus, quod annositas abstulit, pro parte restitut[u]m, videbimus eam scilicet ex honestis atque claris parentibus genitam, non enim 25 illud vnquam degener animus potuit desiderasse vel attigisse plebeius. Hec etenim, si quibus temporibus claruit ignoramus, adeo generose fuit mentis, vt etate florens et forma, non contenta solum litteras iungere nouisse, amplior[e] feruore animi et ingenij suasa viuacitate, cons[c]ens[o] studio vigili per abrupta P[a]rnasi 30 vertice celso, se felici ausu musis non renuentibus immiscuit et

17 perr.] perminimum BU.   18 illius] huius BU.   19 iudicium LS.   20 Sapho] Sapphone B.   21 Mitelena] Mytilena B, Mitilena S, mutilena U.   23 restitutam LS.   26 si] etsi BU. claruit] claruerit BU.   28 ampliori LS.   29 consensu LS. pernasi L.   30 rennuentibus LS.

was acceptyd to be crownede with the lawrell, so that in makynge
of balett*es*, in touchynge the harpe strynge *and* in other musicall
dites she had noo pere, whiche is vnto ryght studiouse men difficill
and harde to attayne to. What shulde I more say? She came to
suche p*er*fectione in thies thynges afore rehersyde that in hyr 5
memory was rasyde certeyn ymages lyke vnto hyr, of coper and
brasse, and hyr name sett emongste the moste renomyde poetes,
whiche surely is more laude to hyre then the diademe to sum
kynges, or the bysshopps myters, or the conquero*ur*s lawrell
braunches. But as in lyke wyse as in those happy thynges she is 10
to be praysede, so is she to be blamyde for the fonde loue she was
taken in. For, were it either by the p*er*sonage or the gesture of a
certeyn yonge man, whiche lytle or nothynge regardyde hyr, she
was so occupyede with that intollerable pestylens, seynge that
neither with hyr lamentable v*er*ses nor with hyr teares she coulde 15
gett hys loue, that it was wonder. This not withstandynge,

---

laureo peruagato nemore in antrum vsque Appollinis euasit et,
Castalio proluta latice, Phebi sumpto plectro, sacris nimphis
choream [trahentibus], son[o]re cithare fid[e]s tangere et expro-
mere modulos puella non dubitauit, que quidem etiam studiosis- 20
simis viris difficili[a] plurimum visa sunt. Quid multa? Eo studio
venit suo, vt vsque in hodiernum clarissimum suum carmen testimonio veterum lucens sit, vt erecta illi fuerit statua enea et suo
dicata nomini, et ipsa inter poetas celebres numerata, quo splendore profecto non clariora sunt regum dyademata, non pontificum 25
infule, nec etiam triumphantium lauree. Verum, si danda fides
est, vti feliciter [studuit], sic infelici amore capta est. Nam seu
facecia, seu decore, seu alia gratia cuiusdam iuuenis dilectione,
ymo intollerabili occupata peste, cum ille desiderio suo non esset
accomodus, ingemiscens in eius obstinatam duriciem, dicunt versus 30
flebiles cecinisse, quos ego elegos fuisse putassem, cum tali sint elegi
attributi materie, ni legissem ab ea, quasi preteritorum carminum

17 peruagato] peruagata B, peruagoto U.   19 trahentibus] *om*. LS.
sonare LS.   fidas LS.   19–20 expromere] exprimere B.
21 difficilimum LS.   22 venit] deuenit BU.   23 vt] et BU.
27 *om*. L.   31 ego] *om*. BU.

beynge oppressyde with thys rage, she fou*n*de a new man*er* of
metre, whiche is called of hyr name the metre of Sapho vnto thys
day.   But what ar the Musys to be accusede for thys—all thoughe
Antheon coulde with hys harpe moue the greate stoones of Ogyges,
f. 46*a* yet the yonge mans harte, though | Sapho songe neuer so swete,
6 wolde not be mouede to loue hyr agayne?

Of Lucres, the wyfe to Collatyne.
The xlvj^{ti} Chapitre.

LVcres, the verey ledare and teacher of the Romaynes chastyte,
10 and the moste holy example of the auncyente wyffes, she was
the doughter of Lucyus Spuryus, a man hyghly extemyde in
honoure emonge the Romaynes, and geuyne to wife to Tarquynus
Collatynus.   Harde to tell, whether in fayre beautie of body or in
swete speche emonge all other matrones she oughte more to be
15 praysed or co*m*mendyde.   Now it was so that Tarquynus, the
Kynge of Romaynes, surnamede the prowde Tarquyne, hade
layde seege vnto a towne callede Ardea, not verey farr frome
Rome.   Ande it chauncyde that, lyinge at the seage, the Kynge

---

formis spretis, nouum adinuentum genus diuersis a ceteris in-
20 cedens pedibus, quod adhuc ex eius nomine Saphicum appellatur.
Sed quid accusande videntur Pyerides, que, tangente Amphione
lyram, Ogigia saxa mouisse potuerunt et adolescentis cor, Sapho
canente, mollisse noluerint?

De Lucrecia, Collatini coniuge. xlvi.

25 LUcrecia Romane pudicicie dux egregia atque sanctissimum
vetuste parsimonie decus, filia fuit Lucrecij Spurij Tricipitini,
clarissimi inter Romanos viri, et coniunx Tarquinij olim Collatini
et Tricipitini filij; incertum vtrum oris formositate an honestate
morum inter Romanas matronas speciosior visa sit.   Que cum,
30 obsidente Tarquin[i]o Superbo Ardeam ciuitatem, apud Collacij
opidum haud longe ab vrbe in viri edes secessisset, actum est, vt
in castris cum obsidio traheretur in longum, cenantibus regijs

20 Saphicum] Sapphicum B, Sapicum S, saphycum U.   21 que]
om. BU.   23 mollisse nol.] mollire uidetur B.   27–8 olim . . . filij]
Collatini, olim Ægerij fratris Tarquinij Prisci filij B, *so* U.   30 Tar-
quino LS.

hauynge with hy*m* at supper dyuers of the noble yonge men of hys
courte, emonge the other Collatyne was oone, and as they had
well eaten and dronken, well warmyde with wyne, that they fell
in co*m*mynynge of their wyfes; and as eche oone of theym sett
furthe hys oune the best he coulde, they fell in pacte that they 5
shulde leepe on theyr horses and so preuyly goo to Rome, to se
what theyr wyfes dyd in theyr absence, and which of theym was
moste honestly occupyede. Now the yonge men comen to Rome,
and fyndynge theyr wyfes makynge goode cheere, and sportynge
and reuelynge, emonge the other, the goode Lucres was founde in 10
hyr house, poorely and sadly appayrelde, spy*n*nynge on the rocke.
Wherfore, by the iudgemente of all the reste, she was extemyd
to be the moste worthy to be praysede. Now Collatyne, hyr
husbond, | callynge all the yonge men vnto hys house, emonge the f. 46*b*
other, Sextus Collatynus, the Kynges son was oone, whiche caste 15
on Lucres a dyshoneste loue and with an vngracyouse mynde
determynede, either by fayre meanes or by force, to fulfyll with
hyr hys pleasure. Nor it was not many days after but the madnes

---

iuuenibus, inter quos et Collatinus erat, et forte nimio calentibus
vino, caderet sermo de coniugum honestate. Et cum suam ceteris, 20
vt moris est, vnusquisque preferret, in consilium hoc itum est, vt
conscensis c[ita]tis equis visisque quibus noctu, eis bella geren-
tibus, ignare coniuges exercerentur officijs, probabiliorem oculata
fide perciperent. Sane, cum iuuenes regias Rome inter equales
ludentes inuenissent, versis equis deuenere Collacium, vbi cum 25
mulieribus suis lanificio vacantem et nullo exornatam cultu inuenere Lucreciam, quamobrem iudicio omnium laudabilior visa
est. Collatinus autem reliquos iuuenes benigne suscepit in domum,
qua dum honorarentur, Sextus, [Tarquinij] Superbi filius, impu-
dicos oculos in honestatem atque formositatem caste mulieris 30
iniecit et nephasto succensus igne per vim opprimendam, si aliter
non daretur, eiusdem venustatem, tacito secum consilio disposuit.

---

22 cunctis L.   24 Rome] Rhomani B, romani U.   equales] coæ-
quales B, coequales U.   28 domum] in *add*. BSU.   29 *om*. LS.
31 opprim.] potiundam BU.   32 daretur] detur BU.   venust.]
vetustatem B.   disposuit] disponit BU.

more and more mouede hym therto, but that, preuely stealynge
frome hys fathers campe, in the nyghte he came to Collatyns
house, and ther the blody prynce [was] honestly receyuyde of
Lucres. Tarquyne, that ment all otherwyse then the chaste lady
5 dyd, when he perceyuyde that all the housholde were at quyete,
he entrede the chambre of Lucres with hys sworde nakyde in hys
hande, shewynge to hyr what he was and threttnynge to sley hyr,
yf eyther she made any noyse, or if she agaynesayde to fullfyll
hys pleasure. And, all thoughe that he perceyuyde that Lucres
10 resystyde hym and lytle fearede to dye, he aduysede hym, as he
was wrestlynge with hyr, of a greate whyle, [and] he sayde to hyr:
'If thow thus withstande me, I shall sley a churle and lay hym
in thy bedde and reporte that for the loue I hade to Collatyn,
fyndynge the enbrasyde in hys armes, that I slewe youe bothe.'
15 The poore Lucres, vppon thyes wordes quakynge all in dreede,
pawsede *and*, fearynge that so greate an infamye myght cum
therof, if so she shulde be slayne, agaynste hyr wyll offrede to
hym hyr chaste body. And thus, when the fowlle, vicyouse prynce
had satisfyede hys desyre, thynkynge that he had escappyde as
20 vyctour, he wentt hys way, leuyng the sayde Lucres a bedde. The

---

Nec multis interpositis diebus, vrgente insania, clam castris
relictis, nocte venit Collatium, vbi, eo quod vir consanguineus esset,
a Lucrecia comiter susceptus et honoratus, postquam domum
omnem tacitam sensit et sic omnes sopitos arbitratus, exempto
25 gladio cubiculum intrauit Lucrecie et quis esset aperuit mina-
tusque est illi mortem, si vocem emitteret aut sue non acquie-
sceret voluntati. Quam cum reluctantem desiderio suo et mortis
inpauidam cerneret, ad damnandam recurrens astuciam, inquit se
illam secus seruum ex suis occisurum et cunctis eam a se ob
30 adulterium cum adultero cesam dicere. Substitit his auditis
tremebunda mulier et a tam obscena infamia terrefacta, timens, si
eo occideretur pacto, purgatorem sue innocentie defuturum, et ob
id aspernanti animo corpus permisit adultero. Qui cum illecebri
voluptati sue satisfecisset et abijsset iudicio suo victor, egra tam

22 vir] viri BU.   24 exempto] exemplo S, exerto BU.   26 est]
om. BU.   29 ob] *om.* B.   34 abijsset] abijssetque U.

day comen, all bewepte with teares, Lucres called to hyr hyr father
and hyr husbonde, and Brutus, verey nyghe a kynne to hyr
husbonde, with the reste of hyr kynsfolkes, declarynge to theym
with a sorowfull and pale, bewepte face what the nyght before
Sextus had doone to hyr. And albeit that they dyd what they 5
coulde to conforte hyr, seynge hyr lamentable sorowe, yet she,
*tha*t was determynede by deathe to shew hyr innocency, drew
owte a sharp knyfe which she had hyd vndre hyr gowne, saynge:
'If I do cleere myselfe of myne offense, yet the infamye shall
neuer be wypyde | away, and therfore, ther shall neuer noone f. 47*a*
vnchaste wome*n* lyue to take example by Lucres', and so saynge, 11
smote the knyfe into hyr innocente stomake, and fallynge downe
vppon hyr blody, wounded breste, afore the face of hyr father and
hyr husbonde *and* hyr freandes exspyrede. Hyr swete beautie, the
more gratiouse it was, the more infortunate was it to hyr. But hyr 15
chastite can neuer be to muche co*m*mendyde and praysede. And all
though the fowlle acte of Sextus was after well reuengyde, yet this
was not all, but for thys acte of Lucres, Rome, that was in
boundage before, by hyr obteynede for euer fredome and lyberty.

---

scelesti facinoris Lucrecia, elucente die, Tricipitinum patrem et 20
Brutum, Collatini affinem amantem vsque in diem illam existi-
matum, aliosque necessarios confestim accersiri iussit et virum.
Quibus aduenientibus, que a Sexto nocte intempesta in eam gesta
sint cum lacrimis ex ordine retulit, et cum eam flentem misere
solarentur affines, cultrum quem sub veste texerat educens, in- 25
quit: 'Ego me, si peccato absoluo, supplicio non libero, nec vlla
deinceps impudica Lucrecie viuet exemplo.' Hisque dictis illum
in pectus impegit innocuum et vulneri incumbens, vidente viro ac
patre, moribunda collapsa est, nec diu animam cum sanguine
fudit. Infelix equidem pulcritudo eius et tanto clarius, nunquam 30
satis laudata pudicicia sua dignis preconijs, extollenda est, quanto
acrius ingesta vi ignominia expiata, cum ex eadem non solum
reintegratum sit decus, quod feditate facinoris iuuenis labefa-
ctarat incestus, sed consecuta sit Romana libertas.

20 scelesti] celesti SU.   elucente] elucescente BS, elucessente U.
24 ex] et BSU.   26 liberor LS.   27 dictis] dominus BU.   29 diu]
et *add*. BU.   31 satis] laudatis *add*. B.   32 ingesta vi ignom.]
vi gesta in ignomina BU.   33–4 labef. incestus] labefactaret ineptus BU.

APPENDIX

I. MORLEY'S PREFACES ADDRESSED TO HENRY VIII

A. *Preface to his Translation of Paolo Giovio's 'Commentario del cose de Turchi'*

(MS. Arundel 8, f. 1 *a,.b*)

To the moste highe, moste myghty and moste Christen Kynge, Henry the VIIIth, by the grace of God Kynge of Englonde and of Fraunce, Lorde of Irelonde, Defendo*ur* of the Feythe, and suppreme heede vnder Gode of the Churche of Englonde. Yo*ur* moste hu*m*ble
5 subiecte Henry P*a*rker, knyght, Lorde Morley, willythe vnto your Grace longe lyf withe perpetuall honour and victorye.

Thys boke, moste Christen Kynge, of the Co*m*mentarys of the Turke, as it apperyth by the prologe next ensuynge, was dedicate vnto Charles the Vth, Empero*ur* of the Almaynes, by Paulus Jouius,
10 Byshope of Nocher, which, as I do here, ys yett lyuynge, and he wrote it in the Italian tonge vnto that entente, as I do suppose, that euery man myght knowe what a puysaunte prynce the greate Turke ys, moste specially that nacion which continually is vexyde withe the Turkes and not withoute cause soore in dreade of theym ; for who
15 so considreth the greate force and myght of thiese people and the innume*r*able threasure that the Turke hathe, wyll meruell though I say not onely Italy, but Fraunce, adioynyde with Spayne and all Christendo*m* besyde, is [vn]abyll[1] to withstande hys infynyte power, for this saide Turke hathe more ryches then all the Christen kynges
20 haue, more horses, more artelery then all they can make. Brefly, hys power is so greate by lande and see that it is oonely Goddes hande that helpyth hys people agaynst hym, for thys Turk not withoute cause is lyke to that dragon that with hys tayle, as Saincte John wryteth in the Apocalipp*es*, pulleth vnto hym the three part*es* of the
25 heuyn, which is to meane the three part*es* of the greate worlde, and by hys so greate power sekythe for noone other thynge but onely to haue the reste and to brynge all the worlde to a monarchy. But with Goddes helpe he shall fayle of his peruers and frowarde wyll, for emongest other moste Christene kynges God hathe electe yo*ur* moste
30 royall p*er*sone, not onely to be victoriouse of yo*ur* ennemyes, but also made youe Defendo*ur* of the Feithe and the verey true setter forthe of hys moste holy and dyuyne wo*ur*de.

To youe than, moste gratiouse souereigne Lorde, I thoughte itt expedyent to translate thys booke oute of the Italion in to oure

[1] MS. abyll.

maternall tonge, that when it shulde please your exellent Mageste
for your recreation and pastyme to see itt, that your hyghe wysdome
myght counsell with other Christen kynges for a remedye agaynste
so perlouse an ennemye to oure feythe. And I darre say, so holy, so
noble and so graciouse a hart haue youe, that yf all the rest wolde 5
folow your holsome ways, all ciuill warres shulde sesse, ande onely
they with youe, moste Christen Kynge, as the chef of theim all,
shulde brynge thys Turke to confusion, which, as the storye tellythe,
with a small and a vyle begynnynge is now comen to so greate an
empyre.   10
  The Sonne of Gode kepe and saue youe, my moste noble souereigne
Lorde, and sende youe a goode Newe Yere with the Nestours yere
to that same. Amen.

B. *Preface to his Translation of Plutarch's Lives of Scipio and Hannibal*

(MS. Royal 17 D. xi, ff. 2a–3b)

  The lives of Scipio and Haniball, writen by Plutarke the Grecian
in the Greke tong, and translated out of the Greke into Laten by 15
Donatus Acciolus, and out of Laten into Englishe by Henry Parker,
knight, Lorde Morleye.
  To the moste highe, moste mightie, moste Cristen King, my good
and gracious soueraign Lorde, King Henry, of that name th'Eight,
King off Englonde and of Fraunce, Defendour of the Faith, Lorde 20
of Yrlonde *etc.* Your moste humble sub[ie]cte[1] Henry Morley desireth honour to your Highnesse, helthe and victorye.
    When I remembred, moste Cristen King and my moste dradde
soveraign Lorde, howe that as well by the lawes of God as by all other
lawes I am bounde to bere to your maiestie love, honour *and* obei- 25
saunce, sithens that I am not of power to do that honour to your
Highnesse that my hart woulde, I haue studied diuers times howe,
as moche as in me is, I might do some thing to your Maiestie pleasing
and acceptable, bounden so to do, as I haue said, ouer and besides
myn alliegeaunce for your moste gracious fauour which you haue so 30
vsed towardes me vnworthie, that if I had, as the facundious Maro
writeth, a houndred mouthes and as many tonges therto, withe as
moche eloquence as Tullius Cicero, I coulde not with wordes nor dedes
give your Highnesse condigne thankes therfore. What shall I then
saie, moste gentle Prince and my good and gracyous soueraign Lorde ? 35
Evin as Seneck telleth, that as the kinges of Perse maie not be saluted
withoute some gifte and that one of the moste renowmed of theim,

[1] MS. subeicte.

when diuers of his subiect*es* presented him with riche gift*es*, one poore
man, having nothing, rann to the water and in the palme of his
handes brought him as moche therof as he coulde holde, the King by
his humanitie well pleased with all, evin so, ouer boldly trusting of
5 yo*ur* moste gracious goodnes, I present to you this traunslacion of the
lyves of the gentle Scipio and of the fierse Affrican Haniball, writen
by the greate clerke and Grecian Plutarke in the Greke tong, and
translated out of the Greke into Laten by that excellent clarke
Donatus Acciolus, and out of Laten into the Englyshe tong by me,
10 Henry, by your goodnesse Lorde Morlei, not doubting but that after
yo*ur* accustomed mekenes your Highnes shall accepte it well, althoughe the storye in Latten be not to your Maiestie vnknowen, for
as this said Plutarke wryteth of Scipio that ouer and besid*es* his
hardines he was of body and shape and of visage wonderfull well pro-
15 porcioned, having in him with thos gift*es* of nature meny vertues,
specially that singuler vertue of mekenesse, so you, most roiall King,
haue in you, ouer and besid*es* suche highe giftes naturall, this
delectable vertue of mekenesse, equall with the gentle Emperour
Traian, that I am well assured, who might attain, althoughe he had
20 grevously offendid your Highnes, to come to your presens, he were
sure to go from you ioyous and mery awaie, so moche of grace resteth
in that roiall harte of yours. Wherfor God, as Lactantius wryteth
to th' Empro*ur* Constantyne, as he hath done hetherto, shall p*r*eserve
you and make you happie aboue all worldly king*es* in this worlde,
25 and after rewarde you with et*er*nall blisse in the other worlde for
your highe demerit*es*, whiche graunte you that hath created you,
my most gentle and gracious soueraigne Lorde. Amen.

C. *Preface to his Translation of Plutarch's Life of Theseus*

(MS. Royal 17 D. ii, ff. 1*a*–3*a*)

To the moste Christen Kynge and my moste dere and moste vic-
toryus soueren Lorde Henry the Eight, by the grace of God, of
30 Inglond, Fraunce and Irelonde Kynge, Defendor of the Faythe, and
in earthe supreme head of the Churche of Inglonde and Irelonde.
Youer moste humble subiect Harry Parker, knyght, Lorde Morley,
desirythe to youer Mageste longe lyfe, perpetuall helthe, honor and
victory. Amen.

35 The Prolog.

Andreas Alciates wrightithe, moste Christe*n* Kinge and my most
dere and redoubted soveren Lorde, that alwayes w*i*th all nasyons the
wrighters of storis were in greate auctorite and were fyrste taken in
hono*ur* withe the Romayns, so that whe*n* as well lawyers as phisicians

and other lernyd in the mathematicall syens were[1] banyshed from
Rome, only the wrighters of storis were admyttyd and taken in
reverens and well cherysyd with greate stypendes amonge them there.
And not with owte greate reasun, for yf that there were no wrighters
of storis[2] eyther to declare the nobyll actes of princes, eyther there 5
highe vertuis or there vices, the worlde sholde be in soche a state as
these barberus pepyll of the late fownde contres, that be more lyke
in maner to beastes then men but that they have the shap of men,
withe owte eny knowlege of thinges paste or thinges to cum at all.
And yf one wolde saye that the wrighters of storis[2] were but meane 10
parsons and soche as that only for luker wrote that whiche was often
fals and vntru, I answere that who so affyrmith that to be tru shall
blame the valyant Julyvs Ceasar, whiche, all thoughe he had a
davngerus war with the Frenshe men and the Bryttons, yet in his
moste warly busynes he lefte not to wright the feates of war of eyther 15
partes in his commentaris, callyd the Commentaris of Ceaser. And
this Ceasar, my moste gracius soveren Lorde, is not to be sett alone,
for, as yt is sayde, Augustus dyd in lyke wise, and a monge other
Alate Zizimus,[3] the greate Turkes brother, a man of a singuler
moderasyon and lerning. Albeyt he was in captiuite and kepte in 20
Rome as a prisoner, yet he delyted to wright the historis of the Turke
and there great conquestes.

Then, brefely to conclude, other to wright the storis of those
worthe princes that be present or paste is a thinge moste commend-
abyll vnto every highe estate, and I dowght not but, my moste 25
gracius Prince and moste dere soveren Lorde, your nobyll, ryall harte
is soche that even so you do accept them that eyther do wright or
translate eny worke worthe of remembrans. And for that all redy
the lyfe of the stronge Hercules and of Jas[o]n[4] that wan the Golden
Flese is in the Inglishe tonge, I thowght yt wolde be greatly and 30
thankfully receyved of your Highnes, the lyfe of Thesius, wrighttun

---

[1] MS. wrere.   [2] MS. stroris.

[3] In MS. Arundel 8, f. 13*b*, we read that 'Zizinio' was the brother of
'Soltan Baiazeto' and a little farther on (f. 14*b*) that after he had been
defeated, Zizinio 'as a man desperate gaue hymself into handes of the
Greate Maister of the Roodes, frome whome he was after sent vnto the
Bysshoppe Innocentius. And thys ys he that the viijth Charles, Kyng of
Fraunce, dyd conducte frome Rome to the border of Naples, the which was
poysonede, as it is sayde, of the Bysshoppe Alexander. He dyede by the
way at Terracyna, whose body was afterwarde sent by Fredryke the kynge
vnto Constantinople to make the Turke to be hys freande for that gentlenes,
which coste hym nothyng. Thys Zizinio was of a graue aspecte and an
exellent wytt and suffrede hys mysfortune with greate prudens and
tranquilite of mynde.'

[4] MS. Jasan.

by the excellent Grecian Plutarke, and translatyd owte of Greke into Latyn by Lappus Florentinus, and by me, your moste humble subiect owte of Laten in to ouer maternall tonge. And suerly, my moste deare and moste victorius soveren, if I had soche science and soche lerning
5 that my pen covlde put in wrighting that whiche my faithefull, tru harte to your Mageste wolde, then wolde I longe or this have wrighttun your Highnes most lawdabyll lyfe and worthi conquestes, well to be reputyd amongest the most worthe princes and conquerors, present or paste. But when I sholde go abowght so highe a thinge,
10 I lacke that whiche Plutark had, that wrote the lyfe of Theseus, the autor and bringer in order of the sage cytezens of Atenes; whiche to reduce in to Inglishe, albeyt the lyfe of Thesius is very obscurely by him sett forthe, yet I have done my devour to sett yt forthe in ouer maternall tonge and to dedicat the same to your moste excellent
15 Mageste, praing your most victorius parson well to accept yt. And I shall praye to Christ Jhesu longe to preserve you in helthe and victory this yere and infenit of yeres. Amen.

D. *Preface to his Translation of Plutarch's Life of Paulus Æmilius*

(MS. Laud Misc. 684, ff. 1a–2b)

To the most hye, most mighty and most pusant prince, Henry the Eight, by the grace of God, of Inglond, Fravnce and Irelond
20 Kynge, Defendor of the Faythe, and supreme hed of the Churche of Inglond and Irelond. Your humble subiect Henry Parker, knight, Lorde Morley, desyrithe to your Highnes honour, helthe and victory.

The Prolog.

Amongest all the lyves of the nobyll Romayns and Gresyans which
25 Plutarke dothe wright of in his boke intytelyd *Plutarchi vitae*, most grasius and most victorius soveren Lorde, there is none in my simpyll opinion that more owght to be notyd then the lyfe of Pavlus Emilius, whiche subduid Parsius and his kingdom of Masydony. And my reason ys soche that although that Scipion, Ceasar and Haniball and
30 Pompius and dyvers other dyd more victorius actes then this Pavlus dyd, yet was there none nother Gresyan nor Romayne that more covlde moderate him selfe in bothe fortunis, that is to saye, the good and the yll fortune, then he of whom we wright.

And suerly, most nobyll Prince, there hathe bene and is dyvers
35 that can and hathe done grete conquestes, butt there be very fewe that when soche good, prosperows fortunes happen vnto them, but that they eyther be to moche prowde thereof, or when yll fortune

cums to them, to moche abasshed thereof, so that the best part, whiche is the meane, is quite sett a parte. Who then he be that dothe not knowe what the meane is in soche a case, let him loke vppon the lyfe of this nobyll Romayne, Pavlus Emilius, and there shall he se as in a glas or myerour the parfect, suer waye howe to governe him 5 with reason in all kynde of prosperite or adversite; whiche sayde lyfe I have translatyd owte of the Laten tonge in to ouer maternall tonge rudely, but truly, I trust, according to the sens, and do presente the same this Newe Yere to your Highnes, most nobyll and most Crysten Kinge and my most dere soveren Lorde, as to a prince honorabyll 10 amongest all other princes in the worlde, that hathe shewed in the ruling of your mighty empiris soche moderasyon, clemens, pyte and marsyfull iustes that ye maye well be comparyd, not only to this Pavlus, but to Traian, Titus and Antoni[n]us[1] Pius, or to eny other Gresyan or Romayn, of what state or dingnite so ever they have 15 bene before this daye.

God preserve your Highnes longe so to contynewe, and the fayer flower of the worlde, your dere sun and ouer comfort to cum, Prince Edwarde, in parpetuall helthe and victory. Amen.

E. *Preface to his Translation of a Tale by Masuccio*
(MS. Royal 18 A. lxii, ff. 1b–3b)

To the most high, most myghty and most Christen King, Kinge 20 Henry th'Eight, by the grace of God King of Englond, Fraunce and Irelande, Defender of the Faith, and in erthe supreme hede of the Churche of England and Ireland. Your most humble subiecte Henry Parker, knyght, Lord Morley, desireth to your Highnes perpetual honour, helthe and victorye. 25

Scenek wryteth in one of hys Epystles that he wrote to Lucil[i]us,[2] moste gratiouse and moste deare souereigne Lorde, that faythe is the sure fundation of mans breste. And albeit that as sum dyuers clerkes wyll that he knew not the verei true faithe, but as other philosophers that by naturall reasone affyrmeth that ther muste 30 neades be one God that muste rule and gouerne all, yet as I do suppose that he coulde not haue wryten so truly of faith, oneles he had had sume perticuler knowlege of Chrystes teachynge by Saincte Paule, as the greate doctoure Saincte Jherome affyrmeth. But lett it be so that he ment it nothynge to the faythe of God, but onely that 35 faithe the whiche a man oughte to kepe, one man to a nother. Yet surely the sentence is worthy allwayes to be pryntede in our herttes. For who so euer he be, poore or ryche, that obserueth not hys faithe,

---

[1] MS. Antonius.   [2] MS. Lucilus.

fyrste to hys superiour, next to hys freandes, and thyrdly *and* generally to all men, what is he to be reputede but, as Isope saith in hys fables, a verey fox, that promyseth frenshyppe and loue to smale, lytle beastes, to noone other entent but for to deuoure theym? Farre
5 frome an honeste Chrysten man so false a condicion! But if it be in a poore man, so ascendynge vp to the greatest of all, a vngoodely and vngodly wyse, what is it to be counted in a spyrytuall man, that by faithe and by hys worde dothe consecrate in fourme of breade the moste blessyd body of God? And not onely hymself to be vnfaithfull,
10 but further to goo aboute to deuoure and to murder the faithfull seruaunt of God, as that false Antecriste, Alexander the iiijth, Bysshope of Rome, dyd, as this lytle hystory declareth, to the moste Chrysten and moste noble Frederyke Barbarouse, Emperour of Rome.[1]
15 Whiche saide hystory, for asmuche as that youe, my moste redoubted and moste graciouse souereigne Lorde, hathe bene in lyke factyon vnfaithefully, vniustly and falsely, by dyuers and sundry tymes, by Paule, Bysshoppe of Rome, with all fraude possible to disturbe your moste godly and moste faithefull wayes, I thought it
20 shulde not be vnpleasaunt to your Highnes, yf so were that ye dyd votesafe to reede it, to se the vngodly faction of the vngodly Bysshoppe, the true faithe of the goode Emperour, the greate noblenes and liberalite of the Sarrasyn Souldan of Babylon, declarede and tolde by Massuccyo Saler[n]ytano[2] in hys Nouelles or tales, whiche
25 he wrote in the Italyan tonge so exellently well that I thynke in noo tonge it can or may be amendyde. Neuertheles, as my poore lernynge is, I haue translatyde the same, as your Hyghnes may perceyue, into our naturall tonge; whiche, if in any poynte it dothe content you, my moste Christen souereigne Lorde, it shall not onely[3] reioyce my verey
30 hert, but further encourage me, as my moste bounden duety requyreth, to pray to Criste Jesu sende youe thys yere to cum, and all your yeres after, perpetuall helthe, vyctory and honour, wyth your noble wyfe, Quene Katheryn, and that hope of this your realme to cum, Prynce Edwarde youre sonne, that after infynyte of yeres in
35 thys worlde ye may cum to that kyngdome that euer shall endure. Amen.

[1] In his *Exposition and Declaration of the Psalme, Deus ultionum Dominus*, Morley alludes to this story. He says: 'What great damage to al Christendom, and what great mischief wrought Honorius agaynst Frederike the good emperour in his iourney ageynste the Turkes? This wycked bysshoppe sente letters to the Soudan, shewynge hym whyche wayes he myght distroy the chrysten armye.'
[2] MS. Salerytano.
[3] MS. shallnot onely.

F. *Preface to his 'Exposition and Declaration of the Psalme, Deus ultionum Dominus'*

(A ii recto–A iiii recto)

To THE MOST HIGH AND myghty prynce, HENRY the.VIII. kynge of Englande and of Fraunce, defendour of the faithe, lorde of Ire-lande, and in erthe supreme heed immediatly vnder Christe of the church of Englande, his most humble subiect, Henry Parker knight, lorde Morley, wyssheth all welth & prosperitie. 5

IF I HAD MOST christyan Prynce, and my most dere and graciouse soueraygne lord, as Virgil saythe, an hundred mouthes, with as many tounges, and therewith as moche swete eloquence, as had the Grecian Demosthenes, or the Romayn Cicero, yet coulde not I expresse halfe the vertue, halfe the rightuousnes, that is in your most royal maiestie, 10 as in a perfecte Arke of all princely goodnes and honour. For where as vnto this presente tyme of your moste happy reigne, this youre Empire mooste triumphant hath ben wrongfully kept[1] as tributarie vnto the Babylonicall seate of the Romyshe byshop, your moste sage and polytike wisedome hath benne suche, that as it maye be well 15 thoughte, by diuine inspiration, ye haue taken a very kynges harte, whiche seketh, as it ought, to rule and nat to be ruled,[2] and hath set the englysshe nation at fredoome and lybertie. What worthy thãkes for so noble a dede, and so beneficial an acte, can your mooste bounden subiectes render vnto your high maiestie? We may moche 20 better say to you, than euer might the Romans vnto the most noble Emperour Augustus, that ye are not onely the noblest kynge that euer reigned ouer the english natiõ, but also *Pater patriæ*, that is, the father of our countrey, one by whose vertue, lernyng, and noble courage, England is newe borne, newly brought from thraldome to 25 freedome. For where as there is nothing more swete than libertie, nothynge more bytter than bondage, in so moche that death hath ofte ben chosen to aduoyde seruitude, what[3] owe we vnto you most gracious soueraigne lorde, which ar by you, as by a most natural father, the bondes broken, set out of danger, from the captiuite Baby- 30 lonical, so that we may say plainly as the Jewes dydde to Judith: You are our beautie, you are oure honour, you are our glorie. Scipio the Affrican dyd moche for the Romayns, Codrus for the Atheniens, Epaminondas moche for yᵉ Thebans, Themistocles moch for the Grecians, Cirus moche for the Persians, Salandine moche for the 35 Egyptians, and yet all these,[4] cõpared with your hyghnes, may seme almost to haue done nothing at al. I therfore, most christẽ king,[5]

[1] *Text comma after* triumphant *and* kept.
[2] *Text comma after* rule *and full stop after* ruled.   [3] *Text* seruitude. What
[4] *Text lacks comma.*   [5] *Text lacks comma.*

beinge a parttaker of all your inestimable benefites, haue and shal always study, whyche wayes, and howe I maye, to the vttermoste of my litel and moste feble puissance, giue thankes to your highnes for the same. And for as moche as I knowe my selfe vnmete to do any
5 bodily seruice, condigne to so vertuous & excellent a prince, yet at ye least I shal gyue vnto your hyghnes[1] y^t thing, which aswel the feble as the stronge maye gyue, that is to saye, hartye prayers to god, for the preseruation of so iust, so mercyfull, and so faythefull a kynge. I than offer vnto your hyghnesse this newe yere, dere and dred
10 soueraygne lorde, this psalme of king Dauid, *Deus ultionum dominus*, with a briefe declaration of the same, moste humbly praienge your high accustomed goodnes[2] to accepte it in gree, & not to regarde the rudenes, but rather the faithfulnes of me your subiect, that wylleth with the very harte, as he writeth, goodnes, and all goodnesse to you:
15 And to youre ennemye the Babylonicall byshoppe of Rome, reproufe, shame, and vtter ruine.

II. Morley's Prefaces addressed to Mary, before and after her Accession

A. *Preface to Richard Rolle's commentary on the Psalms*
(MS. Royal 2 D. xxviii, ff. 1b–2a)

To the moste noble Lady Mary Henry Parker, knyght, Lorde Morley, sendyth gretynge, with many goode yeres, to Goddes pleasure.
20 That singlare vertue and goodnes which ys improprede to youe by the grace of God, enclynethe euery man that heryth the vertuouse lyf that ye do leade, to laude you and prayse youe; as Dauid saithe, to suche as lyuythe well, of ryght they ar to be praysed. Ye then shall-not thynke, moste noble Lady Mary, that I do, as the greate Jherome
25 wrytythe of the Grekys, that by worde I loke to haue fauour of youe, but for my true saynge to be acceptable vnto youe, albe it that I am to bolde to present to so royall and a noble kynges doughter as ye be suche an olde boke and to the fyrst sythe a cast a way. But, moste vertuouse lady, thoughe percase sum that knowythe not what a
30 preciouse thyng ys hyde in thys so rude a letter, thoughe they wolde thynk so, yet that hyghe and exellent wytt of yours wyll in the redynge of thys exposition of thys Psalter deme all other wyse. Orace saythe 'Phisisiens promyse, smythes trete of their forgys.' Euery man wyll say and thynke his fantasy. But your Grace, that
35 vsythe that holy craft of Goddes worde, specially in that that is Catholyke, wyll well wourke with thys holy exposition of thys rude

---

[1] *Text comma after* hyghnes.   [2] *Text comma after* goodnes.

Psalter and fynde thyngs in itt more preciouse then perle or stoone. And surely I do thynke that he that expounde thys Psalter that to avoyde pryde, he neither wolde wryte hys name, nor yett tell in hys boke what tyme he wrote it, which I do greately meruell at, but that the goode man lokyde to haue laude of Hym for hys trauell that for- 5 gettyth noo goode deade vnrewardyde, nor noone euyll deade vn-ponyshede.

I exhorte youe, moste noble Ladye Mary, in Goddes name sumtyme to loke vpon thys when your Grace hathe leysure. And I pray youe, moste noble Lady Mary, accepte my goode wyll, which is, allways to 10 pray, fyrst for your moste royall father, oure souereygne Lorde and Kynge, next for your moste exellent and towarde brother, the Prynce, and thyrde, for youe and the children of hys Grace to cum, to pre-serue and kepe theym and youe in perpetuall felicite and honour. Amen. 15

B. *Preface to his Translation of the Rendering by Angelus Politianus of St. Athanasius' Introduction to the Psalms*

(MS. Royal 17 C. xii, ff. 1b–3b)

To the moste nobyll and moste vertuus Lady Mary. Henry Parcar, knyght, Lorde Morley, desyrythe to youer Grace parpetual helthe and honor.

The Prolog of the Translator.

It shuld seme superfluous, most nobyll and vertuous Lady Mary, 20 to presente to your Grace the tytylles of the Salmes of David, trans-latyd out of the Greke in to the Laten tonge by that fyne-wytted and most excelent orator in the Latten tonge Angelus Polycyanus owte of the worke of the great Athanasius, and that for twayne causes. The one ys, that yt is manefestly knowen to all those that 25 knowe your vertuous lyfe that daly ye exarcyse your selfe in the Salmes, in saynge with your chaplen the service of the daye; the other, that nowe in every printyd boke the tytles of the Salmes be expressed. 'What shold yt nede then', your Grace parcase may say, 'to do a warke that ys everywhere done'? I wyll, withe your accus- 30 tomyd pacyence, make this excuse—that in very dede the tyttyls ar expressed in many printyd Salters, but nothinge to the purpose as this Pollicianus hath set them furthe, nor after that waye. But lyke as here be a great numbre that hath wrytten of the Salter, every one after a dyvers facyon, so in lyke wyse have they done of the tytles 35 of the Salmes, summe one wayes and summe another, as I am very well assuryd that I have sene and daylay do se in redinge of them.

For as moche as in my pore consayte, yf here be VC setters forth of the tytles, this shalbe the flower of them all, I thought that to you,

the very example of this realme in vertu, that yo*ur* Grace wold not
blame, nor take my pore labor but thankefully. And all be yt that
yt ys very harde in all thing*es* to folowe in ou*er* naturall tonge the
exselent style of this Angelus Pollicianus, yet I dare affyrme that I
5 have not moche alteryd from the sence, as, lokinge of the Laten, yo*ur*
Grace shall very well perseave. Then, most nobyll Lady Mare, whom,
next God and yo*ur* moste Christen father and ou*er* nobyll Quene and
yo*ur* swete brother I most honor, moste love, and praye for, loke not
of the gyfte, as I do all ways wryght vnto you, but of the gever, that
10 ys and was and shalbe, as well for the heyghe, excellent bloude that ye
are co*m*me of as also for that vertu in yow, whiche ys suche that ones
yt shalbe manyfest to all the worlde, a parpetuall beadema*n*.

And this with longe lyfe, wi*th* long helthe, and honor, and infynyte
of good yeres, as to a myghty kyng*es* douter yt apartaynyth, I do
15 commyt yo*ur* Grace to God. Amen.

C. *Preface to his Translation of the Exposition of Psalm XXXVI by*
Giovanni de Turrecremata

(MS. Royal 18 A. xv, ff. 1*b*–2*b*)

To the moste noble and vertuouse lady, the Lady Mary, doughter to
oure moste victoriouse and naturall leage Lorde, Kynge Henry the
viijth. Henry Parcare, k*n*ight, Lorde Morley, desyrethe to youre
Grace perpetuall felicite, honor and helthe.
20 I do remembre, moste noble Lady Mary, that I apon a certeyn
tyme waytynge on your Grace at Honesden, and youe, after your
accustomede man*er*s, talkynge with me of thynges 'touchynge to
vertue, that ye dyd greately commende thys same Psalme, 'Noli
emulari in malignantib*us*' etc. And surely, not withoute greate
25 reason youe dyd so prayse it, for asmuche as amonge all other holy
Psalmes of D*au*id thys Psalme onely dothe moste playnly declare how
soone the synner is forsaken of and frome the false felicite of thys
worlde, when he soo trustyth vnto the vane pleas*ur*s therof that he
puttythe noo hope in God, but apon hys ryches and prosperyte. O,
30 how many is ther of those that, hauynge the goodes of this worlde,
weene thay shall neu*er* departe frome theym, yea, and weene that they
be wyser then other and more to be extemyde then other, vntyll
suche tyme as that sodeynly, eyther by fortune, whyche cannot
stande stable, or seknes, or suche lyke aduersyte, they be dispoylede
35 frome all theyr pleasures and lefte in the ryght shappe of men! As
Senek wryteth, that noone be more hono*ur*ede then those that haue
on theym purple robes and golden garment*es* on theyr backes, and
yet, when suche goo to theyr bedd*es* to slepe, as nat*ure* requyrethe,
then cum they vnto the co*m*une shappe of all men. I say to youe,

fayre Lady Mary, that not onely ar fayre in verey deede of outewarde
beautye, but muche fayrer of inwarde vertue, that as for my parte,
seynge the continuall mutation of the worlde, I dreade when I do
here the name of felycyte, as a thynge vncertayne, vnstable, and
thynke myself in felicyte, because I neuer desyrede to haue it. But 5
whether euer I haue it, or haue it not, I pray to oure Lorde for those
that weene thei haue it that they may well remembre thys Psalme,
whyche thys greate clerc hathe so bryfly, so exellently expounyde
that I confesse I haue not redde the lyke.

Your Grace then, I doubte not but wyll take after your gentle 10
facyon thys my rude translation in worthe and allways accepte my
goode wyll that I do beare vnto youe, next youre victoriouse father,
oure naturall and leage Lorde, and your swete and noble, towarde
brother Prynce Edward, afore all other creatures a lyue.

God preserue your Grace in goodenes and vertue, as he haith doone 15
vnto thys day, and sende youe many goode yeres, to Goddes pleasur
and yours, noble Lady Mary. Amen.

D. *Preface to his Translation of Erasmus's Paean in Praise of the Virgin*

(MS. Royal 17 A. xlvi, ff. 1a–3a)

To the moste noble and vertuouse lady, the Lady Mary. Youre
perpetuall oratour and beademan, Henry Parcare, knyghte, Lorde
Morley, praythe to God to geue your Grace perpetuall helthe of body 20
and mynde.

Sayncte Gregory, moste noble Lady Mary, writeth in a certeyn
omely that of verey necessite, when any greate prynce honourably
receyueth the enbassatours sent vnto hym by a nother prynce that
he dothe honour hym that dothe sende theym. And thys clerkes 25
saynge, as I do take it, vtterly dothe confute and blame theym that
do not honour to the holy saynctes in heuen.

But moste in especiall the honour due to the gloriouse mother of
God, whiche, as Anselme writeth, that onely to thynke that Mary
is mother vnto God passith all altitude that either may be thought 30
or spoken. And albeit that sythen Chryste was borne of the Virgyne,
vnnethe was ther noo renoumyde clerke but that he sumthynge saide
in the laude of the mayde, yett we haue clerkes in our tyme that dar
affyrme that to honour hyr is a dymynysshynge of the honour of Godd,
and so, fallynge frome oone hereticall opynyone to another, at last 35
deny the honoure due to God hymsellf in the moste holy and dyuyne
sacrament of the aulter.

And ne were the blessyd stay of our moste victoryouse and moste
Chrysten Kynge, your deare father, I thynk noone other but that
ther be dyuers that wolde be verey Epecurs, that doubted whether

God was, 'Ye' or 'Nay'; and if ther were God, that he was in heuen,
idle and in quyete, nother carynge nor regardynge vs mortall, but
lettynge vs runne at large, and sufferyng vs withoute ordre to do
what we wyll, withoute either to punyshe theym that spende their
5 tyme abhomynably in vyce and synne, or to rewarde theym that
vertuously passe theyr daies in vertuouse lyuynge. O, noble and
vertuouse kynges doughter! How is it that men in oure tyme ar so
blynded? I can thynke noone other but that the ende of the worlde
hastythe apasse, accordynge as Christe saide, that ther shulde cum
10 fals prophettes in the ende of the wourlde that with their false
techynges shulde seduce many. But he addyd to thies soore wordes
a comfortable saynge agayne that who so euer perseuered in true
faythe of the Churche vnto the ende, he shulde be sauede.

   I pray God, moste gentle and honourable Lady, geue vs grace so to
15 do, to perseuer vnto the ende in the faythe of Christes Churche, which
hath, sythens Christe dyede vpon the blessyd crosse, euer had in
honour the gloriouse martyrs and seruauntes of God, and, aboue all
other, the blessyde Virgyne Mary, whose dyuyne holynes and goodnes
this Erasmus soo settyth forthe in this hys Pea[n][1] or praise that I dar
20 affyrme that emonges dyuers other thynges that he haithe wrytten
elegauntly, he neuer wrote with his penne so elegaunte a style as thys,
whiche, all thoughe I cannot sett it forthe in Englishe as he hathe
doone in the Latten, yet as muche as my wytte can serue me, I haue
studyde to sett it furthe in oure tounge and dedicatyd the same to
25 your Grace, the secunde Mary of this wourlde in vertue, grace and
goodenes; humbly besechynge your Grace to accepte my laboures
well and to helpe to supple, wher I haue by any meanes erryde in the
translacion, my faultes.

   And I shall pray, as daily I do pray, not with the lyppes onely, as
30 is sayde, but with the verey harte of me, to God and to the blessid
Virgyne to saue youe and sende youe helthe, and to remoue frome
youe all plag of heuynes and sorowe, and fynally to sende you here
longe lyfe and at the ende to be one of the electe, to accompany
Mary, the mother of Gode, in heuyn.

E. *Preface to his Translation of 'The Angelical Salutacion' by St.*
Thomas Aquinas and 'The stature and forme and lyfe of ouer blessed
Lady and of ouer Sauior Criste Iesu'

(MS. Royal 17 C. xvi, ff. 1b–3a)

35   To the moste nobil and vertuous Lady Mary. Henry Parkar,
knight, Lorde Morley, youer contynuall beadman, desyrithe parpetuall helthe and honour.

[1] MS. Peam.

The Prologe.

So dothe it dayly apeare, moste nobill Lady Marye, to all that be the humble and obedient subiectis to youer most ryall father, the vertue that from youer tender infancy hathe and dothe more and more increase in that beautyfull and most stedfast mynde of youears, that yt may be sayde well of youer Grace that whiche Dauit sayes 5 by those that, dispisinge in maner the fals, worldly plesure, study to loke to nothinge ellis but to increase in goodnes. Thus saythe the ryall profet, they shall go from one vertu in to a nother, and so shall the God of godis be sene in Sion, to proue that youer Grace dothe well fulfyll this profittes saynge. 10

I do well remember that skante ye were cum to xij yeres of age, but that ye were so rype in the Laten tonge, that rathe dothe happen to the women sex, that youer Grace not only coulde perfectly rede, wright and constrewe Laten, but farthermore translate eny harde thinge of the Latin in to ouer Inglysshe tonge. And amonge all other 15 youer most vertuus ocupacions I haue sene one prayer translatyd of youer doynge of Sayncte Thomas Alquyne that, I do ensuer youer Grace, is so well done, so neare to the Laten that when I loke vppon yt, as I haue one of the exemplar of yt, I haue not only meruell at the doinge of yt, but farther, for the well doynge, set yt as well in my 20 boke or bokes as also in my pore wyfes, youer humble beadwoman, and my chyldern, to the entent to gyue them ocasion to remember to praye for youer Grace, to thinke that yt is a honor to all women to se that youer Grace, beinge the moste noblest kinges daughter of the worlde, be to all other a myrrour, to follou so right a waye and 25 soche a vertuus pathe as ye do.

And forbecause that I do imagin by that youer Grace dyd translate that prayer owt of that great clarkes worke, I haue good hope that your meke harte shall take in good gre this Saynte Thomas de Alquino translacion of the 'Aue Maria', whiche I haue translatyd in 30 to Inglyshe, to her honour that is callyd the mother of God, whiche is so highe a worde that, as Anselme sayes, 'only to thinke of the Virgin that she ys the mother of God excedis all height that, nexte God, maye be thought or spoken'.

He that for ouer redemcion was borne of the Virgin saue and pre- 35 serue youer Grace this Newe Yere in helthe and honor, as to a kinges daughter aparteynithe, and after this brefe lyfe graunte ye the ioye that neuer shall ende.

F. *Preface to his Translation from Seneca's 'Epistles'*

(MS. Royal 17 A. xxx, ff. 1a–3a)

I shall most humbly praie vnto you, moste noble and vertuous

Ladye Mary, to accept as for this tyme the translac*i*on [of] thies two Epistles of Senecke ioyned in oon, w*h*ich, althoughe thei be but short, yet for the grete goodnesse that maie be noted in them, thei ar no lesse worthey to be loked vpon then a fayer dyamonde or
5 saphyre, whiche in value farr surmountethe an huge rocke of stone. Not that the matier of them any thing apperteynethe vnto you, being so gratious, so mightye and so victorio*us* a king*es* childe as ye be, and by his fauo*ur* and loue in most highe felicitye, but for other, whiche harde fortune blow*eth* here and there in to so soundry
10 daungiers that when they wene to haue escaped from Sylla, that most perilous monstre, they furthe w*ith* fall in to Caribdis, a farr worse confusion. They then that be so wrapped in suche dysease, lett them loke tha[t][1] can knowe the Latyne tong, of this golden epistle of this vertuous Sen[e]cke;[2] thos that can but rede the mother tong,
15 to loke on this my poore translac*i*on, w*h*ich I nowe w*ith* a loving minde present vnto your Grace, as I am wont yerely to do, praing the same well to take it. And I shall praie vnto God to sende your gentle harte contynuaunce in vertue vnto the laste houre. Amen.

G. *Preface to his Translation of Cicero's 'Somnium Scipionis'*
(MS. Royal 18 A. lx, ff. 1*a*–2*a*)

To the ryght highe and exellent Prynces, the Lady Mary, suster
20 to oure moste redoubted and victoriouse soue*r*eign Lorde, Kyng Edwarde the Syxt. Your humble oratoure Henry Parcar, knyght, Lorde Morley, wyssheth to yo*ur* Grace all prosperouse fortune w*ith* encreasce of vertue.

Moste noble Prynces, I do ymagyne that ye wyll sumwhat meruell
25 that I do present this yer to your goode Grace this litle worke of Tullius Cicero, of my translation into the Englishe tonge, that was accustomed allways afore this present tyme, either to send youe sum notable wo*ur*ke concernynge sum Christen doctours wrytynge in the Laten tonge, or ells sum of their workes by me translated in to our
30 tounge, as my rude knowledge coulde do it. To this, with your patience, moste gentle Prynces, if ye so meruell, I wyll afore hande with all humble reuerence excuse me why that, as saide is, I present to your vertuouse handes thys Tullius Cicero wo*ur*ke, intitled in the Laten Som[n]iu*m* Scipionis, in Englishe, the dreame of Scipion.
35 Surely, to this ententt—yf parcase that when yo*ur* goode Grace had at yo*ur* pleasure redde it, as I thynke that in the Laten ye haue allredy seene yt, that the booke myght be seene of sum of those that by their lyfe shew theymselfes rather to be of Epicurs secte then of Tulli*us*

---

[1] MS. tha.   [2] MS. Sencke

secte, whiche proueth many ways and with wonderfull wourdes the
soule of man to be immortall, and after this lyfe, lyuynge vertuously,
that ther is a place in heauen sure and certeyn, where ther is beatitude
eternall.

And I do professe, noble lady, that I, that am a Christen man, am 5
muche worthy of blame that, seynge a paynyme that knew not
Chryste nor his blessed religion to folow vertue so as Tully dyd, and
I, taught by Chrystes wordes, so often fall frome vertue into vyce.
But all thoughe I confesse me so to do, and haue doone, yett I thank
that eternall God, I neuer had in my hert, nor wyll haue, any false 10
faith to thynke otherwyse but that to theym that beleue well and
in tyme amende their faltes—but that suche shall haue joy eternall,
and contrary, that beleue otherwyse, payne in hell euerlastynge, as,
to my poore vnderstandyng, this moste eloquent paynyme playnly
declareth. Then, exellente Prynces, this is not for youe to looke 15
vppon that so passys your honourable days and with suche vertue
that Fame telleth it frome the Easte to the West, but for theym that
muche commende vertue and folow it nothynge at all.

And I am not ignoraunte but the wordes of Cicero ar so wonderfull
and the sense in many places so diffuse that it passeth my learnynge 20
or capacyte to put it in oure speache as it shulde be. But, brifly, if
your goode Grace be pleased with it, whome my study is allwais,
next our moste gratiouse leage Lorde the Kynge, your deare brother,
aboue all other ladyes in the worlde to please, that no persons ells
wylbe offended therwith, for asmuche as I haue doone in the trans- 25
latynge the best I can, and woll gladly haue don it better, to that
entent that all those that be the Kynges your brother subiectes
myght not onely heere it, but also folowe and vnderstand it as well
as the noble Romayne Macrobius that dyd expounde it.

For to conclude, I doubte not but that yow, noble and vertuous 30
Prynces, shall ryghte well accepte my goode hert and wyll and excuse
in this my faultes. And I shall pray to Cryste continually to preserue
your vertuouse lyfe to Nestor lyfe, and after this transitory and
troubleouse sea to brynge youe to the courte celestiall for youre
merytes. Amen. 35

H. *Preface to his Account of Miracles performed by the Holy Eucharist*

(MS. Add. 12060, ff. 1a–11a)

To the most high, most excellent, and most mighty Princesse, the
Lady Mary, by the grace off God Qvene off Inglonde, Fraunce,
Naples, Jerusalem and Irelond, Defendoresse of the Faythe, Pryn-
cesse off Spayne and Cecyle, Archduches off Austriche, Duches off

Mylayne, Burgundy *and* Brabaunt, Countesse off Haspurge, Flaunders and Tyrole.   Your humble subiect Henry Parker, knyght, Lorde
Morley, prayeth vnto Cryst Jesu and to his blessyd mother to prosper
your Magestye *and* your dere husband, our Lorde and King, longe to
5 raigne togyther in perpetuall honour and felycytie.

The Prologe.

Claudyan, the excellent poete, most gracyous soveraigne lady and
maistres, that was in his flowers in the good Emperour Theodosius
time, albeyt that he was no Cristen man, yet doth he write many
10 notable versys, well worthy to be had in mynde with king*es* and
qvenes and governers off contrees *and* co*m*mon welthes, and among
other his manifolde wise versys this one may well be comparyd to
your excellent Magestie, which is this:

Regis ad exemplum totus componitur orbis.

15 The sence, as I do take yt, is this, that as *the* Prynce or Princesse
gyueth example off vertue or otherwise vnto ther subiect*es*, even
after that sort folowith the people, other to vertue or to vyce.

And suerly in my pore iudgement his sayenge ys most true, for
when the headis doth ensue the happy way to vertue, maintayneth
20 religion, shewith pitye to the pore and miserable, resysteth the provde,
exalteth the meke, and causith true iustyce to be ministred to ther
subiect*es* without parcialytie, remembrith that ther dignytie is no
better then a Maye floure, that to-day shewith fayre and to-morow is
withered and drye, *and* the beauty therof past, and finally, thinketh
25 in ther hartes that death shall devoure the greatest as well as the
porest creature vnd*er* ther subiectyon, oh, such governers or headis
as gyueth such example off liffe to the worlde must off necessytie
be the occasyon and in man*er* a clere light to all the worlde to folowe
that waye; as you, my most deare and gracious lady and maistres
30 hath done, *and* doth, from yo*ur* tender infancy vnto this present day
off your most prosperous raigne.   For which well-doing God shall
kepe you, preserue you and blysse you to the laste age, and all world*es*
shall say and wryte off you laude and co*m*mendatyons and that you
alone aboue all other Cristen qvenes are worthy to haue that honor-
35 able name to be the Defendoresse off the faythe.   And although that
by your [right ?][1] off inheritaunce and by the right off your puissaunt
husband, our gracyous soveraigne Lord and King, ye haue betwixt
you two . . .[1] have the greatest parte of Cristendome vnder your
subiectyon, yet this one tytle [you] have deservyd by your fact, to
40 have the [name] of the Defendoresse off the Faithe, [surpass]yth all
the rest of your tytles and croun[es and i]s *the* very precyous gemme,

[1] MS. illegible.

shinyng ever [stron]gly in your forehead,[1] never to be darkyd in this life nor in the lyfe to come.

For wher that off late dayes this yo*ur* most noble realme was brought to that barbarous estate that ther was in the headis off the people as many dyvers argument*es* as ther hath ben heretyckes synce 5 Christ*es* Churche began, by reason wherof the vulgar was so amased that many thought ther was no religion at all but to do as Epicure or vile Sardanapavlus dyd, that folowed so his vityous liffe *that* vnto this day he is despised off all, lernyd *and* vnlernid—euen in lyke maner this your realme was brought to that sedytion, that first they denyed 10 the head of the Church, the Pope's Holynes, next wolde have no saintes honored but threwe vile matter at the Crucifyx, and, adding mischeife to myscheife, denyed the sevyn sacrament*es* of *th*e Church, some of them willing to have but thre, some none at all, and by ther desertes fyll into so reprobable a will that they not only expulsed the 15 name off the precyous Mary, mother to Christ, out off ther co*m*mon prayers but thervnto wolde not the Aue Maria to be sayde.

This was greatly to be lamentyd, but this *that* folowith moche more, for the most devine Holy Sacrament of the aulter, the very Sancta Sanctoru*m*, which all Cristen realmes hath belevyd to be really the 20 very body off Christ, these heretyckes without sence or wytt, more abhomynable then Machomet, the false prophete, hath so despised yt and handlyd yt, and in such an herytycall sorte that, as the excellent Maro sayeth, to tell yt:

Animus meminisse [h]orret[2] luctuq*ue* refugit,   25

and by ther false doctryne as moche as in them was, hath condemnyd all the king*es* in Cristendome *and* ther p*ro*genitours, with ther subiectes, to be no better then idolaters, for which sayd offence off idolatrye and for false heritycall opynions all Cristen realmes hath ben scourged, eradycate and subvertyd. 30

And here, with your gentle pacyence, moste Cristen Qvene, I wyll somwhat dyvert from my pore oratyon and declare what hurt hathe come by heresyes, what murder, what penurye, to these contryes folowing, that is to say, to the Jewes, to the Grecyans, to the Italyans, to the Egiptians, to the Affricanes, to the Bohemes, to the Span-35 yardes, to the Britaignes, somtyme rulers off this realme, and last, to the empyre of Germany and to this your realme at this present day.

I say therfore that yt is manifest to them *that* haue readde the Byble that from the creatyon off the worlde vnto ther perpetuall rvyne the Jewes were for the most parte evermore idolaters, for which 40 offence God gave them somtyme into the handes of the Philistines,

---

[1] MS. blurred and illegible.   [2] MS. orret.

somtyme to the Assirians, and in processe of tyme they were scourged
by Nabuchodonazer, who toke ther kynge and brought hym and his
people captyue vnto Babylon. This punishment might well haue
ben the cause to have made them left ther idolatrye, and yet, ther
5 cytye reedifyed againe by the favour of God and by the graunt off
Syrus, King of Persia, they lefte not ther olde wayes tyll that by
malyce they had put to death the Savyour of *the* worlde, Christ Jesu,
and in His tyme had thre dyvers sectes among them, that is, the
Pharasyes, the Saduces and the Ess[en]es.[1] What divers opinyons
10 they had Historia Ecclesiastica declareth, and therfore, for brevitye, I
let yt passe. One thing is sure—that Christ blamed them and reprovyd
them for ther inconstancy in manye places off the Holy Gospell *and*
declaryd vnto them how ther perpetuall destrvctyon was at hande,
which folowed in very dede by Titus Vaspasianus, who lefte not one
15 stone of their cytye stonding vpon another and slewe innumerable
off them by famyne and sworde, the rest solde lyke beast*es*, and now
are slaves *and* despised people throughout the vniuersall worlde,
living in captyvytie and vnder trybute.

Thus farre, most excellent lady, is sayd off the Jewes. It folowith
20 off the Grecyans. Our Sauyour Crist hauyng suffred passyon for our
redemptyon, commaunding His Apostles to preach in His name that
all that beleuyd and were baptised shulde haue the kingdome of glory,
innvmerable by fayth were cristenyd. But this faythe lasted not
longe among the Cristen men but that some fyll to heritycall opin-
25 yons and so disturbed Cristes people that many that wolde haue ben
Cristen men, seynge such devisyon off Cristians amonge them selfes,
vtterly forsoke that name and contynved payny*m*mes styll as they
were before. But yet Christ, that promised to Peter that his faith
shuld never fayle, although the M[o]n[tan]ist*es*[2] and Donatist*es* and
30 other tyraunt*es* did impugne the truthe, yet the more they so dyd to
Christ*es* religyon, the more yt florished, but not without the perse-
cutyon and bloudshedding off innumerable saintes, tyll at the last the
great Constantyne, being a Britaine, borne in this your realme, to
the great honour off yt commaundyd through the hole empyre Christ
35 to be honoured, the Holy Crosse to be exaltyd, and S. Sylvester the
Pope to be the head of all the bishopp*es* in the worlde.

I passe over how by the signe of the crosse, which he sawe in
heavyn, shewyd to hym by an angle with these wordes 'Constantine,
in hoc signo uinces', that ys to say, 'In this signe, Constantyne, thou
40 shalt vanquishe', he overcamme Maxentius the tiraun*t*, and, Cristes
flocke set at libertye, all idolatry began to cease, tyll that a newe,

[1] MS. Essayes.
[2] MS. Manatist*es*. But cf. Eusebius, *Historia Ecclesiastica*, V. xiv–xviii.

bytter basilyck, the false herityck Arrian, well nere subvertyd all. What harme that his heresy dyd, what bloudsheding and destrvctyon off kingdomes and contryes came by yt, he that ys any thing lettured knowith yt, and therfore, most gracyous lady, I overpasse yt. And it shall suffise to tell that the Grecyans, being the noblest people in 5 the worlde, forsaking the head of the Church of Rome, the Popes Holynes, fyll from emperour to emperour to innumerable of erronyous opynyons, among whom Julyan the Apostata, seing the strife betwixt the Catholick*es* and the Arryans, forsoke them both—to his perpetuall harme, for, going against the Persians, he was slayne, as it is thought, 10 by the stroke devyne, and, dyeng, sayd in the despite of Christ 'Uicisti, Galil[æ]e'.[1]

To conclude, excellent Qvene, aswell the emperours that folowed for the most part never ensued the Church off Rome till God, being wrothe for ther heresyes, within one hundred yeares pu*n*nished them 15 by Machomet, the greate Turke, in suche wise that he wanne the head cytie of Constantinople and all Grece, slewe ther Emperour, defyled his wife in the temple of Sancta Sophia, and brought the mighty Grecyans into such misery that ther ys not at this day one Grecyan can say that he holdeth one fote within that londe. Oh, Jesu, most 20 noble Qvene, what an example is this for all good Catholick*es* to beware to fall into suche heritycall opynions as the Grecyans dyd!

It folowith off the Egiptyans. Egypt, convertyd vnto the faythe of Christ, having many notable clerkes, great bishopp*es* and holye men, amonge the cheife Athanasius was one, that made that excellent 25 Psalme off 'Quicunq*ue* uult saluus esse'. It was not long after his death but that they, not obeyng the sea of Rome, sent vnto the Pope, onles he wolde agre to ther opinyons, they wolde not take hym the head off the Church. It folowed shortly after in the tyme off the Emperour Eraclius, the Arrabyans, wher fyrst the lawe off Machomet 30 began, vanquished them and chased the bishopp*es* and the Cristen men away, and they at this day are all Machomett*es* and heretyckes, and ther contrey euermore called throughout the worlde 'stultus Egiptus'. I wyll not forgett to declare vnto your Grace what myscheife fyll vnto Eraclius, who, being at his begynnyng a worthy 35 emperour and so fortunate that he vanquished with his owne hande Cosdrus, the Kinge off Persia and brought vnto Jerusalem the Holy Crosse with great pompe and glory, yet, seyng manifestly the miracle that God ther shewid vnto hym, fyll from the true Catholyck relygion vnto the heresy off the Moniclites and perished shortly after by such 40 a straunge death that yt is not honest to tell it. Thus farre off the Egyptyans.

[1] MS. Galileae.

Now, excellent Princesse, I wyll breifly declare how by the Arryans secte mischeife fyll amonge the Italyens and how God suffred them to be scourgyd by the Hvnes, by the Vandales and by the Gotes. And among other Radaga[i]sus,[1] who had in his army two hundred
5 thousand Gotes, entryd Italy and beseiged Rome for no nother cause, as the aucthours wryte, but that in those dayes they were not only heretyck*es* many one of them, but also they were necligent in doing devyne service. Nevertheles, they, crieng to God for mercy, were delyveryd from this tyraunt, and he by the Romaynes was slaine.
10 After this Radaga[i]sus,[1] succedyd Alaricus to be the King of the Gotes and beseigyd Rome and toke it, and albeyt that he was a paynyme, hè vsyd this hvmanytie, that is, he co*m*maundyd all his men of warre, paine of death, not to hurt no Romaine that fledde to the Church of S. Peter *and* S. Paull.
15 Not long after entryd Italy Athala, the King of the Hvnes, who toke Padua, Vincentia, Virona, Milayne and Papia, and at the last going towarde Rome, the Romaynes being in an exceding feare, desyred Leo, then Pope off Rome, the first of that name, to go to hym to appease hym. And he so doing, ther chaunced a wonderous thing off
20 yt, for the barbarous prynce only with the syghte of Leo lefte Rome vntouched; and when certaine of his demaundyd of hym why he, being the scourge of God, wolde not enter Rome and take yt, he aunsweryd that he sawe by this good Pope two men stonding with two nakyd swordes in ther handes, threatyng hym *and* his armey to
25 destroy them if they procedyd any further, wherfore he retourned home agayne. And suerly, most excellent Princesse, this is a wonderous story that he which was so fearfull and mighty a prynce, by the only sight of that holy father, Pope of Rome, was glade to depart away.

And yt is for conclusyon to be remembrid that as long as the
30 Arryans sect was in Italy, they never fayled to be scourgyd other by the Hunes, the Gotes, the Vandales or the Sarasyns; and the contrey once pacifyed from heresy, yt hath prosperyd *and* doth prosper vnto this present day. Thus farre off the Italyens.

And now I shall breifly declare the rvyne of the Affricanes. The
35 great doctour of the Church, S. Austyne, who florishcd in the yeare of grace foure hundred and thirtye, being Bishoppe off Iponense in the sayd contrey of Affryck, had moch to do to stablishe the contrey by his excellent lernyng and to kepe the people from heresy, and specially from the sect of the Arryans. But he could not so bring the
40 matter to passe, for all his great lernyng, but that the people con-tynued in many false opinions styll, vntyll that tyme that Gensericus beseigyd the citye wher as he lay syck, and shortly after his death

[1] MS. radagasus.

toke the cytye and persecutyd so the Catholickes that I haue horrour
to tell yt. And albeyt that his sonne raignyd after hym *and* was even
lykewise off the Arryans sect and more mischeuous then ever was
his father, yet he prosperyd not long, but, dieng miserably, shortly
after hym the Sarasyns conqueryd all the contrey and holde *and* kepe 5
yt styll, to the great rebuke of Cristen men, vnto this present day.
And thus farre of the Affricans.

It folowith of the noble realme of Spayne. The Spanyardes hauyng
many worthy prynces *and* rulers, at last by succession the realme fyll
to Theodoricus, that was descendyd of the bloud off the Goates, who 10
fyll into such heresy and such pride that he vtterly despised the sea
off Rome and sayd that to hym appertayned only to make all the
ecclesiastycall lawes, and vsyd his lyffe so dissolutely that by the
permissyon of God the Sarasyns, that then had gotten by sworde the
gret contrey off Affryke, entryd Spayne; and Theodoricus geving 15
batayle vnto them, albeyt that he was a very valiaunt prynce of his
person *and* dyd many notable actes with his owne hande, yet at the
last his people was put to flyght, and he flyeng away, was drovnyd in
a ryver, and within a lytle while after all Spaine loste, savynge one
lytle contrey in the kingdome off Castyll. How long yt was, or the 20
noble prynces off Castyll could recover againe the contrey of Spayne!
Ther cronycle declareth that in sevyn hundred yeares they had moch
worke to expulse the Sarasyns, tyll at the last Fardinando, that
worthy king your grauntfather gotte Garnado, and so, being lorde
off all Spaine, he *and* his successyon vnto this daye triumphantly 25
enioyeth yt. Thus farre of Spayne.

Now, most Cristen Qvene, although that I can not tell yt without
lamentatyon of my hart what misery the Britaynes, somtyme rulers
of this realme, fyll in by heresy, yet wyll I tell yt, to that intent that
I wolde wishe that your devyne prechers shuld teache the people by 30
the example off the Brytaynes to beware how to fall to vayne argumentes and false beleife, lest that percase might fall to vs that which
fyll to the Brytaynes, which is this. Afore the Incarnatyon of Christ
and after, ther was many a worthy Britayne, as Brenius, Belinus, Vt[h]er
Pendragon,[1] Aureli[us] Ambrose,[2] and the noble Arthur, with dyvers 35
other, that raignyd triumphantly tyll the great Constantyne, in
whose tyme, as Polydorus wryteth, the Brytaynes being in great
prosperitye, an heretyck callyd Pela[g]i[us][3] a monke, preched vnto the
Brytaynes that a man might be savyd by his owne good workes,
without the grace off God, which so infectyd the Britaynes with that 40
heresy that although Lvcivs, a Britayne, was long before that Kinge
off this realme, cristenyd at Rome, wherby in dede the Kinges off

[1] MS. Vterpendragon. [2] MS. Aureliambrose. [3] MS. pelladian.

this realme, your noble progenytours, doth clayme to be the most Cristen kyng*es*, because he was the first cristened king, before any king in Fraunce, yt folowed, the Britaines thus fallen to heresy, the Saxons entryd this londe, and by lytle and lytle expulsed quyte away 5 the Britaynes, and chaungyd the name of the realme, which was afore callyd Brytaine, vnto Inglond, and the Brytaynes, which the Welch men say they be descendyd of, subiectes to your imperiall crovne for ever. Thys example is fearfull, most noble Princesse, well worthye for vs Inglish men to note it well, leste that the like perchaunce may 10 fall to vs. *And* thus farre off the Britaynes.

   Now for the kingdome off Boheme, most excellent Princesse, which yt is not long synce ther heresy began by Wickliff, a scoler of the vniuersitye off Oxforde, whose damnable heresy Luther inespecially hath folowyd, procedyd thus. About the latter dayes of the most 15 worthy prince, King Edward the Third, this Wickliff vsyd, as Randolde, the monke of Chester, writeth, many straunge fashions to cloke his heresy withall, aswell in his apparell, as in vsing a fayned, false, dessembling holynes, and drewe to his company one Jerome, off the kingdome off Boheme, *and* one Hus[s][1]—two bitter poison persons, 20 who, going home into ther contrey, subvertyd all the hole regyon of Boheme. And yt is to be notyd that though this King Edward was the most famous prynce of the worlde, yet, as yt is thought, bycause he dyd not sodenly suppresse this Wicklif, he was nothing so fortunate in his warres at the latter ende of his dayes as he was at his begynning. 25 But, leaving that apart, *and* retournyng againe to the kingdome off Boheme, the head cytye theroff, called Prage, being at that tyme in great welth and prosperytie and one of the head vniuersyties of Cristendome, this Jerome and this Hus[s][1] so subvertyd the religyon ther that they fyll into such a discorde and sodayne batayle among 30 them selues that the hole contrey came vtterly to ruyne, and specyallye by a gentilman whose name is called Johannes Ciskay, who so burnt churches, pulled downe religious houses, defyled virgins, and made suche racket in that realme that it coulde never prosper as it dyd, vnto this present day. And thus farre off the kyngdome off 35 Boheme.

   Now, gracyous lady, to tell the misery off the Germaynes that hath fallen vnto them in these our dayes, it shulde seme superfloous to write yt. Neuertheles, yt is most true that I, beynge embassadour from your most victorious father vnto the noble King of Romaynes, Fardinando, 40 bearing to hym the Garter, Luthers secte then newly begu*n*ne, scant was I retournyd vnto this your realme but that the contrey was in such a rebellion, that is to say, the vilaynes against the lordes, that, or

[1] MS. hust.

they coulde be appeasyd, yt cost of both partes aboue the lyves of an hundred thousand men, and such crueltye was executyd by the vilaynes to certayne of the nobylytye that I haue horrour to tell it. How many religious persons was slayne, how many churches burnt, how many virgines defyled, *and* harmes innumerable done and exe- 5 cutyd, yt is impossible for me to tell. One thing ys that Luther, the aucthor of all mischeife and, as I do thinke, the very Antechrist, for *our* synnes sent from God to persecute Cristendome, in his writing*es* is so vyle *and* abhomynable in certayne places that although, excellent Quene, I professe I haue redde Alkarom, Machomett*es* lawe, 10 lately translatyd into the Italyen tonge, yet is ther nothing so spurke and detestable wordes wryten in that lawe as is writen by hym. And thus farre, vertuous lady, for the Germaynes.

And now to this your realme, most excellent Princesse, I dare not say what I thinke. But thus moche, with your pacyence, I may say. 15 Wher is become all the plentye that was in your wyse grauntfathers daies, King Henry the Seventh, *and* my godly maistres, the Lady Margaret, your great-grandame, and in your worthy fathers dayes, King Henry the Eight? Wher is the plentye off corne, the haboun-daunce of cattall, the frutefulnes of all thing, as well of the water as 20 of the londe? Wher is become the quyetnes of subiect*es and* obedi-ence to ther headis? Wher is the golde and silver that in such haboundaunce was in this realme that, as sayd ys, I being embassa-dour sent by your worthy father to the King Fardinando, ther in reverting home being lodged in a denes house in the cytye of Mastrick 25 in Base Almaine, he sayd vnto me, when I departyd from hym, these wordes: 'God sende the, lorde embassadour, safe *and* sounde to thy golden contrey *and* most plentyfull region in the worlde'? All this, gracious lady, is past *and* gone, our golde is turnyd vnto copper, our sylver to brasse, and ne were the hope that we have in God and you, 30 swete, delycate, red rose, the very maynteyner off faythe, I thinke that we shulde be in worse case then other Grece or Boheme.

But, your Highnes, as I have sayd at the begynnyng of myne oration, ensuing all goodnes and vertue, and folowyng the wise counsell of the vnculpable, vertuous Cardinall, your cosyn, whose 35 conversatyon and life is knowen to be through Cristendome without spotte, I say that your Highnes in folowing his counsell, and with your godly wyt together, the golden worlde shall in processe come againe, and this your realme prosper in peace and in haboundaunce. And if ther be any of your obedient subiect*es* that by false teaching 40 of the heretyck*es* haue had, or have, any vngodly opinyon in ther stomack, with Goddes mercy and your most Cristen example they shall revert home to ther mother, Holy Church, againe, which I pray

to God *and* to his blessyd mother may in your most happy raigne
come to passe, *and* that I may se it, or I die.

Thus hithervnto, most Cristen Qvene, and my most deare *and*
gracyous soveraigne ladye *and* maistres, I haue breifly declared the
5 rvine, the destructyon, the hunger, the penury, the battayles, and
the subvertyon of realmes and empires that hath come by heresy.
And suerly, to write or to tell the matter how it was at lenght, it shuld
fulfyll a hole volume, and a worke that I were not able to bring to an
ende. But this that I haue breifly sayd, I do affirme yt for to be true,
10 as the greatest aucthours that hath ben synce Christ suffred His Death
doth declare yt, and by experience in our tyme we haue sene yt. And
for that intent that divers hath taken opinion against the devine *and*
holy sacrament off the aulter, that it shuld not be really the precious
body of God that was borne of the blissyd Virgin Mary, and also haue
15 despised the Holy Masse, I have translatyd vnto your Highnes certayne examples what wonders God hath wrought to such as hath not
belevid yt, and vsyd the receyving therof vnreverently, prayeng your
excellent Magestye to accept this my pore lytle labour well and in
good part. And I shall contynually pray vnto God and to his blessyd
20 mother to preserve your gracious Highnes and my deare soveraigne
Lorde and Kynge, your husbande, long to lyve together in helth,
glory and vyctorye.

III. MORLEY'S PREFACE TO HIS COMMENTARY ON *ECCLESIASTES* ADDRESSED TO THE DUKE OF SOMERSET

(MS. Royal 17 D. xiii, ff. 1*a*–4*b*)

To the right high and mightie prince Edward, Duke of Somersett,
Erle of Hertford, Vyscounte Beauchampe, Lord Seymour, Governour
25 of the parsone of the Kinge his Maiestie of England, and Protecto*ur*
of all his realmes, domynyons and subiect*es*, his Lieuetena*unt*-
Generall of alle his armyes, bothe by lande and by sea, Threasorour
and Earle Marshall of England, Governo*ur* of the isles of Gernsey and
Gersey, and Knight of the moost noble Order of the Gartier, Henrye
30 Parker, knight, wissheth helthe, honour and felicitie.

Of olde and awntiente vsage, it hathe byn accustomed, most
excellent prince, to dedicate suche bookes as men putt furthe into
light, either made of their owen industrie and studie, orels translated
oute of one language into another, to some noble prince, or otherwise
35 excellent in birthe or renowne, to th'ende that the worke mighte
therebie have more free passage into the hand*es* of other men. This
custome, aswell lawdable as awntient, hathe encouraged me at this
p*re*sent, having dailly experience of your Grac*es* godlie *and* vertuous

maynteynyng of the true preachers for the conducting of alle the
whole bodie of this realme to the purenes and synceritie of the Gospell,
to dedicate this little volume vnto your Grace, entitled 'The Booke
of the Preacher', made by the moost wise and prudent Kinge Salomon, and often declared by the same vnto his nobilitie; who, albeit 5
it apperteigned not vnto his office and dignytie to preache vnto his
subiectes, but vnto the priestes and elders, yett for the zeale he bare
to the advauncemente of Goddes glorie, he accompted it no lesse then
high renowne vnto his maiestie to entreate and comune with his
nobles of suche thinges as mighte be furderaunce vnto the same.   10
  I canne nowe coniecture your Grace being ordeyned of God, of
whome, as Paule saieth in the xiij^th to the Romans is alle aucthoritie
and powre, to be at this tyme over this realme, with alle the Kinges
Highnes domynyons, bearing the same godlie mynde and zeale of
Kinge Salomon, aswell for the wittie defence of vs alle frome our 15
foreyne enymies as for th'advauncement of Goddes veritie, alle vayne
supersticion and Romysshe errour troden vnder foote. Yea, the
veraie same is your Grace vnto this realme at this presente that
Hesekiah and Josia weare vnto Israell, and no lesse bounde in conscience to sett furthe Goddes lyvelie worde then they weare. It is also 20
beleved of many faithfull hartes, the furderaunce of the Gospell also
witnessing the same, that God hathe ordeyned your Grace to make
so godlie a redie waie in the hertes of alle the Kinges Maiesties loving
subiectes, that when God shall appoynte his Highnes to ruele and
governe in his owne parsone, they shall not oonlye receyve hys Grace 25
as their headd and kinge, as other nations are accustomed to do, for
feare of his aucthoritie and sworde, but also throughly enstructed
in the Gospell, therin learnyng their moost bounden dueties, they
shall with alle herte and mynde acknowledge his Maiestie to be the
veraie same their spirituall heade, by whome God hathe appoynted 30
his spirituall temple to be reedified and buylded vp agayne, that
longe hathe lyen waste, overwhelmed with the Romysshe vsurped
aucthoritie and moost pestiferous and erronyous lawes of the same.
For the perfect and fulle perfeccion and perfourmaunce wherof I
shall, as I am mooste bounden, dailly praie vnto the ever-lyving one 35
God, whiche hathe begonne this moost godlie enterprise and purpose,
to prosper it and bringe it to suche effect that the thinge so godlie
begonne may the same persever and contynue, and that throughe
the strength of his almightie hande, no storme of false appostles and
teachers, the onelie disturbers and destroiers of alle godlines, maye 40
hereafter be able to putt owte and exstincte the syncere and pure
light that now begynneth moost purely to shyne, and also that it
may please hym to graunte vnto your Grace for rewarde that

heavenlie ioie whiche no eye hathe seen, no eare hathe harde, nor
canne assende into the herte of manne, prepared of Godd for them
that love hym. So be it.

For asmoche as this boke was translatid out of the Hebrewe tounge
5 more obscurelye then anye other of the Olde Testament, manye well
leornyd men toke in hande to declare and expounde the same, apply-
inge some sentences and sayng*es* therof vnto there owne profession
or rather opinion. Eyther there curiosite was suche that they de-
lightyd in thing*es* that were harde to be vndrestonde, as thing*es* that
10 were newe and rare in vse, or ell*es* for that in suche dark and obscure
writynges yt was easye for them to fayne and holde opinion as they
listed, the philosophers supposid that yt appertayned vnto them
that ys sayd in the first chapter of this boke: 'All thing*es* are so harde
that no man can expresse them', as though Salomon shulde haue
15 spoken of there vayne speculatyue philosophye. Some other were
offendid, for that yt ys said in the thirde chapter: 'As dyethe the
beast, so dyeth the man ; they haue bothe one ende and one birthe',
thinkyng that he was an Epicure, or that at the leaste he spak in the
parson of Epicurus. But there were none that more abused the said
20 boke then the scoles of our diuines, which made a mater of conscience
agaynst God of this place: 'Man knowyt[h] not whether he be worthy
of loue or hatered', greatlye disquietyng w*ith* the wresting of the said
texte the conscienc*es* of all men, extinguishinge the most assurid
faythe in Christ w*ith* all other godlye knowlege, and teaching nothing
25 ell*es* but that we owght to doubt of the grace and loue of God toward*es*
vs. So greate was there blindnes that besides this saynge of Salom*on*
—yea, rather, besydes this there errour apon the same, they wolde
no more see the writyng*es* of th' apostell*es* and evangelist*es*, that w*ith*
soo great authorites of Scriptures, signes and tokens, dothe witnes
30 Christ to be our onlye mediator and saluac*i*on, frelye yeuen vs of
God.

Many also of the holye fathers and doctors of the Churche, not
havynge the trwe intellecc*i*on of the sayd boke, did greatlye depraue
yt, in that they affirmyd and sayd that Salomon tawght the con-
35 tempte of the worlde, as they call yt, that ys to saye, the dispisinge
of the thing*es* creatid and ordeynid of God. And holye Jerome was
one of them who by this boke, or rather by his comment made there
apon, entysid his Blesill vnto a monasticall or solitarye lyff. This
godlye comme*n*t, parteynynge to the establishing of religious men
40 and there monastaries, passid as yt had ben a newe deluge w*ith* most
violent rage thorough the vniue*r*sall Churche, teachinge that yt was
a most Christian thinge to forsake the orderinge and providinge of
thing*es* conce*r*nynge howsholde, to forsake all tempo*r*all authorites,

to forsake the office of a bishope or of an apostéll, and to flee into a desert place, to seperate hym selff from the companye and socyete of men, to lyve in quiete and scilence, and that in the worlde yt was not possible to please and serve God. As though Salomon shulde haue callyd matrimonye, power, office and the administracion of 5 Godes worde vanite, all which thinges hyghlye praysing he callythe the giftes of God. And where as he teacheth that men them selves, there workes, councelles and studies are but vanites, thes our auncient doctors, wrestinge all thinges awrye, call the sayd creatures and thinges ordened by God vanites, and there own imaginacions hygh 10 and holye, dremyng clene contrarye to Salomons intent and mynde.

To conclude, they haue brought out of this excellent worke of Salomon nowght elles but monsters, and of godlye goulde they haue made abhominable idolles. Wherfore, to illuminate thees obscurites and to break in sondre thes filthy idolles, I haue permitted more 15 willinglye thes my annotacions to comme into other mens handes, which, although they be simple and breff, yet vnto thoose that haue no better, or that haue ben deluded affore tyme wyth false gloses and exposicions they maye be occasion of better knowlege. Neyther doubt I but that the taste of this boke shalbe vnto faythfull hartes 20 most pleasant and dilectable, for that yt dothe not onlye set open before our ies the miserable state and condicion, with all the vanites, of this lyff, but also instructyth vs howe to lyue in reste and quietnes of mynde, and howe to commyt our cares and thoughtes vnto the Lorde, the yever of goodnes; as witnessith James in his first chapter, 25 saynge: 'Euery good gyfte and parfayte gyfte ys from aboue and commythe down from the father of light'—vnto whom, for that he hathe wotsauyde to illustrate and renwe with the inestimable light of his worde thes our latter days, be all honor, laude and prayse.

IV. Morley's Preface to *The Pistellis and Gospelles*
addressed to Anne Boleyn

(MS. Harl. 6561, f. 2a, b.)

To the ryght honorable ladye, the Ladye Marchionesse of Pem- 30 brooke, her moost lovyng and fryndely brother sendeth gretyng.

Our frendly dealynges, with so diuers and sondry benifites, besydes the perpetuall bond of blood, haue so often bownd me, Madame, inwardly to loue you, dayly to prayse you, and continually to sarue you, that in euery of theym I must perforce becomme your debtour 35 for want of pooire, but nothyng of my good wyll. And were it not that by experience your gentilnes ys dayly proued, your meeke fachon often tymes put in vre, I myght wel dispaire in my self,

studyeng to acquitt your desertes towardis me, or enboldyng my self
with so poore a thyng to presente you. But, knowyng these perfectly
to raigne in you w*ith* moo, I haue been so bold to send vnto you, not
iewels or gold, wherof you haue plenty, not perle or ryche stones,
5 wherof you haue ynough, but a rude translation of a welwyller, a good
mater meanly handelyd, moost humbly desyryng you with fauour to
way the wekenes of my dull wyt, and paciently to pardon wher*e* any
faute ys, allwayes consideryng that by your co*m*mandement I haue
aduenturyd to do this, without the whiche it had not been in[1] me to
10 haue perfourmyd yt. But that hath had pooire to make me passe my
wit, which lyke as in this I haue been redy to fulfyll, so in all other
thyng*es* at all tymes I shall be redy to obey, prayeng hym oon whoome
this booke treatyth to graunt you many good yeres to his plesure and
shortely to encres in hartes easse with honnor.

V. Morley's Preface to his Translation of Petrarch's *Trionfi*, addressed to Lord Maltravers

(A ii recto–A iii verso)

15 Vnto the mooste towarde yonge gentle Lorde Matrauers, *sonne and
heyre apparaunt to the worthy and noble* Earle of Arundel, your poore
frende Henry Parker knyght, Lorde Morley, prayeth to God that the
vertue whiche doth floryshe in you in this youre tender age, maye
more and more increase in you, to the comfort of all that loue you,
20 vnto the laste age.

The fables of Isope (mooste towarde younge Lorde) are not only
had in commendation amonge the Philosophers, as with Plato,
Aristotle, & diuerse other of y*e* moste excellent of thē: but also the
deuines, when in theyr preachynges there cometh to theyr purpose
25 any matter, to rehearse to the rude people, they alledge the allegorye
sence of them, to the muche edification of the hearers. I saye therfore,
that amonge other his wyttye fables (not to you noble gentleman
vnknowen) he telleth, how that the cocke scrapynge on a dounge hill,
found a precious stone, and when he sawe it, disdayninge, he spurned
30 it from hym, sayinge, what haue I to do with the, thou canste not
serue me to no kynde of vse, and so dispysynge it, left it where as it
laye on the dongehyll styll.

Euen so there be a nomber of that sorte, that percase when they
shall eyther heare redde, or them selfe reade this excellent tryumphes,
35 of this famous clercke Petrarcha, shall lytle set by them, and peraduenture caste it from them, desyrynge rather to haue a tale prynted
of Robyn Hoode, or some other dongehyll matter then this, whiche

[1] MS. in in.

I dare affirme, yea, and the Italians do the same, that the deuine
workes set aparte, there was neuer in any vulgar speche or language,
so notable a worke, so clerckely done as this his worke. And albeit
that he setteth forth these syxe[1] wonderfull made triumphes all to
the laude of hys Ladye Laura, by whome he made so many a swete 5
sonnet, that neuer yet no poete nor gentleman could amend, nor
make the lyke, yet who that doth vnderstande them, shall se in them
comprehended al morall vertue, all Phylosophye, all storyall matters,
and briefely manye deuyne sentences theologicall secretes declared.
But alas who is he that will so reade them, that he wyl marke them, 10
or what prynter wyll not saye, that he may winne more gayne in
pryntynge of a merye ieste, then suche lyke excellente workes? Suerlye[2]
(my good Lorde) very fewe or none, whyche I do lamente at my harte
consyderynge that aswell in French, as in the Italyan (in the whyche
both tongues I haue some lytle knowledge) there is no excellente 15
worke in the latyn, but that strayght wayes they set it forth in the
vulgar, moost commonly to their kynges and noble prynces of theyr
region and countreys: As one of late dayes that was grome of the
chaumber with that renowmed and valyaunte Prynce of hyghe
memorye, Fraunces the Frenche kynge, whose name I haue for- 20
gotten, that dydde translate these tryumphes to that sayde kynge,
whyche he toke so thankefully, that he gaue to hym for hys paynes
an hundred crounes, to hym and to his heyres of inheritaunce to
enioye to that value in lande for euer, and toke suche pleasure in it,
that wheresoeuer he wente amonge hys precyous Iewelles, that booke 25
was alwayes caryed with hym for his pastyme to loke vpon, and as
muche estemed by hym, as the rychest Diamonde he hadde: whiche
sayde booke, when I sawe the coppye of it, I thoughte in my mynde,
howe I beynge an Englyshe man, myght do aswell as the Frenche
man, dyd translate this sayde worke into our maternall tounge, and 30
after much debatyng with my selfe, dyd as your Lordshyppe doth
se, translate the sayde booke to that moost worthy kynge our late
soueraygne Lorde of perpetuall memorye kynge Henrye theyghte,
who as he was a Prynce aboue all other mooste excellente, so toke he
the worke verye thankefullye, merueylynge muche howe I coulde do 35
it, and thynkynge verelye I hadde not doone it, wythoute helpe of
some other, better knowynge the Italyen tounge then I: but when
he knewe the verye treweth, that I hadde traunslated the worke my
selfe, he was more pleased therewith then he was before, and so what
his highnes dyd with it, is to me vnknowen, one thynge is, that I dyd 40
it in suche hast, that doubtles in many places (yf it were agayne in
my handes) I thynke I coulde well amende it, albeit that I professe,

---

[1] *Text* syxte. [2] *Text* workes, suerlye.

I haue not erred moche from the letter, but in the ryme, whiche is
not possible for me to folow in the translation, nor touche the least
poynt of the elegancy that this elegant Poete hath set forth in his
owne maternall tongue. But as it is, if in the translation there be
5 anye thynge to be amended, or any wyll depraue it, I shall praye you
(mooste noble younge Lorde) the very myrroure of al the yonge noble
gentelmen of this realme in vertue, in learnynge, and in all other
feates appertayning to such a Lorde as you be, to defende it agaynst
those that will more by enuy then by knowledge depraue it, and then
10 I do not feare but those that knowe and can speake the Italian, will
beare with the simple translation, and commende the worke, as it is
so muche commendable, that it can not be to dere bought, I desyre
god noble yonge gentleman, to make the lorde Matrauers an olde
gentleman, and then thy worthy father the Earle of Arundell my
15 most speciall good Lorde and frend, shall make an olde Earle and
lyue *vsque in senium et senectu[te]m.*

Dixi Henry Morelye.

¹ *Text* senectum.

ADDENDA

p. 3, *l.* 4. The *Epistola ad Andream de Acciarolis*, prefixed by Boccaccio to his work, but untranslated by Morley, shows that *De claris mulieribus* was not dedicated to Queen Johanna. This was Boccaccio's original intention, but in the end he dedicated it to the Countess Andrea degli Acciaiuoli. As he himself explains: 'quia adeo vigens regius fulgor est et opusculi tenuitas et fere semisopita fauillula, timens ne a potiori lumine minus omnino fugaretur in tenebras, sensim retraxi consilium et noua indagine multis alijs perquisitis ad extremum ab illustri regina in te votum deflexi meum.' It is probable, as Mr. Victor Scholderer suggests, that Morley's error arose from a confused recollection of this passage and another in the *Conclusio*, where the 'tam clara regina' is mentioned in passing.

p. 11, *l.* 14, hym] hyr MS.

p. 40, *l.* 4, vnneth so wylde that any man MS.

p. 61, *l.* 9, Ceon MS.

p. 68, *l.* 17, of] on MS.

p. 95, *l.* 5, wytte MS.

p. 130, *l.* 7, Eurmaaus MS.

p. 130, *l.* 8, Angelau*m* MS

GLOSSARY

The glossary, which is based on *The Oxford English Dictionary*, is selective and records only the more important forms and meanings. Some familiarity with Tudor English spelling is presupposed. As a rule, only the infinitive of a verb is given. Reference is made to the page and the line where the form occurs.

a, *vb.* have, 143/17.
a, *prep.* of, a kynne, 159/2.
abashede, *ppl. adj.* confounded, disconcerted, 106/15.
abaytede, *pp.* decreased, 88/11.
abedde, *adv.* to bed, 150/13.
abhomynable, *adj.* abominable, 15/9.
abowght, *prep.* about, 164/9.
abroode, *adv.* out of one's house, 37/5.
acceptyde, *ppl. adj.* acceptable, 3/11.
accompany, *vb.* abide with, 172/33; *pp.* **accompanede**, joined in sexual intercourse, 53/1.
accomptyd, *pp.* accounted, 9/9.
accorn, *sb.* acorn, 21/13.
accustomed, *ppl. adj.* customary, 184/31.
acquitt, *vb.* requite, 188/1.
adioynyde, *pp.* joined, 160/17.
admiratione, *sb.* astonishment, 82/15–16.
aduenture, see **auenture**.
aduertese, *vb.* perceive, 51/9; **aduertyse**, 93/13.
aduoulterer, *sb.* adulterer, 112/10.
aduoultry, *sb.* adultery, 113/1.
aduyse, *sb.* design, 101/3.
aduyse, *vb. refl.* bethink oneself, 158/10.
advoyde, *vb.* avoid, escape, 56/14.
aferde, *ppl. adj.* afraid, 53/6.
afore, *adv.* before, 11/18.
afore, *prep.* before, 13/13.
aforehande, *adv.* beforehand, 174/31.
after, *adv.* afterwards, 31/12.
agayne, *adv.* in return, 156/6.
agaynesay, *vb.* gainsay, refuse, 139/16.
alegaunse, *sb.* allegiance, 56/5.
all, *adv.* entirely, 45/15.
alonely, *adv.* only, 65/9.
amendyd, *pp.* improved, 64/5.
and, *conj.* if, 72/3.
angle, *sb.* nook, remote corner, 147/4.
angle, *sb.* angel, 178/38.
Antecriste, Antichrist, 166/11.
antiquyte, *sb.* the ancients, 27/11.

apon, *prep.* upon, 23/1.
apte, *adj.* fit, 126/4; suitable, 143/7.
arsmetryke, *sb.* arithmetic, 87/11.
artelery, *sb.* artillery, 160/20.
asqwynte, *adv.* squinting, 28/1.
assaute, *vb.* attack, 75/11.
assautynge, *vbl. sb.* attacking, 13/10.
assay, *vb.* try, 45/20.
assoyl, *vb.* solve, clear up, 147/10–11.
astonyde, *ppl. adj.* astounded, 45/19.
Athenes, Athenians, 27/13.
aucthour, *sb.* author, 180/6; **aucthor**, 183/7.
auctorite, *sb.* authority, 162/38.
auenture, *sb.* at **auenture**, by chance, 92/4; on chance, 136/7–8; at **aduenture**, at a venture, 92/8.
aulter, *sb.* altar, 145/16.
auncyenty, *sb.* the ancients, 146/7.
awntiente, *adj.* ancient, 184/31.

balett, *sb.* song, 155/2.
banke, *sb.* coast, shore, 32/7; **bancke**, 37/12; **bounke**, 37/1.
bankett, *sb.* banquet, 48/16.
basilyck, *sb.* basilisk, 179/1.
bawme, *sb.* balm, 147/15.
be, *vb. pr. ind. 1 pl.* be, 83/18; *pr. ind. 3 pl.* be, 8/8; *pr. ind. 3 pl.* is, 3/26, 164/34; *pt. ind. 3 pl.* was, 10/11, 19/10, 24/1, 28/16 and 17, 129/10, 136/5, 155/6, 183/4.
beademan, *sb.* beadsman, 170/12.
beadwoman, *sb.* beadswoman, 173/21.
beastly, *adv.* like a beast, 15/6.
beck, *vb.* beckon, 92/6.
beere, *vb.* bear 54/13, *pt. 3 sg.* bare, 185/7.
belayde, *pp.* waylaid, 33/16.
benygne, *adj.* gracious, 65/6.
besydes, *prep.* in spite of, 93/19.
better, *adv.* rather, 68/16.
bettynge, *vbl. sb.* beating, 142/10.
betyne, *pp.* beaten, 109/11.
bitter, *adv.* 182/19.
blame, *vb.* reprove, 171/26.

blissyd, *ppl. adj.* blessed, 184/14.
blody, *adj.* cruel, 158/3.
blottynge, *vbl. sb.* stain, tarnish, 62/11.
blowe, *vb.* proclaim, 62/8.
blysse, *vb.* bless, 176/32.
Boheme, Bohemia, 182/11.
Bohemes, Bohemians, 177/35.
borde, *sb.* table, 57/13.
borne, *vb.* burn, 59/11; *pp.* brunte, burnt, 108/2.
boundage, *sb.* bondage, serfdom, 24/5.
bounde, *adj.* in bondage, 41/1.
bounde, *sb.* bond, 96/7.
bounke, see banke.
brasyn, *adj.* shameless, 25/8.
brawl, *vb. tr.* chide, 49/9.
brear, *sb.* briar, 10/9.
breeke, *vb.* break, 51/2; breake, disclose, 138/17.
bremble, *sb.* bramble, 10/9.
breue, *adj.* short, 49/17.
breuely, *adv.* briefly, 4/2; brefly, 160/20; brifly, 30/7; in short, brifly, 175/21; soon, breuely, 74/2.
broker, *sb.* pander, 130/5.
brunte, see borne.
Brytaynes, Britons, 181/31; Britaynes, 181/28; Britaignes, 177/36.
by, *prep.* concerning, 101/13; during, 18/16; according to, 43/6.
bytte, *sb.* bite, 6/5.

Caldeys, Chaldaeans, soothsayers, 77/16.
Capitall, Capitol, 21/2, 28/18; Capitoll, 87/2.
carecte, *sb.* character, letter, 35/3.
carecter, *sb.* character, letter, 86/9.
caruyde, *ppl. adj.* carved, 125/11.
castaway, *sb.* something thrown away, 168/28.
caste, *vb.* devise, 100/15; consider, 92/2.
charge, *vb.* burden, 120/8.
charyte, *sb.* love, affection, 102/3.
chastese, *vb.* subdue, 125/10; chastyse, punish, 109/11.
chastesynge, *vbl. sb.* breaking in, training, 41/19.
cherysyd, *pp.* made much of, 163/3.
cheualerouse, *adj.* of warlike renown, 137/19.
Chrysten, *adj.* Christian, 142/1; Cristen, 176/34.
churle, *sb.* serf, 158/12.

chyldre, *sb.* children, 48/3; chyldern, 173/22.
clarytude, *sb.* splendour, 25/11.
cleene, *adv.* entirely, 99/14.
cleere, *adj.* illustrious, 96/9.
clemens, *sb.* clemency, 165/12.
clerke, *sb.* scholar, 2/4; clarke, 173/28.
clerkly, *adv.* in learned fashion, 2/29.
cloysterar, *sb.* cloisterer, nun, 151/2.
clyft, *sb.* crack, 43/17.
coartyd, *pp.* coerced, 12/3.
comen, *pp.* come, 86/2.
commun, *vb.* converse, 43/16; comune, 185/9; comon, 55/9; commyn, 129/9.
commyxtion, *sb.* mingling, 6/11.
company, *vb.* copulate, 32/8.
compas, *sb.* extent, 13/16.
compass, *vb.* surround, 13/15.
competente, *adj.* fitting, 154/13.
complexion, *sb.* constitution, 25/2.
conclude, *vb.* decide, 130/1.
condescende, *vb.* agree, 107/8.
condicion, *sb.* disposition, 166/5; quality, 107/12; condiciones, manners, 6/6.
condigne, *adj.* fitting, 161/34.
conforte, *vb.* comfort, 58/11.
congruente, *adj.* proper, 5/7.
consayte, *sb.* opinion, 169/38.
consecrate, *pp.* consecrated, 27/18.
contrary, *adv.* contrariwise, 108/11.
conuenaunte, *sb.* agreement, 17/12.
conuenyent, *adj.* proper, fitting, 11/11; suitable, 22/18.
coppewebb, *sb.* cobweb, 64/15.
couetouse, *sb.* lust, 62/7; covetousness, 72/9.
couple, *vb. intr.* come together sexually, 110/4.
craft, *sb.* contrivance, 8/18; skill, 42/2.
credyde, *pp.* believed, 69/13.
Cristen, see Chrysten.
culter, *sb.* coulter, 21/10.
cure, *sb.* care, anxiety, 23/12.
cyuylyte, *sb.* culture, 22/15.

dalyaunce, *sb.* toying, amour, 32/4.
darke, *vb. tr.* darken, 31/15.
daungyer, *sb.* danger, 96/2.
deare, *adv.* dearly, 73/7.
debate, *sb.* strife, dissension, 61/5.
declare, *vb.* make known, state, aver, 14/4; relate, 15/1.
decorate, *ppl. adj.* adorned, 8/7.
dedicate, *ppl. adj.* dedicated, 18/1.

O

dedicate, *vb.* dedicate, *pt. 3 pl.*
dedicate, 31/4.
deface, *vb.* mar, 129/4; *pp.* defacyte,
destroyed, 151/1.
deformydly, *adv.* in a disfigured way,
108/1.
defourmyde, *ppl. adj.* deformed, 18/8.
delicacy, *sb.* luxury, 25/1.
delycate, *adj.* self-indulgent, 75/3.
delycatnes, *sb.* voluptuousness, 75/5.
delyce, *sb.* delight, pleasure, 8/17.
demerite, *sb.* merit, 162/26.
departe, *vb.* divide, 42/10.
depraue, *vb. tr.* pervert, 186/33;
decry, disparage, 190/5.
descryue, *vb.* describe, 113/14.
deserte, *sb.* good deed, 188/1.
desolate, *adj.* disconsolate, 91/16.
despite, *sb.* contempt, 179/11.
dessembling, *ppl. adj.* dissembling,
182/18.
deuowred, *pp.* destroyed, 106/3.
devine, *adj.* divine, 177/19.
devisyon, *sb.* dissension, 178/26.
devour, *sb.* do one's devour, endea-
vour, 164/13.
deyntines, *sb.* fastidiousness, 125/11.
diffamy, *sb.* dishonour, 37/8, 50/15,
51/11.
difficill, *adj.* difficult, 155/3.
diffuse, *adj.* obscure, 175/20.
diligens, *sb.* care, 18/9.
diligently, *adv.* carefully, 41/11.
dingnite, *sb.* rank, 165/15.
disconuenyence, *sb.* disadvantage,
25/4.
discordance, *sb.* disagreement, 33/13.
discrepante, *adj.* inconsistent, 34/
5–6; discrepant, different, 59/13.
dishoneste, see dyshoneste.
dispyse, *vb.* set at nought, 45/9.
dissemylynge, *ppl. adj.* dissembling,
73/9.
dissymyl, *vb.* pretend, feign, 103/8.
distresse, *vb.* overwhelm, 40/10.
dite, *sb.* ditty, poem, 155/3.
doctryne, *sb.* knowledge, 35/4.
douter, *sb.* daughter, 170/14.
dowght, *vb.* doubt, 163/25.
dradde, *ppl. adj.* redoubted, 161/23.
dradde, *pp.* feared, 42/6.
drawe, *vb.* proceed, *pt. 3 pl.* drew,
41/8.
dressyd, *pp.* prepared, 26/12.
dronken, *pp.* drunk, 157/3.
dygge, *vb.* dig, *pt. 3 pl.* dyggedde,
137/17.

dysdaynously, *adv.* disdainfully, 91/1.
dysease, *sb.* trouble, 174/12.
dyshoneste, *adj.* immoral, wicked,
157/16; dishoneste, unchaste, 144/
6–7.
dyvert, *vb.* digress, 177/32.

eare, *vb.* plough, till, 10/15.
easely, *adv.* readily, without difficulty, 129/2.
effabilite, *sb.* affability, 114/13.
eglogge, *sb.* eclogue, 2/20
eight, *adj.* eighth, 119/6.
elatyde, *ppl. adj.* proud, 53/4.
elders, *sb.* ancestors, 103/15.
elect, *sb.* one chosen by God, 172/33.
electe, *pp.* chosen, 111/4; chosen by
God, 160/29.
eleuate, *ppl. adj.* proud, 100/4.
emonge, *prep.* among, 4/3; emonges,
130/13; emongest, 115/14;
emongste, 3/14.
emperour, *sb.* commander, 111/1.
enbassatour, *sb.* ambassador, 171/
24; embassadour, 183/23–4.
enbolde, *vb. refl.* embolden oneself,
188/1.
enbrase, *vb.* embrace, 45/18.
endytyd, *pp.* set down, 4/4.
enhaunce, *vb.* exalt, 66/1.
enherytour, *sb.* heir, 104/7.
ensue, *vb. tr.* follow, 176/19.
ensuer, *vb.* assure, 173/17.
ensyne, *sb.* token, 66/16.
entermedle, *vb.* intermingle, 137/4.
entreate, *vb. intr.* treat, 185/9.
eny, *adj.* any, 163/9.
Epecur, *sb.* follower of Epicurus,
171/40.
eradycate, *pp.* eradicated, 177/30.
eschewe, *vb.* achieve, 12/18.
especiall, *adj.* in especiall, particularly, 171/28.
examplar, *sb.* model, 1/25; exemplar,
114/5; exemplar, copy, 173/19.
exarcyse, *vb. refl.* employ oneself,
169/26.
exedynge, *adj.* excessively great,
82/14.
exellent, *adv.* excellently, 97/1.
exeptyde, *pp.* received, accepted,
90/9.
experte, *adj.* experienced, 10/16.
exposicion, *sb.* explanation, 187/19.
expoune, *vb.* expound, interpret,
169/2.
expressyd, *pp.* mentioned, 11/18.

Glossary

195

expulsed, *pp.* expelled, 10/12.
exstincte, *vb.* extinguish, 185/41.
exteme, *sb.* esteem, 128/2.
exteme,*vb.* esteem, 2/16; think, 45/11.
extyncte, *adj.* dead, 145/12.
eyare, *sb.* heir, 143/7.
eyen, *sb. pl.* eyes, 34/2.

fachon, *sb.* way, 187/38.
fact, *sb.* course of conduct, 176/39.
factyon, *sb.* fashion, 166/17.
facundious, *adj.* eloquent, 161/31.
falle, *vb.* fall, *pt. 3 sg.* fyll, 179/35; *pt. 3 pl.* fyll, 178/24.
fantasy, *sb.* liking, desire, 73/11; opinion, 112/15.
farse, *vb.* stuff, 24/10.
father, *sb. gen.* father's, 60/3.
faute, *sb.* fault, 188/8; faulte, offence, 16/14.
faynede, *ppl. adj.* fictitious, 11/7.
felowe, *sb.* companion, 9/3; equal, associate, 52/5.
felysshypp, *sb.* band, 50/6.
fleynge, *pr. p.* flying, 24/6.
flie, *vb.* flee, 56/13.
flower, *sb.* prime of life, in his flowers, 176/8.
fonde, *adj.* foolish, 151/10.
forbecause, *conj.* because, 38/8–9.
forbed, *vb.* forbid, 46/13.
forboden, *pp.* forbidden, 9/17.
forderynge, *vbl. sb.* furtherance, 12/8.
forgeunes, *sb.* forgiveness, 91/19.
forneys, *sb.* furnace, 142/4.
fortitude, *sb.* strength, 73/16.
fortune, *vb.* happen, 59/14.
forwythe, *adv.* forthwith, 77/9.
foullyd, *pp.* defiled, 45/5.
fraunkyncens, *sb.* frankincense, 30/18.
frenshyppe, *sb.* friendship, 166/3.
freshe, *adj.* vigorous, 51/10.
fret, *vb.* gnaw, 19/6.
fro, *prep.* from, 124/10.
fronter, *sb.* frontier, 67/4.
fructe, *sb.* fruit, 10/6.
fruicyon, *sb.* pleasant possession, 9/15.
fryndely, *adj.* friendly, 187/31.
fulfyll, *vb.* fill, 184/8.
furderaunce, *sb.* furtherance, 185/10.
furthe, *adv.* forth, 157/5.
furthwythe, *adv.* forthwith, 138/4.
fyle, *vb.* defile, pollute, 56/11.
fyll, see falle.
fylthe, *sb.* vileness, 15/9.

fynde, *vb.* provide, for, maintain, 152/9.
fyne, *adj.* sheer, by fyne force, 14/11.
fyne-wytted, *adj.* of subtle understanding, 169/22.
fyrme, *vb.* make firm, 144/3.

gamme, *sb.* sport, 30/13.
gentle, *adj.* kind, 132/17.
gentlely, *adv.* kindly, tenderly, 70/14.
gentlenes, *sb.* kindness, 99/11; gentylnes, 133/1.
gentyles, *sb.* pagans, 11/10; gentylls, 19/5.
gerdle, *sb.* belt, 66/14.
geste, *sb.* deed, 88/12.
geuen, *pp.* given, 27/3.
geuer, *sb.* giver, 27/12.
glose, *sb.* exposition, 187/18.
godlye, *adj.* goodly, excellent, 27/13.
gotten, *pp.* begotten, 33/5.
Gotes, Goths, 180/3; Goates, 181/10.
gouernauns, *sb.* control, rule, 11/19.
goulde, *sb.* gold, 187/13.
gratynge, *ppl. adj.* wearing, 19/6.
graunte, *sb.* consent, 73/2.
graunte, *vb. intr.* consent, 48/13.
grauntfather, *sb.* grandfather, 181/24.
greatenes, *sb.* thickness, 13/16.
great-grandame, *sb.* great-grandmother, 183/18.
gre, *sb.* in good gre, in good part, 173/29; in gree, 168/12.
gryfte, *sb.* graft, 147/14.
guydour, *sb.* guide, director, 55/14.
guyse, *sb.* custom, 100/11.

habyttes, *sb. pl.* clothes, 101/5.
handlede, *pp.* treated, 129/13.
handsome, *adj.* apt, 21/9.
hange, *vb. refl.* hang, *pt. 3 sg.* honge, 127/13; hangede, 132/10.
hardy, *adj.* courageous, 4/7; bold, 126/8.
harnes, *sb.* armour, 28/5.
headlynge, *adv.* headlong, 15/13.
helth, *sb.* salvation, well-being, deliverance, 18/5.
herd, *adj.* hard, 83/14.
heredytour, *sb.* heir, 131/14.
heretofore, *adv.* previously, 15/2.
heritycall, *adj.* heretical, 179/22.
hert, *sb.* heart, 45/10.
hetherto, *adv.* hitherto, 162/23.
heuely, *adv.* grievously, 80/21.
heuy, *adj.* sorrowful, 54/8.

O 2

holpen, *pp.* helped, 140/10.
holsome, *adj.* beneficial, 161/6.
honeste, *adj.* commendable, 22/15;
  decent, 78/6; chaste, 111/12;
  honourable, 141/3.
honeste, *sb.* chastity, 126/9.
honestly, *adv.* worthily, 157/8;
  honourably, 158/3.
honge, see hange.
humanyte, *sb.* civilized ways, 23/2;
  humanitie, kindness, 162/4.
hundrithe, *adj.* hundred, 1/32.
husbounde, *sb.* husband, 12/2.
hyde, *pp.* hidden, 168/30; hydden,
  94/5.

illustrate, *vb.* illuminate, 187/28.
imbecillyte, *sb.* weakness, 74/13.
improprede,*pp.* appropriated,168/20.
impugne, *vb.* assail, dispute, 178/30.
incongruente, *adj.* unfitting, 8/5.
incontynent, *adv.* forthwith, 140/1.
inconuenience, *sb.* misfortune,
  trouble, 11/1–2.
indignacion, *sb.* wrath, 16/16.
inespecially, *adv.* especially, 182/13.
infection, *sb.* corrupt faith, 19/4–5.
infortunate, *adj.* luckless, 55/13; un-
  happy, 72/10.
ingrate, *adj.* ungrateful, 90/1.
innocency, *sb.* innocence, 159/7.
instore, *vb.* repair, 13/15.
intelleccion, *sb.* understanding, 186/
  33.
inuenimyde, *ppl. adj.* poisoned, 79/6.
inuentour, *sb.* inventor, 149/6.
inuoluyde, *pp.* wrapped up, 69/6.

kept, *pp.* protected, 112/7.
kerue, *vb.* carve, 113/16.
keruer, *sb.* sculptor, 113/15.
ketche, *vb.* catch, 36/13.
knyffes, *sb. pl.* knives, 48/16.
kynde, *sb.* sex, 13/5.
kynred, *sb.* kindred, 11/6.

lacrimable, *adj.* lamentable, 8/8.
large, *sb.* at large, at length, 133/10.
lase, *sb.* strip, 137/14.
lengar, *adv.* longer, 130/3.
lerne, *vb.* teach, 26/10.
lese, *vb.* lose, 84/9; leese,144/12.
lette, *vb.* desist, 13/2.
lettured, *adj.* educated, 179/3.
lodyne, *ppl. adj.* laden, 71/14.
loke, *vb.* loke of, look at, 6/3, 75/15,
  170/5 and 8–9, 174/13.

lombe, *sb.* loom, 26/13.
londe, *sb.* land, take londe, land,
  57/12.
longe, *vb.* belong, pertain, 30/12.
loste, *sb.* loss, 54/8.
lyen, *pp.* lain, 185/32.
lyffes, *sb. pl.* lives, 4/2; lyfes, 7/3.
lyft, *adj.* left, 125/4.
lyfte, *vb.* lift, *pt. 3 sg.* lyft, 46/8.
lyght, *adj.* slight, 44/15; lyghte,
  ready, 37/6.
lyghtnede, *ppl. adj.* enlightened, 128/
  14.
lyghtnes, *sb.* levity, 10/2.
lytle and litle, little by little, 15/12;
  by lytle and lytle, 182/4.
lyue, *sb.* life, 45/9.
lyvelie, *adj.* living, 185/20.

Machomettes, Mahometans, 179/32.
maistres, *sb.* mistress, 176/8.
make, *sb.* mate, consort, 9/4.
malle, *sb.* club, 74/7.
manyfestly, *adv.* openly, publicly,
  96/4.
mariable, *adj.* marriageable, 43/14.
marsyfull, *adj.* merciful, 165/13.
mastrie, *sb.* achievement, 1/24.
matier, *sb.* matter, 174/6.
maynteyner, *sb.* supporter, 75/5.
meane, *adj.* inferior, 163/10.
meanly, *adv.* poorly, badly, 188/6.
meeke, *adj.* gentle, 51/3.
mekenes, *sb.* gentleness, 3/7.
mengle, *vb.* mingle, 46/14.
menglysshe, *vb.* mingle, 3/14.
meny, *adj.* many, 162/15.
meruelede, *pp.* astonished, 104/16.
mesure, *sb.* satisfaction, 143/3.
metely, *adv.* fairly, moderately, 59/4.
monstruouse, *adj.* monstrous, 18/13.
monycyone, *sb.* warning, 100/13;
  monytion, direction, 112/3.
moo, *adj.* more, 32/10.
more, *adj.* greater, 33/13.
muche, *adv.* very, 12/6.
muchewhat, *sb.* many things, 121/1.
muete, *adj.* mute, 54/9.
mundayne, *adj.* earthly, 100/3.
mynde, *sb.* desire, 49/14.
mynyshede, *pp.* diminished, 72/8.
myschife, *sb.* evil-doing, 121/12.

nat, *adv.* not, 167/17.
naturall, *adj.* native, 99/7.
ne, *adv.* not, ne were, had it not been,
  171/38, 183/30.

Glossary

Glossary 197

neclecte, *vb.* neglect, *pt. 3 sg.* neclecte, 55/8.
necligent, *adj.* negligent, 180/7.
neuow, *sb.* grandson, 10/17; neuowe, nephew, 48/6.
newe, *adv.* newly, 153/14.
neybourhed, *sb.* proximity, 43/9.
norishe, *vb.* rear, nurture, 57/17.
notable, *adj.* conspicuous, 107/16.
nother, *adj.* other, 105/6.
nother, *adv.* neither, 13/2.
nothynge, *adv.* in no way, 175/18; not at all, 5/9.
nouelle, *sb.* tale, 166/24.
numbers, *sb.* metrical periods, 27/4.
nyll. *vb.* to be unwilling; wylde she, nylde she, 57/15; wyll they, nyll they, 102/3-4.

obeysaunce, *sb.* obedience, 42/13.
obiectyde, *pp.* brought against, 133/12.
obprobry, *sb.* disgrace, 133/12.
obscure, *adj.* dark, 152/1.
occupye, *vb.* seize, take possession of, 71/10.
of, *adv.* off, 28/9.
off, *prep.* of, 161/20.
omely, *sb.* homily, 171/23.
on, *prep.* on wayte, in wait, 36/13.
onles, *conj.* unless, 179/28; oneles, 83/9.
open, *vb.* reveal, 91/13.
oppen, *adj.* open, 112/2.
oppressyde, *pp.* violated, 34/8; suppressed, 63/1; oppressyd, killed, 108/3.
or, *conj.* before, 24/7.
or, *prep.* before, 164/6.
oratour, *sb.* beadsman, suppliant, 171/19.
orbate, *adj.* bereaved, 54/4.
other, *pron. pl.* others, 8/8.
other, *adv.* either, 63/2.
ouerpasse, *vb.* pass over, 2/22.
ouerthrowe, *sb.* defeat, 42/17.
ouerwhelmyde, *pp.* covered, 150/17.
ourselfe, *pron. 1 pl.* ourselves, 57/3; oureself, 23/16; ourselffes, 57/4.
owe, *vb.* owe, *pt. 3 pl.* oughte, 56/5.

pagente, *sb.* part, role, 60/8.
paine, see peyne.
parcase, see percase.
parelle, *sb.* peril, 77/8.
parfayte, *adj.* perfect, 187/26.
parfect, *adj.* perfect, 165/5.

parpetual, *adj.* perpetual. 169/17.
parson, *sb.* person, 164/15.
parte, *sb.* party, 102/2.
passage, *sb.* road, way, 94/15.
passe, *vb.* surpass, 9/13.
passynge, *adv.* exceedingly, 43/10.
paysan, *sb.* peasant, 150/4.
pean, *sb.* paean, 172/19.
peax, *sb.* peace, 41/7.
pensyll, *sb.* brush, 114/3.
perauenture, *adv.* perchance, 50/9.
percase, *adv.* perhaps, 44/10; parcase, 169/29.
perfyte, *adj.* perfect, 103/2.
perfytly, *adv.* perfectly, 114/9.
perlouse, *adj.* dangerous, 161/4.
persever, *vb.* continue, 185/38.
personage, *sb.* handsome appearance, 15/9.
persyde, *pp.* pierced, 105/14.
pertaker, *sb.* partaker, 93/15.
perticuler, *adj.* particular, 165/33.
perysshed, *pp.* destroyed, 110/5.
peyne, *sb.* penalty; peyne of deathe, on pain of death, 95/1; paine of death, 180/13.
peynture, *sb.* painting, 64/4.
philozophy, *sb.* philosophy, 87/12.
picture, *sb.* effigy, 14/14.
platt, *sb.* place, 98/2.
poison, *adj.* poisonous, 182/19.
pollicy, *sb.* prudence, 40/10; shrewdness, 89/6; pollecy, device, 135/13.
pooire, *sb.* power, 187/36.
poynte, *vb.* fix, 102/9.
praysewourthely, *adj.* praiseworthy, 57/1.
precelle, *vb.* excel, 26/1.
preferre, *vb. refl.* advance, 104/2.
pretende, *vb.* tend, 28/2.
preuentyde, *pp.* provided with aid, 28/11.
priste, *sb.* priest, 18/2.
procreate, *ppl. adj.* begotten, 11/12.
procurer, *sb.* one who persuades or incites, 141/15.
profet, *sb.* prophet, 173/8; profitt, 173/10.
profyte, *sb.* advantage, 48/15.
progenytour, *sb.* ancestor, 148/12.
proheme, *sb.* preface, 3/13.
prolonge, *vb.* delay, postpone, 128/15.
promytte, *vb.* promise, 44/2-3.
propre, *adj.* own, 8/15.
proue, *sb.* trial, 76/2.
proue, *vb.* try, 124/9.

prouoker, *sb.* irritator, 129/3; pro-
uocar, 129/13.
prowyse, *sb.* prowess, 88/4.
prycke, *sb.* mark, 2/8.
pryncelyke, *adj.* princely, 53/12.
pryncelyke, *adv.* in princely fashion,
96/4.
pryncelylyke,   *adv.*   in   princely
fashion, 142/13.
pusant, *adj.* puissant, 164/18.
put, *vb.* put to, exert, apply, 4/7.
pye, *sb.* magpie, 122/9.
pyte, *sb.* piety, 52/7, 55/12, 56/20.
pyteouse, *adj.* merciful, 50/16.

queuer, *sb.* quiver, 103/16.
quycke, *adj.* active, vigorous, 4/18;
alive, 150/17.

raath, *adv.* rarely, 28/1.
race, *vb.* erase, 15/14.
racket, *sb.* disturbance, 182/33.
ragyde, *adj.* enraged, 56/9.
rapyne, *sb.* love of plunder, 89/5.
rasyde, *pp.* raised, 14/13, 155/6.
rathe, *adv.* rarely, 173/12.
ratyde, *pp.* arranged, 6/7.
Redemptor, *sb.* Redeemer, 142/2.
redifie, *vb.* build, 20/3; redyfye, 138/
14; reedifie, 185/31; reedifye,
20/15; reedyfye, 85/17.
reduce, *vb.* translate, 164/12.
refraynyde, *pp.* restrained, 47/7.
reherse, *vb.* mention, 1/18; relate,
26/14.
rendred, *pp.* given back, restored,
14/11.
renoume, *sb.* renown, 153/11.
renoumyde, *adj.* renowned, 3/29;
renowmed, 161/37; renomede, 13/
17.
renwe, *vb.* renew, 187/28.
reprobable, *adj.* deserving of reproof,
177/15.
reproufe, *sb.* disgrace, 168/15.
requyre, *vb.* request, 128/15.
reuerente, *adj.* venerable, 93/7.
reuerte, *vb.* return, 67/9.
rocke, *sb.* distaff, 157/11.
rore, *sb.* outcry, vpp on a rore, in an
uproar, 117/10.
rughe, *adj.* rough, 73/13.
rumor, *sb.* tumult, 60/2.
rutylant, *adj.* shining, 115/6.
ryall, *adj.* royal, 163/26.

sadd, *adj.* grave, 139/6.
sadly, *adv.* quietly, soberly, 157/11.

sarue, *vb. tr.* serve, 187/34.
scant, *adv.* almost, 24/6; scante,
hardly, 25/5.
scenate, *sb.* senate, 88/2.
science, *sb.* knowledge, 1/22; scyens,
64/8.
sclaundre, *sb.* disgrace, 37/9.
sclaundre, *vb.* slander, 130/15.
scorne, *vb.* scorne with, jeer at,
speak contemptuously of, 55/3.
scornefull, *adj.* contemptible, 26/3.
sea, *sb.* see, 179/27.
seeke, *vb. intr.* sue, 41/7.
seknes, *sb.* illness, 170/34.
selle, *sb.* cell, 151/15.
sentence, *sb.* saying, 165/37.
seruyde, *pp.* preserved, 88/14.
sex, *sb. pl.* sexes, 16/1.
sex, *adj.* six, 1/32.
sexten, *adj.* sixteen, 86/11.
shamefastness, *sb.* decency, 76/18.
shappe, *sb.* shape, 154/13; shap,
form, 163/8.
shett, *vb.* shut, 63/3.
shipman, *sb.* sailor, 120/10.
shorte, *vb.* grow short, 24/15.
shue, *vb.* show, 106/16.
singler, *adj.* singular, 15/8; singlare,
168/20; synglar, 52/16.
sithens, see sythens.
slaknes, *sb.* remissness, 98/14.
slypper, *adj.* fickle, unstable, 49/16.
smyte, *vb.* thrust, 159/12.
so, *conj.* provided, 75/13, 76/6.
solempne, *adj.* solemn, 140/2.
sondre, in sondre, in pieces, 187/15.
soore, *adv.* very, 71/9.
sorte, *sb.* fashion, 12/15; band, company, 99/15.
soundry, *adj.* various, 174/9.
sownde, *vb.* signify, 138/1.
speciall, *adv.* especially, 147/14.
speede, *vb.* prosper, 77/16.
spoyle, *sb.* spoliation, 111/12.
spoyled, *pp.* seized, 66/16; robbed,
72/6.
spurke, *adj.* foul, 183/11.
spyede, *pp.* found out, discovered,
101/8.
spynnar, *sb.* spider, 64/14.
spyrytuall, *adj.* ecclesiastical, 166/7.
stark, *adv.* utterly, 79/16.
stay, *sb.* control, 171/38.
stay, *vb. tr.* hold back, delay, 60/13.
stere, *vb.* stir, 6/4.
stomake, *sb.* heart, 46/11; breast,
159/12.

Glossary

199

stonde, *vb.* stand, 178/15; *pp.*
stonde, 63/7.
storyall, *adj.* historical, 189/8.
strayte, *adj.* rigorous, strictly moral,
5/10.
streight, *adv.* at once, 41/10.
streightways, *adv.* immediately, 94/
13.
stryke, *vb.* strike, *pt. 3 sg.* strooke,
79/7.
stryue, *vb.* strive, *pt. 3 sg.* straue, 27/
2; *pt. 3 pl.* straue, 60/4.
study, *sb.* effort, 75/17.
studye, *vb.* ponder, 50/17.
styll, *sb.* stillness, 44/12, 45/3.
suffise, *vb.* suffice, 179/5.
superstitione, *sb.* rite, observance,
53/9.
supple, *vb.* make up for, 172/27.
sure, *adv.* securely, 49/2; with certainty, 51/12.
surmounte, *vb.* surpass, 70/7–8.
suspectione, *sb.* suspicion, 72/8.
suster, *sb.* sister, 33/3.
swerde, *sb.* sword, 24/8.
swete, *adv.* sweetly, 156/5.
syeth, *sb.* scythe, 24/7.
syncere, *adj.* pure, 185/41.
synceritie, *sb.* purity, 185/2.
synge, *vb.* sing, *pt. 3 sg.* songe, 156/
5.
sythe, *sb.* time, 168/28.
sythens, *conj.* since, 172/16; sithens,
161/26; sythen, 171/31.
syttynge, *ppl. adj.* fitting, 56/21.
syxt, *adj.* sixth, 174/21.

taare, see teare.
take, *pp.* taken, 99/13.
tary, *vb. tr.* wait for, 44/9.
teare, *vb.* tear, *pt. 3 sg.* taare, 45/1.
telde, *pp.* told, 69/2.
terme, *sb.* bound, 55/2.
than, *adv.* then, 57/9.
the, *pers. pron.* they, 100/10.
then, *conj.* than, 1/22.
there, *poss. adj.* their, 163/5; ther,
176/16.
theymselfe, *refl. pron. 3 pl.* themselves, 66/1–2; theymself, 23/6;
theimself, 10/6; theymselffes, 6/6;
theymselfes, 174/38.
thorow, *prep.* throughout, 128/2.
thorowoute, *prep.* throughout, 113/8.
threasorour, *sb.* treasurer, 184/27.
threasure, *sb.* treasure, 71/10; treasoure, 71/14.

threate, *vb.* threaten, *pr. p.* threatyng,180/24; *pt. 3 sg.* threte,120/16.
throughly, *adv.* thoroughly, 185/27.
thynge, *sb.* things, 19/6.
to, *prep.* to this, in addition, 12/7.
to-cum, *vb.* come to, 58/11–12.
tofore, *adv.* before, 86/4.
togedre, *adv.* together, 90/11;
togyther, 176/5.
tone, *pron.* one, 43/12.
too, *adj.* two, 42/10.
toone, *adj.* one, 14/14.
tother, *pron.* other, 43/12.
tother, *adj.* other, 2/24.
touche, *vb.* treat of, 4/12.
toyes, *sb. pl.* amorous sport, 73/10.
towardes, *adj.* promising, 127/4;
towarde, 99/5.
towardnes, *sb.* promise, 131/16.
translatyd, *pp.* conveyed, 8/16.
trauell, *sb.* trouble, 13/2.
troubleouse, *adj.* stormy, 175/34.
tryfyll, *sb.* trifle, 140/17.

vagabounde, *sb.* vagabond, 22/14.
vallyauntnes, *sb.* valour, 104/11.
variete, *sb.* variation, 106/17.
vastyde, *pp.* put forth unprofitably,
143/15.
vastynge, *vbl. sb.* laying waste, destroying, 139/11.
vaynquyshe, *vb.* vanquish, 26/8.
venerall, *adj.* venereal, 16/1; venereall, 31/15; veneriall, 151/3.
vertue, *sb.* power, 59/7.
vestementes, *sb. pl.* clothes, 100/17.
vesture, *sb.* garment, 24/9.
vexyde, *pp.* afflicted, harassed, 160/
13.
viage, *sb.* voyage, 136/16.
viduate, *adj.* widowed, 79/17.
vilayne, *sb.* peasant, 183/3.
virago, *sb.* female warrior, 104/17;
wicked woman, 111/9; virile
woman, 135/7.
vnabyll, *adj.* unable, 160/18.
vnclosed, *ppl. adj.* unenclosed, 24/1.
vncorrupte, *adj.* uncorrupted, 63/9.
vnculpable, *adj.* free from fault,
183/35.
vndo, *vb.* ruin, 143/1.
vndrestonde, *pp.* understood, 186/9.
vngoodely, *adj.* wicked, 166/6.
vngraciousnes, *sb.* wickedness, 15/
16.
vngracyouse, *adj.* wicked, 9/15; evil,
72/2.

vnhappely, *adv.* evilly, 15/5.
vnhoneste, *adj.* indecent, unchaste, 63/10; immoral, 151/13.
vnkynde, *adj.* ungrateful, 90/2.
vnmeate, *adj.* unsuitable, 11/18.
vnmouable, *adj.* immovable, 70/15.
vnnethe, *adv.* scarcely, 2/17.
vnpatiently, *adv.* impatiently, 134/17.
vnstedfaste, *adj.* fickle, unreliable, 55/4.
vnwayres, *sb.* at vnwayres, without warning, 134/16.
vnwytty, *adj.* foolish, 15/12.
vnyte, *ppl. adj.* united, 102/4.
votesafe, *vb.* vouchsafe, 166/21; *pp.* wotsauyde, 187/28.
voyde, *adj.* bereaved, 54/4.
vre, *sb.* practice, put in vre, 187/38.
vse, *sb.* custom, 140/4.
vse, *vb. tr.* accustom, 41/18; practise, carry on, 31/13; spend, 181/13; *vb. refl.* behave oneself, 15/5.
vulgar, *adj.* common, 52/11.
vulgar, *sb.* common people, 177/6; vernacular, 189/17.
vyle, *adj.* mean, poor, 100/17; low, 154/10.
vyly, *adv.* vilely, 17/1.

waare, *adj.* aware, 36/12.
wakynge, *ppl. adj.* vigilant, 84/5.
wan, wanne, see winne.
warke, *sb.* work, 169/30.
warly, *adj.* warlike, 163/15.
was, see be.
wastyde, *pp.* ravaged, 110/5.
wauerynge, *ppl. adj.* wandering, 120/14.
way, *vb.* weigh, 188/7.
weare, *vb.* wear, *pt. 3 sg.* waare, 66/14.
weife, *vb.* weave, 64/1; weeue, 65/2.
weike, *adj.* weak, 4/17.
well, *sb.* fountain, 44/14.
wellnere, *adv.* well-nigh, 47/10.
welthe, *sb.* well-being, 24/4; welth, welfare, 48/15.
welwyller, *sb.* well-wisher, 188/5.
wery, *adv.* very, 15/10.
wex, *vb.* grow, wax, 24/13.
weyke, *vb. refl.* weaken, 50/5.
weyuynge, *vbl. sb.* weaving, 64/7.
whether, *pron.* which, 78/2.
whether, *adv.* whither, 62/2.
whyle, *sb.* ruse, wile, 158/11.

whyles, *conj.* whilst, 44/3; whiles, 50/17.
willfully, see wylfully.
winne, *vb.* win, *pt. 3 sg.* wan, 163/29; wanne, 179/16.
withstonde, *pp.* withstood, 57/11.
wittie, *adj.* wise, 185/15.
wodde, *sb.* wood, 21/14.
woll, see wyll.
womanly, *adv.* like a woman, 15/7.
wonder, *adj.* wondrous, 127/7.
wonder, *adv.* wondrously, 125/2; wondre, 90/13.
wonder, *vb.* wander, 97/15.
wonderfull, *adv.* wonderfully, 162/14.
wonderly, *adv.* wondrously, 20/7.
wonders, *adv.* wondrously, 30/17; wondres, 73/5; wounders, 49/7; woundres, 8/7.
wondersly, *adv.* wondrously, 42/11.
woodenes, *sb.* madness, 56/2.
worke, *vb.* plan, contrive, *pt. 3 sg.* wroughte, 12/13.
workemaister, *sb.* master workman, 8/14.
worlde, *sb.* century, generation, 55/9.
worshipfull, *adj.* distinguished, 129/3.
worthe, *adj.* worthy, 163/24.
worthe, *sb.* take in worthe, be content with, 171/11.
wose, *pron.* whose, 40/11.
wotsauyde, see votesafe.
wounders, *adj.* wondrous, 65/13.
woundre, *sb.* marvel, 146/16.
woundre, *vb.* wonder, 13/7.
wrastlynge, *vbl. sb.* wrestling, 41/19.
wresting, *vbl. sb.* distortion, 186/22.
wrighte, *vb.* write, 162/36; *pp.* wrighttun, 163/31.
wrighter, *sb.* writer, 162/38.
wrighting, *vbl. sb.* writing, 164/5.
wydowhede, *sb.* widowhood, 133/13.
wyffes, *sb. pl.* wives, 98/11; wyfes, 95/12.
wyle, *adj.* cunning, 5/14.
wylfully, *adv.* deliberately, 79/16; willfully, voluntarily, 141/4.
wyll, *conj.* while, 144/11.
wyll, *vb.* will, *pr. ind. 1 sg.* woll, 175/26; *pr. subj. 2 sg.* wyll, 142/7.
wytte, *sb.* wisdom, 68/12.

yere, *sb. pl.* years, 161/12.
yeven, *pp.* given, 186/30.
yever, *sb.* giver, 187/25.
ymagen, *vb. intr.* plot, 48/12.